Propeller Manual

Version 1.0

DISCLAIMER OF LIABILITY

Parallax Inc. is not responsible for special, incidental, or consequential damages resulting from any breach of warranty, or under any legal theory, including lost profits, downtime, goodwill, damage to or replacement of equipment or property, or any costs of recovering, reprogramming, or reproducing any data stored in or used with Parallax products. Parallax Inc. is also not responsible for any personal damage, including that to life and health, resulting from use of any of our products. You take full responsibility for your Propeller microcontroller application, no matter how life-threatening it may be.

INTERNET DISCUSSION LISTS

We maintain active web-based discussion forums for people interested in Parallax products. These lists are accessible from www.parallax.com via the Support → Discussion Forums menu. These are the forums that we operate from our web site:

- Propeller chip – This list is specifically for our customers using Propeller chips and products.
- BASIC Stamp – This list is widely utilized by engineers, hobbyists and students who share their BASIC Stamp projects and ask questions.
- Stamps in Class® – Created for educators and students, subscribers discuss the use of the Stamps in Class curriculum in their courses. The list provides an opportunity for both students and educators to ask questions and get answers.
- Parallax Educators – A private forum exclusively for educators and those who contribute to the development of Stamps in Class. Parallax created this group to obtain feedback on our curricula and to provide a place for educators to develop and obtain Teacher's Guides.
- Robotics – Designed for Parallax robots, this forum is intended to be an open dialogue for robotics enthusiasts. Topics include assembly, source code, expansion, and manual updates. The Boe-Bot®, Toddler®, SumoBot®, HexCrawler and QuadCrawler robots are discussed here.
- SX Microcontrollers and SX-Key – Discussion of programming the SX microcontroller with Parallax assembly language SX – Key® tools and 3rd party BASIC and C compilers.
- Javelin Stamp – Discussion of application and design using the Javelin Stamp, a Parallax module that is programmed using a subset of Sun Microsystems' Java® programming language.

ERRATA

While great effort is made to assure the accuracy of our texts, errors may still exist. If you find an error, please let us know by sending an email to editor@parallax.com. We continually strive to improve all of our educational materials and documentation, and frequently revise our texts. Occasionally, an errata sheet with a list of known errors and corrections for a given text will be posted to our web site, www.parallax.com. Please check the individual product page's free downloads for an errata file.

SUPPORTED HARDWARE, FIRMWARE AND SOFTWARE

This manual is valid with the following hardware, software, and firmware versions:

Hardware	Software	Firmware
P8X32A-D40 P8X32A-Q44 P8X32A-M44	Propeller Tool v1.0	P8X32A v1.0

CREDITS

Authorship: Jeff Martin. Format & Editing, Stephanie Lindsay.
Cover Art: Jen Jacobs; Technical Graphics: Rich Allred; with many thanks to everyone at Parallax Inc.

Table of Contents

Table of Contents

Table of Contents

Table of Contents

Table of Contents

Table of Contents

Table of Contents

Preface

Thank you for purchasing a Propeller chip. You will be spinning your own programs in no time!

Propeller chips are incredibly capable multiprocessor microcontrollers; the much-anticipated result of over eight years of the intense efforts of Chip Gracey and the entire Parallax Engineering Team.

This book is intended to be a complete reference guide to Propeller chips and their programming languages, Spin and Propeller Assembly. Have fun!

Despite our best efforts, there are bound to be questions unanswered by this manual alone. Check out our Propeller chip discussion forum – (accessible from www.parallax.com via the Support → Discussion Forums menu) – this is a group especially for Propeller users where you can post your questions or review discussions that may have already answered yours.

Chapter 1: Introducing the Propeller Chip

This chapter describes the Propeller chip hardware. To fully understand and use the Propeller effectively, it's important to first understand its hardware architecture. This chapter presents the details of the hardware such as package types, package sizes, pin descriptions, and functions.

Concept

The Propeller chip is designed to provide high-speed processing for embedded systems while maintaining low current consumption and a small physical footprint. In addition to being fast, the Propeller provides flexibility and power through its eight processors, called cogs, that can perform simultaneous independent or cooperative tasks, all while maintaining a relatively simple architecture that is easy to learn and utilize.

The resulting design of the Propeller frees application developers from common complexities of embedded systems programming. For example:

- The memory map is flat. There is no need for paging schemes with blocks of code, data or variables. This is a big time-saver during application development.

- Asynchronous events are easier to handle than they are with devices that use interrupts. The Propeller has no need for interrupts; just assign some cogs to individual, high-bandwidth tasks and keep other cogs free and unencumbered. The result is a more responsive application that is easier to maintain.

- The Propeller Assembly language features conditional execution and optional result writing for each individual instruction. This makes critical, multi-decision blocks of code more consistently timed; event handlers are less prone to jitter and developers spend less time padding, or squeezing, cycles here and there.

Package Types

The Propeller chip is available in the package types shown here.

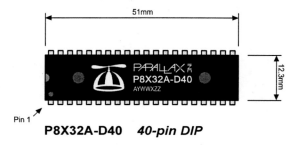

P8X32A-D40   *40-pin DIP*

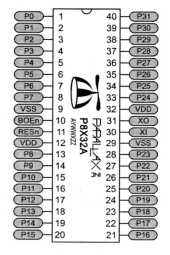

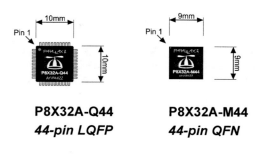

P8X32A-Q44   **P8X32A-M44**

44-pin LQFP   *44-pin QFN*

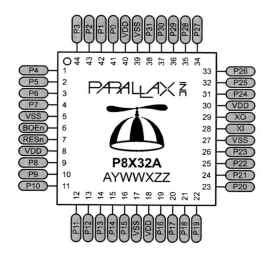

Pin Descriptions

Table 1-1: Pin Descriptions		
Pin Name	**Direction**	**Description**

P0 – P31	I/O	General purpose I/O Port A. Can source/sink 30 mA each at 3.3 VDC. Do not exceed 100 mA source/sink total across any group of I/O pins at once. Logic threshold is ≈ ½ VDD; 1.65 VDC @ 3.3 VDC.
		
		The pins shown below have a special purpose upon power-up/reset but are general purpose I/O afterwards.
		    P28 - I2C SCL connection to optional, external EEPROM.
		    P29 - I2C SDA connection to optional, external EEPROM.
		    P30 - Serial Tx to host.
		    P31 - Serial Rx from host.

VDD	---	3.3 volt power (2.7 – 3.3 VDC).
VSS	---	Ground.
BOEn	I	Brown Out Enable (active low). Must be connected to either VDD or VSS. If low, RESn becomes a weak output (delivering VDD through 5 KΩ) for monitoring purposes but can still be driven low to cause reset. If high, RESn is CMOS input with Schmitt Trigger.
RESn	I/O	Reset (active low). When low, resets the Propeller chip: all cogs disabled and I/O pins floating. Propeller restarts 50 ms after RESn transitions from low to high.
XI	I	Crystal Input. Can be connected to output of crystal/oscillator pack (with XO left disconnected), or to one leg of crystal (with XO connected to other leg of crystal or resonator) depending on CLK Register settings. No external resistors or capacitors are required.
XO	O	Crystal Output. Provides feedback for an external crystal, or may be left disconnected depending on CLK Register settings. No external resistors or capacitors are required.

The Propeller (P8X32A) has 32 I/O pins (Port A, pins P0 through P31). Four of these I/O pins, P28-P31 have a special purpose upon power-up/reset. At power-up/reset, pins P30 and P31 communicate with a host for programming and P28 and P29 interface to an external 32 KB EEPROM (24LC256).

Specifications

Table 1-2: Specifications	
Model	P8X32A
Power Requirements	3.3 volts DC
External Clock Speed	DC to 80 MHz (4 MHz to 8 MHz with Clock PLL running)
System Clock Speed	DC to 80 MHz
Internal RC Oscillator	12 MHz or 20 kHz (approximate; may range from 8 MHz – 20 MHz, or 13 kHz – 33 kHz, respectively)
Main RAM/ROM	64 K bytes; 32 KB RAM + 32 KB ROM
Cog RAM	512 x 32 bits each
RAM/ROM Organization	Long (32-bit), Word (16-bit), or Byte (8-bit) addressable
I/O pins	32 CMOS signals with VDD/2 input threshold.
Current Source/Sink per I/O	30 mA
Current Source/Sink per 8 pins	100 mA
Current Draw @ 3.3 vdc, 70 °F	500 µA per MIPS (MIPS = Freq in MHz / 4 * Number of Active Cogs)

Hardware Connections

Figure 1-1 shows an example wiring diagram that provides host and EEPROM access to the Propeller chip. In this example the host access is achieved through the Propeller Clip device (a USB to TTL serial converter).

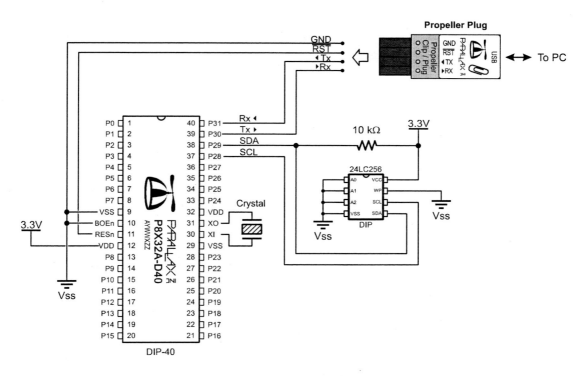

Figure 1-1: Example wiring diagram that allows for programming the Propeller chip and an external 32 Kbyte EEPROM, and running the Propeller with an external crystal.

Boot Up Procedure

Upon power-up (+ 100 ms), RESn low-to-high, or software reset:

1. The Propeller chip starts its internal clock in slow mode (≈ 20 KHz), delays for 50 ms (reset delay), switches the internal clock to fast mode (≈ 12 MHz), and then loads and runs the built-in Boot Loader program in the first processor (Cog 0).

2. The Boot Loader performs one or more of the following tasks, in order:

    a. Detects communication from a host, such as a PC, on pins P30 and P31. If communication from a host is detected, the Boot Loader converses with the host to identify the Propeller chip and possibly download a program into Main RAM and optionally into an external 32 KB EEPROM.

    b. If no host communication was detected, the Boot Loader looks for an external 32 KB EEPROM (24LC256) on pins P28 and P29. If an EEPROM is detected, the entire 32 KB data image is loaded into the Propeller chip's Main RAM.

    c. If no EEPROM was detected, the boot loader stops, Cog 0 is terminated, the Propeller chip goes into shutdown mode, and all I/O pins set to inputs.

3. If either step 2a or 2b was successful in loading a program into the Main RAM, and a suspend command was not given by the host, then Cog 0 is reloaded with the built-in Spin Interpreter and the user code is run from Main RAM.

Run-Time Procedure

A Propeller Application is a user program compiled into its binary form and downloaded to the Propeller chip's RAM and, possibly, external EEPROM. The application consists of code written in the Propeller chip's Spin language (high-level code) with optional Propeller Assembly language components (low-level code). Code written in the Spin language is interpreted during run time by a cog running the Spin Interpreter while code written in Propeller Assembly is run in its pure form directly by a cog. Every Propeller Application consists of at least a little Spin code and may actually be written entirely in Spin or with various amounts of Spin and assembly. The Propeller chip's Spin Interpreter is started in Step 3 of the Boot Up Procedure, above, to get the application running.

Once the boot-up procedure is complete and an application is running in Cog 0, all further activity is defined by the application itself. The application has complete control over things like the internal clock speed, I/O pin usage, configuration registers, and when, what and how many cogs are running at any given time. All of this is variable at run time, as controlled by the application, including the internal clock speed. See Chapter 3: Propeller Programming Tutorial.

Shutdown Procedure

When the Propeller goes into shutdown mode, the internal clock is stopped causing all cogs to halt and all I/O pins are set to input direction (high impedance). Shutdown mode is triggered by one of the three following events:

1) VDD falling below the brown-out threshold (≈2.7 vdc), when the brown-out circuit is enabled,

2) the RESn pin going low, or

3) the application requesting a reboot (see the REBOOT command, page 292).

Shutdown mode is discontinued when the voltage level rises above the brown-out threshold and the RESn pin is high.

Block Diagram

Figure 1-2: Propeller Chip Block Diagram

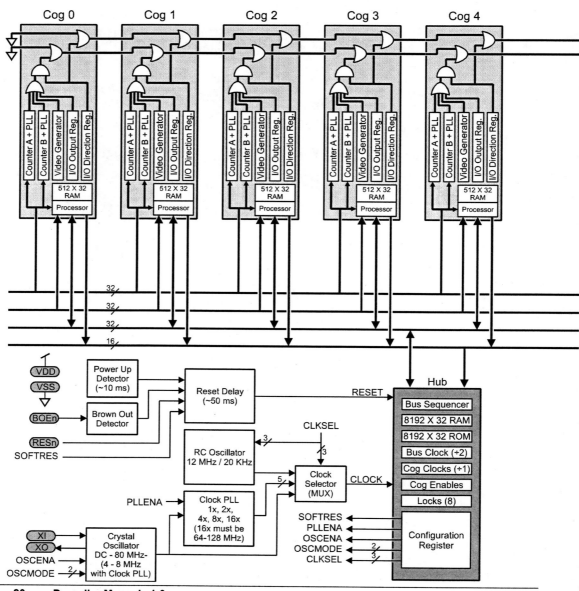

Cog and Hub interaction is critical to the Propeller chip. The Hub controls which cog can access mutually-exclusive resources, such as Main RAM/ROM, configuration registers, etc. The Hub gives exclusive access to every cog one at a time in a "round robin" fashion, regardless of how many cogs are running, in order to keep timing deterministic.

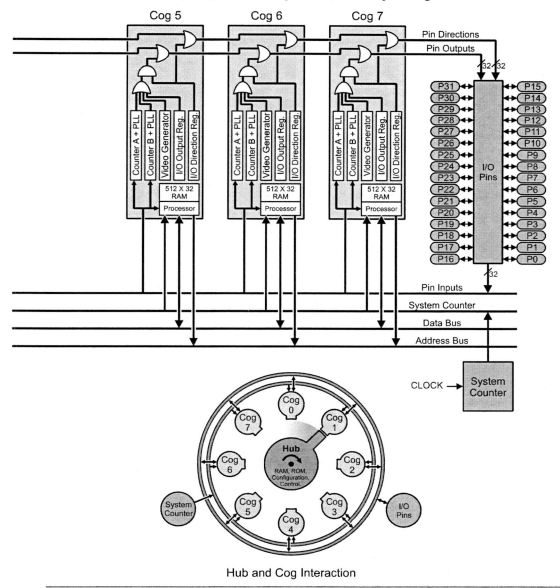

Hub and Cog Interaction

Shared Resources

There are two types of shared resources in the Propeller: 1) common, and 2) mutually-exclusive. Common resources can be accessed at any time by any number of cogs. Mutually-exclusive resources can also be accessed by any number of cogs, but only by one cog at a time. The common resources are the I/O pins and the System Counter. All other shared resources are mutually-exclusive by nature and access to them is controlled by the Hub. See the Hub section on page 24.

System Clock

The System Clock (shown as "CLOCK" in Figure 1-2) is the central clock source for nearly every component of the Propeller chip. The System Clock's signal comes from one of three possible sources: 1) the Internal RC Oscillator, 2) the Clock Phase-Locked Loop (PLL), or 3) the Crystal Oscillator (an internal circuit that is fed by an external crystal or crystal/oscillator pack). The source is determined by the CLK register's settings, which is selectable at compile time or at run time. The only components that don't use the System Clock directly are the Hub and Bus; they divide the System Clock by two (2).

Cogs (processors)

The Propeller contains eight (8) processors, called cogs, numbered 0 to 7. Each cog contains the same components (see Figure 1-2): a Processor block, local 2 KB RAM configured as 512 longs (512 x 32 bits), two I/O Assistants with PLLs, a Video Generator, I/O Output Register, I/O Direction Register, and other registers not shown in the diagram. See Table 1-3 for a complete list of cog registers. Each cog is designed exactly the same and can run tasks independently from the others.

All eight cogs are driven from the same clock source, the System Clock, so they each maintain the same time reference and all active cogs execute instructions simultaneously. See System Clock, above. They also all have access to the same shared resources, like I/O pins, Main RAM, and the System Counter. See Shared Resources, above.

Cogs can be started and stopped at run time and can be programmed to perform tasks simultaneously, either independently or with coordination from other cogs through Main RAM. Regardless of the nature of their use, the Propeller application designer has full control over how and when each cog is employed; there is no compiler-driven or operating system-driven splitting of tasks between multiple cogs. This method empowers the developer to deliver absolutely deterministic timing, power consumption, and response to the embedded application.

Each cog has its own RAM, called Cog RAM, which contains 512 registers of 32 bits each. The Cog RAM is all general purpose RAM except for the last 16 registers, which are special purpose registers, as described in Table 1-3. The Cog RAM is used for executable code, data, variables, and the last 16 locations serve as interfaces to the System Counter, I/O pins, and local cog peripherals.

When a cog is booted up, locations 0 ($000) through 495 ($1EF) are loaded sequentially from Main RAM / ROM and its special purpose locations, 496 ($1F0) through 511 ($1FF) are cleared to zero. After loading, the cog begins executing instructions, starting at location 0 of Cog RAM. It will continue to execute code until it is stopped or rebooted by either itself or another cog, or a reset occurs.

Table 1-3: Cog RAM Special Purpose Registers				
Cog RAM Map	**Address**	**Name**	**Type**	**Description**
	$1F0	PAR	Read-Only[1]	Boot Parameter
	$1F1	CNT	Read-Only[1]	System Counter
	$1F2	INA	Read-Only[1]	Input States for P31 - P0
	$1F3	INB	Read-Only[1]	Input States for P63- P32[2]
	$1F4	OUTA	Read/Write	Output States for P31 - P0
	$1F5	OUTB	Read/Write	Output States for P63 – P32[2]
General Purpose Registers (496 x 32)	$1F6	DIRA	Read/Write	Direction States for P31 - P0
	$1F7	DIRB	Read/Write	Direction States for P63 - P32[2]
	$1F8	CTRA	Read/Write	Counter A Control
	$1F9	CTRB	Read/Write	Counter B Control
	$1FA	FRQA	Read/Write	Counter A Frequency
	$1FB	FRQB	Read/Write	Counter B Frequency
Special Purpose Registers (16 x 32)	$1FC	PHSA	Read/Write	Counter A Phase:
	$1FD	PHSB	Read/Write	Counter B Phase
	$1FE	VCFG	Read/Write	Video Configuration
	$1FF	VSCL	Read/Write	Video Scale

Cog RAM Map addresses: $000, $1EF, $1F0, $1FF

Note 1: Only accessible as a Source Register (i.e. MOV DEST, SOURCE).
Note 2: Reserved for future use.

Each Special Purpose Register may be accessed via:

1) its physical register address,

2) its predefined name, or

3) a register array variable with an index of 0 to 15.

The following are examples in Propeller Assembly:

```
MOV    $1F4, #$FF        'Set OUTA 7:0 high
MOV    OUTA, #$FF        'Same as above
```

The following are examples in Spin:

```
SPR[$4] := $FF           'Set OUTA 7:0 high
OUTA := $FF              'Same as above
```

Hub

To maintain system integrity, mutually-exclusive resources must not be accessed by more than one cog at a time. The Hub maintains this integrity by controlling access to mutually-exclusive resources, giving each cog a turn to access them in a "round robin" fashion from Cog 0 through Cog 7 and back to Cog 0 again. The Hub, and the bus it controls, runs at half the System Clock rate. This means that the Hub gives a cog access to mutually-exclusive resources once every 16 System Clock cycles. Hub instructions, the Propeller Assembly instructions that access mutually-exclusive resources, require 7 cycles to execute but they first need to be synchronized to the start of the Hub Access Window. It takes up to 15 cycles (16 minus 1, if we just missed it) to synchronize to the Hub Access Window plus 7 cycles to execute the hub instruction, so hub instructions take from 7 to 22 cycles to complete.

Figure 1-3 and Figure 1-4 show examples where Cog 0 has a hub instruction to execute. Figure 1-3 shows the best-case scenario; the hub instruction was ready right at the start of that cog's access window. The hub instruction executes immediately (7 cycles) leaving an additional 9 cycles for other instructions before the next Hub Access Window arrives.

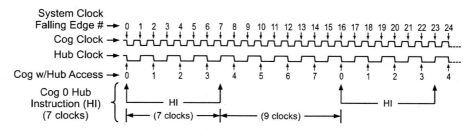

Figure 1-3: Cog-Hub Interaction – Best Case Scenario

Figure 1-4 shows the worst-case scenario; the hub instruction was ready on the cycle right after the start of Cog 0's access window; it just barely missed it. The cog waits until the next Hub Access Window (15 cycles later) then the hub instruction executes (7 cycles) for a total of 22 cycles for that hub instruction. Again, there are 9 additional cycles after the hub instruction for other instructions to execute before the next Hub Access Window arrives. To get the most efficiency out of Propeller Assembly routines that have to frequently access mutually-exclusive resources, it can be beneficial to interleave non-hub instructions with hub instructions to lessen the number of cycles waiting for the next Hub Access Window. Since most Propeller Assembly instructions take 4 clock cycles, two such instructions can be executed in between otherwise contiguous hub instructions.

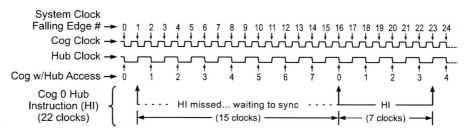

Figure 1-4: Cog-Hub Interaction – Worst Case Scenario

Keep in mind that a particular cog's hub instructions do not, in any way, interfere with other cogs' instructions because of the Hub mechanism. Cog 1, for example, may start a hub instruction during System Clock cycle 2, in both of these examples, possibly overlapping its execution with that of Cog 0 without any ill effects. Meanwhile, all other cogs can continue executing non-hub instructions, or awaiting their individual hub access windows regardless of what the others are doing.

I/O Pins

The Propeller has 32 I/O pins, 28 of which are entirely general purpose. Four I/O pins (28 - 31) have a special purpose at Boot Up and are available for general purpose use afterwards; see the Boot Up Procedure section on page 18. After boot up, any I/O pins can be used by any cogs at any time since I/O pins are one of the common resources. It is up to the application developer to ensure that no two cogs try to use the same I/O pin for different purposes during run-time.

Each cog has its own 32-bit I/O Direction Register and 32-bit I/O Output Register. The state of each cog's Direction Register is OR'd with that of the previous cogs' Direction Registers. Similarly, each cog's output states is OR'd with that of the previous cogs' output states. Note that each cog's output states are made up of the OR'd states of its internal I/O hardware and that is all AND'd with its Direction Register's states. The result is that each I/O pin's direction and output state is the "wired-OR" of the entire cog collective. No electrical contention between cogs is possible, yet they can all still access the I/O pins simultaneously!

The result of this I/O pin wiring configuration can easily be described in the following simple rules:

> A. A pin is an input <u>only</u> if no active cog sets it to an output.
>
> B. A pin outputs low <u>only</u> if all active cogs that set it to output also set it to low.
>
> C. A pin outputs high if <u>any</u> active cog sets it to an output and also sets it high.

Table 1-4 demonstrates a few possible combinations of the collective cogs' influence on a particular I/O pin, P12 in this example. For simplification, these examples assume that bit 12 of each cog's I/O hardware, other than its I/O Output Register, is cleared to zero (0).

Table 1-4: I/O Sharing Examples				
	Bit 12 of Cogs' I/O Direction Register	Bit 12 of Cogs' I/O Output Register	State of I/O Pin P12	Rule Followed
Cog ID	0 1 2 3 4 5 6 7	0 1 2 3 4 5 6 7		
Example 1	0 0 0 0 0 0 0 0	0 0 0 0 0 0 0 0	Input	A
Example 2	1 0 0 0 0 0 0 0	0 0 0 0 0 0 0 0	Output Low	B
Example 3	1 0 0 0 0 0 0 0	1 0 0 0 0 0 0 0	Output High	C
Example 4	1 0 0 0 0 0 0 0	0 1 0 0 0 0 0 0	Output Low	B
Example 5	1 1 0 0 0 0 0 0	0 1 0 0 0 0 0 0	Output High	C
Example 6	1 1 1 1 1 1 1 1	0 1 0 1 0 0 0 0	Output High	C
Example 7	1 1 1 1 1 1 1 1	0 0 0 1 0 0 0 0	Output High	C
Example 8	1 1 1 0 1 1 1 1	0 0 0 1 0 0 0 0	Output Low	B

Note: For the I/O Direction Register, a 1 in a bit location sets the corresponding I/O pin to the output direction while a 0 sets it to an input direction.

Any cog that is shut down has its Direction Register and output states cleared to zero, effectively removing it from influencing the final state of the I/O pins that the remaining active cogs are controlling.

Each cog also has its own 32-bit Input Register. This input register is really a pseudo-register; every time it is read, the actual states of the I/O pins are read, regardless of their input or output direction.

System Counter

The System Counter is a global, read-only, 32-bit counter that increments once every System Clock cycle. Cogs can read the System Counter (via their CNT register, page 184) to perform timing calculations and can use the WAITCNT command (page 322) to create effective delays within their processes. The System Counter is a common resource. Every cog can read it simultaneously. The System Counter is not cleared upon startup since its practical use is for differential timing. If a cog needs to keep track of time from a specific, fixed moment in time, it simply needs to read and save the initial counter value at that moment in time, and compare all of the later counter values against that initial value.

CLK Register

The CLK register is the System Clock configuration control; it determines the source of and the characteristics for the System Clock. More precisely, the CLK register configures the RC Oscillator, Clock PLL, Crystal Oscillator, and Clock Selector circuits. (See Figure 1-2: Propeller Chip Block Diagram on page 20.) It is configured at compile time by the _CLKMODE declaration and is writable at run time through the CLKSET command. Whenever the CLK register is written, a global delay of ≈75 µs occurs as the clock source transitions.

Whenever this register is changed, a copy of the value written should be placed in the Clock Mode value location (which is BYTE[4] in Main RAM) and the resulting master clock frequency should be written to the Clock Frequency value location (which is LONG[0] in Main RAM) so that objects which reference this data will have current information for their timing calculations. (See CLKMODE, page 179, and CLKFREQ, page 175.) When possible, it is recommended to use the CLKSET command (page 183), since it automatically updates all the above-mentioned locations with the proper information.

Table 1-5: CLK Register Structure								
Bit	7	6	5	4	3	2	1	0
Name	RESET	PLLENA	OSCENA	OSCM1	OSCM0	CLKSEL2	CLKSEL1	CLKSEL0

Table 1-6: RESET (Bit 7)	
Bit	**Effect**
0	Always write '0' here unless you intend to reset the chip.
1	Same as a hardware reset – reboots the chip. The Spin command REBOOT writes a '1' to the RESET bit.

Table 1-7: PLLENA (Bit 6)

Bit	Effect
0	Disables the PLL circuit. The RCFAST and RCSLOW settings of the _CLKMODE declaration configure PLLENA this way.
1	Enables the PLL circuit. Each of the PLLxx settings of the _CLKMODE declaration configures PLLENA this way at compile time. The Clock PLL internally multiplies the XIN pin frequency by 16. OSCENA must also be '1' to propagate the XIN signal to the Clock PLL. The Clock PLL's internal frequency must be kept within 64 MHz to 128 MHz – this translates to an XIN frequency range of 4 MHz to 8 MHz. Allow 100 µs for the Clock PLL to stabilize before switching to one of its outputs via the CLKSELx bits. Once the Crystal Oscillator and Clock PLL circuits are enabled and stabilized, you can switch freely among all clock sources by changing the CLKSELx bits.

Table 1-8: OSCENA (Bit 5)

Bit	Effect
0	Disables the Crystal Oscillator circuit. The RCFAST and RCSLOW settings of the _CLKMODE declaration configure OSCENA this way.
1	Enables the Crystal Oscillator circuit so that a clock signal can be input to XIN, or so that XIN and XOUT can function together as a feedback oscillator. The XINPUT and XTALx settings of the _CLKMODE declaration configure OSCENA this way. The OSCMx bits select the operating mode of the Crystal Oscillator circuit. Note that no external resistors or capacitors are required for crystals and resonators. Allow a crystal or resonator 10 ms to stabilize before switching to a Crystal Oscillator or Clock PLL output via the CLKSELx bits. When enabling the Crystal Oscillator circuit, the Clock PLL may be enabled at the same time so that they can share the stabilization period.

Table 1-9: OSCMx (Bits 4:3)

OSCMx		_CLKMODE	XOUT	XIN/XOUT	Frequency Range
1	0	Setting	Resistance	Capacitance	
0	0	XINPUT	Infinite	6 pF (pad only)	DC to 128 MHz Input
0	1	XTAL1	2000 Ω	36 pF	4 to 16 MHz Crystal/Resonator
1	0	XTAL2	1000 Ω	26 pF	8 to 32 MHz Crystal/Resonator
1	1	XTAL3	500 Ω	16 pF	20 to 60 MHz Crystal/Resonator

Table 1-10: CLKSELx (Bits 2:0)						
CLKSELx			_CLKMODE Setting	Master Clock	Source	Notes
2	**1**	**0**				
0	0	0	RCFAST	~12 MHz	Internal	No external parts. May range from 8 MHz to 20 MHz.
0	0	1	RCSLOW	~20 kHz	Internal	Very low power. May range from 13 kHz to 33 kHz.
0	1	0	XINPUT	XIN	OSC	OSCENA must be '1'.
0	1	1	XTALx and PLL1x	XIN x 1	OSC+PLL	OSCENA and PLLENA must be '1'.
1	0	0	XTALx and PLL2x	XIN x 2	OSC+PLL	OSCENA and PLLENA must be '1'.
1	0	1	XTALx and PLL4x	XIN x 4	OSC+PLL	OSCENA and PLLENA must be '1'.
1	1	0	XTALx and PLL8x	XIN x 8	OSC+PLL	OSCENA and PLLENA must be '1'.
1	1	1	XTALx and PLL16x	XIN x 16	OSC+PLL	OSCENA and PLLENA must be '1'.

Locks

There are eight lock bits (also known as semaphores) available to facilitate exclusive access to user-defined resources among multiple cogs. If a block of memory is to be used by two or more cogs at once and that block consists of more than one long (four bytes), the cogs will each have to perform multiple reads and writes to retrieve or update that memory block. This leads to the likely possibility of read/write contention on that memory block where one cog may be writing while another is reading, resulting in misreads and/or miswrites.

The locks are global bits accessed through the Hub via the Hub Instructions: LOCKNEW, LOCKRET, LOCKSET, and LOCKCLR. Because locks are accessed only through the Hub, only one cog at a time can affect them, making this an effective control mechanism. The Hub maintains an inventory of which locks are in use and their current states, and cogs can check out, return, set, and clear locks as needed during run time. See LOCKNEW, 230; LOCKRET, 233; LOCKSET, 234; and LOCKCLR, 228 for more information.

Main Memory

The Main Memory is a block of 64 K bytes (16 K longs) that is accessible by all cogs as a mutually-exclusive resource through the Hub. It consists of 32 KB of RAM and 32 KB of

ROM. The 32 KB of Main RAM is general purpose and is the destination of a Propeller Application either downloaded from a host or uploaded from the external 32 KB EEPROM. The 32 KB of Main ROM contains all the code and data resources vital to the Propeller chip's function: character definitions, log, anti-log and sine tables, and the Boot Loader and Spin Interpreter. The Main Memory organization is shown in Figure 1-5.

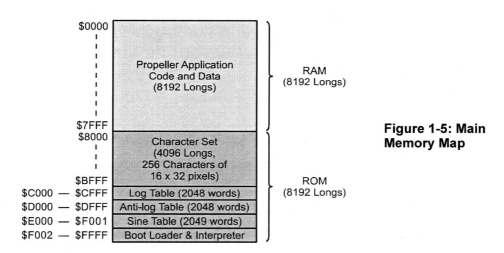

Figure 1-5: Main Memory Map

Main RAM

The first half of Main Memory is all RAM. This space is used for your program, data, variables and stack(s); otherwise known as your Propeller Application.

When a program is loaded into the chip, either from a host or from an external EEPROM, this entire memory space is written. The first 16 locations, $0000 – $000F, hold initialization data used by the Boot Loader and Interpreter. Your program's executable code and data will begin at $0010 and extend for some number of longs. The area after your executable code, extending to $7FFF, is used as variable and stack space.

There are two values stored in the initialization area that might be of interest to your program: a long at $0000 contains the initial master clock frequency, in Hertz, and a byte following it at $0004 contains the initial value written into the CLK register. These two values can be read/written using their physical addresses (LONG[$0] and BYTE[$4]) and can be read by using their predefined names (CLKFREQ and CLKMODE). If you change the CLK register without using the CLOCKSET command, you will also need to update these two locations so that objects which reference them will have current information.

Main ROM

The second half of Main Memory is all ROM. This space is used for character definitions, math functions, and the Boot Loader and Spin Interpreter.

Character Definitions

The first half of ROM is dedicated to a set of 256 character definitions. Each character definition is 16 pixels wide by 32 pixels tall. These character definitions can be used for video displays, graphical LCD's, printing, etc. The character set is based on a North American / Western European layout (Basic Latin and Latin-1 Supplement), with many specialized characters inserted. The special characters are connecting waveform and schematic building-blocks, Greek symbols commonly used in electronics, and several arrows and bullets.

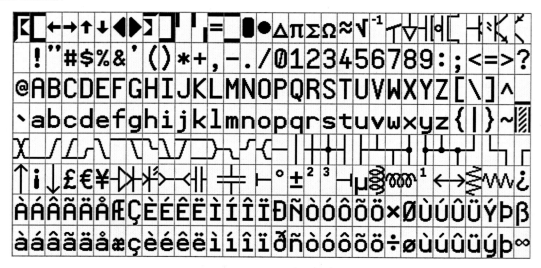

Figure 1-6: Propeller Font Characters

The character definitions are numbered 0 to 255 from left-to-right, top-to-bottom in Figure 1-6, above. In ROM, they are arranged with each pair of adjacent even-odd characters merged together to form 32 longs. The first character pair is located in bytes $8000-$807F. The second pair occupies bytes $8080-$80FF, and so on, until the last pair fills $BF80-$BFFF. The Propeller Tool includes an interactive character chart (Help → View Character Chart...) that has a ROM Bitmap view which shows where and how each character resides in ROM.

The character pairs are merged row-by-row such that each character's 16 horizontal pixels are spaced apart and interleaved with their neighbors' so that the even character takes bits 0, 2, 4, ...30, and the odd character takes bits 1, 3, 5, ...31. The leftmost pixels are in the lowest bits, while the rightmost pixels are in the highest bits, as shown in Figure 1-7. This forms a long (4 bytes) for each row of pixels in the character pair. 32 such longs, building from the character's top row down to the bottom, make up the complete merged-pair definition. The definitions are encoded in this manner so that a cog's video hardware can handle the merged longs directly, using color selection to display either the even or the odd character. It also has the advantage of allowing run-time character pairs (see next paragraph) that are four-color characters used to draw beveled buttons, lines and focus indicators.

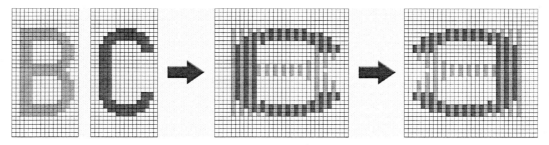

Figure 1-7: Propeller Character Interleaving

Some character codes have inescapable meanings, such as 9 for Tab, 10 for Line Feed, and 13 for Carriage Return. These character codes invoke actions and do not equate to static character definitions. For this reason, their character definitions have been used for special four-color characters. These four-color characters are used for drawing 3-D box edges at run time and are implemented as 16 x 16 pixel cells, as opposed to the normal 16 x 32 pixel cells. They occupy even-odd character pairs 0-1, 8-9, 10-11, and 12-13. Figure 1-8 shows an example of a button with 3D beveled edges made from some of these characters.

Figure 1-8: Button with 3-D Beveled Edges

The Propeller Tool includes, and uses, the Parallax True Type® font which follows the design of the Propeller Font embedded in the hardware. With this font, and the Propeller Tool, you can include schematics, timing diagrams and other diagrams right in the source code for your application.

Log and Anti-Log Tables

The log and anti-log tables are useful for converting values between their number form and exponent form.

When numbers are encoded into exponent form, simple math operations take on more complex effects. For example 'add' and 'subtract' become 'multiply' and 'divide.' 'Shift left' becomes 'square' and 'shift right' becomes 'square-root.' 'Divide by 3' will produce 'cube root.' Once the exponent is converted back to a number, the result will be apparent.

See Appendix B: Accessing Math Function Tables on page 420 for more information.

Sine Table

The sine table provides 2,049 unsigned 16-bit sine samples spanning from 0° to 90°, inclusively (0.0439° resolution). Sine values for all other quadrants covering > 90° to < 360° can be calculated from simple transformations on this single-quadrant sine table. The sine table can be used for calculations related to angular phenomena.

See Appendix B: Accessing Math Function Tables on page 420 for more information.

Boot Loader and Spin Interpreter

The last section in Main ROM contains the Propeller chip's Boot Loader and Spin Interpreter programs.

The Boot Loader is responsible for initializing the Propeller upon power-up/reset. When a Boot Up procedure is started, the Boot Loader is loaded into Cog 0's RAM and the cog executes the code starting at location 0. The Boot Loader program first checks the host and EEPROM communication pins for code/data to download/upload, processes that information accordingly and finally it either launches the Spin Interpreter program into Cog 0's RAM (overwriting itself) to run the user's Propeller Application, or it puts the Propeller into shutdown mode. See the Boot Up Procedure section on page 18.

The Spin Interpreter program fetches and executes the Propeller Application from Main RAM. This may lead to launching additional cogs to run more Spin code or Propeller Assembly code, as is requested by the application. See Run-Time Procedure, page 18.

Chapter 2: Using the Propeller Tool

This chapter describes the features of the Propeller Tool software starting with the concept and structure, followed by the software's screen organization and purpose, details of menu functions, and advanced features, and finishing with shortcut keys.

Concept

The engineering staff at Parallax has used many development environments over a period of more than 20 years. On many occasions we found ourselves thinking things like:

- It sure would be nice if feature "x" were easier to find/invoke.

- Where are my project files and why are there so many of them?

- Can I legally install/recompile/maintain this on another computer, years from now?

- Isn't there a less expensive solution?

This experience has driven us to renew our determination to create simple, inexpensive tools for our products.

The Propeller Tool was designed with those ideas in mind to provide many useful functions while maintaining a simple, consistent development environment that encourages quick and easy development of Propeller chip firmware objects.

The Propeller Tool software consists of a single executable file, some on-line help files and Propeller library files, all stored in the same folder by the installer, typically: C:\Program Files\Parallax Inc\Propeller. The Propeller Tool's executable file "Propeller.exe" can be copied and run from any folder on the computer; it does not rely on special system files other than what comes standard with the operating system.

Each library file (files with a ".spin" extension) is a self-contained object, available for use by your Propeller Projects, with both source code and documentation built-in. These are really just text files, either ANSI- or Unicode-encoded, that may be edited in any text editor that supports the encoding type; even Notepad in Windows® 2000 (and above) supports both ANSI and Unicode-encoded text files.

Did you notice we mentioned that an object's documentation is "built-in" to the object file? We encourage writing the user documentation for an object right inside the object's source file. This means fewer files to maintain and a higher likelihood that the documentation will stay in sync with the source code revision. To further enable this process, we've created:

- Two types of source comments, 1) code comments (for commenting portions of the source code), and 2) document comments (entered in code also, but intended for reading through the "documentation view" feature).

- A "documentation view" mode in the Propeller Tool that extracts an object's documentation from its source code for viewing purposes.

- A special font, the Parallax font, which contains special characters for things like schematics, timing diagrams, and tables within the object's documentation.

The Parallax font is a True Type® font built right into the Propeller Tool executable. It was designed in the same style as the font built into the Propeller chip's ROM. Using the special characters of the font, the object's documentation can include helpful diagrams for engineering purposes such as these:

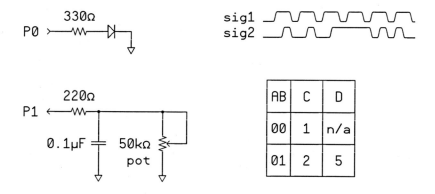

Figure 2-1: Graphics Built with the Parallax Font

After running the Propeller Tool at least once, this font becomes available for other programs on that computer as well so that you can see these special diagrams using other text editors, such as Notepad, or even within your email software, provided it supports Unicode-encoded text (a requirement of the special characters).

Every object you create for your project will also be stored in the same format as library files (with a ".spin" extension) but in the working directory of your choice. This is all designed to promote sharing and learning from existing objects, whether they were designed by us or by users of the Propeller products.

For more information about files, objects, object documentation, library files and source code, see Chapter 3: Propeller Programming Tutorial.

Screen Organization

The Propeller Tool software's main window is split into four sections, called "panes," each having a specific function.

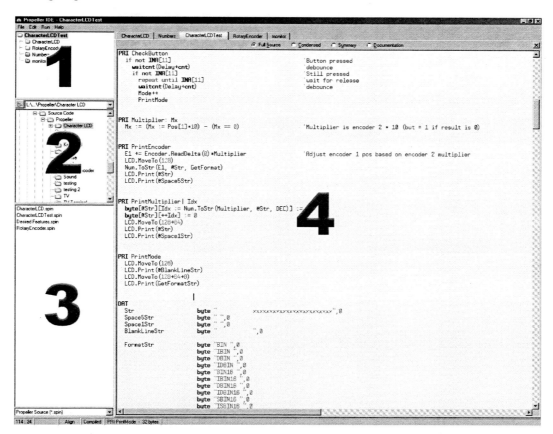

Figure 2-2: The Propeller Tool software's main window contains four major sections, or "panes."

Using the Propeller Tool

Panes one, two and three are all part of the Integrated Explorer. The Integrated Explorer is the region to the left of the Editor pane (pane four) that provides views of the project you're working on as well as folders and files on disk. The Integrated Explorer is separated from the Editor pane by a tall, vertical splitter bar that can be resized with the mouse at any time. The Integrated Explorer can even be hidden by resizing it down to nothing (left-click and drag its vertical splitter bar), by selecting File → Hide Explorer, or by pressing Ctrl+E. The menu and shortcut options toggle the Integrated Explorer between: 1) Visible (set to its last known size), and 2) Invisible (completely collapsed into the left edge of the Propeller Tool).

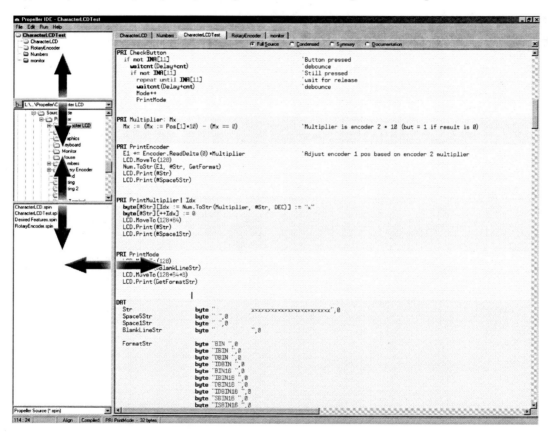

**Figure 2-3: The Integrated Explorer and its components
can be resized via the splitter bars.**

Pane 1: Object View Pane

Pane one is the Object View pane. The Propeller chip's language, Spin, is object-based and a Propeller Project can be made up of multiple objects. The Object View displays the hierarchical view of the project you most recently compiled successfully, providing valuable feedback on the relational structure of your project. Using the Object View, you can determine what objects are used, how they fit together with other objects, their physical location on disk (work folder, library folder or editor only), redundancy optimization results (if any) and any potential object collision issues. See "Object View" on page 52 for more information.

Pane 2: Recent Folders field and Folder List

Pane two contains two components: 1) the Recent Folders field, and 2) the Folder List. These two components work together to provide navigational access to the disk drives available to your computer. The Folder List displays a hierarchical view of folders within each disk drive and can be manipulated in a similar fashion as the left pane of Windows® Explorer.

The Recent Folders field (above the Folder List) provides a drop-down list of special folders as well as the most recent folders you've loaded files from. Selecting a folder from the Recent Folders field causes the Folder List to immediately navigate to that folder. In addition, if you select a folder in the Folder List which exists in the Recent Folders list, the Recent Folder field will automatically update itself to display that item.

The first items in the Recent Folders list are "Propeller Library" and "Propeller Library – Demos." These are automatically included to point to the folders where the Propeller library files exist and where the demos for the library files exist. Those files are included by the Propeller Tool installer.

If you select a folder that is not in the Recent Folders list, the Recent Folder field will be blank. The button to the left of the Recent Folders field toggles the function of both the Recent Folders and Folder List between: 1) showing every drive and folder, and 2) showing only drives and folders recently used. Setting the mode to show recent folders only is a convenient way to quickly navigate to commonly used Propeller Project folders among a large set of unrelated folders on a particular drive or network.

Pane 3: File List and Filter Field

Pane three contains two components: 1) the File List, and 2) the Filter field. The File List displays all the files contained in the folder selected from the Folder List which match the filter criteria of the Filter field. The File List can be used in a similar fashion as the right pane of Windows Explorer.

Using the Propeller Tool

The Filter field (below the File List) provides a drop-down list of file extensions, called filters, to display in the File List. Typically it will be set to show Spin files only (those with ".spin" file extensions) but can also be set to show text files or all files. If you navigate to a folder and don't see the files you expect to see, make sure that the current filter in the Filter field is set appropriately.

Files in the Files List can be opened into the editor by: 1) double-clicking them, 2) selecting and dragging them into the Editor pane (pane four), or 3) right-clicking them and selecting Open from the shortcut menu.

Pane 4: Editor Pane

Pane four is the Editor pane. The Editor pane provides a view of the Spin source code files you've opened and is the area where you can review, edit, or otherwise manipulate, all the source code objects for your project. Each file (source code object) you open is organized within the Editor pane as an individual edit tab named after the file it contains. The currently active edit tab is highlighted differently than the rest. You can have as many files open at once as you wish, limited only by memory.

Clicking on an edit tab brings its edit page into view. You can switch between open files by: 1) pressing Alt+CrsrLeft or Alt+CrsrRight, or 2) pressing Ctrl+Tab or Ctrl+Shift+Tab. If you let the mouse pointer hover over an edit tab long enough it will display a hint message with the full path and filename of the file it represents. The source code in the edit page is automatically syntax highlighted, both in foreground and background colors, to help distinguish block types, element types, comments vs. executable code, etc.

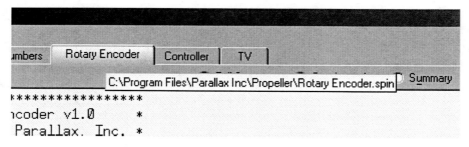

Figure 2-4: Hover the mouse over an edit tab to see the full path and file name that tab contains.

Each edit page can display source code in one of four views:

1) Full Source

2) Condensed

3) Summary

4) Documentation.

The view mode can be seen or changed, individually for each edit tab, by:

1) selecting the respective radio button with the mouse,

2) pressing Alt+Up or Alt+Down,

3) pressing Alt+<letter>, where <letter> is the underlined hot key of the desired view, or

4) pressing Alt and moving the mouse wheel up or down.

Note that the Documentation view can not be entered if the object can not be fully compiled at that moment. See the View Modes, Bookmarks and Line Numbers section beginning on page 61 for more information about view modes.

Since a project can consist of many objects, developing a project can be awkward unless you can see both the object you're working on and the object you're interfacing to at the same time. The Editor pane helps here by allowing its edit tabs to be dragged and dropped to different locations. For example, once multiple objects are open, you can use the left mouse button to select and drag the edit tab of an object down towards the bottom half of the Editor pane and simply drop it there. The display changes to show you a new edit tab region where you just dropped that edit tab. You can continue to drag and drop edit tabs to this new region if you wish. These steps are illustrated in Figure 2-5.

Figure 2-5: Viewing and Arranging Multiple Objects

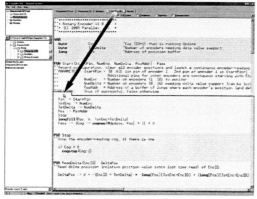

Step 1: To see more than one object's source code simultaneously, left-click and drag an edit tab to a lower region of the Editor Pane.

Step 2: Release the button to drop the edit tab. The edit tab and its contents now appear in the new region.

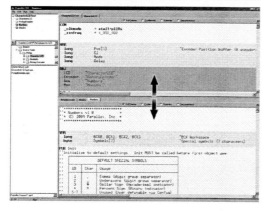

Step 3: Repeat steps 1 and 2 as necessary for other edit tabs and resize both regions using the horizontal splitter between them.

The vertical size of these two regions can be changed by dragging the horizontal splitter bar separating them. Of course, the objects you're interfacing to can be viewed in whatever mode is convenient at the moment (Full Source, Condensed, Summary, or Documentation) while the object you're developing remains in the Full Source view (the only editable view).

The Editor pane even allows its edit tabs to be dragged and dropped completely outside of the Propeller Tool. When this is done, the new edit tabs occupy a new window that can be manipulated independently of the Propeller Tool application window. This is particularly useful for development on computers with more than one monitor; edit tabs can be dragged from the application in one monitor and dropped onto the desktop of a second monitor.

Figure 2-6: Arranging Objects

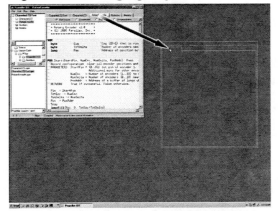

Step 1: If desktop space allows, you can even drag edit tabs outside the application itself; left-click and drag an edit tab to a region outside the Propeller Tool.

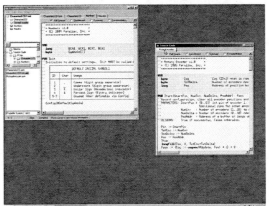

Step 2: Release the button to drop the edit tab; it will drop into a form of its own that can be moved and sized independent of the Propeller Tool. You can drag and drop more edit tabs into this new form also.

Using the Propeller Tool

The Status Bar at the bottom of the Propeller Tool, is separated into six panels, each displaying useful information at various stages of the development process.

Panel one of the Status Bar always displays the row and column position of the editor's caret in the currently active edit tab.

Figure 2-7: Status Bar

Panel two displays the modified status of the current edit tab: 1) blank, meaning not modified, 2) modified, or 3) read-only.

Panel three shows the current edit mode: 1) Insert (default), 2) Align, or 3) Overwrite. The edit mode can be changed by pressing the Insert key. See the Edit Modes section beginning on page 65 for more information about how the different edit modes work.

Panel four shows the compiled status of the current edit tab: 1) blank, meaning uncompiled, or 2) compiled. This panel indicates whether or not the source code it represents is still in the form it was in when it was last compiled. If the code has not been changed in any way since the last compile operation, this panel will say "Compiled."

Panel five displays context sensitive information about the current edit tab's source code if that code has not been changed since the last compile operation. Move the edit page's caret to CON or DAT block symbols or anywhere within PUB/PRI blocks to see information pertaining to that region.

Panel six displays temporary messages about the most recent operation. This is the area of the Status Bar where the error message, if any, from the last compile operation is displayed until another message overwrites it. This area also indicates successful compilations, font size changes and other status.

The entire Status Bar displays hints describing the function of each menu item on the menu bar as well as various other items when you let the mouse pointer hover over those items.

Menu Items

File Menu

New Create a new edit tab with a blank page. Any existing edit tabs are unaffected.

Open... Open a file in a new edit tab with the Open file dialog.

Open From... Open a file in a new edit tab from a recently accessed folder using the Open file dialog.

Save Save current edit tab's contents to disk using the existing file name, if applicable.

Save As... Save current edit tab's contents to disk with a new file name using the Save As dialog.

Save To... Save current edit tab's contents to disk in a recently accessed folder using the Save As dialog.

Save All Save all unsaved edit tab's contents to disk using their existing names, if applicable.

Close Close current edit tab (will prompt if file is unsaved).

Close All Close all edit tabs (will prompt for any files unsaved).

Select Top Object File... Select the top object file of current project. This setting is used for all of the Compile Top... operations and remains until changed.

Archive

→ Project... Collect all objects and data files for the project shown in Object View and store them in a compressed (.zip) file along with a "readme" file containing archive and structure information. The compressed file is named after the project's top file with "Archive" plus the date/time stamp appended and is stored in the top file's work directory.

→ Project + Propeller Tool... Perform the same task as above but add the entire Propeller Tool executable to the compressed file.

Using the Propeller Tool

Hide/Show Explorer   Hide or show the Integrated Explorer panels (left side of the application window).

Print Preview...   View a sample of the output before printing.

Print...   Print the current edit tab's contents.

<recent files>   The menu area between the Print... and Exit items displays the most recently accessed files, up to ten. Selecting one of these items opens that file. Point the mouse at a recent file menu item to see the full path and file name in the status bar.

Exit   Close the Propeller Tool.

Edit Menu

Undo   Undo the last edit action on the current edit page. Each edit page retains its own undo history buffer until closed. Multiple undo actions are allowed, limited only by memory.

Redo   Redo the last undone action on the current edit page. Each edit page retains its own redo history buffer until closed. Multiple redo actions are allowed, limited only by memory.

Cut   Delete the selected text from the current edit page and copy it to the Windows clipboard.

Copy   Copy the selected text from the current edit page to the Windows clipboard.

Paste   Paste text from the Windows clipboard to the current edit page at the current caret position.

Select All   Select all text in the current edit page.

Find / Replace...   Open the Find/Replace dialog; see Find/Replace Dialog on page 49 for details.

Find Next   Find the next occurrence of the last search string entered into the Find/Replace dialog.

Replace   Replace the current selection with the string entered into the Replace field of the Find/Replace dialog.

Go To Bookmark   Go to bookmark 1, 2, 3... (visible only when bookmarks are shown).

Text Bigger	Increase the font size in every edit page.
Text Smaller	Decrease the font size in every edit page.
Preferences…	Open the Preferences window. Users can customize many settings within the Propeller Tool using this feature.

Run Menu
Compile Current

→ **View Info…**	Compile source code in current edit tab and, if successful, display Object Info form with the results. The Object Info form displays many details about the resulting object including object structure, code size, variable space, free space and redundancy optimizations.
→ **Update Status**	Compile source code in current edit tab and, if successful, update the status info on the Status Bar for every object in the project.
→ **Load RAM**	Compile source code in current edit tab and, if successful, download the resulting application into Propeller chip's RAM and run it.
→ **Load EEPROM**	Compile source code in current edit tab and, if successful, download the resulting application into Propeller chip's EEPROM (and RAM) and run it.

Compile Top

→ **View Info…**	Same as Compile Current → View Info except compilation is started from the file designated as the "Top Object File."
→ **Update Status**	Same as Compile Current → Update Status except compilation is started from the file designated as the "Top Object File."
→ **Load RAM**	Same as Compile Current → Load RAM + Run except compilation is started from the file designated as the "Top Object File."
→ **Load EEPROM**	Same as Compile Current → Load EEPROM + Run except the compilation is started from the file designated as the "Top Object File."

| **Identify Hardware...** | Scan available ports for the Propeller chip and, if found, display the port it is connected to and the hardware version number. |

Help Menu

Propeller Tool...	Display on-line help about the Propeller Tool.
Spin Language...	Display on-line help about the Spin language.
Assembly Language...	Display on-line help about the Propeller Assembly language.
Example Projects...	Display on-line help containing example Propeller Projects.
View Character Chart...	Display the interactive Parallax Character Chart. This character chart shows the Parallax font's character set in three possible views: Standard Order, ROM Bitmap and Symbolic Order. Standard Order is the standard ANSI order. ROM Bitmap demonstrates how the character data is organized in the Propeller chip's ROM. Symbolic Order lists the characters in a categorical order (i.e.: alpha characters, numerics, punctuation, schematic symbols, etc). See Character Chart on page 58.
View Parallax Website...	Open up the Parallax website using the computer's default web browser.
E-mail Parallax Support...	Open up the computer's default email software and start a new message to Parallax support.
About...	Displays the About window with details about the Propeller Tool.

Find/Replace Dialog

The Find/Replace dialog is used to find and/or replace text in the current edit page.

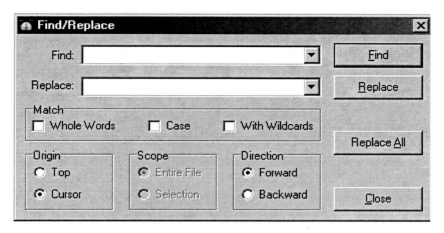

Figure 2-8: The Find/Replace Dialog

Find:

The Find: field is where to enter the string you wish to search for. If a word or phrase was selected in the current edit page when the Find/Replace dialog was opened, that word or phrase will automatically be entered in the Find: field. The Find: field remembers the last ten unique items entered into it. To select a previous entry, click the Find: field's down arrow and choose it from the drop-down list.

Replace:

The Replace: field is where to enter the string you wish to replace the found string with. The Replace: field remembers the last ten unique items entered into it. To select a previous entry, click the Replace: field's down arrow and choose it from the drop-down list.

Match

The Match group controls how the string in the Find: field is matched to text in the edit page. The Match options are: 1) Whole Words, 2) Case, and 3) With Wildcards.

Whole Words

Select the Whole Words checkbox if you want the string in the Find: field to match only characters of entire words rather than both characters of entire words and characters within larger words.

Case

Select the Case checkbox if you want the string in the Find: field to match only text of the same case; a case-sensitive search.

With Wildcards

Select the With Wildcards checkbox if you want the search to be performed using regular expression wildcards from the string in the Find: field.

The Origin, Scope and Direction groups all work together to dictate the start, range and direction the search process should use.

Origin

The Origin group controls where the search begins from; from the Top or from the Cursor. Selecting Top starts the search from the top of the file (or from the top of the selection if Selection is set in the Scope group). Selecting Cursor starts the search from the current cursor (caret) position in the file. Note: The "Top" option changes to "Bottom" if the Direction group is set to Backward.

Scope

The Scope group controls the range of the search: the Entire File or just the current Selection. This is a convenient way to perform a find, or a find and replace, within only a limited region of the file. The Scope group is set to Entire File by default and is disabled unless a selection is made prior to opening the Find/Replace dialog. The Scope group is set to Selection automatically if a selection of at least one entire line is made prior to opening the Find/Replace dialog.

Direction

The Direction group controls the direction of the search; in the Forward direction (towards the bottom of the file) or the Backward direction (towards the top of the file). If set to Backward, the Origin group's first option changes from "Top" to "Bottom," meaning the origin is from the bottom of the file or selection.

Find Button

The Find button starts the search process based on all the settings in the Find/Replace dialog. If text in the edit page matches the criteria, it is selected and moved into view, and then the Find button changes to a Find Next button. Additional clicks on the Find Next button result in the next matching text being selected and shown. You can also use the F3 key, with or without the Find/Replace dialog open, to perform more Find Next searches.

Replace Button

The Replace button is enabled if a string was entered in the Replace: field and a matching string was found (via Find button or F3). Clicking Replace, or pressing F4 with or without the Find/Replace dialog open, causes the currently matched string in the file to be replaced with the string in the Replace: field. After a replace, the Find Next button, or F3 key, needs to be used before Replace becomes available again. Holding the Control (Ctrl) key down changes the Replace button to "Replace/Find" and clicking it, or pressing Ctrl+F4 with or without the Find/Replace dialog open, causes the currently matched string to be replaced and then another Find Next operation to be performed immediately.

Replace All Button

The Replace All button is enabled if a string was entered in the Replace: field. Clicking on Replace All causes every matching string in the file to be found and replaced with the string in the Replace field, the dialog closes, and a results dialog appears indicating the number of occurrences found and replaced.

Close Button

The Close button closes the Find/Replace dialog.

Object View

The Object View displays a hierarchical view of the project you most recently compiled successfully. There are two Object Views in the Propeller Tool: 1) The Object View at the top of the Integrated Explorer in the main application's window (see Pane 1: Object View Pane on page 39), and 2) The Object Info View in the upper left of the Object Info form (see Object Info on page 55). Both of these Object Views function in a similar fashion.

The Object View provides visual feedback on the structure of the most recent successful compilation as well as information for each object within the compiled project.

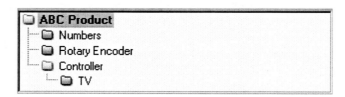

**Figure 2-9: Example Object View display showing
the structure of the ABC Product compilation**

In Figure 2-9 above, the Object View indicates the structure of the ABC Product application. In this example, the ABC Product object is the "top object file" (see Objects and Applications, page 87) and it uses the Numbers, Rotary Encoder and Controller objects. Additionally, the Controller object uses the TV object.

The object names shown are their actual file names without the extension. The name includes their file extension only if they are data files (see FILE, page 215) and is shown in italics as well.

The icons to the left of each object name indicate the folder that the object exists in. This list shows the four possibilities:

- (yellow): Object is within the Work Folder.
- (blue) : Object is within the Library Folder.
- (striped): Object is in Work Folder but another object with the same name is also being used from the Library Folder.
- (hollow): Object is not in any folder because it has never been saved.

Work Folder

The Work Folder (yellow) is the folder where the top object file exists. Every project has one, and only one, work folder.

Library Folder

The Library Folder (blue) is where the Propeller Tool's library objects exist, such as those that came with the Propeller Tool software. The Library Folder is always the folder that the Propeller Tool executable started from, and every object (file with .spin extension) within it is considered to be a library object.

Striped Folders

Objects with striped icons indicate that an object from the work folder and an object from the library folder each refer to a sub-object of the same name and that sub object happens to exist in both the work and library folders. This same-named object may be: 1) an exact copy of the same object, 2) two versions of the same object, or 3) two completely different objects that just happen to have the same name. Regardless of the situation, it is recommended that you resolve this potential problem as soon as possible since it may lead to problems later on, such as not being able to use the Archive feature.

Hollow Folders

Objects with hollow icons indicate that the object was created in the editor and has never been saved to any folder on the hard drive. This situation, like the one mentioned above, is not an immediate problem but can lead to future problems if it is not addressed soon.

Using the mouse to point at and select objects can provide additional information as well. Clicking on an object within the Object View opens that object into the Editor pane. Left-clicking opens that object in Full Source view, right-clicking opens it in Documentation view and double-clicking opens it, and all its sub-objects, in Full Source view. If the object was already open, the Editor pane simply makes the related edit tab active and switches to the appropriate view; Full Source for a left-click or double-click, or Documentation for a right-click.

Using the Propeller Tool

Hovering the mouse over an object in the Object View displays a hint with additional information for that object. Figure 2-10a shows the hint for the ABC Product object. This hint indicates 1) the ABC Product object is the top object file of the project, 2) it exists in the work folder, and 3) its path and file name are: C:\Source\ABC Product.spin. From this information you can also infer that the work folder for this project is:

> C:\Source

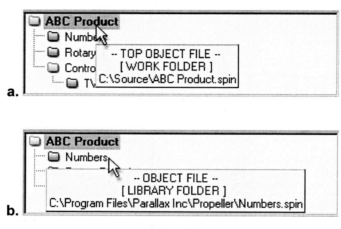

**Figure 2-10: Hover the mouse over an object
to see hints with additional information**

Figure 2-10b shows the hint for the Numbers object: 1) it's an object file (i.e.: a sub object, rather than the top object), 2) it's in the library folder, and 3) it's at the path and file name: C:\Program Files\Parallax Inc\Propeller\Numbers.spin. From this information you can also infer that the library folder for this project is:

> C:\Program Files\Parallax Inc\Propeller.

It's a good idea to review the hints in the Object View occasionally since they may also contain additional helpful information, such as warnings about conflicts and optimization results.

Object Info

The Object Info form displays details about the project you just compiled successfully using the Compile Current/Top → View Info… function. At the top is an Info Object View very similar to that of the Integrated Explorer's Object View (see Object View, p. 52). Below the Info Object View are two panels with summary information.

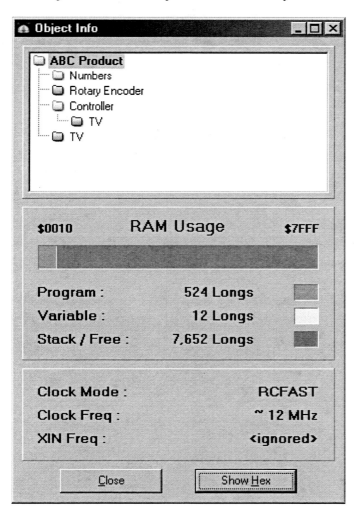

Figure 2-11: Object Info Form

This example Object Info display shows details about the "ABC Product" project compilation.

Info Object View

The Info Object View works exactly like the Object View (see Object View, p. 52) with a few exceptions:

- Clicking on an object within the Info Object View updates the Object Info display with information pertaining to that object.

- Double-clicking on an object within the Info Object View opens that object in the Edit pane.

- Data files are not selectable in the Info Object View.

RAM Usage Panel

The RAM Usage panel displays statistics about RAM allocation by the object currently selected in the Info Object View. The horizontal bar gives a summary view of the entire RAM with its color legend and numerical details below it. For example, Figure 2-11 shows that the ABC Product object consumes 524 longs (2096 bytes) for program space and 12 longs (48 bytes) for variable space, leaving over 7k longs (over 30k bytes) free.

Clock Panel

The clock panel, under the RAM Usage panel, displays the clock/oscillator settings of the object currently selected in the Info Object View. For example, Figure 2-11 shows that the ABC Product object configured the clock for RCFAST, approximately 12 MHz and no XIN frequency.

Hex View

The Show/Hide Hex button shows or hides the detailed object hex view, as in Figure 2-12 on the next page. The hex view shows the actual compiled object data, in hexadecimal, that are loaded into the Propeller chip's RAM/EEPROM upon download.

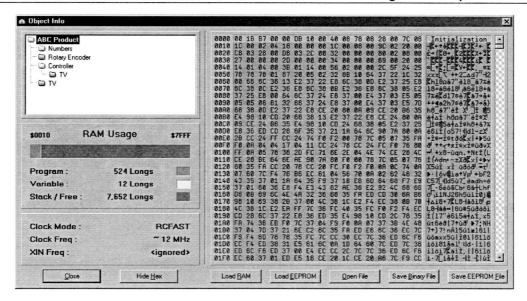

Figure 2-12: Example Object Info Form display with the object Hex View open showing the hex values of the ABC Product compilation.

The buttons under the hex display allow for downloading and saving of the currently displayed hex data.

The first two buttons, Load RAM and Load EEPROM, perform the same function as the similarly named menu items under the Compile Current/Top menu. It's important to note that they use the current object (the one selected in the Info Object View) as the source to download. In other words, you can actually select a sub-object from the project and download just that; a practical procedure only if that object were designed to run completely on its own.

The last three buttons, Open File, Save Binary File, and Save EEPROM File, either open a file or save a file to disk. The Open File button opens a previously saved Binary or EEPROM file into the Object Info window. The "save" buttons save the hex data from the currently selected object to a file on disk. Save Binary File saves only the portion actually used by the object; the program data, but not variable or stack/free space. Save EEPROM File saves the entire EEPROM image, including variable and stack/free space. Use Save EEPROM File if you wish to have a file that you can load into an EEPROM programmer for production purposes.

Character Chart

The Character Chart window is available from the Help → View Character Chart... menu item. It shows the entire character set for the Parallax Font that is used by the Propeller Tool and is also built into the ROM of the Propeller chip. There are three views in the Character Chart: 1) Standard Order, 2) ROM Bitmap, and 3) Symbolic Order.

In each of the three views, the mouse, left mouse button, cursor keys and enter button can be used to highlight and select a character. If clicked (or enter pressed), the highlighted character will be entered into the current edit page at the current cursor location. As a new character is highlighted, the title bar and info bar of the window updates to show the name, size and address information for that character. Moving the mouse wheel up or down changes the font size displayed in this window.

Standard Order

Standard Order, shown in Figure 2-13, displays the characters in the order that follows that of the ANSI set typically used by modern day computers.

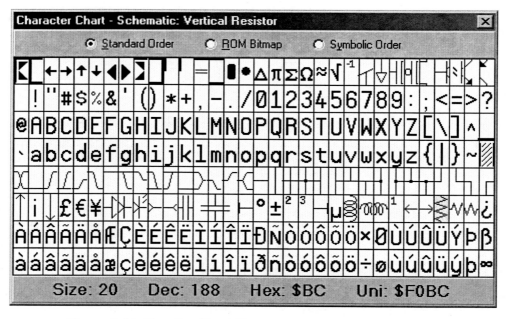

Figure 2-13: Parallax Font Character Chart, Standard Order

The Vertical Resistor character (near the lower right of the display) is selected in this example. The information at the bottom of the window shows the font size, in points, and the character's location in the character set in decimal, hexadecimal, and Unicode. Note: The Unicode value is the address of the character in the True Type® Font file that is used by the Propeller Tool. The decimal and hexadecimal values are the logical addresses of the character in the character set within the Propeller chip and correspond to that location in the ANSI character set used by most computers.

ROM Bitmap

The ROM Bitmap, Figure 2-14, shows the characters in a way representative of how they are stored in the Propeller chip's ROM. This view uses four colors, white, light gray, dark gray, and black, to represent the bit pattern of each font character. Each character, in the Propeller chip's ROM, is defined with two bits of color (four colors per row in each character cell). The rows of each pair of adjacent characters are overlapped in memory for the purpose of creating the run-time characters used to draw 3D buttons with hot key and focus indicators; see Character Definitions on page 32. The information at the bottom of the window shows the font size, in points, and the selected character's pixel data address range in the Propeller chip's ROM.

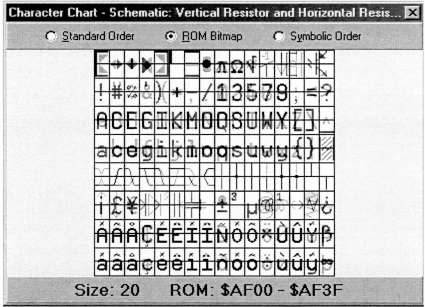

Figure 2-14: Parallax Font Character Chart, ROM Bitmap

Symbolic Order

Symbolic Order, Figure 2-15, shows the characters arranged categorically. This is useful for finding the special characters in the Parallax font for depicting timing diagrams, lines, arrows, and schematics.

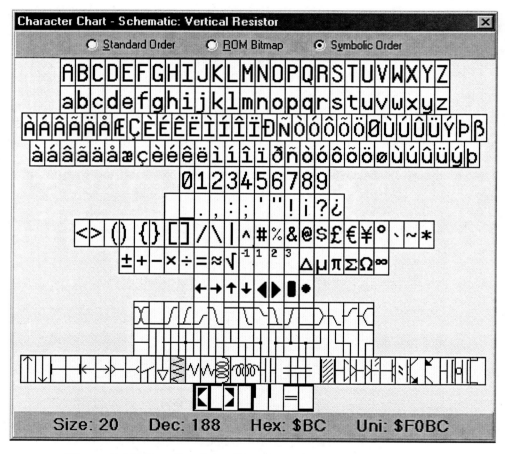

Figure 2-15: Parallax Font Character Chart, Symbolic Order

View Modes, Bookmarks and Line Numbers

While developing objects, or conversing about them with other users, it may sometimes be difficult to quickly navigate to certain regions of code simply because of the size of the file itself or because large sections of code and comments obscure the desired section. There are a number of features built into the Propeller Tool to assist with this problem, including different View Modes, Bookmarks and Line Numbers.

View Modes

Each edit tab can display an object's source in one of four view modes: 1) Full Source, 2) Condensed, 3) Summary, and 4) Documentation.

- Full Source view displays every line of source code within the object and is the only view that supports editing.

- Condensed view hides every line that contains only a code comment as well as contiguous lines that are blank, showing only compilable lines of code.

- Summary view displays only the block heading lines (CON, VAR, OBJ, PUB, PRI, and DAT); a convenient way to see the entire object's structure at a glance.

- Documentation view displays the object's documentation generated by the compiler from the source code's doc comments (see Exercise 3: Output.spin - Comments on page 100 for more information).

By briefly switching to another view you may be able to locate the routine or region of code desired. For example, Figure 2-16a shows the Graphics object open in an edit page. If you were having trouble finding the "plot" routine within the source code, you could switch to the Summary view (Figure 2-16b) locate the "plot" routine's header line and click the mouse on that line to place the cursor there, then switch back to Full Source view (Figure 2-16c). Keep your eye on the line with the cursor because the code will expand to full view above and below the line where the cursor is.

The view mode can be changed a number of ways; see the Shortcut Keys listing beginning on page 75. For example, while in any view mode other than Full Source, pressing the Escape key will take you back to Full Source view. While in Condensed or Summary view modes, double-clicking on a line will switch back to Full Source view; expanding above and below that line. Also, the view mode bar items act like a toggle so that clicking on the Summary item switches back and forth between Summary view and the previous view mode.

Figure 2-16: View Modes Example

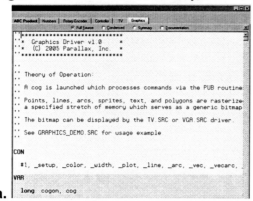

a.

Can't find a routine in an object?

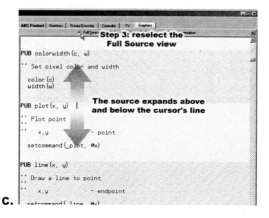

b.

Step 1: Select Summary Mode

Step 2: Click on the routine's line.

c.

Step 3: Select Full Source mode again; the code re-expands around the cursor's line,

-or-

Double-click on the desired line from Step 2.

Bookmarks

You can also set bookmarks on various lines of each edit page's source code to quickly jump to desired locations. Figure 2-17 shows an example of two bookmarks set in the Graphics object's edit tab. To enable bookmarks, press Ctrl+Shift+B to make the Bookmark Gutter visible; a blank area to the left of the edit page. Then click the mouse in the Bookmark Gutter next to each line you want to be able to navigate to quickly. Finally, from anywhere in the page, press Ctrl+# where # is the bookmark number that you want to go to; the cursor will instantly jump to that location. Up to 9 bookmarks (1 – 9) can be set in each edit tab. The bookmarks are not saved in the source code; however, the bookmark settings of the last 10 files accessed are remembered by the Propeller Tool and restored upon reopening those files.

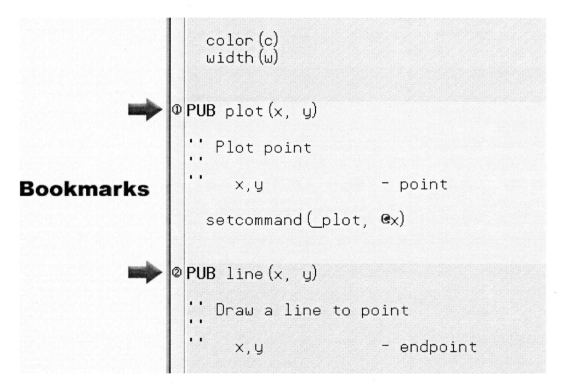

Figure 2-17: Example edit page with Bookmarks enabled and two bookmarks set.
Click on Bookmark Gutter (blank area left of edit page) to set or clear bookmarks. Press Ctrl+# where # is the desired bookmark number to instantly navigate to an existing bookmark.

Line Numbers

Maybe it is easier to remember a region of code by its line number. At any time, you can enable or disable line numbers in the edit page. Line Numbers show up in the Line Number Gutter, next to the Bookmark Gutter (see Figure 2-18), and can be made visible/invisible by pressing Ctrl+Shift+N. Lines are automatically numbered as they are created; they are a visual item only and are not stored in the source code. Though Line Numbers share space with Bookmarks, the two are independent of each other and can be enabled or disabled individually. Line numbers can be printed, if desired.

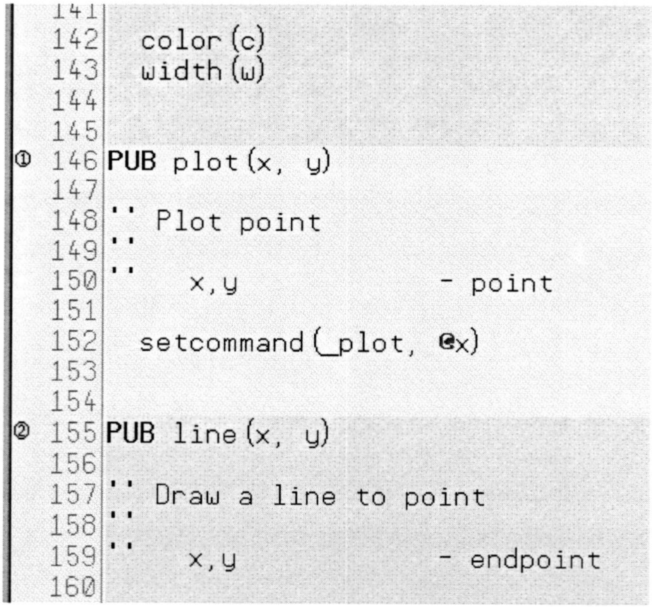

```
    141
    142    color (c)
    143    width (w)
    144
    145
①   146 PUB plot (x, y)
    147
    148 '' Plot point
    149 ''
    150 ''    x,y              - point
    151
    152    setcommand (_plot, @x)
    153
    154
②   155 PUB line (x, y)
    156
    157 '' Draw a line to point
    158 ''
    159 ''    x,y              - endpoint
    160
```

**Figure 2-18: Example Edit Page with Bookmarks
and Line Numbers Enabled**

Edit Modes

There are three edit modes provided by the Editor pane: 1) Insert (default), 2) Align (available for ".spin" objects only), and 3) Overwrite. You can switch between each mode by using the Insert key. The current mode is reflected by both the caret shape and by panel three of the status bar.

Figure 2-19: Edit Modes

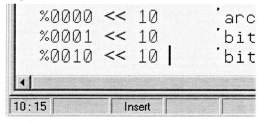

Insert Edit Mode

Caret is the standard blinking, vertical bar and the status bar shows "Insert."

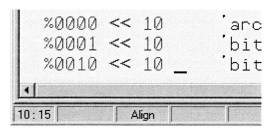

Align Edit Mode

Caret is a blinking underline and the status bar shows "Align."

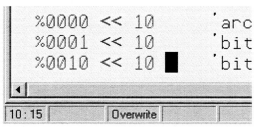

Overwrite Edit Mode

Caret is a blinking, solid block and the status bar shows "Overwrite."

Insert and Overwrite Modes

The Insert and Overwrite modes are similar to that of many other text editors. These are the only two modes available to edit tabs containing files other than Propeller ".spin" objects, such as ".txt" files.

Align Mode

The Align mode is a special version of the Insert mode designed specifically for maintaining source code. To understand Align mode, we first need to consider common programming techniques. There are two very common practices used when writing modern source code: indention of code and alignment of comments to the right of code. It is also common for source code to be viewed and edited using more than one editor application. Historically, programmers have used either tabs or spaces for indention and alignment purposes, both of which prove problematic. Tab characters cause alignment issues because some editors use different sized tab settings than others. Both tab and space characters cause alignment issues because future edits cause right-side comments to shift out of alignment. Here are some examples; Figure 2-20 is our original code.

Figure 2-20: Common Alignment Issues – Original Code

```
PRI CheckButton
    if not INA[11]              'Button pressed
       waitcnt(Delay+cnt)       'debounce
       if not INA[11]           'Still pressed
          repeat until INA[11]  'wait for release
          waitcnt(Delay+cnt)    'debounce
          Mode++
          PrintMode
```

If the original code used tab characters to align the comments, changing "Delay" to "BtnDelay" will cause a comment to shift right if the altered text crosses a tab boundary.

Figure 2-21: Common Alignment Issues – Tab Aligned

```
PRI CheckButton
    if not INA[11]              'Button pressed
       waitcnt(BtnDelay+cnt)            'debounce
       if not INA[11]           'Still pressed
          repeat until INA[11]  'wait for release
          waitcnt(BtnDelay+cnt) 'debounce
          Mode++
          PrintMode
```

If the original code had been made with tab characters to align the comments, changing "Delay" to "BtnDelay" results in the second comment suddenly being pushed out by another tab width.

If the original code used space characters to align the comments, changing "Delay" to "BtnDelay" will cause the comments to shift right by three characters.

Figure 2-22: Common Alignment Issues – Space Aligned

```
PRI CheckButton
    if not INA[11]                'Button pressed
       waitcnt(BtnDelay+cnt)      ➞'debounce
       if not INA[11]             'Still pressed
          repeat until INA[11]    'wait for release
             waitcnt(BtnDelay+cnt) ➞'debounce
          Mode++
          PrintMode
```

If the original code had been made with space characters to align the comments, and a standard Insert edit mode is used, changing "Delay" to "BtnDelay" results in the second and fifth comments being pushed out by 3 spaces.

For Spin code, the Propeller Tool solves this problem first by disallowing tab characters (Tab key presses emit the proper number of space characters), and second by providing the Align edit mode. While in the Align mode, characters inserted into a line affect neighboring characters but not characters separated by more than one space. The result is that comments and other items separated by more than one space maintain their intended alignment for as long as possible, as shown in Figure 2-23.

Figure 2-23: Effects of the Align Edit Mode

```
PRI CheckButton
    if not INA[11]                'Button pressed
       waitcnt(BtnDelay+cnt)      'debounce
       if not INA[11]             'Still pressed
          repeat until INA[11]    'wait for release
             waitcnt(BtnDelay+cnt) 'debounce
          Mode++
          PrintMode
```

Using the Align edit mode, changing "Delay" to "BtnDelay" leaves all the comments in their original, aligned, location. No manual re-aligning of comments is necessary in this case.

Since the Align mode maintains existing alignments as much as possible, much less time is wasted realigning elements due to future edits by the programmer. Additionally, since spaces are used instead of tab characters, the code maintains the same look and feel in any editor that displays it with a mono-spaced font.

The Align mode isn't perfect for all situations, however. We recommend you use Insert mode for most code writing and briefly switch to Align mode to maintain existing code where alignment is a concern. The Insert key rotates the mode through Insert → Align → Overwrite and back to Insert again. The Ctrl+Insert key shortcut toggles only between Insert and Align modes. A little practice with the Align and Insert modes will help you program more time-efficiently.

Note that non-Spin source (without a .spin extension) does not allow the Align mode. This is because, for non-Spin source, the Propeller Tool is designed to maintain any existing tab characters and to insert tab characters when the Tab key is pressed in order to maintain the original intent of the file, which may be a tab-delimited data source for a Spin program or other use where tab characters are desired.

Block Selection and Selection Moving

In addition to normal text selections made with the mouse, the Propeller Tool allows block selections (rectangular regions of text). To make a block selection, first press and hold the Alt key, then left-click and drag the mouse to select the text region. After the selection is made, cut and copy operations behave as they do with other selections. Figure 2-24 demonstrates block selection and movement of the text block with the mouse.

Figure 2-24: Block Selection and Selection Moving

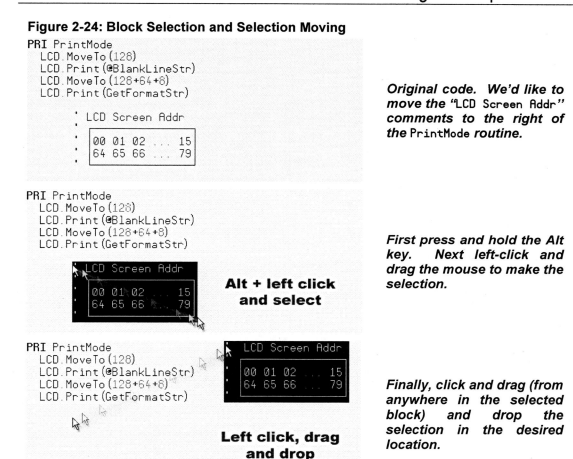

```
PRI PrintMode
   LCD.MoveTo (128)
   LCD.Print (@BlankLineStr)
   LCD.MoveTo (128+64+8)
   LCD.Print (GetFormatStr)

          LCD Screen Addr

          00 01 02 ... 15
          64 65 66 ... 79
```

Original code. We'd like to move the "LCD Screen Addr" comments to the right of the PrintMode *routine.*

```
PRI PrintMode
   LCD.MoveTo (128)
   LCD.Print (@BlankLineStr)
   LCD.MoveTo (128+64+8)
   LCD.Print (GetFormatStr)

          LCD Screen Addr

          00 01 02 ... 15
          64 65 66 ... 79
```

Alt + left click and select

First press and hold the Alt key. Next left-click and drag the mouse to make the selection.

```
PRI PrintMode
   LCD.MoveTo (128)
   LCD.Print (@BlankLineStr)
   LCD.MoveTo (128+64+8)
   LCD.Print (GetFormatStr)
```

```
          LCD Screen Addr

          00 01 02 ... 15
          64 65 66 ... 79
```

Left click, drag and drop

Finally, click and drag (from anywhere in the selected block) and drop the selection in the desired location.

Indenting and Outdenting

A common programming practice is to indent blocks of code that are either in loops or are conditionally executed in order to make that code easier to read. The act of doing this is called "indenting." We'll call the opposite action, shifting code to the left, "outdenting." The Spin language requires this kind of formatting to indicate which lines are within loops or conditional blocks. The Propeller Tool includes the following features to make this easier to accomplish while creating or maintaining code.

Single Lines

For Spin code, the Propeller Tool uses a set of fixed tab positions that you can change via the Edit → Preferences menu. Each Spin block (CON, VAR, OBJ, PUB, PRI, and DAT) has its own Fixed Tab settings.

The Tab key moves the cursor to the next tab position (to the right) and Shift + Tab moves the cursor to the previous tab position (to the left). Additionally, the Backspace key moves to the previous tab position depending on the text around it; more on this later.

The default tab settings for the PUB and PRI blocks include tab positions for every two characters near the start of the line to support common code indentions. For example, Figure 2-25, below, shows a public method, FSqr, containing lines at various levels of indention, each two characters apart.

```
PUB FSqr
  repeat 31
    result |= root
    if result ** result > m
      result ^= root
    root >>= 1
  m := result >> 1
```

Figure 2-25: Fixed Tab Default Setting for PUB and PRI Blocks

Using the Tab key, this code could have quickly been entered with the following sequence on the keyboard:

- Type: "PUB FSqr" <Enter>

- Type: <Tab> "repeat 31" <Enter>

- Type: <Tab> "result |= root" <Enter>, etc.

Note that the Enter key automatically aligns the cursor to the level of indention currently in use; this means the Tab key needs to be pressed only once to indent to the next level.

If there are characters to the right of the cursor when the Tab key is pressed, they are shifted to the right as well, as in Figure 2-26.

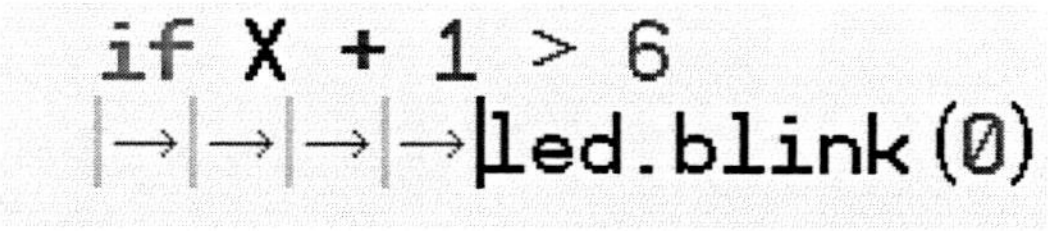

Figure 2-26: Indenting

If the cursor is immediately to the left of the first character on a line, both the Shift + Tab and the Backspace keys cause the cursor and the text to be shifted left to the previous tab position; i.e.: outdenting. If, however, the cursor is not immediately to the left of the first character on a line, Backspace acts normally (deleting the previous character) and Shift + Tab moves only the cursor to the previous tab position.

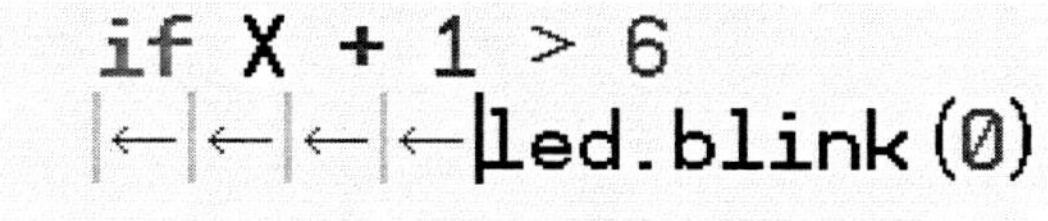

Figure 2-27: Outdenting

Multiple Lines

In addition to affecting single lines, multiple lines of code can be indented or outdented to fixed tab positions easily. Take a look at Figure 2-28.

```
result |= root
if result ** result > m
  result ^= root
root >>= 1
m := result >> 1
```

Figure 2-28: Sample Code Block. We want to make the first four lines repeat 31 times.

Suppose we wanted to take the first four lines of this example and encase them in a "repeat 31" loop; to repeat those lines 31 times. You can quickly achieve this with the following steps: 1) enter the "repeat 31" line above the existing lines, 2) using the mouse, select the four lines to indent, and 3) press the Tab key. These steps are illustrated in Figure 2-29.

Figure 2-29: Code Block Indenting

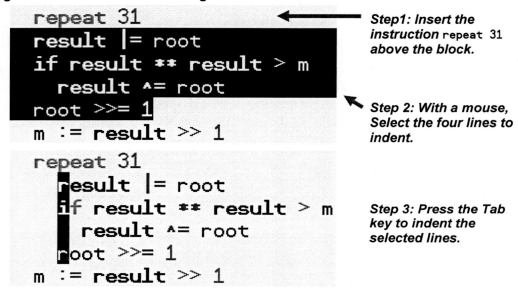

Step1: *Insert the instruction* repeat 31 *above the block.*

Step 2: *With a mouse, Select the four lines to indent.*

Step 3: *Press the Tab key to indent the selected lines.*

Note that the four lines we had selected in the second step are now indented to the next fixed tab position (two spaces to the right of the start of the "repeat") and the selection changed to a single column surrounding the first characters of the lines. The selection changed to indicate that we performed a multi-line indention action. Pressing the Tab key again will indent that group of lines further and pressing Shift + Tab will outdent that group of lines.

Any contiguous group of lines can be indented or outdented in this fashion. The selection itself doesn't have to include the entire line either; it only needs to include at least one character of more than one line to work. This type of selection is called a "stream" selection.

The second type of selection, a "block" selection (see Block Selection and Selection Moving, page 68), can also be used to indent or outdent portions of lines. For example, Figure 2-30 shows our example with comments to the right of the lines.

Figure 2-30: Sample Code Block with Comments to the Right

```
repeat 31                        'loop 31 times
   result |= root                'OR result w/root
   if result ** result > m 'calculate square
      result ^= root
   root >>= 1                     'shift root right
 m := result >> 1
```

If we block select the first few characters of the comments (Alt + Left Mouse Button and Drag, Figure 2-31), we can press the Tab key to indent those comments to the next fixed tab position. Pressing Shift + Tab will outdent them, at least up to any characters they bump into on their left, as in Figure 2-32.

Figure 2-31: Using Block Selection to Outdent Comments

```
repeat 31                        'loop 31 times
   result |= root                'OR result w/root
   if result ** result > m 'calculate square
      result ^= root
   root >>= 1                     'shift root right
 m := result >> 1
```

Step 1: Block-select the comment lines (Alt + Left Mouse Button and Drag).

```
repeat 31                        'loop 31 times
   result |= root                'OR result w/root
   if result ** result > m  'calculate square
      result ^= root
   root >>= 1                     'shift root right
 m := result >> 1
```

Step 2: Press the Tab key to outdent the comments.

Block–Group Indicators

Sometimes it may be hard to see exactly how groups of code are logically arranged simply by their level of indention. The Propeller Tool can optionally indicate the logical block-groups of conditional blocks or loop blocks as shown in Figure 2-32. To toggle this feature on or off, press Ctrl + I.

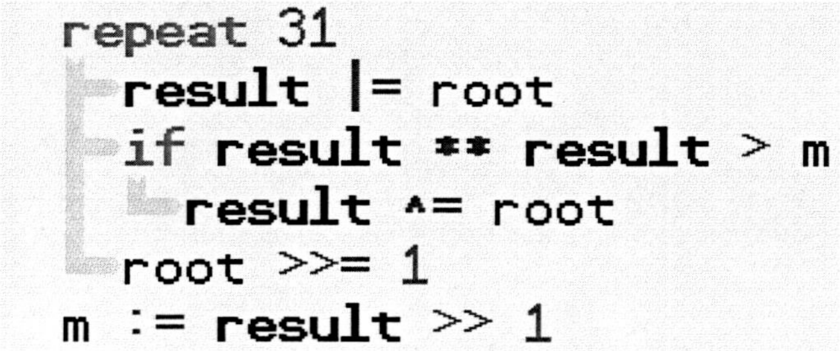

```
repeat 31
  result |= root
  if result ** result > m
    result ^= root
  root >>= 1
m := result >> 1
```

Figure 2-32: Block Group Indicators

Note that only compilable code that is actually within a conditional block or a loop block is actually enhanced with the indention indicators. Also, this is simply a visual aid to see how the code will be executed; it does not affect the code or the source file physically; only the actual levels of indention do that.

Shortcut Keys

Categorical Listings

In Table 2-1, keyboard shortcuts are grouped by related functions. In Table 2-2, which begins on page 80, the keyboard shortcuts are grouped by key rather than by function.

Table 2-1: Shortcut Keys – Categorical Listing	
Tool Shortcuts	
Function	**Keys**
New	Ctrl + N
Open	Ctrl + O
Close	Alt + Q -or- Ctrl + W
Save	Ctrl + S
Save All	Ctrl + Alt + S
Print	Ctrl + P
Toggle Show/Hide Bookmarks	Ctrl + Shift + B
Toggle Bookmark on current line	Ctrl + B
Toggle Block Group Indicators	Ctrl + I
Toggle Show/Hide Explorer	Ctrl + E
Toggle Show/Hide Line Numbers	Ctrl + Shift + N
Increase font size	Ctrl + Up -or- Ctrl + Mouse Wheel Up
Decrease font size	Ctrl + Down -or- Ctrl + Mouse Wheel Down
Select Full Source view mode	Alt + S
Select Condensed view mode	Alt + C
Select Summary view mode	Alt + U
Select Documentation view mode	Alt + D
Select alternate view (towards Full Source)	Alt + Up
Select alternate view (towards Documentation)	Alt + Down -or- Alt + Mouse Wheel Down
Set focus on active edit	Esc

Table 2-1: Shortcut Keys – Categorical Listing (continued)	
Compiler Shortcuts	
Function	**Keys**
Select Top File	Ctrl + T
Identify Hardware	F7
Compile Current File and View Information	F8
Compile Current File and Update Status	F9
Compile Current File, Load RAM and Run	F10
Compile Current File, Load EEPROM and Run	F11
Compile Top File and View Information	Ctrl + F8
Compile Top File and Update Status	Ctrl + F9
Compile Top File, Load RAM and Run	Ctrl + F10
Compile Top File, Load EEPROM and Run	Ctrl + F11
Navigation Shortcuts	
Select next edit tab	Alt + Right -or- Ctrl + Tab
Select previous edit tab	Alt + Left -or- Ctrl + Shift + Tab
Scroll up one page size	Page Up
Scroll down one page size	Page Down
Scroll left	Shift + Mouse Wheel Up
Scroll right	Shift + Mouse Wheel Down
Jump to start of next word	Ctrl + Right
Jump to start of previous word	Ctrl + Left
Jump to start of line	Home
Jump to end of line	End
Jump to start of page	Ctrl + Page Up
Jump to end of page	Ctrl + Page Down
Jump to start of file	Ctrl + Home
Jump to end of file	Ctrl + End

Table 2-1: Shortcut Keys – Categorical Listing (continued)	
Navigation Shortcuts (cont.)	
Function	**Keys**
Select word	Double-Click
Select line	Triple-Click
Select to start of next word	Ctrl + Shift + Right
Select to start of previous word	Ctrl + Shift + Left
Select to start of line	Shift + Home
Select to end of line	Shift + End
Select to start of page	Ctrl + Shift + Page Up
Select to end of page	Ctrl + Shift + Page Down
Select to previous page above	Shift + Page Up
Select to next page below	Shift + Page Down
Select to start of file	Ctrl + Shift + Home
Select to end of file	Ctrl + Shift + End
Editing Shortcuts	
Undo	Ctrl + Z
Redo	Ctrl + Shift + Z
Select All	Ctrl + A
Copy to Clipboard	Ctrl + C
Cut to Clipboard	Ctrl + X
Paste from Clipboard	Ctrl + V
Find / Replace	Ctrl + F
Find Next	F3
Replace	F4
Replace then Find Next	Ctrl + F4
Change edit mode to Align, Insert or Overwrite	Insert
Toggle edit mode between Align and Insert	Ctrl + Insert
Insert white space up to next tab position	Tab
Delete white space back to previous tab position	Shift + Tab

Table 2-1: Shortcut Keys – Categorical Listing (continued)	
Editing Shortcuts (cont.)	
Function	**Keys**
Delete current line	Ctrl + Y
Delete to end of line	Ctrl + Shift + Y
Rename Folder/File (in Folder List or File List)	F2
Symbol Shortcuts	
Insert Negative One Superior Character ($^{-1}$)	Ctrl + Alt + 1
Insert One Superior Character (^{1})	Ctrl + Shift + 1
Insert Two Superior Character (^{2})	Ctrl + Shift + 2
Insert Three Superior Character (^{3})	Ctrl + Shift + 3
Insert Bullet Character (•)	Ctrl + Shift + .
Insert Rectangle Bullet Character (▌)	Ctrl + Alt + .
Insert Left Bullet Character (◀)	Ctrl + Shift + Alt + <
Insert Right Bullet Character (▶)	Ctrl + Shift + Alt + >
Insert Left Arrow Bullet Character (←)	Ctrl + Shift + Alt + Left
Insert Right Arrow Bullet Character (→)	Ctrl + Shift + Alt + Right
Insert Up Arrow Bullet Character (↑)	Ctrl + Shift + Alt + Up
Insert Right Arrow Bullet Character (→)	Ctrl + Shift + Alt + Right
Insert Euro Character (€)	Ctrl + Shift + $
Insert Yen Character (¥)	Ctrl + Alt + $
Insert Sterling Character (£)	Ctrl + Shift + Alt + $
Insert Left Arrow Character (←)	Ctrl + Alt + Left
Insert Right Arrow Character (→)	Ctrl + Alt + Right
Insert Up Arrow Character (↑)	Ctrl + Alt + Up
Insert Down Arrow Character (↓)	Ctrl + Alt + Down
Insert Degree Character (°)	Ctrl + Shift + %
Insert Plus/Minus Character (±)	Ctrl + Shift + -

Table 2-1: Shortcut Keys – Categorical Listing (continued)	
Symbol Shortcuts (cont.)	
Function	**Keys**
Insert Multiply Character (×)	Ctrl + Shift + *
Insert Divide Character (÷)	Ctrl + Shift + /
Insert Radical Character (√)	Ctrl + Shift + R
Insert Infinity Character (∞)	Ctrl + Shift + I
Insert Delta Character (△)	Ctrl + Shift + D
Insert Mu Character (μ)	Ctrl + Shift + M
Insert Omega Character (Ω)	Ctrl + Shift + O
Insert Pi Character (π)	Ctrl + Shift + P
Insert Sigma Character (Σ)	Ctrl + Shift + S

Using the Propeller Tool

Listing by Key

Table 2-2: Shortcuts By Key	
Single Key or Mouse	
Function	**Keys**
F2	Rename Folder/File (in Folder List or File List)
F3	Find Next
F4	Replace
F7	Identify Hardware
F8	Compile Current File and View Information
F9	Compile Current File and Update Status
F10	Compile Current File, Load RAM and Run
F11	Compile Current File, Load EEPROM and Run
End	Jump to end of line
Esc	Select Full Source view mode or set focus on active edit
Home	Jump to start of line
Insert	Change edit mode to Align (default), Insert or Overwrite
Page Down	Scroll down one page size
Page Up	Scroll up one page size
Tab	Insert white space up to next tab position
Double-Click	Select word
Triple-Click	Select line
Ctrl + ...	
Ctrl + A	Select All
Ctrl + B	Toggle Bookmark on current line
Ctrl + C	Copy to Clipboard
Ctrl + E	Toggle Show/Hide Explorer
Ctrl + F	Find / Replace
Ctrl + I	Toggle Block Group Indicators

Table 2-2: Shortcuts By Key (continued)	
Ctrl + … (cont.)	
Function	**Keys**
Ctrl + N	New
Ctrl + O	Open
Ctrl + S	Save
Ctrl + P	Print
Ctrl + T	Select Top File
Ctrl + V	Paste from Clipboard
Ctrl + W	Close
Ctrl + X	Cut to Clipboard
Ctrl + Y	Delete current line
Ctrl + Z	Undo
Ctrl + F4	Replace then Find Next
Ctrl + F8	Compile Top File and View Information
Ctrl + F9	Compile Top File and Update Status
Ctrl + F10	Compile Top File, Load RAM and Run
Ctrl + F11	Compile Top File, Load EEPROM and Run
Ctrl + F4	Replace then Find Next
Ctrl + Down	Decrease font size
Ctrl + End	Jump to end of file
Ctrl + Home	Jump to start of file
Ctrl + Insert	Toggle edit mode between Align and Insert
Ctrl + Left	Jump to start of previous word
Ctrl + Page Down	Jump to end of page
Ctrl + Mouse Wheel Down	Decrease font size
Ctrl + Mouse Wheel Up	Increase font size
Ctrl + Up	Increase font size

Table 2-2: Shortcuts By Key (continued)	
Alt + ...	
Alt + C	Select Condensed view mode
Alt + D	Select Documentation view mode
Alt + S	Select Full Source view mode
Alt + Q	Close
Alt + U	Select Summary view mode
Alt + Down	Select alternate view mode (towards Documentation)
Alt + Left	Select previous edit tab
Alt + Mouse Wheel Down	Select alternate view mode (towards Documentation)
Alt + Mouse Wheel Up	Select alternate view mode (towards Full Source view)
Alt + Right	Select next edit tab
Alt + Up	Select alternate view mode (towards Full Source view)
Shift + ...	
Shift + End	Select to end of line
Shift + Home	Select to start of line
Shift + Page Down	Select to next page below
Shift + Page Up	Select to previous page above
Shift + Tab	Delete white space back to previous tab position
Shift + Mouse Wheel Down	Scroll right
Shift + Mouse Wheel Up	Scroll left
Ctrl + Alt + ...	
Ctrl + Alt + .	Insert Rectangle Bullet Character (▮)
Ctrl + Alt + $	Insert Yen Character (¥)
Ctrl + Alt + 1	Insert Negative One Superior Character ($^{-1}$)
Ctrl + Alt + S	Save All
Ctrl + Alt + Down	Insert Down Arrow Character (↓)
Ctrl + Alt + Left	Insert Left Arrow Character (←)
Ctrl + Alt + Right	Insert Right Arrow Character (→)
Ctrl + Alt + Up	Insert Up Arrow Character (↑)

Table 2-2: Shortcuts By Key (continued)	
Ctrl + Shift + ...	
Function	**Keys**
Ctrl + Shift + $	Insert Euro Character (€)
Ctrl + Shift + %	Insert Degree Character (°)
Ctrl + Shift + *	Insert Multiply Character (×)
Ctrl + Shift + -	Insert Plus/Minus Character (±)
Ctrl + Shift + .	Insert Bullet Character (•)
Ctrl + Shift + /	Insert Divide Character (÷)
Ctrl + Shift + =	Insert Approximate Character (≈)
Ctrl + Shift + 1	Insert One Superior Character (^{1})
Ctrl + Shift + 2	Insert Two Superior Character (^{2})
Ctrl + Shift + 3	Insert Three Superior Character (^{3})
Ctrl + Shift + B	Toggle Show/Hide Bookmarks
Ctrl + Shift + D	Insert Delta Character (Δ)
Ctrl + Shift + I	Insert Infinity Character (∞)
Ctrl + Shift + M	Insert Mu Character (μ)
Ctrl + Shift + N	Toggle Show/Hide Line Numbers
Ctrl + Shift + O	Insert Omega Character (Ω)
Ctrl + Shift + P	Insert Pi Character (π)
Ctrl + Shift + R	Insert Radical Character (√)
Ctrl + Shift + S	Insert Sigma Character (Σ)
Ctrl + Shift + Y	Delete to end of line
Ctrl + Shift + Z	Redo
Ctrl + Shift + End	Select to end of file
Ctrl + Shift + Home	Select to start of file
Ctrl + Shift + Left	Select to start of previous word
Ctrl + Shift + Page Down	Select to end of page
Ctrl + Shift + Page Up	Select to start of page
Ctrl + Shift + Right	Select to start of next word

Ctrl + Shift + ... (cont.)	
Function	**Keys**
Ctrl + Shift + Tab	Select previous edit tab

Table 2-2: Shortcuts By Key (continued)	
Ctrl + Shift + Alt...	
Function	**Keys**
Ctrl + Shift + Alt + $	Insert Sterling Character (£)
Ctrl + Shift + Alt + <	Insert Left Bullet Character (◀)
Ctrl + Shift + Alt + >	Insert Right Bullet Character (▶)
Ctrl + Shift + Alt + Down	Insert Down Arrow Bullet Character (↓)
Ctrl + Shift + Alt + Left	Insert Left Arrow Bullet Character (←)
Ctrl + Shift + Alt + Right	Insert Right Arrow Bullet Character (→)
Ctrl + Shift + Alt + Up	Insert Up Arrow Bullet Character (↑)

Chapter 3: Propeller Programming Tutorial

This chapter assumes you are familiar with the general programming concepts of other programming languages, including object-oriented languages. Discussion of some basic concepts will be presented, but some prior knowledge and programming experience is recommended.

In addition to the above, this material should be read only after reading Chapters 1 and 2. If you have not read through all of Chapter 1 and at least most of Chapter 2, please do so before continuing with this chapter. Many items presented in Chapters 1 and 2 will be referred to here, but will not be described in detail.

The following Propeller Programming Tutorial describes Propeller chip programming concepts in a step-by-step fashion with quick review notes along the way. It is best to read this chapter from its start to its finish, without skipping around, while working with your computer and the Propeller chip and trying each example as it is taught. The earlier exercises are basic in nature and each later exercise covers more advanced material.

Concept

The Propeller product (hardware, firmware and software) was designed with many well-known and also many brand-new concepts in mind. To this end, we designed the hardware, firmware, software and the two programming languages that go with it (Spin and Propeller Assembly) completely from scratch to give users the most direct and efficient control over the Propeller device.

To fully understand and utilize these tools and languages, it is best that you approach it all with an open mind. In other words, please be careful not to let legacy programming concepts and methods prevent you from experiencing the advantages made available by the Propeller chip and its programming languages. We believe that some legacy concepts do not belong in true real-time processing environments since they tend to bring turmoil to those who rely on them.

Propeller Languages (Spin and Propeller Assembly)

The Propeller chip is programmed using two languages designed specifically for it: 1) Spin, a high-level object-based language, and 2) Propeller Assembly, a low-level, highly-optimized assembly language. There are many hardware-based commands in Propeller Assembly that have direct equivalents in the Spin language. This makes learning both languages, and the use of the Propeller chip overall, much easier to handle.

The Spin language is compiled by the Propeller Tool software into tokens that are interpreted at run time by the Propeller chip's built-in Spin Interpreter. Those familiar with other programming languages usually find that Spin is easy to learn and is well-suited for many applications. With Spin you can easily perform high-level/low-bandwidth tasks and can even create code to handle some typically higher-bandwidth features like asynchronous serial communication at 19200 baud.

The Propeller Assembly language is assembled into pure machine code by the Propeller Tool and is executed in its pure form at run time. Assembly language programmers enjoy Propeller Assembly's nature and its ability to achieve high-bandwidth tasks with very little code.

Propeller Objects (see below) can be written entirely in Spin or can use various combinations of Spin and Propeller Assembly. It's possible to write objects almost entirely in Propeller Assembly as well, but at least two lines of Spin code are required to launch the final application.

Propeller Objects

The Propeller chip's Spin language is object-based and serves as the foundation for every Propeller Application.

What is an Object?

Objects are really just programs written in a way that: 1) create a self-contained entity, 2) perform a specific task, and 3) may be reused by many applications.

For example, the Keyboard object and Mouse object each come with the Propeller Tool software. The Keyboard object is a program that interfaces the Propeller chip to a standard PC-style keyboard. Similarly, the Mouse object interfaces to a standard computer mouse. Both of these objects are self-contained programs with carefully designed software interfaces that allow other objects, and developers, to use them easily.

By using existing objects, more sophisticated applications can be built very quickly. For instance, an application can include both the Keyboard and Mouse objects, and with just a few additional lines of code, a standard user interface is realized. Since the objects are self-contained and provide a concise software interface, application developers don't necessarily need to know exactly how an object achieves its task just to be able to use it. In a similar way, a driver of a car doesn't necessarily know how the engine works, but as long as that driver understands the interface (the ignition key, gas pedal, brakes, etc.) he or she can make the car accelerate and decelerate.

Well-written objects can be created by one developer and easily used by many different applications from many different developers.

Objects and Applications

A Propeller Object consists of Spin code and, optionally, Propeller Assembly code; see Figure 3-1. We'll simply call these "objects" from now on.

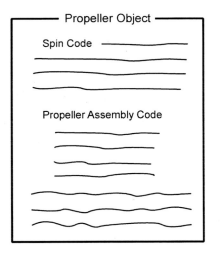

Figure 3-1: Propeller Object

Objects are stored on your computer as files with ".spin" extensions, therefore you should always think of each Spin file as an object.

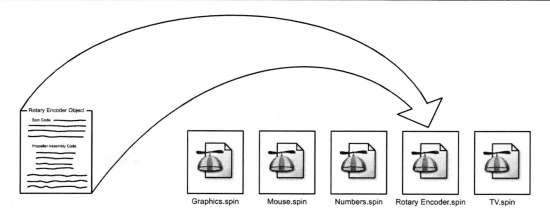

Figure 3-2: Object Files consist of Spin, and possibly Propeller Assembly, and are stored as ".spin" files on your computer's hard drive.

Each object can be thought of as a "building block" for an application. An object may choose to utilize one or more other objects in order to build a more sophisticated application. This is loosely called "referencing" or "including" another object. When an object references other objects it forms a hierarchy where it is the object at the top, as in Figure 3-3. The topmost object is referred to as the "Top Object File" and is the starting point for compiling a Propeller Application.

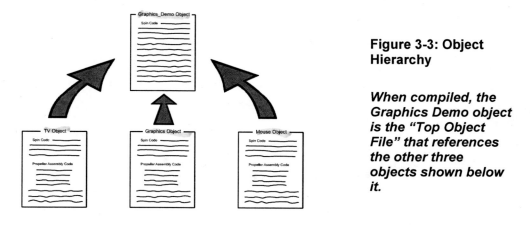

Figure 3-3: Object Hierarchy

When compiled, the Graphics Demo object is the "Top Object File" that references the other three objects shown below it.

In the above figure, the Graphics Demo object references three other objects: TV, Graphics, and Mouse. If the Graphics Demo object is compiled by the user, it is considered the Top

Object File and the other three objects are loaded and compiled with it resulting in a finished program called a Propeller Application, or "application" for short.

Applications are formed from one or more objects. The application is really a specially compiled binary stream that consists of executable code and data and can be run by the Propeller chip.

When downloaded, the application is stored in the Propeller chip's Main RAM and optionally into an external EEPROM. At run time, the application is executed by one or more of the Propeller chip's processors, called cogs, as directed by the application itself.

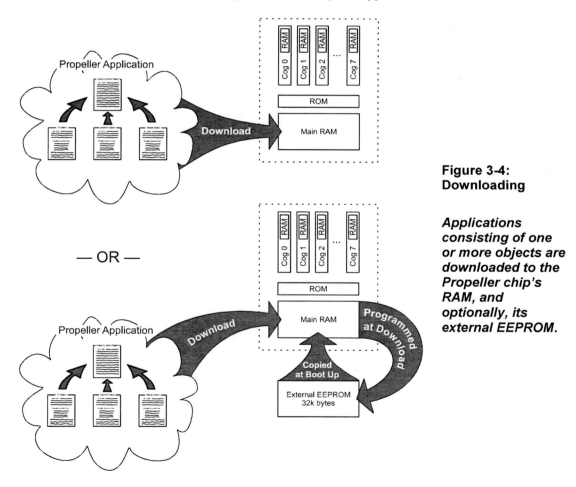

**Figure 3-4:
Downloading**

Applications consisting of one or more objects are downloaded to the Propeller chip's RAM, and optionally, its external EEPROM.

Connect for Downloading

In order to download a Propeller Application from the PC, you first need to connect the Propeller chip properly.

- If you have a Propeller Demo Board (Rev C or D), it includes the Propeller chip and all the necessary circuitry. Connect it to a power supply and the PC's USB cable and switch the power on. You may also need to install the USB drivers as directed by the Propeller Demo Board's documentation.

- If you do not have the Propeller Demo Board, we'll assume you have the Propeller chip and that you are experienced with wiring prototype circuits. Refer to Package Types on page 14 (showing the Propeller pinout) and Hardware Connections on page 17 for an example circuit showing the connections for power and programming. If you are using the Propeller Plug device, you may also need to install the USB drivers as directed by its documentation. The rest of this chapter relies heavily on circuitry similar to that of the Propeller Demo Board. In addition to the above power and programming connections, include the components and connections of the following schematic in your prototype circuit. You may also refer to the Propeller Demo Board's schematic; downloadable from the Parallax website.

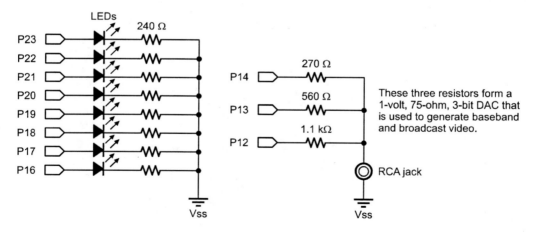

Figure 3-5: Propeller Tutorial Schematic

If you have made the connections suggested above, you should be able to verify and identify the Propeller chip via the Propeller Tool software. Start the Propeller Tool software (Version 1.0) and then press the F7 key (or select Run → Identify Hardware... from the menu). If the

Propeller chip is powered and connected to the PC properly, you should see an "Information" dialog similar to Figure 3-6.

Figure 3-6: The Information Dialog

The port (COM5) may be different on your computer.

Quick Review: Intro

- The Propeller is programmed using two custom-designed languages: Spin and Propeller Assembly.
    - Spin is a high-level, object-based language interpreted at run time.
    - Propeller Assembly is a low-level, optimized assembly language which is executed directly at run time.
- Objects are programs that:
    - are self-contained.
    - perform a specific task.
    - may be reused by many applications.
- Well-written objects from one developer can easily be used by other developers and applications.
- A Propeller Object:
    - consists of two or more lines of Spin code and possibly Propeller Assembly code.
    - is stored on the computer as a file with a ".spin" extension.
    - may use one or more other objects to build a sophisticated application.
- Propeller Applications:
    - consist of one or more objects.
    - are compiled binary streams containing executable code and data.
    - are run by the Propeller chip in one or more cogs (processors) as directed by the application.
- The topmost object in a compiled application is called the "Top Object File."

Exercise 1: Output.spin – Our First Object

The following is a simple object, written in Spin, that will toggle an I/O pin high and low repeatedly. Start the Propeller Tool software and enter this program into the editor. We'll explain how it works in a moment. Make sure the "PUB" line begins in column 1 (the leftmost edge of the edit pane) and pay very close attention to each line's indention; it's important for proper operation.

```
PUB Toggle
  dira[16]~~
  repeat
    !outa[16]
    waitcnt(3_000_000 + cnt)
```

While indentation is critical, capitalization is not. Propeller code is not case-senitive. However, throughout this book, reserved words appear in bold all-captials, except in code snippets and excerpts, to help you become familiar with them.

After checking that you've typed it in properly, press the F10 key (or select Run → Compile Current → Load RAM + Run from the menu) to compile and download our example program. If the program you entered is syntactically correct and the Propeller chip is properly powered and connected to the PC, you should see a "Propeller Communication" dialog appear momentarily on the screen, like the one in Figure 3-7, and now the LED on I/O pin 16 of the Propeller chip should be blinking about twice per second. What we just accomplished is what is shown at the top of Figure 3-4: Downloading on page 89.

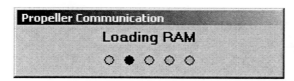

Figure 3-7: Propeller Communication Dialog

What really happened was probably too fast to see because the example program we entered is so small. When you pressed F10 it caused the Propeller Tool to compile the source code you entered and turn it into a Propeller Application. The Propeller Tool then searched for a Propeller chip connected to the PC and downloaded the application into its RAM. Finally, the Propeller started running the application from RAM, blinking the LED on I/O pin 16.

Downloading to RAM vs. EEPROM

Before we explain the code, let's take a closer look at the downloading process. Since our code was downloaded to RAM only, power cycling or resetting the Propeller will cause RAM contents to be lost and the program to stop permanently. Try pressing the reset button. The LED should turn off and never turn on again.

What if we don't want it to stop permanently? We could download to EEPROM instead of just RAM. Let's download again, but this time press the F11 key (or select Run → Compile Current → Load EEPROM + Run from the menu) to compile and download our example program to EEPROM. This is what is shown at the bottom of Figure 3-4: Downloading on page 89. As you may see from the figure, this actually downloaded to RAM first, then the Propeller chip programmed its external EEPROM, then started running the application from RAM, blinking the LED on I/O pin 16.

You probably noticed that the "Propeller Communication" dialog stayed on the screen much longer; EEPROMs take much longer to program than RAMs do.

Try pressing the reset button now. When you release the reset button, you'll notice a delay of about 1 ½ seconds and then the LED starts blinking. This is exactly what we wanted; a more permanent application in our Propeller chip.

Upon waking up from reset, the Propeller chip performed the boot-up procedure detailed on page 18. During that procedure, it determined it needed to boot up from the external EEPROM and then it took approximately 1½ seconds to completely copy the 32 Kbytes of content into its RAM and start running it.

Downloading only to RAM is convenient for development sessions because it is much faster. Downloading to both RAM and EEPROM to make the application more permanent is best done only when necessary because of the extra download time required.

A word of caution: If you download to EEPROM one or more times then revise your program and download to RAM only, when manually reset, the Propeller will boot up with your old program. This may make sense now, but that result can be very confusing when you're not paying attention. If things don't work right after a reset occurs, suspect the program in EEPROM first.

Exercise 1: Output.spin Explanation

Now for an explanation of the source code:

```
PUB Toggle
  dira[16]~~
  repeat
    !outa[16]
    waitcnt(3_000_000 + cnt)
```

The first line, PUB Toggle, declares that we're creating a "public" method called "Toggle." A method is the object-oriented term for "procedure" or "routine." We chose the name Toggle simply because it is descriptive of what the method does and we knew it is a unique symbol; it must be a unique symbol and conform to the Symbol Rules on page 159. We'll describe the term PUB, "public," in more detail later, but it's important to note that every object must contain at least one public (PUB) method.

The rest of the code is logically part of the Toggle method. We indented each line by two spaces from the PUB's column to make that more clear; this indenting isn't required but is a good habit for clarity.

The first line of the Toggle method (second line of our example), dira[16]~~, sets the direction of I/O pin 16 to output. The DIRA symbol is the direction register for I/O pins P0 through P31; clearing or setting bits within it changes the corresponding I/O pin's direction to input or output. The [16] following dira indicates we want to access only the direction register's bit 16; the one that corresponds to I/O pin 16. Finally, the ~~ is the Post-Set operator that causes direction register bit 16 to be set to high (1); which makes I/O pin 16's direction an output. The Post-Set operator is a shorthand way of saying something like dira[16] := 1 which may look familiar to you from other languages.

The next line, repeat, creates a loop consisting of the two lines of code below it. This REPEAT loop runs infinitely, toggling P16, waiting ¼ second, toggling P16, waiting ¼ second, etc.

The next line, !outa[16], toggles the state of I/O pin 16 between high (VDD) and low (VSS). The OUTA symbol is the output state register for I/O pins P0 through P31. The [16] in !outa[16] indicates we want to access only the output register's bit 16; the one that corresponds to I/O pin 16. The ! at the start of this statement is the Bitwise Not operator; it toggles the state of all bits specified to its right (the bit corresponding to I/O pin 16 in this case).

The last line, waitcnt(3_000_000 + cnt), causes a delay of 3 million clock cycles. WAITCNT means "Wait for System Counter." The cnt symbol is the System Counter register; CNT returns the current value of the System Counter, so this line means "wait for System Counter to equal 3 million plus its current value." In this code example, we didn't specify any clock settings for the Propeller chip, so by default it runs with its internal fast clock (about 12 MHz) meaning a delay of 3 million clock cycles is about ¼ second.

Remember how we said to pay close attention to each line's indenting? Here is where indenting *is* required: the Spin language uses levels of indention on lines following conditional or loop commands (IF, CASE, REPEAT, etc.) to determine which lines belong to that structure. In this case, since the two lines following repeat are indented to the right by at least one space beyond repeat's column, those two lines are considered to be a part of the repeat loop. If you have trouble recognizing these structural groupings, the Propeller Tool can make them more visible on-screen through the Block-Group Indicators feature. Use Ctrl+I to toggle this feature on or off. Figure 3-8 shows our example code with these indicators visible.

```
PUB Toggle
  dira[16]~~
  repeat
    !outa[16]
    waitcnt(3_000_000 + cnt)
```

Figure 3-8: Block-Group Indicators

Ctrl+I toggles them on and off.

If you haven't saved this example object yet, you may do so by pressing Ctrl+S (or selecting File → Save from the menu). You may save it in a folder of your choosing but make sure to save it with the filename "Output.spin" since some exercises below rely on it.

Quick Review: Ex 1

- Applications are downloaded to either Propeller RAM only or RAM and EEPROM.
  - Those in RAM will not survive power cycling or resetting the Propeller chip.
  - Those in EEPROM are loaded into RAM on boot-up in approximately 1½ seconds.
  - To download the current object to:
    - RAM only: press F10 or select Run → Compile Current → Load RAM + Run.
    - RAM + EEPROM: press F11 or select Run → Compile Current → Load EEPROM + Run.
- Spin language:
  - Method means "procedure" or "routine."
  - PUB *Symbol* declares a public method called *Symbol*. Every object must contain at least one public (PUB) method. See PUB on page 287 and Symbol Rules on page 159.
  - DIRA is the direction register for I/O pins 0-31. Each bit sets the corresponding I/O pin's direction to input (0) or output (1). See DIRA, DIRB on page 212.
  - OUTA is the output state register for I/O pins 0-31. Each bit sets the corresponding I/O pin's output state to low (0) or high (1). See OUTA, OUTB on page 280.
  - Registers can use indexes, like [16], to access individual bits within them. See DIRA, DIRB on page 212 or OUTA, OUTB on page 280.
  - ~~ following a register/variable sets its bit(s) high. See Sign-Extend 15 or Post-Set '~~' on page 263 in the Operators section.
  - ! preceding a value/register/variable sets its bit(s) opposite their current state. See Bitwise NOT '!' on page 272 in the Operators section.
  - REPEAT creates a loop structure. See REPEAT on page 293.
  - WAITCNT creates a delay. See WAITCNT on page 322.
  - Indention at the start of lines:
    - indicates they belong to the preceding structure; it is required for lines following conditional or loop commands (like REPEAT). (Indenting is *optional* after block indicators, such as PUB.)
    - Ctrl+I toggles visible block-group "structure" indicators on and off.

Cogs (Processors)

The Propeller has eight identical processors, called cogs. Each cog can be individually set to run or stop at any time as directed by the application it is running. Each cog can be programmed to run independent tasks or cooperative tasks with other cogs, as needed, and this can change as desired during the application's run time.

But we didn't specify which cog(s) to run in our Output.spin example, so how did it work? For a review, you could read Boot Up Procedure, page 18, and Run-Time Procedure, page 18, in Chapter 1, but we'll discuss it a bit more here.

For our example, upon power-up, the Propeller chip starts the first processor (Cog 0) and loads it with a built-in Boot Loader program. The Boot Loader program is copied from the Propeller chip's ROM into Cog 0's internal RAM memory. Cog 0 then runs the Boot Loader program in its internal memory and the Boot Loader soon determines it should copy user-code from the external EEPROM. So Cog 0 copies the entire 32 K byte EEPROM contents into the Propeller chip's 32 K byte main RAM memory (separate from the cog's internal memory). Then the Boot Loader program makes Cog 0 reload itself with the built-in Spin Interpreter; the Boot Loader program in Cog 0 halts at this point while it is being overwritten with the Spin Interpreter program.

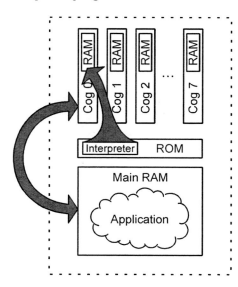

Figure 3-9: Running Output.spin

Notice that the Spin Interpreter, not the Spin Application, is loaded into Cog RAM. The Spin Application resides in Main RAM and is interpreted by the Spin Interpreter program that is running in the cog.

Now, Cog 0 is running the Spin Interpreter, which fetches and executes our application's code from main memory (RAM). This is shown in Figure 3-9. Since our application consists entirely of interpreted Spin code, it continues to reside only in main memory while a cog running the Spin Interpreter (Cog 0 in this case) reads, interprets and effectively executes it. No other cogs were started during boot up or during our application's execution; the other seven cogs remain in a dormant state consuming virtually no current at all. Later, we'll change our application to start other cogs as well.

Exercise 2: Output.spin – Constants

Let's enhance our program a little. Suppose we want to make it easy to change the I/O pin and the length of the delay used. As it is written currently, we'd have to find and change the pin number in two places and the delay in yet another place. We can make it better by defining those items in a separate place that is easy to find and edit. Look at the following example and edit your code to match (we highlighted every new or modified element).

```
CON
  Pin   = 16
  Delay = 3_000_000

PUB Toggle
  dira[Pin]~~
  repeat
    !outa[Pin]
    waitcnt(Delay + cnt)
```

The new `CON` block at the top of the code defines global constants for the object (see `CON`, page 194.) In it, we created two symbols, `Pin` and `Delay`, and assigned the constant values 16 and 3,000,000 to them, respectively. We can now use the symbols `Pin` and `Delay` elsewhere in the code to represent our constant values 16 and 3,000,000. Notice that we used underscores (_) to separate the "thousands" groups in the number 3,000,000? Commas are not allowed there but underscores are allowed anywhere inside of constant values; this makes large numbers more readable.

In the `Toggle` method, we replaced both occurrences of 16 with the symbol `Pin`, and replaced the `3_000_000` with the symbol `Delay`. When compiled, the Propeller Tool will use the constant values in place of their respective symbols. This makes it easy, later on, to change the pin number or delay at will since we only have to change it up at the top of code in a place that is easy to find and understand.

Try changing the `Delay` constant from 3,000,000 to 500,000 and download again; the LED should now flicker at a rate of 12 blinks per second (24 toggles per second). You can also change the `Pin` constant from 16 to 17 and download again to see a different LED blink. NOTE: you can try 18 through 23 as well, but on the Propeller Demo Board they are connected in pairs with resistors for the VGA driver circuit, so two LEDs will blink at once.

Block Designators

You may have noticed that the backgrounds of the `CON` and `PUB` blocks of code were colored differently when you entered them into the editor. This is the Propeller Tool's way to indicate these are distinct blocks of code.

Spin code is organized in blocks that have distinct purposes. `CON` and `PUB` are block designators that indicate the start of a "constant block" and "public method block", respectively. Every block designator must start in the first column of text (the leftmost edge of the edit pane) on a line. There are six types of blocks in the Spin language: `CON`, `VAR`, `OBJ`, `PUB`, `PRI`, and `DAT`. The following is a list of the block designators and their purpose:

`CON`	Global Constant Block. Defines symbolic constants that can be used anywhere within the object (and in some cases outside the object) wherever numeric values are allowed.
`VAR`	Global Variable Block. Defines symbolic variables that can be used anywhere within the object wherever variables are allowed.
`OBJ`	Object Reference Block. Defines symbolic references to other existing objects. These are used to access those objects and the methods and constants within them.
`PUB`	Public Method Block. Public methods are code routines that are accessible both inside and outside the object. Public routines provide the interface to the object; the way methods outside of the object interact with the object. There must be at least one `PUB` declaration in every object.
`PRI`	Private Method Block. Private methods are code routines that are accessible only inside the object. Since they are not visible from the outside, they provide a level of encapsulation to protect critical elements within the object and help maintain the integrity of the object's purpose.
`DAT`	Data Block. Defines data tables, memory buffers, and Propeller Assembly code. The data block's data can be assigned symbolic names and can be accessed via Spin code and assembly code.

There can be multiple occurrences of each block type, arranged in any order desired, but there must be at least one `PUB` block per object. Even though the number of blocks and their order is quite flexible, typically there is only one occurrence of CON, VAR, OBJ and DAT blocks, multiple occurrences of PUB and PRI blocks, and the suggested order for typical programs is the order they are given in the list above.

The very first PUB block in the very first object (the Top Object File where compilation starts from) automatically becomes the Propeller Application's starting point; it is executed first when the application starts. No other public or private method is executed automatically, but rather they are executed only as determined by the natural flow of the application.

The Propeller Tool automatically colors the backgrounds of each block differently, even two consecutive occurrences of the same block type, in order to make it easy to identify the type, start, and end of each block. This in no way affects the actual source code itself, it is simply an indicator for on-screen use that is intended to solve a typical problem with source code; that is, as the code gets larger, it is harder to find a particular method quickly as you scroll up and down through the code unless you have some kind of separator between methods. The background color coding serves as an automatic separator that prevents you from having to waste time typing in text-based separators manually.

Exercise 3: Output.spin – Comments

Our Output object is better now, but it still could be more readable. How about adding some comments to the code to make it easier for other readers to understand? The next example functions the same as before, but with a number of comments (human-readable, non-executable text) above and to the right of our existing code.

These comments should help people figure out what it does. There are four types of comments supported by the Propeller Tool (all of which are shown in this example):

'...   – Single-line code comment (apostrophe).

''...   – Single-line document comment (two apostrophes, NOT a quotation mark).

{...}   – Multi-line code comment (curly braces).

{{...}}   – Multi-line document comment (two curly braces).

```
{{Output.spin

Toggles Pin with Delay clock cycles of high/low time.}}

CON
  Pin   = 16              { I/O pin to toggle on/off }
  Delay = 3_000_000       { On/Off Delay, in clock cycles}

PUB Toggle
''Toggle Pin forever
{Toggles I/O pin given by Pin and waits Delay system clock cycles
in between each toggle.}

  dira[Pin]~~            'Set I/O pin to output direction
  repeat                 'Repeat following endlessly
    !outa[Pin]           '   Toggle I/O Pin
    waitcnt(Delay + cnt) '   Wait for Delay cycles
```

Single line comments begin with at least one apostrophe (') and continue until the end of the line. Executable code can be to the left of a single-line comment but not to the right of it since that would make it "commented out." The "'Set I/O pin..." and "'Repeat following..." comments are examples of single-line comments.

Multi-line comments begin with at least one open curly brace ({) and end with at least one close curly brace (}). Unlike single-line comments, executable code can be to the left and the right of multi-line comments. Multi-line comments can actually be entirely on one line, or can span across multiple lines. The "{On/Off Delay...}" and "{Toggles I/O pin given...}" comments are both examples of a multi-line comments.

If a comment begins with just one apostrophe (') or one open curly brace ({), it is a "code" comment. This is a comment meant to be read by code developers while reviewing the source code itself.

If a comment begins with either two apostrophes ('') or two open curly braces ({{), with no spaces in between, it is a "document" comment. This is a special type of comment that is visible within the code, but can also be extracted by the Propeller Tool into a document formatted for easier reading, containing no executable code.

As discussed in Chapter 2View Modes on page 61, the Propeller Tool's editor has a Documentation view mode. With the above code entered into the editor, if the Documentation view mode is selected, the code is compiled and the document comments are shown along with some statistics about the compiled code. The following is what this looks like:

```
Output.spin

Toggles Pin with Delay clock cycles of high/low time.
Object "Output" Interface:

PUB  Toggle

Program:      8 Longs
Variable:     0 Longs
_____
PUB  Toggle

Toggle Pin forever
```

If you compare this to our code you should recognize all the text that came directly from our document comments. The section "Object "Output" Interface:" is created automatically by the Propeller Tool; it lists all the public methods (just PUB Toggle in this case) and shows that the program size is 8 longs (32 bytes) and no variables were used. Following that, it lists all the public methods again, with an overbar above each method, and the document comments that belong with them. This section shows the public Toggle method and our last document comment, "Toggle Pin forever," indicating what the Toggle method does.

Adding document comments to your code allows you to create just one file that contains both source code and documentation for an object. This is extremely convenient for developers since they can easily switch to Documentation view to learn how to use an object they are unfamiliar with. To support this further, the Propeller Tool's Parallax font has many special characters for including schematics, timing diagrams, and mathematical symbols right in the objects that they relate to, like those shown in Figure 2-1 on page 36.

Quick Review: Ex 2 & 3

- The Propeller has eight identical processors, called cogs.
  - Any number of cogs can be running or halted at any time as directed by the application.
  - Each cog can run independent or cooperative tasks.
  - At boot-up, Cog 0 runs the Spin Interpreter to execute the main memory-based Spin application.
- Spin language:
  - Organized in blocks that have distinct purposes.
    - `CON` – Defines global constants, see page 194.
    - `VAR` – Defines global variables, see page 315.
    - `OBJ` – Defines object references, see page 247.
    - `PUB` – Defines a public method, see page 287.
    - `PRI` – Defines a private method, see page 286.
    - `DAT` – Defines data, buffers, and assembly code, see page 208.
  - Block designators must be in column 1 of a line.
  - Each block type can occur multiple times and can be arranged in any order.
  - The very first `PUB` block in the very first object is the Propeller Application's starting point.
  - Underscores "_" in constants denote logical groupings, like thousands in decimal numbers.
  - Types of comments:
    - Code comments; visible in source code only. Great for notes to developers regarding function of specific code.
      - `'...` – Single-line; starts at apostrophe and continues to end of line.
      - `{...}` – Multi-line; starts and ends with single curly braces.
    - Document comments; visible in source code and documentation view. Great for object documentation. Can even include schematics, timing diagrams and other special symbols.
      - `''...` – Single-line; starts at double-apostrophe and continues to end of line.
      - `{{...}}` – Multi-line; starts and ends with double-curly braces.

Exercise 4: Output.spin – Parameters, Calls, and Finite Loops

Our current object from Exercise 3 is interesting, but still isn't very flexible; after all, the Toggle method only works with a specific pin and delay. Let's make the Toggle method more flexible and also give it the ability to toggle a specific, finite number of times. Look at the following example and edit your code to match. We've crossed out the elements that should be removed, and highlighted every new element.

```
{{Output.spin

Toggles Pin with Delay clock cycles of high/low time.}}
Toggles two pins, one after another.}}

CON
  Pin   = 16                    { I/O pin to toggle on/off }
  Delay = 3_000_000             { On/Off Delay, in clock cycles}

PUB Main
  Toggle(16, 3_000_000, 10)   'Toggle P16 ten times, 1/4 s each
  Toggle(17, 2_000_000, 20)   'Toggle P17 twenty times, 1/6 s each


PUB Toggle(Pin, Delay, Count)
''Toggle Pin forever
{Toggles I/O pin given by Pin and waits Delay system clock cycles
in between each toggle.}
{{Toggle Pin, Count times with Delay clock cycles in between.}}

  dira[Pin]~~                 'Set I/O pin to output direction
  repeat Count                'Repeat for Count iterations
    !outa[Pin]                '  Toggle I/O Pin
    waitcnt(Delay + cnt)      '  Wait for Delay cycles
```

Compile and download this application to see the results. The LED on pin 16 should blink five times (10 toggles) with 1/4th second durations and intervals, then it will stop and the LED on pin 17 will blink ten times (20 toggles) at 1/6th second durations and intervals.

In this example we removed the constant (CON) block, added a new method called Main, and made some minor modifications to the Toggle method. The Toggle method still performs the actual pin-toggling action, but the Main method tells it when and how to do so.

The Toggle Method

Let's look closely at the `Toggle` method first. In its declaration, we added (`Pin`, `Delay`, `Count`) immediately to the right of its name. This creates a "parameter list" for our `Toggle` method consisting of three parameters, `Pin`, `Delay` and `Count`. A parameter list is one or more symbols that must be filled with values when the method is called; more on that in a moment. Each parameter symbol is a long-sized (4-byte) variable that is local to the method; they are all accessible within the method but not outside of the method. Parameter variables can be modified within the method but those modifications do not affect anything outside the method.

Now, our `Toggle` method can be called by other methods and given unique values to use as its `Pin`, `Delay` and `Count` symbols; it is more flexible since we can adjust its operational parameters.

Inside of `Toggle`, nothing changed except the `REPEAT` command, which is now `repeat Count`. Remember, in our previous examples the `REPEAT` loop was an infinite loop; it never stopped. Well, if you immediately follow `REPEAT` with an expression, it becomes a finite loop that iterates the number of times indicated by the expression. In this case our `REPEAT` loop will execute `Count` times, then it will stop, and any lines of code below the end of the loop will begin to execute.

The Main Method

Now look at the `Main` method. `Main`'s first line, `Toggle(16, 3_000_000, 10)`, is a method call; it causes the `Toggle` method to execute using 16 for its `Pin` parameter, 3 million for its `Delay` parameter, and 10 for its `Count` parameter. The following line looks similar, `Toggle(17, 2_000_000, 20)`, but it calls the `Toggle` method with different values: 17 for `Pin`, 2 million for `Delay`, and 20 for `Count`.

Notice that we put the `Main` method above `Toggle`? Remember that the first public method in the first object is automatically executed when the application is started by the Propeller. We are only using one object in this case, so `Main` is automatically executed after we download this application.

When `Main`'s first line, `Toggle(16, 3_000_000, 10)`, is executed, the `Toggle` method is called and it executes its function: blinking the LED on pin 16 five times with a delay of 1/4th second in between. Then, because `Toggle` has no more code to execute after the loop, it returns to the caller, `Main`, and execution continues at the next line of `Main`: `Toggle(17, 2_000_000, 20)`. When that line executes, the `Toggle` method is called, and it blinks the LED on pin 17 ten times with a delay of 1/6th second in between. Finally, the `Toggle` method returns to `Main` again, but `Main` has no more code to execute so it exits and the application terminates; the cog stops and the Propeller goes into a low-power mode until the next reset or power cycle.

Don't be confused by the look of the code. The two methods, Main and Toggle, are shown one right after another, but they are treated as distinct routines starting at their PUB block declarations and ending at the next block declaration or the end of the source code, whichever comes first. In other words, the Propeller knows that the Toggle method is not a part of the Main method's executable code.

Also note we've still used just one cog in our example, and the entire application is executed serially: first blink P16, then stop, blink P17, then stop. We'll begin to use multiple cogs in the next exercise.

Exercise 5: Output.spin – Parallel Processing

In exercises 1 through 4 we've used just one cog to process the application; it toggles P16 only, then stops and toggles P17 only, then terminates. This is called "serial processing."

Suppose, however, that we want to do things in parallel; simultaneously toggling pins 16 and 17, each at different rates and for different finite periods. Tasks like this can certainly be done with serial processing and clever programming but it is easier with parallel processing by having the Propeller activate two cogs. Look at the following example and edit your code to match. We added a variable block (VAR) and made a slight change to the Main method.

```
{{Output.spin
Toggle two pins, one after another simultaneously.}}

VAR
  long   Stack[9]                'Stack space for new cog

PUB Main
  cognew(Toggle(16, 3_000_000, 10), @Stack)      'Toggle P16 ten...
  Toggle(17, 2_000_000, 20)                      'Toggle P17 twenty...

PUB Toggle(Pin, Delay, Count)
{{Toggle Pin, Count times with Delay clock cycles in between.}}

  dira[Pin]~~                'Set I/O pin to output direction
  repeat Count               'Repeat for Count iterations
    !outa[Pin]               '   Toggle I/O Pin
    waitcnt(Delay + cnt)     '   Wait for Delay cycles
```

The VAR Block

In the VAR block we defined an array of longs, Stack, which is 9 elements in length. This is used by the Main method.

The Main Method

We modified the Main method's first line such that its original code, the call to Toggle, is encased in a COGNEW command. The COGNEW command starts a new cog to run either Spin or Propeller Assembly code. In this case, we entered Toggle(16, 3_000_000, 10), for COGNEW's first parameter, and @Stack for its second parameter. This means COGNEW will start a new cog to run the Toggle method and will use the memory starting at the address of Stack for run-time stack space. The @ is the Symbol Address operator; it returns the actual address of the variable following it.

To run Spin code, the new cog needs some run-time workspace, called "stack space," where it can store temporary things like return addresses, return values, intermediate expression values, etc. We chose to reserve 9 longs of space (36 bytes), and passed the address of that space as COGNEW's second parameter, @Stack. How much stack space is needed? It varies depending on the Spin code being executed, but we'll discuss those details later. For now, rest assured that 9 longs of space is enough for our Toggle method.

Compile and download Output.spin. You should see that the LEDs on P16 and P17 now simultaneously blink at different rates, 5 times and 10 times, respectively. This is because we now have two cogs running simultaneously; one toggles P16 while the other toggles P17.

Here's how it works: Cog 0 starts executing our application's Main method. The first line of Main uses the COGNEW command to activate a new cog (Cog 1) to run the Toggle method with the parameters (16, 3_000_000, 10) passed to it. While Cog 1 is starting up, Cog 0 continues on with the second line of the Main method, the direct call to Toggle with the parameters (17, 2_000_000, 20) passed to it. Ultimately, Cog 0 is left executing Toggle on P17 while Cog 1 executes Toggle on P16, simultaneously. When their individual tasks have expired, they each terminate due to lack of code. Cog 1 terminates the moment it finishes Toggle. Cog 0 finishes Toggle, returns to Main and then terminates. Cog 1 happens to terminate earlier than Cog 0 in this case.

Figure 3-10 illustrates this. The Propeller loads the Spin Interpreter into Cog 0 to execute the application (the two leftmost arrows in the figure). Then the application requests a new cog to activate, via the COGNEW command, which causes the Propeller to load the Spin Interpreter into the next available cog, Cog 1, to execute a smaller portion of Spin code from the application, the Toggle method (the two rightmost arrows in the figure). Each cog executes its code completely independently of the other; true parallel processing. Note that towards the end of the application both cogs are executing the same piece of Spin code, the Toggle method, but each is using its own workspace and its own values for Pin, Delay and Count.

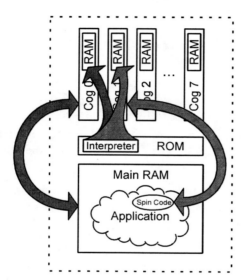

Figure 3-10: Two Cogs Running Output Application and Toggle method.

Notice that the Spin Interpreter is loaded into each Cog's RAM. The Spin Application, Output, resides in Main RAM interpreted by Cog 0 and it launches Cog 1 to run just the Toggle method.

Quick Review: Ex 4 & 5

- Spin language:
  - Methods:
    - To call methods in the same object, use *method* where method is the method's name, see PUB on page 287.
    - Methods automatically exit, returning to their caller, when they run out of code to execute.
    - When an application's first method exits, the application and the cog it is running in terminate.
  - Parameter Lists
    - Methods declare parameters in the form: *method(param1, param2, etc.)* , see PUB on page 287.
    - Parameters are long-sized, local variables that are accessible from within the method only.
      - They can be modified within the method but any corresponding variables used in the call are left unaffected.
  - REPEAT command:
    - Infinite loop: repeat
    - Finite loop: repeat *expression* where *expression* evaluates to the desired number of loops to iterate through, see REPEAT on page 293.
  - Arrays:
    - Arrays are defined with the form *symbol [count]* where *symbol* is the array's symbolic name and *count* is the number of elements in the array, see VAR on page 315.
  - COGNEW command:
    - Activates another cog (processor) to run either Spin or Propeller Assembly code, see COGNEW on page 189.
    - Allows for true parallel processing.
    - Requires an address to reserve run-time stack space for Spin code.
  - The Symbol Address operator (@) returns the address of the variable following it. See Symbol Address '@' on page 278.

Exercise 6: Output.spin & Blinker1.spin – Using Our Object

Now let's explore the power of objects. All of the preceding exercises created an application that contained only one object; the Output.spin object is the entire application. This is typical of how new objects begin their development. Suppose that the motivation behind all this work was really to create an object other developers could use to easily toggle one or more I/O pins. Yes, it may be silly to create an object for such a use, but let's have fun with it anyway!

It's time to make our Output object easily interface with other objects. Edit your code to look like the following:

Example Object: Output.spin

```
{{ Output.spin }}
Toggle two pins, one after another.}}

VAR
  long   Stack[9]              'Stack space for new cog

PUB Main
  cognew(Toggle(16, 3_000_000, 10), @Stack)       'Toggle P16 ten...
  Toggle(17, 2_000_000, 20)                        'Toggle P17 twenty...

PUB Start(Pin, Delay, Count)
{{Start new toggling process in a new cog.}}

  cognew(Toggle(Pin, Delay, Count), @Stack)

PUB Toggle(Pin, Delay, Count)
{{Toggle Pin, Count times with Delay clock cycles in between.}}

  dira[Pin]~~                  'Set I/O pin to output direction
  repeat Count                 'Repeat for Count iterations
    !outa[Pin]                 '  Toggle I/O Pin
    waitcnt(Delay + cnt)       '  Wait for Delay cycles
```

Be sure to save this object with the filename "Output.spin" for later use by our next object.

The Start Method

Here we replaced the Main method with a Start method. The Start method activates another cog to run the Toggle method independently and passes along the Pin, Delay, and Count parameters.

The interface to an object is made up of its public (PUB) methods, so our Output object now has two interface components, the Start method and the Toggle method.

Now our Output object can be used by other objects to toggle any pin at any rate for any number of times they want. They can also choose to do this serially, by calling Output's Toggle method, or in parallel with other tasks, by calling Output's Start method.

Let's create another object that uses Output. To create a new object, select File → New from the menu and a new edit tab will appear. In this new edit page, enter the following code. Pay attention to the bold items, as we will discuss them soon.

Example Object: Blinker1.spin

```
{{ Blinker1.spin }}

OBJ
  LED : "Output"

PUB Main
{Toggle pins at different rates, simultaneously}
  LED.Start (16, 3_000_000, 10)
  LED.Toggle (17, 2_000_000, 20)
```

Save this new object as "Blinker1.spin" in the same folder as you saved Output.spin. Now, with Blinker1's edit tab active, press F10 to compile and download. The LEDs should have blinked in the same way they did in Exercise 5, but a different technique was used by the code; Blinker1 used our Output object and simply called Output's Start and Toggle methods.

Here's how it worked. In Blinker1 we have an object block (OBJ) and a public method (PUB). The object block's LED : "Output" line declares that we're going to use another object called Output and that we'll refer to it as LED within this Blinker1 object.

The Object-Method Reference

In the public method, Main, we have two method calls. Remember how we learned in Exercise 4 that one method can call another just by referencing its name? That works for methods that are in the same object, but now we need to call a method that is in another object. To do this, we use the form *object.method* where *object* is the symbolic name we gave the object in the OBJ block (LED in this case) and *method* is the name of that object's method. This is called an Object-Method reference. Blinker1 refers to the Output object as LED, so LED.Start calls Output's Start method, and LED.Toggle calls Output's Toggle method.

When Blinker1 is compiled, since it references Output, the two objects get compiled into one application. Figure 3-11 illustrates this. This structure is also shown in the Object View, which we'll learn about next.

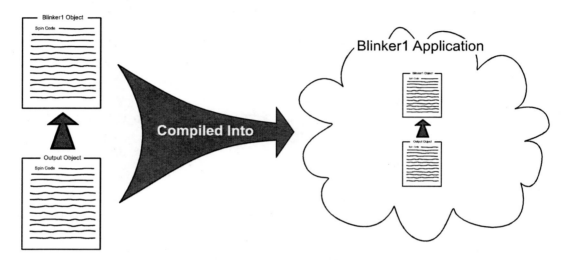

Figure 3-11: Blinker1 Hierarchy and Blinker1 Application

The Object View

When you compiled Blinker1, the Object View pane updated to indicate the application's structure. The Object View is in the upper left corner of the Propeller Tool if you have the Integrated Explorer pane open (see Pane 1: Object View Pane on page 39.) Figure 3-12 shows what it should look like now.

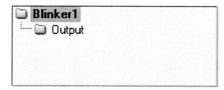

Figure 3-12: Blinker1 Object View

The Object View updates itself each time an application is successfully compiled to show you the logical structure of that application. The view shown in Figure 3-12 is the Object View's way of illustrating the logical structure in Figure 3-11. It is necessary to check the Object View once in a while to troubleshoot or to verify proper compilation.

Your entire application is displayed in the Object View, or at least what it looked like after the last successful compile. You can also use it to explore the application. For example, pointing the mouse at each object in the Object View gives you hint information about that object. Left-clicking each of those objects either opens them up or switches the active edit tab to that object. Right-clicking each of those objects does the same as left-clicking but it makes the object switch to Documentation view instead of Full Source view.

Top Object File

The object at the top of the Object View is always the "Top Object File" for that particular compilation. That means the compilation started from Blinker1, in this case. When we compile by using the F10 or F11 shortcut keys, or their corresponding menus, the Propeller Tool starts the compile operation using whatever edit tab is active at that moment. The active edit tab is the one that is highlighted differently than the rest; see Pane 4: Editor Pane on page 40 and Figure 2-4 on page 40 for an example.

If we had accidentally clicked on the Output object's tab first and then compiled with F10 or F11 the compile would have started from that object instead. This would not have resulted in the application we desired and the Object View would have shown only one object, Output, in its structure. This is all because the compile functions we've been using are the "Compile Current" options; meaning they compile from the currently active object, or edit tab.

There are other compile functions that can help us. Select the Run menu and look at the options. You should see a "Compile Current" and "Compile Top" flyout menu (Figure 3-13).

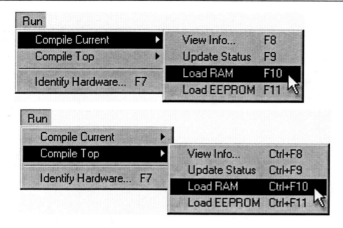

Figure 3-13: Compile Current Menu (top) and Compile Top Menu (bottom)

Each menu, Compile Current and Compile Top, has the same sub-options but they start their compilation from different places. Compile Current starts from the active edit tab and Compile Top starts from the designated Top Object File.

You can tell the Propeller Tool which object to treat as the "designated Top Object File" at any time. You do this by any one of the following methods:

1) Right-click the desired object's edit tab and select "Top Object File," or

2) Right-click the desired object from the File List (in the Integrated Explorer) and select "Top Object File," or

3) Choose the File → Select Top Object File... menu option and select the desired file from the browse window, or

4) Press Ctrl+T and select the desired file from the browse window.

We used option #1 to select Blinker1 as the Top Object File, in the figure below. Note that afterwards, the Blinker1 tab's text is bold; see Figure 3-14b. The file the Propeller Tool knows as the Top Object File always appears in bold.

Now, if we use one of the Compile Top options, such as Ctrl+F10 or Ctrl+F11, regardless of which edit tab is active, the Propeller Tool will compile starting from the Top Object File. For example, in Figure 3-14b the Output object is the active edit tab. If we press Ctrl+F10, the application will be compiled starting with the Blinker1 object, however. If we had pressed F10 instead, the Output object would have been compiled.

Each of the shortcut keys for the Compile Current options, F8, F9, F10, etc., has a similar variation for the Compile Top options, Ctrl+F8, Ctrl+F9, Ctrl+10, etc.

Figure 3-14: Setting Blinker1 to be the Top Object File

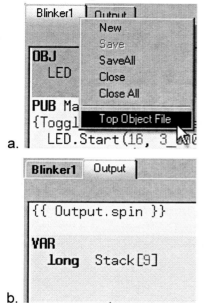

a.

One way to set the Top Object File is by right-clicking the desired edit tab, and choosing Top Object File.

b.

The Top Object File's name will show in bold on its Edit Tab.

Which Objects Were Compiled?

If there's ever a question of which object files were compiled in the last successful compile operation, use the mouse to explore the resulting application's structure in the Object View.

It's important to keep track of which file you've designated as the Top Object File and what compile option you chose; Current vs. Top. Only one file can be designated as the Top Object File at a time and the Propeller Tool remembers that file even between sessions.

Also, keep in mind that an object doesn't really need to be open in the Propeller Tool just to be compiled. If an object you compiled references another object, that object will be compiled whether or not it is currently open. Even the Top Object File can be compiled without it being open. For example, pressing Ctrl+F10 will compile the last designated Top Object File regardless of whether or not it even belongs to the current application you are working on.

Quick Review: Ex 6

- Spin language:
  - Methods:
    - To call methods in anoTher object, use *object.method* where *object* is the object's symbolic name (given to it in the OBJ block) and *method* is the method's name within that other object. See OBJ on page 247.
    - Public (PUB) methods are an object's interface; other objects call its public methods. See PUB on page 287.
- Object View
  - Illustrates the structure of the most recent successfully compiled application. See Object View, page 52.
  - Pointing the mouse at displayed objects displays hints about them.
  - Left-clicking a displayed object either opens it up or makes it the active edit tab.
  - Right-clicking a displayed object opens or switches to it in Documentation view.
- Compile Current – (F8 through F11) - compiles starting from the current object (active edit tab).
- Compile Top – (Ctrl+F8 through Ctrl+F11) - compiles starting from the Top Object File.
- Top Object File:
  - Appears with a bold name in the edit tab and File List.
  - Can be designated by one of the following (and compiled via Compile Top operation):
  1) Right-click object's edit tab and select "Top Object File," or
  2) Right-click object in the File List and select "Top Object File," or
  3) Choose File → Select Top Object File… menu and select object from browser, or
  4) Press Ctrl+T and select object from browser.
- Objects don't have to be open to be compiled; they may be compiled as the result of another object's compilation or as the result of a Compile Top operation.

Objects vs. Cogs

It's important to understand that there is no direct relationship between objects and cogs. Remember, Exercise 5 used just one object but two cogs and Exercise 6 used two objects and two cogs, but each of these exercises could have used only one cog if they wanted to process everything serially. When and how cogs are used is completely determined by the application and the developer(s) who wrote it.

Exercise 7: Output.spin – More Enhancements

Let's add some significant enhancements to our Output object. Currently the Toggle method can be called to toggle a pin serially, or the Start method can be called to launch the Toggle method as a separate process, to run in parallel. But we haven't provided a way to stop that process once it is going or even a way to determine if it's running in the first place. Also, it would be nice to have the option of toggling the pin endlessly, in addition to the finite count feature we already have.

Let's add a Stop method to stop the active process and an Active method to test whether a parallel process is currently running. In addition, we'll enhance our Toggle method as described above.

For objects like this one, it is a common and recommended convention to use the name "Start" for a method that activates a new cog and the name "Stop" for a method that deactivates a cog previously started by that object. This way, while scanning an object in summary or documentation view, other developers can more quickly understand how to use your object; when they see Start and Stop they can infer that the object activates/deactivates another cog. For objects that don't activate another cog but still need some kind of initialization, it is recommended to use the name "Init" for the key method.

This code is loaded with clever changes; be prepared, it will take a lot to explain it but the knowledge you'll gain is well worth it.

Here's the code; modify yours to match:

```
{{ Output.spin }}

VAR
  long  Stack[9]                          'Stack space for new cog
  byte  Cog                               'Hold ID of cog in use, if any


PUB Start(Pin, Delay, Count): Success
{{Start new blinking process in new cog; return TRUE if successful}}

  Stop
  Success := (Cog := cognew(Toggle(Pin, Delay, Count), @Stack) + 1)


PUB Stop
{{Stop toggling process, if any.}}

  if Cog
    cogstop(Cog~ - 1)


PUB Active: YesNo
{{Return TRUE if process is active, FALSE otherwise.}}

  YesNo := Cog > 0


PUB Toggle(Pin, Delay, Count)
{{Toggle Pin, Count times with Delay clock cycles in between.}}
  If Count = 0, toggle Pin forever.}}

  dira[Pin]~~                             'Set I/O pin to output...
  repeat Count                            'Repeat for Count iterations
  repeat                                  'Repeat the following
    !outa[Pin]                            '  Toggle I/O Pin
    waitcnt(Delay + cnt)                  '  Wait for Delay cycles
  while Count := --Count #> -1            'While not 0 (make min -1)
  Cog~                                    'Clear Cog ID variable
```

The VAR Block

In the VAR block we've added a byte-sized variable, Cog. This will be used to keep track of the ID of the cog started by the Start method, if any. Both Stack and Cog variables are global to the object; they can be used within any PUB or PRI block in the Output object. If they are modified by one method, other methods will see the new value when they are referenced.

The Start Method

For the Start method, we've decided it may be nice to know if it was successful or not. Since there are a limited number of cogs in the Propeller, the Start method may not be able to activate another cog every time it is called. For this reason, we'll make it return a Boolean (TRUE or FALSE) value as an indication of its outcome; the ": Success" in its declaration indicates it will return this value we chose to call Success. Each PUB and PRI method always returns a long value (4 bytes) whether or not it is specified to have one. When a method is designed to return a meaningful value, it is always good practice to declare a return value as we have done here. Our Success symbol becomes an alias for the method's built-in RESULT variable, so we can assign either Success or RESULT a value to have that value returned upon exit.

The body of the Start method now does two things: first it stops any existing process and then it starts a new process. It calls the Stop method first just in case Start has been called multiple times without first calling Stop from outside the object. Without that, a new cog would start up and overwrite another cog's workspace variables, such as Stack.

The next line is similar to our original but may seem a bit overwhelming because it is a compound expression. We'll dissect it a piece at a time from the inside out. The COGNEW portion of the line is exactly as it was before: cognew(Toggle(Pin, Delay, Count), @Stack). It activates another cog to run the Toggle method. What you may not have known is that COGNEW always returns the ID of the cog it started; 0 to 7, or -1 if no cog was available to start. In the prior version of the Output object, we simply ignored the return value. This time, however, we use COGNEW's return value in this expression and assign the result to a variable: Cog := cognew(Toggle(Pin, Delay, Count), @Stack) + 1. This expression says to execute COGNEW, take its returned value and add it to 1, then assign that result to the variable named Cog. The ':='is the assignment operator; similar to the equal sign '=' in other languages.

We'll use the Cog variable to remember the ID of the cog we started so we can later stop it if necessary. We'll explain why we added 1 to it in a moment.

We're not done with that line yet. To the left of the Cog := ... part is the Success := assignment statement. So after the new cog's ID is returned, added to 1 and stored in Cog, that final value is also stored in the Success variable. Remember how Success is supposed to be our Start method's Boolean return value? A Boolean result of FALSE is actually the numerical value 0 and TRUE is -1, but Boolean comparisons treat zero (0) as FALSE and any non-zero value (≠0) as TRUE. This is very convenient and is the reason we added 1 to COGNEW's return value; the range -1 to 7 becomes 0 to 8, and 0 (FALSE) means no cog was started while 1 to 8 (TRUE) means a cog was started.

So, in that single line of code we launched a new cog (hopefully), passed it the reference to the Toggle routine and stack space to use, stored the newly activated cog ID plus 1 in the variable Cog and used that final result to set Start's return value, the Success variable! This line demonstrates one of the most powerful features of the Spin language: compound expressions with assignable intermediate results.

The outer parentheses encasing the Cog :=… part are not required but we added them to help separate the two different variable assignments; Cog is assigned first then that result is assigned to Success. To assist you in studying complex expressions such as this one, the Propeller Tool temporarily bolds the matching pairs of parentheses that surround the current cursor position. Place the cursor in various positions on the line to see the effect. The figure below illustrates this; the star shows the cursor position, arrows show the bolded parentheses, and the shaded area is what is contained within those parentheses.

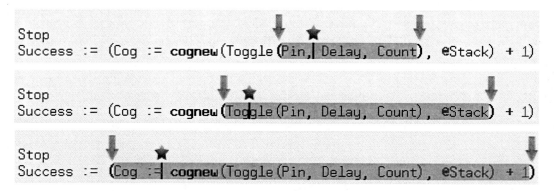

Figure 3-15: Matching Parentheses Bolded
Matching parentheses are temporarily displayed in bold for the expression group the cursor is currently within. Use this feature to study complex expressions.

The Stop Method

Our Stop method needs to stop the cog that was started by Start. The if Cog statement is a conditional structure meaning "if the Cog variable is TRUE execute the following indented block." Remember, Cog was set to 0 if no cog was started, and set to 1 through 8 if a cog was started. Since 0 means FALSE and non-0 means TRUE, the IF statement is true only if we actually started a cog.

The COGSTOP statement is indented below the IF statement so it is executed only when the IF statement is true. The COGSTOP command deactivates the cog whose ID is indicated by its parameter: Cog~ - 1. This is another tricky but powerful expression in Spin. Remember the Post-Set operator, ~~, from earlier exercises? Well, a single ~ following a variable is the Post-Clear operator; it clears the variable preceding it to zero (0). These are called "post" operators because they perform their duty "after" the variable's original value is used by the expression that it is involved in. So Cog~ - 1 takes the value of Cog, subtracts 1, gives that value to the COGSTOP command, then clears Cog to zero (0). In effect, the cogstop (Cog~ - 1) statement stops the cog whose ID is Cog-1, then clears the Cog variable to 0 so future references to Cog reflect that there is no additional cog running.

The Active Method

The Active method is simple, it sets its return value, YesNo, to TRUE if Cog is greater than 0, FALSE otherwise. The > symbol is the Is Greater Than operator. Note that we could also have just set YesNo equal to Cog since zero is considered to be FALSE and non-zero is considered to be TRUE; that would have the additional advantage of being a true/false return value as well as the actual ID of the cog in use by this object.

The Toggle Method

We made a couple of minor but significant enhancements to the Toggle method. First, let's look at the last line, Cog~. Remember that if Start is called, it runs the Toggle method in another cog and stores the ID of that cog in the Cog variable. When Toggle terminates, that cog terminates as well, but the Cog variable would be left holding the ID of that cog, fooling the Active and Start methods into thinking its cog was still active. We put Cog~ at the end of Toggle to clear the Cog variable to zero (0) to maintain the code's integrity.

Remember we said we'd like to change Toggle to allow for an infinite loop as well as a finite loop? Our next change achieves that in a clever way. The Count parameter is the number of times to toggle the pin. That means it doesn't make sense to set Count equal to 0... who would want to toggle a pin zero times? So, we'll make 0 an exception case that means "toggle the pin infinitely."

We changed the loop from `repeat Count` to `repeat..while`. The `while` is at the end of the loop, three lines below `repeat`. This is another form of REPEAT loop structure called a "conditional one-to-many loop." It executes the statement block within it at least once, and iterates again and again as long as the "while" condition is true. In this case it repeats while `Count := --Count #> -1` is TRUE (ie: non-zero). This condition is another compound expression. The double-minus, '`--`' 'preceding `Count` is the Pre-Decrement operator; it decrements `Count` by 1 before its value is used by the expression. The `#>` is the Limit Minimum operator; it takes the value on its left and returns either that value, or the number on its right, whichever is greater. So each time this expression is evaluated, `Count` is decremented by 1, that result is limited to -1 or higher, and that final result is assigned back into `Count`. This has a clever effect that we'll explain next.

If `Toggle` was called with `Count` set to 2, the loop would execute two times, just like we want. After the first iteration, the `while Count := --Count #> -1` would decrement `Count`, making it 1, then would limit it to -1 or higher (still 1) and store that value in `Count`. Since the result, 1, is non-zero (TRUE) the loop would execute again. After the second iteration, the WHILE statement would decrement `Count`, making it 0, would limit that to -1 or higher (still 0) and store that in `Count`. Since 0 is FALSE, the WHILE condition terminates the loop.

That works for all normal `Count` values, but what about when `Toggle` is called with a `Count` of 0? After the first iteration, the `while Count := --Count #> -1` would decrement `Count`, making it -1, then would limit it to -1 or higher (still -1) and store that value in `Count`. Since the result, -1, is non-zero (TRUE) the loop would execute again. After the second iteration, the WHILE statement decrements `Count`, making it -2, limits that to -1 or higher (it is changed to -1) and stores that in `Count`. Once again, since the result, -1, is non-zero (TRUE) the loop would execute again.

So, if `Count` started out as 0, the loop iterates endlessly! If `Count` started out as greater than 0, it loops only that number of times!

Quick Review: Ex 7

- Objects:
  - o Have no direct relationship with cogs.
  - o Should call interface methods "Start" and "Stop" if they affect other cogs.
  - o Should call interface method "Init" if it needs initialization.
- Spin language:
  - o Variables defined in variable blocks are global to the object so modifications by one method are visible by other methods. See VAR, page 315.
  - o Booleans: (See Constants (pre-defined), page 202 and Operators, page 249).
    - ▪ FALSE = 0
    - ▪ TRUE = -1; any non-zero (≠0) value is True for Boolean comparisons.
  - o Compound expressions can include Intermediate Assignments, see page 253.
  - o Operators:
    - ▪ "Pre"/"Post" operators perform their duty before/after the variable's value is used by the expression.
    - ▪ Assignment ':=' is similar to equal '=' in other languages, see Variable Assignment ':=', page 255.
    - ▪ Post-Clear '~' clears the variable preceding it to zero (0), see Sign-Extend 7 or Post-Clear '~', page 262.
    - ▪ Pre-Decrement '--' decrements the variable following it, giving the expression the result, see Decrement, pre- or post- '- -', page 257.
    - ▪ Is Greater Than '>' returns True if value on left-side is greater than that of right-side, see Boolean Is Greater Than '>', '>=', page 276.
    - ▪ Limit Minimum '#>' returns the greater of either the value on its left or its right, see Limit Minimum '#>', '#>=', page 260.
  - o Methods: (See PUB, page 287).
    - ▪ Always return a long value (4 bytes) whether or not one is specified.
    - ▪ Contain a built-in local variable, RESULT, that holds its return value.
    - ▪ Return values are declared by following the method's name and parameters with a colon (:) and a descriptive return value name.
  - o COGNEW returns the ID (0 to 7) of cog started; -1 if none, see COGNEW, page 189.
  - o COGSTOP deactivates a cog by ID, see COGSTOP, page 193.
  - o IF is a conditional structure that executes the indented block of code following it if the conditional statement is true, see IF, page 220.
  - o REPEAT's conditional, one-to-many form: REPEAT WHILE *Condition* executes at least once and continue while *Condition* is true. See REPEAT, page 293.
- The Propeller Tool bolds matching parentheses pairs surrounding the cursor.

Exercise 8: Blinker2.spin – Many Objects, Many Cogs

Now let's make a new object that takes advantage of the enhancements to Output to use many cogs for many parallel processes. Here's the code:

Example Object: Blinker2.spin

```
{{ Blinker2.spin }}

CON
  MAXLEDS = 6                      'Number of LED objects to use

OBJ
  LED[6] : "Output"


PUB Main
{Toggle pins at different rates, simultaneously}

  dira[16..23]~~                                   'Set pins to outputs
  LED[NextObject].Start(16, 3_000_000,   0)        'Blink LEDs
  LED[NextObject].Start(17, 2_000_000,   0)
  LED[NextObject].Start(18,   600_000, 300)
  LED[NextObject].Start(19, 6_000_000,  40)
  LED[NextObject].Start(20,   350_000, 300)
  LED[NextObject].Start(21, 1_250_000, 250)
  LED[NextObject].Start(22,   750_000, 200)        '<-Postponed
  LED[NextObject].Start(23,   400_000, 160)        '<-Postponed
  LED[0].Start(20, 12_000_000, 0)                  'Restart object 0
  repeat                                           'Loop endlessly


PUB NextObject : Index
{Scan LED objects and return index of next available LED object.
 Scanning continues until one is available.}

  repeat
    repeat Index from 0 to MAXLEDS-1
      if not LED[Index].Active
        quit
  while Index == MAXLEDS
```

Compile and download Blinker2. You should see six LEDs start blinking with different, independent, rates and periods. Look carefully, after about 8 seconds P20 will stop blinking and P22 will start. A few seconds later, P18 will stop and P23 will start, then P16 will stop and P20 will start again, but at a different rate. Eventually, all but P17 and P20 will cease. Can you figure out why it behaves this way? We'll explain it below.

The OBJ Block

In the object block we defined an array of Output objects, called LED, with six elements. This is so we can have six simultaneous processes running, each operating independently.

The Main Method

The first line of Main, dira[16..23]~~, sets I/O pins 16 through 23 to outputs. The I/O registers, DIRA, OUTA, and INA, can use this form to affect multiple contiguous pins. We are setting this group of I/O pins to outputs only to prevent confusing results due to the Propeller Demo Board's resistors between the I/O pairs in 18 to 23. If a cog is the only one making a particular pin an output, upon shutting down that pin becomes an input again which allows the resistor between it and its neighbor to affect the LED on it. We'll keep this application's cog active so results are clear.

The next nine lines, LED[..., call the Output object's Start method to activate a new cog and toggle different I/O pins at different rates. The lines in the form LED[NextObject].Start..., call the NextObject method to get an index value for the array. We'll explain the NextObject method in more detail soon, but simply put, it returns the index of the next available Output object in the LED array (i.e. the index of the first idle object) and pauses until one is available.

We only have six Output objects defined for the LED array, so the first six calls to Start are going to execute quickly, each one accessing LED indexes 0 through 5 and activating a total of 6 additional cogs. The first two have a Count parameter of 0, so they will toggle infinitely; the last four will terminate after the given number of toggles is performed.

The seventh line, LED[NextObject].Start(22, 750_000, 200) will first call NextObject to get the index of the next available object, but since all six objects are busy toggling pins, NextObject will wait and won't return to Main until it finds that an object has finished. As it turns out, the object at index 4 (I/O pin 20) finishes its task first and shuts down. The NextObject method then returns the number 4, allowing that object's Start method to execute, which will re-launch another cog to toggle pin 22. A similar process happens with the eighth line, LED[NextObject].Start(23, 400_000, 160); all objects are busy so NextObject postpones further operation until one becomes available, index 2 in this case.

Immediately after the eighth line is executed, the ninth line executes, LED[0].Start(20, 12_000_000, 0). This statement is unlike the previous in that it doesn't call NextObject, but rather it uses a fixed index of 0. This means the LED object at index 0, which is busy toggling I/O pin 16 endlessly, suddenly has its Start method called again. This causes the cog that is toggling P16 to immediately stop and start again but with P20 instead.

The final line, repeat, is only there to keep the application's cog alive. It creates an endless loop that executes no additional code since there is nothing indented underneath it. If the application cog stopped, the I/O pins it directed to be outputs may switch back to inputs, causing strange-looking results due to the resistors between some pairs of LEDs on the Propeller Demo Board. If you are not using the Propeller Demo Board, the first line and last line of Main are not necessary.

The NextObject Method

We have six LED objects in this code and any number of them can be processing in parallel at any time. The point of the NextObject method is to tell us which one is available and to postpone future operations until one is available. To do this, it scans through all six LED objects looking for the first one that is not running as a parallel process and returns the LED-based index of that object. If all are currently running, it continues scanning until one becomes available. NextObject uses our Output object's Active method to assist with this.

There are two nested REPEAT loops. The outer loop, repeat..while Index == MAXLEDS iterates as long as Index equals MAXLEDS, 6 in this case. We learned how this type of REPEAT loop works in the previous exercise.

The inner REPEAT loop, repeat Index from 0 to MAXLEDS-1, is new to us, however. It is called a "counted loop" and repeats the indented block below it but for each iteration it sets the variable Index to a new value. Index is set to 0 for the first iteration, 1 for the second, etc., until the last iteration where Index equals MAXLEDS-1, or 5. This is an excellent way to adjust the operation within a loop based on how many times the loop has executed.

The next line, if not LED[Index].Active, is a conditional statement that executes the indented code below it if the LED object at Index is "not active." Since the inner loop changes the value of Index from 0 through 5 as it executes, this conditional statement calls the Active method of each of our LED objects, in order.

Once the condition is true (the LED object at Index is not active) the next line, quit, executes. The QUIT command is a special command for REPEAT loops only; it causes the REPEAT loop it is contained within to terminate immediately. When this happens, execution continues with the end of the outer REPEAT loop, the "while" condition.

If all LED objects are active, the inner loop will count, with Index, from 0 to 5, then Index will be 6 (MAXLEDS) when it exits, causing the outer loop to iterate again and the whole process starts over. If, however, an inactive LED object is found, the Index value will be less than

MAXLEDS, and the outer loop will terminate, causing the NextObject method to return the Index of the available object. That value is used by Main to select the right LED object to start.

Behind the Scenes

In the object block, we created an array of six Output objects. Each object that an application uses needs to be treated as its own individual entity with its critical data kept separate from that of any other object. So, since we needed the capabilities of six Output objects, we declared the need for six of them in the object block.

After compiling Blinker2, the Object View shows that there are six occurrences of the Output object in our application; the "[6]" that appears to the right of the Output object image. This is the Object View's way of illustrating the structure of our application, indicated by Figure 3-16.

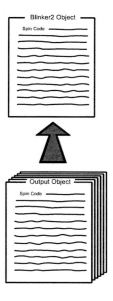

**Figure 3-16:
Blinker2 Application**

There are six instances of the Output object. The application actually uses only one copy of its executable code and six copies of its global variable space.

Does this mean our application grew by the size of the Output object times six? Fortunately, the answer is no. The Propeller Tool optimizes the application's code such that, for every occurrence of an object only one copy of the object's code is included, but multiple copies of the object's global variables are created. This is because the code is considered to be static (unchanging) and exactly the same for each object. However, the object's global variables (defined in its VAR block), are not static; each object needs its own variable space in order to work independently without interference from other instances of itself.

Object Info Window

We can see this effect using the Propeller Tool's Object Info feature. First, change the object block in Blinker2 to specify only one instance of the Output object; LED[1] : "Output". Don't run the code this way, it will not work, we're just experimenting for a moment.

Now, press the F8 key (or select Run → Compile Current → View Info...) to compile the application and display the Object Info window. Figure 3-17 shows how this should look.

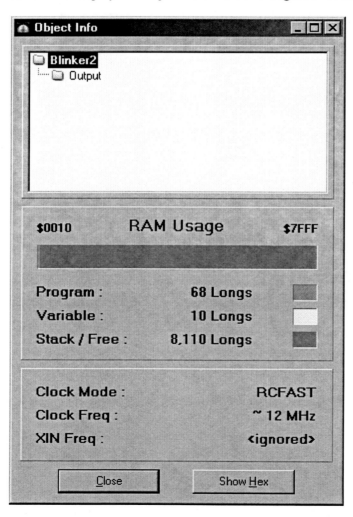

Figure 3-17:
Object Info Window for Blinker2 Application

The top part of the window is the Info Object View; it is similar to the Object View. The center part of the window shows the application's RAM Usage. Notice that the "Program" (the compiled source code) itself consumes 68 longs of RAM and the "Variable" (the global variables) consumes 10 longs of space.

Now, close this window and change the object block back to the way it was, specifying six instances of the Output object; LED[6] : "Output". Compile and view info again (F8 or Run → Compile Current → View Info…). Notice that now the program consumes 73 longs of RAM and the variable space consumes 60 longs. This is only 5 additional longs of program space but 50 additional longs of variable space. The extra program space is just overhead to deal with five additional objects but the variable space is six times its previous size; each object has its own global variable space. Our Blinker2 object doesn't define any global variable space, but Output defines nine longs for Stack and one byte for Cog for a total of 10 longs of space since an object's variable space is always long-aligned.

In the Object Info window, you can also click on the Output object to see how much space each individual instance of that object consumes. We can see that Output's program size is 21 longs and variable space is 10 longs.

Object Lifetime

When applications are compiled a binary image of the executable code is created. That binary image is what is actually downloaded into the Propeller and is usually what we are referring to when we say "application" or "Propeller Application."

The compiled code for each object used by an application is included within that binary image along with variable space for each instance of each of those objects.

During run time, the application may use any object for any amount of time; some may be used always and others only on occasion but all are consuming a static amount of memory for their code and variables.

For developers accustomed to programming with objects on a computer, this is an important concept to understand. On the Propeller an object's lifetime is static; whether or not it is actively in use at the time, it always requires a specific amount of memory in the application's binary image. On desktop/laptop computers, objects require a dynamic amount of memory because they are "created" and "destroyed" during the run-time process as is needed. On the Propeller, the objects are "created" at compile time and are never "created" or "destroyed" at run time because the act of doing so would fragment memory and cause indeterministic behaviour in real-time embedded systems.

This means that every instance of an object that is, or may be, required must be declared at compile time in the OBJ block, just as we did in Exercise 8 with the array of Output objects.

Quick Review: Ex 8

- Applications:
  - o Use unique symbols, or elements of an array, for each distinct object in use.
  - o Use one copy of an object's code and one or more copies of its global variables.
- Objects:
  - o An object array may be created in object blocks similar to a variable array in variable blocks.
  - o An object's lifetime is static, consuming a specific, static amount of memory regardless of whether or not it is active. This eliminates the possibility of fragmented memory during normal run-time use and ensures deterministic behavior in real-time systems.
- Spin language:
  - o REPEAT command: (See REPEAT, page 293).
    - ▪ Finite, counted loop: REPEAT *Variable* FROM *Start* TO *Finish* where *Variable* is the variable to use as the counter and *Start* and *Finish* indicate the range.
    - ▪ The QUIT command works inside REPEAT loops only and causes the loop to terminate immediately, see QUIT, page 291.
  - o I/O registers (DIRx, OUTx, and INx) may use the form *reg[a..b]* to affect multiple contiguous pins; where *reg* is the register (DIRx, OUTx, or INx) and *a* and *b* are I/O pin numbers, see DIRA, DIRB on page 212, OUTA, OUTB on page 280, and INA, INB on page 225.
- I/O pins are set to outputs only while a cog that set them that way remains active, see DIRA, DIRB, page 212.
- Compile & View Info: F8 key (or select Run → Compile Current → View Info...), see Object Info, page 55.

Exercise 9: Clock Settings

The Propeller chip's internal clock has two speeds, slow ($\approx$ 20 KHz) and fast ($\approx$ 12 MHz). Since we never specified any clock settings for our application, all previous exercises used the Propeller chip's default, internal RC clock in fast mode.

To specify the clock settings for the application, the top object file must set values for one or more special constants in a CON block. These constants are: _CLKMODE, _CLKFREQ and _XINFREQ.

We'll start with _CLKMODE first. Refer to Table 4-3: Clock Mode Setting Constants on page 180 for a listing of pre-defined symbolic values to set _CLKMODE to. For example, continuing with our Blinker2 object, changing the CON block as follows sets the clock mode to use the internal slow clock (only the CON block is shown here).

```
{{ Blinker2.spin }}

CON
  _CLKMODE = RCSLOW              'Set to internal slow clock
  MAXLEDS  = 6                   'Number of LED objects to use

<remaining code unchanged>
```

Try compiling and downloading Blinker2 now. Once the Propeller finishes the download/boot-up process, it switches to the RCSLOW clock mode and executes the application. Since the application is now running with a clock that is hundreds of times slower that before, the application will run much slower, taking more than 20 seconds for the fastest toggling pin, P20, to toggle off for the first time.

You can replace _CLKMODE = RCSLOW with _CLKMODE = RCFAST to have the application run with the internal fast clock (the default).

If you'd like to use an external clock, there are many more options for _CLKMODE. We'll assume you're using a 5 MHz external crystal, like the one that comes with the Propeller Demo Board.

Modify your code to match the following:

```
{{ Blinker2.spin }}

CON
  _CLKMODE = RCSLOW            'Set to internal slow clock
  _CLKMODE = XTAL1             'Set to ext. low-speed crystal
  _XINFREQ = 5_000_000         'Frequency on XIN pin is 5 MHz
  MAXLEDS  = 6                 'Number of LED objects to use

<remaining code unchanged>
```

Here we set _CLKMODE to XTAL1 which configures the clock mode for an external low-speed crystal and configures the Propeller internal oscillator gain circuitry to drive a 4 MHz to 16 MHz crystal. Besides the crystal itself (which should be connected to the XI and XO pins), no other external circuitry is required for this clock configuration.

Whenever external crystals or clocks are used, either _XINFREQ or _CLKFREQ must be specified in addition to _CLKMODE. _XINFREQ specifies the frequency coming into the XI pin (Crystal Input pin). _CLKFREQ specifies the System Clock frequency. The two are related by PLL settings which we'll discuss later.

In this example we specified an _XINFREQ value of 5 million to indicate that the frequency on the XI pin is 5 MHz, since we have a 5 MHz crystal connected to XI and XO. Once that is specified, the _CLKFREQ value is automatically calculated and set by the Propeller Tool.

You could also have specified a _CLKFREQ of 5 MHz (instead of _XINFREQ) and the proper _XINFREQ value would automatically be set by the Propeller Tool. However, it is more typical to specify the _XINFREQ value since _CLKFREQ is directly affected by PLL settings. In our example, both _XINFREQ and _CLKFREQ end up with the same value, but a later example will show how they can typically differ.

If you compile and download Blinker2 now, you should see the LEDs toggle at slightly less than half the speed as in Exercise 8. Our settings specified an external 5 MHz crystal instead of the internal 12 MHz oscillator.

So why would anyone want to use an external crystal that is slower than the internal clock? Two reasons: 1) for accuracy; the internal clock is not very accurate from chip to chip or across voltage variances but external crystals or clock/oscillators are typically very accurate, and 2) the phase-locked loop (PLL) can only be used with external clock sources.

Try the following example:

```
{{ Blinker2.spin }}

CON
  _CLKMODE = XTAL1 + PLL4X      'Set to ext low-speed crystal, 4x PLL
  _XINFREQ = 5_000_000         'Frequency on XIN pin is 5 MHz
  MAXLEDS  = 6                 'Number of LED objects to use

<remaining code unchanged>
```

Here we changed the _CLKMODE setting slightly by adding the + PLL4X value. This configures the clock mode to use the internal phase-locked loop (PLL) to wind up the XIN frequency by four times, resulting in a System Clock frequency of 5 MHz * 4 = 20 MHz.

Try compiling and downloading Blinker2 with these settings. You should see the LEDs blink at a faster rate than you've seen before.

NOTE: Since we specified _XINFREQ here, _CLKFREQ is automatically calculated to be 20 MHz. If we had specified a _CLKFREQ value of 5 MHz instead, adding the PLL4X setting would have calculated an _XINFREQ value of 1.25 MHz, which doesn't match our external crystal's frequency. This is why it is more common to specify an XIN frequency (_XINFREQ) rather than a clock frequency (_CLKFREQ).

The Clock PLL circuit, when enabled, always winds up the frequency by 16 times, but you can select any of the 1x, 2x, …16x taps for the final System Clock frequency using the settings PLL1X, PLL2X, PLL4X, PLL8X and PLL16X.

Try changing _CLKMODE from XTAL1 + PLL4x to XTAL1 + PLL16x and download again. That configures the System Clock to be 5 MHz * 16 = 80 MHz! Most of the LEDs blink so quickly that they appear to be solidly on.

Exercise 10: Clock–Related Timing

The last exercise may have made you aware of something; our Output object is easily affected by the clock frequency. It relies on a specific, hard-coded time-base but subordinate objects (those that are not the top object) should never do that because they cannot predict what the clock frequency will be for the many applications they may be used for. Additionally, the Propeller application can change the System Clock frequency a number of times throughout its run time.

Suppose that we really intended to make an Output object that toggles pins at a specific rate that is essentially clock independent. This means that it must respond dynamically to the System Clock frequency. Below is the modified code; make sure to edit your code to match.

Propeller Programming Tutorial

Example Object: Output.spin

```
{{ Output.spin }}

VAR
  long   Stack[9]                       'Stack space for new cog
  byte   Cog                            'Hold ID of cog in use, if any


PUB Start(Pin, DelayMS, Count): Success
{{Start new blinking process in new cog; return True if successful.}}

  Stop
  Success := (Cog := cognew(Toggle(Pin, DelayMS, Count), @Stack) + 1)


PUB Stop
{{Stop toggling process, if any.}}

  if Cog
    cogstop(Cog~ - 1)


PUB Active: YesNo
{{Return TRUE if process is active, FALSE otherwise.}}

  YesNo := Cog > 0


PUB Toggle(Pin, DelayMS, Count)
{{Toggle Pin, Count times with DelayMS milliseconds ~~clock cycles~~
  in between.  If Count = 0, toggle Pin forever.}}

  dira[Pin]~~                           'Set I/O pin to output...
  repeat                                'Repeat the following
    !outa[Pin]                          '  Toggle I/O Pin
    waitcnt(clkfreq / 1000 * DelayMS + cnt)  '  Wait for DelayMS...
  while Count := --Count #> -1          'While not 0 (make min...
  Cog~                                  'Clear Cog ID variable
```

We modified the Start and Toggle methods by changing the Delay parameter to DelayMS, meaning "delay in units of milliseconds." Then we modified the waitcnt... statement such that instead of waiting a fixed number of clock cycles, it calculates the number of clock cycles that there are in DelayMS milliseconds of time. CLKFREQ is a command that returns the current System Clock frequency in Hertz (cycles per second). Its value is set by the Propeller Tool at compile time and also by the CLKSET command at run time; see CLKSET on page 183. There are 1,000 milliseconds per second and CLKFREQ is the number of clock cycles per second, so clkfreq / 1000 * DelayMS is the number of clock cycles in DelayMS milliseconds of time.

With this modification, regardless of the application's start-up frequency, or how often the application changes the frequency during run time, the Output object will recalculate the proper delay each time through its loop.

Now, of course, we need to modify our Blinker2 object to adjust the DelayMS parameters appropriately. Enter the code modifications shown in the listing on page 136. Note that we entered the _CLKMODE and _XINFREQ settings just as we had left them from the last exercise.

Example Object: Blinker2.spin

```
{{ Blinker2.spin }}

CON
  _CLKMODE = XTAL1 + PLL4X        'Set to ext low-speed crystal, 4x PLL
  _XINFREQ = 5_000_000            'Frequency on XIN pin is 5 MHz
  MAXLEDS = 6                     'Number of LED objects to use


OBJ
  LED[6] : "Output"


PUB Main
{Toggle pins at different rates, simultaneously}

  dira[16..23]~~                                'Set pins to outputs
  LED[NextObject].Start(16, 250,   0)           'Blink LEDs
  LED[NextObject].Start(17, 500,   0)
  LED[NextObject].Start(18,  50, 300)
  LED[NextObject].Start(19, 500,  40)
  LED[NextObject].Start(20,  29, 300)
  LED[NextObject].Start(21, 104, 250)
  LED[NextObject].Start(22,  63, 200)           '<-Postponed
  LED[NextObject].Start(23,  33, 160)           '<-Postponed
  LED[0].Start(20, 1000, 0)                     'Restart object 0
  repeat                                        'Loop endlessly

PUB NextObject : Index
{Scan LED objects and return index of next available LED object.
 Scanning continues until one is available.}

  repeat
    repeat Index from 0 to MAXLEDS-1
      if not LED[Index].Active
        quit
  while Index == MAXLEDS
```

In `Main`, we adjusted the second parameter of the all the calls to `Start` from "delay in clock cycles" to "delay in milliseconds." Compile and download the Blinker2 object now. Notice that the rate at which each LED blinks is the same as it was when we used the internal fast clock. Try increasing the clock speed by changing `_CLKMODE` from `XTAL1 + PLL4X` to `XTAL1 + PLL16X`. You should not see any change in the blink rates even though we just multiplied the clock frequency by four!

Keep in mind that the accuracy of the internal clock on your particular Propeller chip can play a big role in the way this example looks, especially when using the `RCSLOW` mode.

There are two techniques for using the `WAITCNT` command but we only demonstrated one of them. For further tips regarding timing, see the `WAITCNT` command on page 322.

Quick Review: Ex 9 & 10

- Clock:
  - The internal clock has two speeds, slow (≈ 20 KHz) and fast (≈ 12 MHz).
  - To specify clock settings for an application, the top object file sets values for one or more special constants: `_CLKMODE`, `_CLKFREQ` and `_XINFREQ`.
  - Whenever external crystals or clocks are used, either `_XINFREQ` or `_CLKFREQ` must be specified in addition to `_CLKMODE`.
  - `_CLKMODE` specifies the clock mode: internal/external, oscillator gain, PLL settings, etc. See `_CLKMODE`, page 180.
  - `_XINFREQ` specifies the frequency coming into the XI pin (Crystal Input pin). See `_XINFREQ`, page 337.
  - `_CLKFREQ` specifies the System Clock frequency. See `_CLKFREQ`, page 177.
  - Use the internal clock for convenience where accuracy doesn't matter. Use an external clock for accuracy or when the phase-locked loop (PLL) is needed.
- Timing:
  - Subordinate objects can't rely on a specific, hard-coded time-base since applications which use them may change the clock frequency.
  - Use the `CLKFREQ` command to get the current System Clock frequency in Hertz for timing calculations. See `CLKFREQ`, page 175.

Exercise 11: Library Objects

The Propeller Tool comes with a library of objects created by Parallax engineers. These objects perform many useful functions such as serial communication, floating-point math, number-to-string and string-to-number conversion, and TV display generation, using standard PC-style keyboards, mice and monitors, etc.

The Propeller Object Library is simply a folder containing Propeller object files that are automatically created during the Propeller Tool software installation. You can get to the Propeller Library folder by selecting "Propeller Library" from the Recent Folders list; see Figure 3-18. After selecting the Propeller Library, the Files List will display all the available objects.

Figure 3-18:
Propeller Library Browsing

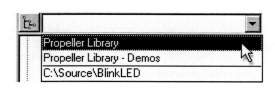

Select "Propeller Library" from the Integrated Explorer's Recent Folders list to quickly browse to the library folder.

Let's use some of them now. Create a new file and enter the code below. The highlighted items are important for the discussion following the code.

Example Object: Display.spin

```
{{ Display.spin }}

CON
  _clkmode = xtal1 + pll16x
  _xinfreq = 5_000_000

OBJ
  Num   :       "Numbers"
  TV    :       "TV_Terminal"

PUB Main | Temp
  Num.Init                                      'Initialize Numbers
  TV.Start(12)                                  'Start TV Terminal

  Temp := 900 * 45 + 401                        'Evaluate expression
  TV.Str(string("900 * 45 + 401 = "))          'then display it and
  TV.Str(Num.ToStr(Temp, Num#DDEC))            'its result in decimal
  TV.Out(13)
  TV.Str(string("In hexadecimal it's  = "))    'and in hexadecimal
  TV.Str(Num.ToStr(Temp, Num#IHEX))
  TV.Out(13)
  TV.Out(13)

  TV.Str(string("Counting by fives:"))         'Now count by fives
  TV.Out(13)
  repeat Temp from 5 to 30 step 5
    TV.Str(Num.ToStr(Temp, Num#DEC))
    if Temp < 30
      TV.Out(",")
```

Save this object as "Display.spin" in a folder of your choice; for this example we'll use the "C:\Source\" folder.

In this example we use two Propeller Library objects, Numbers and TV_Terminal, to convert numeric values to strings and display them on a TV. Compile and download this example object and connect a TV (NTSC) display to the composite output (RCA jack) on the Propeller Demo Board. The TV display should show the following text:

```
900 * 45 + 401 = 40,901
In hexadecimal it's  = $9FC5
Counting by fives:
 5, 10, 15, 20, 25, 30
```

Look at what we just achieved! Using just a few lines of our own code plus two existing library objects and three resistors (on the Propeller Demo Board) we converted numeric values to text strings and generated a TV-compatible signal to display that text in real time on a standard TV! In fact, while you are reading this, a cog is keeping busy constantly generating an NTSC signal at 60 frames per second that the TV can lock onto.

The TV_Terminal object provides a great display for debugging purposes. Since the Propeller has many processors and can run quite fast, a real-time display such as a TV monitor (CRT or LCD) used for debugging purposes goes a long way toward developing optimal source code. We recommend using this technique along with the usual debugging techniques to speed up development time.

Let's look at some important parts of our code now. The first new item in our code is the | Temp that appears in Main's declaration line. Don't be fooled, this may look like a return variable declaration, but it is not. The pipe symbol '|' indicates we are declaring local variables next. So, | Temp declares that Temp is a long-sized local variable for Main.

Next we have two very important statements, Num.Init and TV.Start(12). These two statements initialize the Numbers object and start the TV_Terminal object (on pins 12, 13 and 14), respectively. Each of these objects requires some kind of initialization before using it. Numbers requires that its Init method is called to initialize some internal registers. TV_Terminal requires that its Start method is called to configure the proper output pins and to start two more cogs to generate the display signals. Objects typically indicate these requirements in their documentation, but it is common that they include an Init or a Start method if they require some initial setup before use.

The next line performs some arithmetic and sets our local variable, Temp, to the result. We'll use this result soon.

The next three statements create the first line of text on the TV display: 9 * 45 + 401 = 40,901. The TV.Str method outputs a zero-terminated string to the display. Its parameter, string("900 * 45 + 401 = ") is new to us. STRING is a directive that creates a zero-terminated string of characters (multiple bytes of character data followed by a zero; sometimes called a z-string) and returns the address of that string. Most methods that deal with strings require just the address of the starting character and for the string to end with a byte equal to zero. TV.Str method's parameter requires exactly that, the address of a zero-terminated string. So the line TV.Str(string("900 * 45 + 401 = ")) causes the string "900 * 45 + 401 = " to be displayed on the TV.

The next statement, TV.Str(Num.ToStr(Temp, Num#DDEC)) prints the "40,901" part of the line. The Num.ToStr method converts the numeric value in Temp into a string using delimited decimal format and returns the address of that string. Temp, of course, holds the long-sized result of our earlier expression: 40901. The Num#DDEC part is new to us, however. The # symbol when used this way is an Object-Constant reference; it is used to reference a constant that was defined in another object. In this case, Num#DDEC refers to the "format constant" DDEC that is declared within the Numbers object. As defined by Numbers, DDEC stands for Delimited Decimal and holds a value that indicates to the ToStr method that it should format the number with a thousands-group delimiter; a comma in this case. So, ToStr creates a z-string equal to "40,901" and returns the address of it. TV.Str then outputs that string onto the display. Read the documentation in the Numbers object for more information about this and other format constants.

TV.Out(13) outputs a single byte, 13, to the display. The 13 is the ASCII code for a carriage return (a non-visible character) and causes the TV_Terminal object to move to the next text line. We do this in preparation for the next string we'll print afterward.

Work and Library Folders

When our Display object is compiled, the Object View displays the structure shown below. This shows us that our Display object uses the Numbers and TV_Terminal objects and the TV_Terminal object uses the TV and Graphics objects.

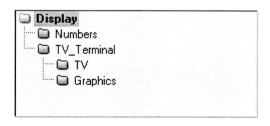

Figure 3-19:
Object View of
Display Application

Yellow folders
indicate objects in the
"work" folder. Blue
folders indicate
objects in the
"library" folder.

The folder icons in front of each object are different colors to indicate their individual folder locations. Objects with yellow folders are in the "work" folder while those with blue folders are in the "library" folder. From this display we can see that the Propeller Tool found the Numbers, TV_Terminal, TV and Graphics objects in the library folder and the Display object in the work folder.

Remember that we saved our Display object in the C:\Source folder? When an application is compiled, the folder that the top object file is stored within becomes known as the work folder. If that file refers to other objects, the work folder is the first place where the Propeller Tool looks for them. If the referenced object is not in the work folder, the library folder is searched next. If an object in the library folder refers to another object, the library folder is searched for that other object. An error occurs if referenced objects are not found in either the work folder or the library folder.

Due to this nature, it can be said that every application is composed entirely of files from as many as two folders; the work folder and/or the library folder. Keep this in mind while building your applications.

You can find out the location of each object, and the work and library folders, by pointing the mouse at each object in the Object View. In the figures below we see that Display is in C:\Source (the "work" folder) and Numbers is in C:\Program Files\Parallax Inc\Propeller Tool (the "library" folder).

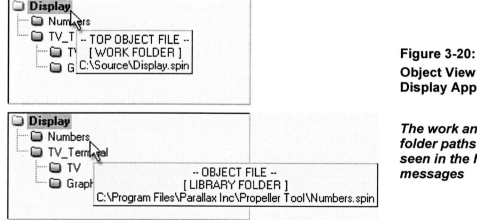

Figure 3-20:
Object View Hints for Display Application

The work and library folder paths can be seen in the hint messages

Exercise 12: Whole and Real Numbers

The Propeller is a 32-bit device and can naturally handle whole numbers as signed integers (-2,147,483,648 to 2,147,483,647) both in constants or in run-time math expressions. However, for real numbers (those with both integer and fraction components) the compiler supports floating-point format (single-precision, IEEE-754 compliant) for constants, and there are library objects that allow for run-time floating-point math operations.

Pseudo–Real Numbers

For handling real numbers, there are many possible techniques. One technique is to use integer math in a way that accommodates your real values as well as the run-time expressions involved. We call this pseudo-real numbers.

Having 32-bit integers built in to the Propeller provides us with a lot of "elbow room" for calculations. For example, perhaps we have an equation to multiply and divide values that have 2-digit fractions, like the following:

$A = B * C / D$

For our example, let's use $A = 7.6 * 38.75 / 12.5$ which evaluates to 23.56.

To solve this at run time, we can adjust all the equation's values upward by 2 digits to make them all integers, perform the math and then treat the rightmost 2 digits of the result as being the fractional portion. Multiplying each value by 100 achieves this. Here's the algebraic proof:

$A = (B * 100) * (C * 100) / (D * 100)$

$A = (7.6 * 100) * (38.75 * 100) / (12.5 * 100)$

$A = 760 * 3875 / 1250$

$A = 2356$

Since we multiplied all the original values by 100, we know that the final value is really $2356 / 100 = 23.56$, but for most purposes we can keep it in integer form knowing that the rightmost two digits are really to the right of the decimal point.

The above solution works as long as each of the original values and each of the intermediate results never exceed the signed integer boundaries: -2,147,483,648 to 2,147,483,647.

The example presented next includes code that uses both the pseudo-real number technique as well as floating-point numbers.

Floating–Point Numbers

In many cases, expressions involving real numbers can be solved without using floating-point values and methods, such as with the pseudo-real number technique. Since solutions like the one above tend to execute much faster and consume less memory, it is recommended that you think carefully about whether or not you really need floating-point support before you actually use it. If you can afford the extra execution time and memory usage, floating-point support may be the best solution.

The Propeller Tool supports floating-point constants directly. The Propeller chip supports floating-point run-time expressions through the use of objects; ie: at run time the Spin Interpreter can only directly process integer-based expressions.

The next example object, RealNumbers.spin, demonstrates using integer constants (iB, iC, and iD) that are pre-translated to pseudo-real numbers, floating-point constants (B, C, and D) used in their native form by the FloatMath and FloatString library objects, and also those same floating-point constants translated to pseudo-real numbers at compile time.

Example Object: RealNumbers.spin

```
{{ RealNumbers.spin}}
CON
  _clkmode = xtal1 + pll16x
  _xinfreq = 5_000_000

  iB    =  760                      'Integer constants
  iC    = 3875
  iD    = 1250

  B     =  7.6                      'Floating-point constants
  C     = 38.75
  D     = 12.5

  K     = 100.0                     'Real-to-Pseudo-Real multiplier
OBJ
  Term  :          "TV_Terminal"
  F     :          "FloatMath"
  FS    :          "FloatString"

PUB Math
  Term.Start(12)

  {Integer constants (real numbers * 100) to do fast integer math}
  Term.Str(string("Pseudo-Real Number Result: "))
  Term.Dec(iB*iC/iD)

  {Floating-point constants using FloatMath and FloatString objects}
  Term.Out(13)
  Term.Str(string("Floating-Point Number Result: "))
  Term.Str(FS.FloatToString(F.FDiv(F.FMul(B, C), D)))

  {Floating-point constants translated to pseudo-real for fast math}
  Term.Out(13)
  Term.Str(string("Another Pseudo-Real Number Result: "))
  Term.Dec(trunc(B*K)*trunc(C*K)/trunc(D*K))
```

Compile and download RealNumbers.spin. It will display the following on a TV display:

```
Pseudo-Real Number Result: 2356
Floating-Point Number Result: 23.56
Another Pseudo-Real Number Result: 2356
```

The pseudo-real results, of course, each represent the value 23.56 but the entire value is shifted upwards by two digits to maintain integer math compatibility. With some additional code we could output it as 23.56 for display purposes.

The constants iB, iC, and iD are standard integer constants as we've seen before, but their values are really pseudo-real numbers representing the values in our example equation.

The constants B, C, D, and K, are floating-point constants (real numbers). The compiler automatically recognizes them as such and stores them in 32-bit single-precision floating-point format. They can be used in other compile-time floating-point expressions directly but at run time they should only be used with floating-point methods such as those found in the FloatMath and FloatString objects.

The statement Term.Dec(iB*iC/iD) uses the pre-translated pseudo-real constants as suggested by the Pseudo-Real Numbers technique, above. This is evaluated about 1.6 times faster than with the floating-point technique and takes much less code space.

The statement Term.Str(FS.FloatToString(F.FDiv(F.FMul(B, C), D))) calls FloatMath's FMul method to multiply the floating-point values B and C, then calls FloatMath's FDiv method to divide that result by the floating-point value D, translates the result to a string using FloatString's FloatToString method and displays that on the TV.

The statement Term.Dec(trunc(B*K)*trunc(C*K)/trunc(D*K)) uses compile-time expressions inside of TRUNC directives to shift the floating-point constants B, C, and D upwards by two digits and truncate the values to integers. The resulting expression is equivalent to that of the first pseudo-real number equation Term.Dec(iB*iC/iD) but has the added benefit of allowing its component values to be defined in floating-point terms.

The TRUNC directive truncates fully resolved floating-point expressions to their integer form at compile time. It is required here since floating-point constant values can not be used directly by run-time expressions.

Context–Sensitive Compile Information

After an object has been compiled, the Propeller Tool displays context-sensitive compile information on the status bar (panel 5) about the source item the cursor is currently near or within. This is very useful in verifying and understanding the values of constants declared in an object. For example, compile this example by pressing F9 (or selecting the Run → Compile Current → Update Status menu option) and then place the cursor on the iB constant in the CON block. The status bar will temporarily highlight the context information and should look similar to the figure below.

Figure 3-21:
Status Bar with
Compile Information

| 5 : 4 | | Insert | Compiled | CON iB = 760 ($0000_02F8) |

After a compile operation, the status bar's panel 5 displays information about the source item nearest the cursor.

This tells us that our iB constant is defined by the CON block to be 760 decimal, or $2F8 hexadecimal.

Try placing the cursor on the B constant. The compile information should now read "CON B = 7.6 ($40F3_3333) Floating Point" to indicate this is a real number, in floating-point form, equal to 7.6 decimal ($40F3_3333 hexadecimal) This illustrates that floating-point values are encoded into 32 bits in a way that makes them incompatible with integer values.

In addition to symbols in CON and DAT blocks, the compile information displays shows the size, in bytes, of PUB/PRI/DAT blocks when the cursor is within that block. In our case, the Math method is 196 bytes long. This is a great feature to use when optimizing code for size; make small changes to code, press F9, check size against that of the previous code, and so on.

Quick Review: Ex 11 & 12

- Propeller Library:
  - Is a folder automatically created by the Propeller Tool installer.
  - Contains Parallax-made Propeller objects that perform useful functions.
  - The "Propeller Library" item in the Recent Folders list allows for quick access.
- Spin Language:
  - The pipe symbol '|' on method declaration lines declares a list of local variables for the method; see Parameters and Local Variables, page 289.
  - The STRING directive creates a zero-terminated string and returns its address; see STRING, page 310.
  - The # symbol forms an Object-Constant reference used to access constants defined in other objects; see Scope of Constants, page 199.
  - The TRUNC directive truncates floating-point constants to integers; see TRUNC, page 314.
- Work and Library Folders:
  - The Object View's folder icons indicate the object's location.
    - Objects with yellow folders are in the "work" folder.
    - Objects with blue folders are in the "library" folder.
  - Every application is composed entirely of files from as many as two folders; the work folder and/or the library folder.
- Integers and Real Numbers: (See CON, page 194, or Operators, page 249)
  - Integers are directly supported both in constants and in run-time expressions.
  - Real numbers, in floating-point format, are directly supported in constants and are indirectly supported at run time by special library objects.
  - In many cases, expressions involving real numbers can be solved without using floating-point values and methods.
- The Status Bar displays compile information about the source item nearest to the cursor. This includes CON/DAT block symbol's size/address and PUB/PRI/DAT block's size.

Where to go from here...

You should now have the knowledge you need to explore the Propeller chip on your own and develop your first applications. Use the rest of this manual as a reference to the Spin and Propeller Assembly languages, explore every existing library object that interests you and join the Propeller Forum to keep learning and sharing with other active Propeller chip users.

Chapter 4: Spin Language Reference

This chapter describes all elements of the Propeller chip's Spin language and is best used as a reference for individual elements of the Spin language. For a general tutorial of the use of the Spin language, first read Chapter 3: Propeller Programming Tutorial, then return here for more details.

The Spin Language Reference is divided into three sections:

1) **The Structure of the Propeller Objects**. Propeller Objects consist of Spin code, optional Assembly Code, and data. An object's Spin code provides it with structure, consisting of special-purpose blocks. This section lists these blocks and the elements that may be used in each. Each listed element has a page reference for more information.

2) **The Categorical Listing of the Propeller Spin Language**. All elements, including operators and syntax symbols, are grouped by related function. This is a great way to quickly realize the breadth of the language and what features are available for specific uses. Each listed element has a page reference for more information. Some elements are marked with a superscript "a" indicating that they are also available in Propeller Assembly, though syntax may vary. Such marked elements are also included in Chapter 5: Assembly Language Reference.

3) **The Spin Language Elements**. Most elements have their own dedicated sub-section, alphabetically arranged to ease searching for them. Those individual elements without a dedicated sub-section, such as Operators, Symbols and some constants, are grouped within other related sub-sections but can be easily located by following their page reference from the Categorical Listing.

Structure of Propeller Objects

Each Propeller object has an inherent structure consisting of up to six different special-purpose blocks: CON, VAR, OBJ, PUB, PRI, and DAT. These blocks are shown below (in the order that they typically appear in objects) along with the set of elements usable within each.

For detailed examples of the object structure and usage, refer to Chapter 3: Propeller Programming Tutorial which begins on page 85.

CON: Constant blocks define global constants (page 194).

_CLKFREQ	p 177	NEGX	p 202	PLL16X	p 180	XINPUT	p 180
_CLKMODE	p 180	Operators*	p 249	POSX	p 202	XTAL1	p 180
_FREE	p 218	PI	p 202	RCFAST	p 180	XTAL2	p 180
_STACK	p 307	PLL1X	p 180	RCSLOW	p 180	XTAL3	p 180
_XINFREQ	p 337	PLL2X	p 180	ROUND	p 303		
FALSE	p 202	PLL4X	p 180	TRUE	p 202		
FLOAT	p 216	PLL8X	p 180	TRUNC	p 314		

*Non-assignment operators only.

VAR: Variable blocks define global variables (page 315).

BYTE	p 165	LONG	p 236	ROUND	p 303	TRUNC	p 314
FLOAT	p 216	Operators*	p 249	WORD	p 331		

*Non-assignment operators only.

OBJ: Object blocks define referenced objects (page 247).

FLOAT	p 216	Operators*	p 249	ROUND	p 303	TRUNC	p 314

*Non-assignment operators only.

PUB/PRI: Public and Private method blocks define Spin routines (pages 287/286).

ABORT	p 161	FLOAT	p 216	**Operators**	p 249	ROUND	p 303
BYTE	p 165	FRQA	p 219	OUTA	p 280	SPR	p 305
BYTEFILL	p 169	FRQB	p 219	OUTB	p 280	STRCOMP	p 308
BYTEMOVE	p 170	IF	p 220	PAR	p 283	STRING	p 310
CASE	p 171	IFNOT	p 225	PHSA	p 285	STRSIZE	p 311
CHIPVER	p 174	INA	p 225	PHSB	p 285	TRUE	p 202
CLKFREQ	p 175	INB	p 225	PI	p 202	TRUNC	p 314
CLKMODE	p 179	LOCKCLR	p 228	PLL1X	p 180	VCFG	p 317
CLKSET	p 183	LOCKNEW	p 230	PLL2X	p 180	VSCL	p 320
CNT	p 184	LOCKRET	p 233	PLL4X	p 180	WAITCNT	p 322
COGID	p 186	LOCKSET	p 234	PLL8X	p 180	WAITPEQ	p 326
COGINIT	p 187	LONG	p 236	PLL16X	p 180	WAITPNE	p 328
COGNEW	p 189	LONGFILL	p 240	POSX	p 202	WAITVID	p 329
COGSTOP	p 193	LONGMOVE	p 241	QUIT	p 291	WORD	p 331
CONSTANT	p 200	LOOKDOWN	p 242	RCFAST	p 180	WORDFILL	p 335
CTRA	p 204	LOOKDOWNZ	p 242	RCSLOW	p 180	WORDMOVE	p 336
CTRB	p 204	LOOKUP	p 244	REBOOT	p 292	XINPUT	p 180
DIRA	p 212	LOOKUPZ	p 244	REPEAT	p 293	XTAL1	p 180
DIRB	p 212	NEGX	p 202	RESULT	p 299	XTAL2	p 180
FALSE	p 202	NEXT	p 246	RETURN	p 301	XTAL3	p 180

DAT: Data blocks define data and Propeller Assembly code (page 208).

Assembly	p 339	FRQB	p 219	PI	p 202	TRUNC	p 314
BYTE	p 165	INA	p 225	PLL1X	p 180	VCFG	p 317
CNT	p 184	INB	p 225	PLL2X	p 180	VSCL	p 320
CTRA	p 204	LONG	p 236	PLL4X	p 180	WORD	p 331
CTRB	p 204	NEGX	p 202	PLL8X	p 180	XINPUT	p 180
DIRA	p 212	**Operators***	p 249	PLL16X	p 180	XTAL1	p 180
DIRB	p 212	OUTA	p 280	POSX	p 202	XTAL2	p 180
FALSE	p 202	OUTB	p 280	RCFAST	p 180	XTAL3	p 180
FILE	p 215	PAR	p 283	RCSLOW	p 180		
FLOAT	p 216	PHSA	p 285	ROUND	p 303		
FRQA	p 219	PHSB	p 285	TRUE	p 202		

* Non-assignment operators only.

Categorical Listing of Propeller Spin Language

Elements marked with a superscript "a" are also available in Propeller Assembly.

Block Designators

CON	Declare constant block; p 194.
VAR	Declare variable block; p 315.
OBJ	Declare object reference block; p 247.
PUB	Declare public method block; p 287.
PRI	Declare private method block; p 286.
DAT	Declare data block; p 208.

Configuration

CHIPVER	Propeller chip version number; p 174.
CLKMODE	Current clock mode setting; p 179.
_CLKMODE	Application-defined clock mode (read-only); p 180.
CLKFREQ	Current clock frequency; p 175.
_CLKFREQ	Application-defined clock frequency (read-only); p 177.
CLKSET[a]	Set clock mode and clock frequency; p 183.
_XINFREQ	Application-defined external clock frequency (read-only); p 337.
_STACK	Application-defined stack space to reserve (read-only); p 307.
_FREE	Application-defined free space to reserve (read-only); p 218.
RCFAST	Constant for _CLKMODE: internal fast oscillator; p 180.
RCSLOW	Constant for _CLKMODE: internal slow oscillator; p 180.
XINPUT	Constant for _CLKMODE: external clock/osc (XI pin); p 180.
XTAL1	Constant for _CLKMODE: external low-speed crystal; p 180.
XTAL2	Constant for _CLKMODE: external med-speed crystal; p 180.
XTAL3	Constant for _CLKMODE: external high-speed crystal; p 180.
PLL1X	Constant for _CLKMODE: external frequency times 1; p 180.
PLL2X	Constant for _CLKMODE: external frequency times 2; p 180.
PLL4X	Constant for _CLKMODE: external frequency times 4; p 180.

| PLL8X | Constant for _CLKMODE: external frequency times 8; p 180. |
| PLL16X | Constant for _CLKMODE: external frequency times 16; p 180. |

Cog Control

COGID[a]	Current cog's ID (0-7); p 186.
COGNEW	Start the next available cog; p 189.
COGINIT[a]	Start, or restart, a cog by ID; p 187.
COGSTOP[a]	Stop a cog by ID; p 193.
REBOOT	Reset the Propeller chip; p 292.

Process Control

LOCKNEW[a]	Check out a new lock; p 230.
LOCKRET[a]	Release a lock; p 233.
LOCKCLR[a]	Clear a lock by ID; p 228.
LOCKSET[a]	Set a lock by ID; p 234.
WAITCNT[a]	Wait for System Counter to reach a value; p 322.
WAITPEQ[a]	Wait for pin(s) to be equal to value; p 326.
WAITPNE[a]	Wait for pin(s) to be not equal to value; p 328.
WAITVID[a]	Wait for video sync and deliver next color/pixel group; p 329.

Flow Control

IF
  ...ELSEIF
  ...ELSEIFNOT
  ...ELSE
	Conditionally execute one or more blocks of code; p 220.

IFNOT
  ...ELSEIF
  ...ELSEIFNOT
  ...ELSE
	Conditionally execute one or more blocks of code; p 225.

CASE ...OTHER	Evaluate expression and execute block of code that satisfies a condition; p 171.

Spin Language Reference

REPEAT	Execute block of code repetitively an infinite or finite number of times
...FROM	with optional loop counter, intervals, exit and continue conditions; p
...TO	293.
...STEP	
...UNTIL	
...WHILE	

NEXT	Skip rest of REPEAT block and jump to next loop iteration; p 246.
QUIT	Exit from REPEAT loop; p 291.
RETURN	Exit PUB/PRI with normal status and optional return value; p 301.
ABORT	Exit PUB/PRI with abort status and optional return value; p 161.

Memory

BYTE	Declare byte-sized symbol or access byte of main memory; p 165.
WORD	Declare word-sized symbol or access word of main memory; p 331.
LONG	Declare long-sized symbol or access long of main memory; p 236.
BYTEFILL	Fill bytes of main memory with a value; p 169.
WORDFILL	Fill words of main memory with a value; p 335.
LONGFILL	Fill longs of main memory with a value; p 240.
BYTEMOVE	Copy bytes from one region to another in main memory; p 170.
WORDMOVE	Copy words from one region to another in main memory; p 336.
LONGMOVE	Copy longs from one region to another in main memory; p 241.
LOOKUP	Get value at index (1..N) from a list; p 244.
LOOKUPZ	Get value at zero-based index (0..N−1) from a list; p 244.
LOOKDOWN	Get index (1..N) of a matching value from a list; p 242.
LOOKDOWNZ	Get zero-based index (0..N−1) of a matching value from a list; p 242.
STRSIZE	Get size of string in bytes; p 311.
STRCOMP	Compare a string of bytes against another string of bytes; p 308.

Directives

STRING	Declare in-line string expression; resolved at compile time; p 310.
CONSTANT	Declare in-line constant expression; resolved at compile time; p 200.
FLOAT	Declare floating-point expression; resolved at compile time; p 216.
ROUND	Round compile-time floating-point expression to integer; p 303.
TRUNC	Truncate compile-time floating-point expression at decimal; p 314.
FILE	Import data from an external file; p 215.

Registers

DIRA[a]	Direction Register for 32-bit port A; p 212.
DIRB[a]	Direction Register for 32-bit port B (future use); p 212.
INA[a]	Input Register for 32-bit port A (read only); p 225.
INB[a]	Input Register for 32-bit port B (read only) (future use); p 226.
OUTA[a]	Output Register for 32-bit port A; p 280.
OUTB[a]	Output Register for 32-bit port B (future use); p 282.
CNT[a]	32-bit System Counter Register (read only); p 184.
CTRA[a]	Counter A Control Register; p 204.
CTRB[a]	Counter B Control Register; p 204.
FRQA[a]	Counter A Frequency Register; p 219.
FRQB[a]	Counter B Frequency Register; p 219.
PHSA[a]	Counter A Phase-Locked Loop (PLL) Register; p 285.
PHSB[a]	Counter B Phase-Locked Loop (PLL) Register; p 285.
VCFG[a]	Video Configuration Register; p 317.
VSCL[a]	Video Scale Register; p 320.
PAR[a]	Cog Boot Parameter Register (read only); p 283.
SPR	Special-Purpose Register array; indirect cog register access; p 305.

Spin Language Reference

Constants

TRUE[a]	Logical true: -1 ($FFFFFFFF); p 202.
FALSE[a]	Logical false: 0 ($00000000) ; p 202.
POSX[a]	Maximum positive integer: 2,147,483,647 ($7FFFFFFF); p 202.
NEGX[a]	Maximum negative integer: -2,147,483,648 ($80000000); p 202.
PI[a]	Floating-point value for PI: ~3.141593 ($40490FDB); p 202.

Variable

RESULT	Default result variable for PUB/PRI methods; p 299.

Unary Operators

+	Positive (+X); unary form of Add; p 256.
−	Negate (-X); unary form of Subtract; p 256.
−−	Pre-decrement (--X) or post-decrement (X--) and assign; p 257.
++	Pre-increment (++X) or post-increment (X++) and assign; p 257.
^^	Square root; p 261.
||	Absolute Value; p 261.
~	Sign-extend from bit 7 (~X) or post-clear to 0 (X~); p 262.
~~	Sign-extend from bit 15 (~~X) or post-set to -1(X~~); p 263.
?	Random number forward (?X) or reverse (X?); p 264.
|<	Decode value (modulus of 32; 0-31) into single-high-bit long; p 265.
>|	Encode long into magnitude (0 - 32) as high-bit priority; p 266.
!	Bitwise: NOT; p 272.
NOT	Boolean: NOT (promotes non-0 to -1); p 274.
@	Symbol address; p 278.
@@	Object address plus symbol value; p 279.

Binary Operators

NOTE: All right-column operators are assignment operators.

`=`	--and--	`=`	Constant assignment (`CON` blocks); p 254.
`:=`	--and--	`:=`	Variable assignment (`PUB/PRI` blocks); p 255.
`+`	--or--	`+=`	Add; p 255.
`−`	--or--	`−=`	Subtract; p 256.
`*`	--or--	`*=`	Multiply and return lower 32 bits (signed); p 258.
`**`	--or--	`**=`	Multiply and return upper 32 bits (signed); p 259.
`/`	--or--	`/=`	Divide (signed); p 259.
`//`	--or--	`//=`	Modulus (signed); p 259.
`#>`	--or--	`#>=`	Limit minimum (signed); p 260.
`<#`	--or--	`<#=`	Limit maximum (signed); p 261.
`~>`	--or--	`~>=`	Shift arithmetic right; p 264.
`<<`	--or--	`<<=`	Bitwise: Shift left; p 266.
`>>`	--or--	`>>=`	Bitwise: Shift right; p 267.
`<-`	--or--	`<-=`	Bitwise: Rotate left; p 267.
`->`	--or--	`->=`	Bitwise: Rotate right; p 268.
`><`	--or--	`><=`	Bitwise: Reverse; p 268.
`&`	--or--	`&=`	Bitwise: AND; p 269.
`|`	--or--	`|=`	Bitwise: OR; p 270.
`^`	--or--	`^=`	Bitwise: XOR; p 271.
`AND`	--or--	`AND=`	Boolean: AND (promotes non-0 to -1); p 272.
`OR`	--or--	`OR=`	Boolean: OR (promotes non-0 to -1); p 273.
`==`	--or--	`===`	Boolean: Is equal; p 275.
`<>`	--or--	`<>=`	Boolean: Is not equal; p 275.
`<`	--or--	`<=`	Boolean: Is less than (signed); p 276.
`>`	--or--	`>=`	Boolean: Is greater than (signed); p 276.
`=<`	--or--	`=<=`	Boolean: Is equal or less (signed); p 277.
`=>`	--or--	`=>=`	Boolean: Is equal or greater (signed); p 277.

Spin Language Reference

Syntax Symbols

%	Binary number indicator, as in %1010; p 312.
%%	Quaternary number indicator, as in %%2130; p 312.
$	Hexadecimal number indicator, as in $1AF; p 312.
""	String designator "Hello"; p 312.
_	Group delimiter in constant values, or underscore in symbols; p 312.
#	Object-Constant reference: obj#constant; p 312.
.	Object-Method reference: obj.method(param) or decimal point; p 312.
..	Range indicator, as in 0..7; p 312.
:	Return separator: PUB method : sym, or object assignment, etc.; p 312.
|	Local variable separator: PUB method | temp, str; p 313.
\	Abort trap, as in \method(parameters); p 313.
,	List delimiter, as in method(param1, param2, param3); p 313.
( )	Parameter list designators, as in method(parameters); p 313.
[ ]	Array index designators, as in INA[2]; p 313.
{ }	In-line/multi-line code comment designators; p 313.
{{ }}	In-line/multi-line document comment designators; p 313.
'	Code comment designator; p 313.
''	Document comment designator; p 313.

Spin Language Elements

The remainder of this chapter describes the elements of the Spin Language, shown above, in alphabetical order. A few elements are explained within the context of others for clarity; use the page references from the categorical listing, above, to find those discussions. Many elements are available both in Spin and Propeller Assembly. Those elements are described in detail within this section, with references to them, and any differences, in the appropriate areas of Chapter 5: Assembly Language Reference beginning on page 339.

Symbol Rules

Symbols are case-insensitive, alphanumeric names either created by the compiler (reserved word) or by the code developer (user-defined word). They represent values (constants or variables) to make source code easier to understand and maintain. Symbols must fit the following rules:

1) Begins with a letter (a – z) or an underscore '_'.
2) Contains only letters, numbers, and underscores (a – z, 0 – 9, _); no spaces allowed.
3) Must be 32 characters or less.
4) Is unique to the object; not a reserved word (p. 419) or previously user-defined symbol.

Value Representations

Values can be entered in binary (base-2), quaternary (base-4), decimal (base-10), hexadecimal (base-16), or character formats. Numerical values can also use underscores, '_', as a group separator to clarify numbers. The following are examples of these formats.

Base	Type of Value	Examples				
2	Binary	%1010	–or–	%11110000_10101100		
4	Quaternary	%%2130_3311	–or–	%%3311_2301_1012		
10	Decimal (integer)	1024	–or–	2_147_483_647	–or–	-25
10	Decimal (floating-point)	1e6	–or–	1.000_005	–or–	-0.70712
16	Hexadecimal	$1AF	–or–	$FFAF_126D_8755		
n/a	Character	"A"				

Table 4-1: Value Representations

Separators can be used in place of commas (in decimal values) or to form logical groups, such as nibbles, bytes, words, etc.

Syntax Definitions

In addition to detailed descriptions, the following pages contain syntax definitions for many elements that describe, in short terms, all the options of that element. The syntax definitions use special symbols to indicate when and how certain element features are to be used.

BOLDCAPS	Items in bold uppercase should be typed in as shown.
Bold Italics	Items in bold italics should be replaced by user text; symbols, operators, expressions, etc.
. .. : , # | \ [ ] ( )	Periods, double-periods, colons, commas, pound signs, pipes, back slashes, square brackets and parentheses should be typed in where shown.
〈 〉	Angle bracket symbols enclose optional items. Enter the enclosed item if desired. Do not enter the angle brackets.
((¦))	Double parentheses symbols enclose mutually-exclusive items, separated by a dash-bar. Enter one, and only one, of the encoded items. Do not enter the double parentheses or dash-bar.
...	Repetition symbol indicates that the previous item, or group, can be repeated numerous times. Repeat the last item(s) if desired. Do not enter the repetition symbol.
↳	New Line/Indent symbol indicates following items should appear on the next line, indented by at least one space.
→|	Indent symbol indicates following items should be intended by at least one space.
Single line	Separates various syntax structure options.
Double line	Separates instruction from the value it returns.

Since elements are limited to specific Spin blocks, all syntax definitions begin with an indication of the type of block required. For example, the following syntax indicates that the BYTEFILL command and its parameters must appear in either a PUB or PRI block, but it may be one of many commands within that block.

```
((PUB ¦ PRI))
    BYTEFILL (StartAddress, Value, Count )
```

ABORT

Exit from PUB/PRI method using abort status with optional return *Value*.

((PUB | PRI))
   ABORT ⟨*Value*⟩

Returns: Either the current RESULT value, or *Value* if provided.

- *Value* is an optional expression whose value is to be returned, with abort status, from the PUB or PRI method.

Explanation

ABORT is one of two commands (ABORT and RETURN) that terminate a PUB or PRI method's execution.

ABORT causes a return from a PUB or PRI method with abort status; meaning it pops the call stack repeatedly until either the call stack is empty or it reaches a caller with an Abort Trap, (\ ), and delivers a value in the process.

ABORT is useful for cases where a method needs to terminate and indicate an abnormal or elevated status to the immediate caller or one its previous callers. For example, an application may be involved in a complicated chain of events where any one of those events could lead to a different branch of the chain or a final action decision. It may be easier to write that application using small, specialized methods that are called in a nested fashion, each meant to deal with a specific sub-event in the chain. When one of the simple methods determines a course of action, it can issue an abort that completely collapses the nested call chain and prevents all the intermediate methods from continuing.

When ABORT appears without the optional *Value*, it returns the current value of the PUB/PRI's built-in RESULT variable. If the *Value* field was entered, however, the PUB or PRI aborts and returns that *Value* instead.

About the Call Stack

When methods are called simply by referring to them from other methods, there must be some mechanism in place to store where to return to once the called method is completed. This mechanism is a called a "stack" but we'll use the term "call stack" here. It is simply RAM memory used to store return addresses, return values, parameters and intermediate results. As more and more methods are called, the call stack logically gets longer. As more and more methods are returned from (via RETURN or by reaching the end of the method) the call stack gets shorter. This is called "pushing" onto the stack and "popping" off of the stack, respectively.

The RETURN command pops the most recent data off the call stack to facilitate returning to the immediate caller; the one who directly called the method that just returned. The ABORT command, however, repetitively pops data off the call stack until it reaches a caller with an Abort Trap (see below); returning to some higher-level caller that may have just been one call, or many calls, up the nested chain of calls. Any return points along the way between an aborting method and an abort trapping method are ignored and essentially terminated. In this way, ABORT allows code to back way out of a very deep and potentially complicated series of logic to handle a serious issue at a high level.

Using ABORT

Any method can choose to issue an ABORT command. It's up to the higher-level code to check for an abort status and handle it. This higher-level code can be either that which called an aborting method directly, or via some other set of methods. To issue an ABORT command, use something like the following:

```
if <bad condition>
   abort                    'If bad condition detected, abort
```

—or—

```
if <bad condition>
   abort <value>            'If bad condition detected, abort with value
```

...where <bad condition> is a condition that determines the method should abort and <value> is a value to return upon aborting.

The Abort Trap (\ )

To trap an ABORT, the call to the method or method chain that could potentially abort must be preceded with the Abort Trap symbol, a backslash (\). For example, if a method called MayAbort could abort, or calls other methods that may abort, a calling method could trap this with the following:

```
if \MayAbort             'Call MayAbort with abort trap

   abort <value>         'Process abort
```

The type of exit that MayAbort actually used, ABORT or RETURN, is not automatically known by the trapping call; it may have just happened to be the destination of a RETURN command. Therefore, the code must be written in a way to detect which type was used. Some possibilities are: 1) code may be designed such that a high-level method is the only place that traps an abort and other mid-level code processes things normally without allowing RETURNs to propagate higher, or 2) aborting methods may return a special value that can not occur in any normal circumstance, or 3) a global flag can be set by the aborting method prior to aborting.

Example Use Of Abort

The following is an example of a simple-minded robot application in which the robot is designed to move away from an object it senses with its four sensors (Left, Right, Front and Back). Assume that CheckSensors, Beep, and MotorStuck are methods defined elsewhere.

```
CON
  #0, None, Left, Right, Front, Back   'Direction Enumerations

PUB Main | Direction
  Direction := None
  repeat
    case CheckSensors                  'Get active sensor
      Left  : Direction := Right       'Object on left? Let's go right
      Right : Direction := Left        'Object on right? Let's go left
      Front : Direction := Back        'Object in front? Let's go back
      Back  : Direction := Front       'Object in back? Let's go front
      other : Direction := None        'Otherwise, stay still
    if not \Move(Direction)            'Move robot
      Beep                             'We're stuck?  Beep

PUB Move(Direction)
  result := TRUE                       'Assume success
  if Direction == None
    return                             'Return if no direction
  repeat 1000
    DriveMotors(Direction)             'Drive motor 1000 times

PUB DriveMotors(Direction)
  <code to drive motors>
  if MotorStuck
    abort FALSE                        'If motor is stuck, abort
```

```
<more code>
```

The above example shows three methods of various logical levels, Main ("high-level"), Move ("mid-level") and DriveMotors ("low-level"). The high-level method, Main, is the decision maker of the application; deciding how to respond to events like sensor activations and motor movements. The mid-level method, Move, is responsible for moving the robot a short distance. The low-level method, DriveMotors, handles the details of driving the motors properly and verifying that it is successful.

In an application like this, critical events could occur in low-level code that needs to be addressed by high-level code. The ABORT command can be instrumental in getting the message to the high-level code without requiring complicated message-passing code for all the mid-level code in-between. In this case, we have only one mid-level method but there could be many nested mid-level methods between the high-level and the low-level.

The Main method gets sensor inputs and decides what direction to move the robot via the CASE statement. It then calls Move in a special way, with the Abort Trap symbol, \ , preceding it. The Move method sets its RESULT to TRUE and then calls DriveMotors in a finite loop. If it successfully completes, Move returns TRUE. The DriveMotors method handles the complication of moving the robot's motors to achieve the desired direction, but if it determines the motors are stuck, it cannot move them further and it aborts with a FALSE value. Otherwise it simply returns normally.

If everything is fine, the DriveMotors method returns normally, the Move method carries on normally and eventually returns TRUE, and the Main method continues on normally. If, however, DriveMotors finds a problem, it ABORTs which causes the Propeller to pop the call stack all the way through the Move method and up to the Main method where the Abort Trap was found. The Move method is completely oblivious to this and is now effectively terminated. The Main method checks the value returned by its call to Move (which is now the FALSE value that was actually returned by the aborted DriveMotors method deep down the call stack) and it decides to Beep as a result of the detected failure.

If we had not put the Abort Trap, (\ ), in front of the call to Move, when DriveMotors aborted, the call stack would have been popped until it was empty and this application would have terminated immediately.

BYTE

Declare byte-sized symbol, byte aligned/sized data, or read/write a byte of main memory.

VAR
    BYTE *Symbol* ⟨[*Count*]⟩

DAT
    BYTE *Data*

((PUB ⦙ PRI))
    BYTE [*BaseAddress*] ⟨[*Offset*]⟩

((PUB ⦙ PRI))
    Symbol.BYTE ⟨[*Offset*]⟩

- **Symbol** is the desired name for the variable (Syntax 1) or the existing name of the variable (Syntax 4).
- **Count** is an optional expression indicating the number of byte-sized elements for *Symbol*, arranged in an array from element 0 to element *Count*-1.
- **Data** is a constant expression or comma-separated list of constant expressions. Quoted strings of characters are also allowed; they are treated as a comma-separated list of characters.
- **BaseAddress** is an expression describing the address of main memory to read or write. If *Offset* is omitted, *BaseAddress* is the actual address to operate on. If *Offset* is specified, *BaseAddress* + *Offset* is the actual address to operate on.
- **Offset** is an optional expression indicating the offset from *BaseAddress* to operate on, or the offset from byte 0 of Symbol.

Explanation

BYTE is one of three multi-purpose declarations (BYTE, WORD, and LONG) that declare or operate on memory. BYTE can be used to:

    1) declare a byte-sized (8-bit) symbol or a multi-byte symbolic array in a VAR block, or
    2) declare byte-aligned, and possibly byte-sized, data in a DAT block, or
    3) read or write a byte of main memory at a base address with an optional offset, or
    4) access a byte within a word-sized or long-sized variable.

BYTE – Spin Language Reference

Byte Variable Declaration (Syntax 1)

In VAR blocks, syntax 1 of BYTE is used to declare global, symbolic variables that are either byte-sized, or are any array of bytes.

For example:

```
VAR
   byte   Temp                  'Temp is a byte
   byte   Str[25]               'Str is a byte array
```

The above example declares two variables (symbols), Temp and Str. Temp is simply a single, byte-sized variable. The line under the Temp declaration uses the optional *Count* field to create an array of 25 byte-sized variable elements called Str. Both Temp and Str can be accessed from any PUB or PRI method within the same object that this VAR block was declared; they are global to the object. An example of this is below.

```
PUB SomeMethod
   Temp := 250                  'Set Temp to 250
   Str[0] := "A"                'Set first element of Str to "A"
   Str[1] := "B"                'Set second element of Str to "B"
   Str[24] := "C"               'Set last element of Str to "C"
```

For more information about using BYTE in this way, refer to the VAR section's Variable Declarations (Syntax 1) on page 315, and keep in mind that BYTE is used for the *Size* field in that description.

Byte Data Declaration (Syntax 2)

In DAT blocks, syntax 2 of BYTE is used to declare byte-aligned, and/or byte-sized data that is compiled as constant values in main memory. DAT blocks allow this declaration to have an optional symbol preceding it, which can be used for later reference (See DAT, page 208). For example:

```
DAT
   MyData      byte   64, $AA, 55    'Byte-aligned and byte-sized data
   MyString    byte   "Hello",0      'A string of bytes (characters)
```

The above example declares two data symbols, MyData and MyString. Each data symbol points to the start of byte-aligned and byte-sized data in main memory. MyData's values, in main memory, are 64, $AA and 55, respectively. MyString's values, in main memory, are "H", "e", "l", "l", "o", and 0, respectively. This data is compiled into the object and resulting application as part of the executable code section and may be accessed using the read/write form, syntax 3, of BYTE (see below). For more information about using BYTE in this way, refer to the DAT section's Declaring Data (Syntax 1) on page 208, and keep in mind that BYTE is used for the *Size* field in that description.

Reading/Writing Bytes of Main Memory (Syntax 3)

In PUB and PRI blocks, syntax 3 of BYTE is used to read or write byte-sized values of main memory. In the following two examples, we'll assume our object contained the DAT block from the example above, and we will demonstrate two different ways to access that data.

First, let's try accessing the data directly using the labels we provided in our data block.

```
PUB GetData | Index, Temp
  Temp := MyData                   'Read 1st byte of MyData to Temp
  <do something with Temp>         'Perform task with Temp

  Index := 0
  repeat
    Temp := MyString[Index++]      'Read chars into Temp
    <do something with Temp>       'Perform task with character
  while Temp > 0                   'Loop until end found
```

The first line inside of the GetData method, Temp := MyData, reads the first value in the MyData list (the byte-sized value 64) and stores it in Temp. Further down, in the REPEAT loop, the Temp := MyString[Index++] line reads a byte of from the location of MyString + Index. Since Index is earlier set to 0, the first byte of MyString is read, "H". On that same line Index is post incremented with ++, so the next time through the loop it reads the next byte, effectively MyString + 1 (the "e"), and the next time MyString + 2 (the "l"), etc.

Similar to the above, we can use the BYTE declaration to achieve our goal, as in the following example.

```
PUB GetData | Index, Temp
  Temp := BYTE[@MyData]            'Read 1st byte of MyData to Temp
  <do something with Temp>         'Perform task with Temp

  Index := 0
  repeat
    Temp := BYTE[@MyString][Index++] 'Read chars into Temp
    <do something with Temp>       'Perform task with character
  while Temp > 0                   'Loop until end found
```

This example works just like the previous, except that we use the BYTE declaration to read a byte of main memory from the address of MyData and the address of MyString + Index.

With a similar syntax, bytes of main memory can be written to as well, as long as they are RAM locations. For example:

```
BYTE[@MyString][0] := "M"    'Write M to first character of MyString
```

This line writes the character "M" to the first byte of string data at MyString, changing the string to be "Mello",0.

Accessing Bytes of Larger–Sized Variables (Syntax 4)

In PUB and PRI blocks, syntax 4 of BYTE is used to read or write byte-sized components of word-sized or long-sized variables. For example:

```
VAR
    word    WordVar
    long    LongVar


PUB Main
    WordVar.byte := 0           'Set first byte of WordVar to 0
    WordVar.byte[0] := 0        'Same as above
    WordVar.byte[1] := 100      'Set second byte of WordVar to 100
    LongVar.byte := 25          'Set first byte of LongVar to 25
    LongVar.byte[0] := 25       'Same as above
    LongVar.byte[1] := 50       'Set second byte of LongVar to 50
    LongVar.byte[2] := 75       'Set third byte of LongVar to 75
    LongVar.byte[3] := 100      'Set fourth byte of LongVar to 100
```

This example accesses the byte-sized components of both WordVar and LongVar, individually. The comments indicate what each line is doing. At the end of the Main method, WordVar will equal 25,600 and LongVar will equal 1,682,649,625.

BYTEFILL

Fill bytes of main memory with a value.

((PUB ¦ PRI))
  BYTEFILL (*StartAddress*, *Value*, *Count*)

- *StartAddress* is an expression indicating the location of the first byte of memory to fill with *Value*.
- *Value* is an expression indicating the value to fill bytes with.
- *Count* is an expression indicating the number of bytes to fill, starting with *StartAddress*.

Explanation

BYTEFILL is one of three commands (BYTEFILL, WORDFILL, and LONGFILL) used to fill blocks of main memory with a specific value. BYTEFILL fills *Count* bytes of main memory with *Value*, starting at location *StartAddress*.

Using BYTEFILL

BYTEFILL is a great way to clear large blocks of byte-sized memory. For example:

```
VAR
  byte    Buff[100]

PUB Main
  bytefill(@Buff, 0, 100)      'Clear Buff to 0
```

The first line of the Main method, above, clears the entire 100-byte Buff array to all zeros. BYTEFILL is faster at this task than a dedicated REPEAT loop is.

BYTEMOVE

Copy bytes from one region to another in main memory.

((PUB ¦ PRI))
  BYTEMOVE (*DestAddress*, *SrcAddress*, *Count*)

- *DestAddress* is an expression specifying the main memory location to copy the first byte of source to.
- *SrcAddress* is an expression specifying the main memory location of the first byte of source to copy.
- *Count* is an expression indicating the number of bytes of the source to copy to the destination.

Explanation

BYTEMOVE is one of three commands (BYTEMOVE, WORDMOVE, and LONGMOVE) used to copy blocks of main memory from one area to another. BYTEMOVE copies *Count* bytes of main memory starting from *SrcAddress* to main memory starting at *DestAddress*.

Using BYTEMOVE

BYTEMOVE is a great way to copy large blocks of byte-sized memory. For example:

```
VAR
  byte    Buff1[100]
  byte    Buff2[100]

PUB Main
  bytemove(@Buff2, @Buff1, 100)     'Copy Buff1 to Buff2
```

The first line of the Main method, above, copies the entire 100-byte Buff1 array to the Buff2 array. BYTEMOVE is faster at this task than a dedicated REPEAT loop.

CASE

Compare expression against matching expression(s) and execute code block if match found.

```
((PUB ┊ PRI))
    CASE CaseExpression
      →ı MatchExpression :
        →ı Statement(s)
    ⟨→ı MatchExpression :
        →ı Statement(s) ⟩
    ⟨→ı OTHER :
        →ı Statement(s) ⟩
```

- *CaseExpression* is the expression to compare.
- *MatchExpression* is a singular or comma-delimited set of value- and/or range-expressions, to compare *CaseExpression* against. Each *MatchExpression* must be followed by a colon (:).
- *Statement(s)* is a block of one or more lines of code to execute when the *CaseExpression* matches the associated *MatchExpression*. The first, or only, statement in *Statement(s)* may appear to the right of the colon on the *MatchExpression* line, or below it and slightly indented from the *MatchExpression* itself.

Explanation

CASE is one of the three conditional commands (IF, IFNOT, and CASE) that conditionally executes a block of code. CASE is the preferred structure to use, as opposed to IF..ELSEIF..ELSE, when you need to compare the equality of *CaseExpression* to a number of different values.

CASE compares *CaseExpression* against the values of each *MatchExpression*, in order, and if a match is found, executes the associated *Statement(s)*. If no previous matches were found, the *Statement(s)* associated with the optional OTHER command are executed.

Indention is Critical

IMPORTANT: Indention is critical. The Spin language relies on indention (of one space or more) on lines following conditional commands to determine if they belong to that command or not. To have the Propeller Tool indicate these logically grouped blocks of code on-screen, you can press Ctrl + I to turn on block-group indicators. Pressing Ctrl + I again will disable that feature. See Indenting and Outdenting, page 69, and Block-Group Indicators, page 74.

Using CASE

CASE is handy where one of many actions needs to be performed depending on the value of an expression. The following example assumes A, X and Y are variables defined earlier.

```
case X+Y            'Test X+Y
   10, 15:  !outa[0]   'X+Y = 10 or 15? Toggle P0
   A*2   :  !outa[1]   'X+Y = A*2? Toggle P1
   30..40:  !outa[2]   'X+Y in 30 to 40? Toggle P2
X += 5              'Add 5 to X
```

Since the *MatchExpression* lines are indented from the CASE line, they belong to the CASE structure and are executed based on the *CaseExpression* comparison results. The next line, X += 5, is not indented from CASE, so it is executed regardless of the CASE results.

This example compares the value of X + Y against 10 or 15, A*2 and the range 30 through 40. If X + Y equals 10 or 15, P0 is toggled. If X + Y equals A*2, P1 is toggled. If X + Y is in the range 30 through 40, inclusive, then P2 is toggled. Whether or not any match was found, the X += 5 line is executed next.

Using OTHER

The optional OTHER component of CASE is similar to the optional ELSE component of an IF structure. For example:

```
case X+Y            'Test X+Y
   10, 15:  !outa[0]   'X+Y = 10 or 15? Toggle P0
   25    :  !outa[1]   'X+Y = 25? Toggle P1
   20..30:  !outa[2]   'X+Y in 20 to 30? Toggle P2
   OTHER :  !outa[3]   'Othewise toggle P3
X += 5              'Add 5 to X
```

This example is similar to the last one except that the third *MatchStatement* checks for the range 20 to 30 and there's an OTHER component. If X + Y does not equal 10, 15, 25, or is not in the range 20 to 30, the *Statement(s)* block following OTHER is executed. Following that, the X += 5 line is executed.

There is an important concept to note about this example. If X + Y is 10 or 15, P0 is toggled, or if X + Y is 25, P1 is toggled, or if X + Y is 20 to 30, P2 is toggled, etc. This is because the *MatchExpressions* are checked, one at a time, in the order they are listed and only the first expression that is a match has its block of code executed; no further expressions are tested after that. This means that if we had rearranged the 25 and 20..30 lines, so that the range of 20..30 is checked first, we'd have a bug in our code. We did this below:

```
case X+Y            'Test X+Y
   10, 15: !outa[0]  'X+Y = 10 or 15? Toggle P0
   20..30: !outa[2]  'X+Y in 20 to 30? Toggle P2
   25    : !outa[1]  'X+Y = 25? Toggle P1  <-- THIS NEVER RUNS
```

The above example contains an error because, while X + Y could be equal to 25, that match expression would never be tested since the previous one, 20..30 would be tested first, and since it is true, its block is executed and no further match expressions are checked.

Variations of Statement(s)

The above examples only use one line per *Statement(s)* block, but each block can be many lines of course. Additionally, the *Statement(s)* block may also appear below, and slightly indented from, the *MatchExpression* itself. The following two examples show these variations.

```
case A               'Test A
   4     : !outa[0]   'A = 4? Toggle P0
   Z+1   : !outa[1]   'A = Z+1? Toggle P1
           !outa[2]   'And toggle P2
   10..15: !outa[3]   'A in 10 to 15? Toggle P3


case A               'Test A
  4:                  'A = 4?
     !outa[0]         'Toggle P0
  Z+1:                'A = Z+1?
     !outa[1]         'Toggle P1
     !outa[2]         'And toggle P2
  10..15:             'A in 10 to 15?
     !outa[3]         'Toggle P3
```

CHIPVER

Get the Propeller chip's version number.

```
((PUB ¦ PRI))
   CHIPVER
```

Returns: Version number of the Propeller chip.

Explanation

The `CHIPVER` command reads and returns the version number of the Propeller chip. For example:

```
V := chipver
```

This example sets V to the version number of the Propeller chip, 1 in this case. Future Propeller Applications can use this to determine the version and type of Propeller chip they are running on and make modifications to their operation as necessary.

CLKFREQ

Current System Clock frequency; the frequency at which each cog is running.

((PUB ⦙ PRI))
    CLKFREQ

Returns: Current System Clock frequency, in Hz.

Explanation

The value returned by CLKFREQ is the actual System Clock frequency as determined by the current clock mode (oscillator type, gain, and PLL settings) and the external XI pin frequency, if any. Objects use CLKFREQ to determine the proper time delays for time-sensitive operations. For example:

```
waitcnt(clkfreq / 10 + cnt)   'wait for .1 seconds (100 ms)
```

This statement divides CLKFREQ by 10 and adds the result to CNT (the current System Counter value) then waits (WAITCNT) until the System Counter reaches the result value. Since CLKFREQ is the number of cycles per second, a divide by 10 yields the number of clock cycles per 0.1 seconds, or 100 ms. So, disregarding the time it takes to process the expression, this statement pauses the cog's program execution for 100 ms. The table below shows more examples of System Clock tick verses Time calculations.

Table 4-2: System Clock Ticks vs. Time Calculations	
Expression	**Result**
clkfreq / 10	Clock ticks per 0.1 seconds (100 ms)
clkfreq / 100	Clock ticks per 0.01 seconds (10 ms)
clkfreq / 1_000	Clock ticks per 0.001 seconds (1 ms)
clkfreq / 10_000	Clock ticks per 0.0001 seconds (100 µs)
clkfreq / 100_000	Clock ticks per 0.00001 seconds (10 µs)
clkfreq / 9600	Clock ticks per serial bit period at 9,600 baud (~ 104 µs)
clkfreq / 19200	Clock ticks per serial bit period at 19,200 baud (~ 52 µs)

The value that CLKFREQ returns can change whenever the application changes the clock mode, either manually or via the CLKSET command. Objects that are time-sensitive should check CLKFREQ at strategic points in order to adjust to new settings automatically.

CLKFREQ vs. _CLKFREQ

CLKFREQ is related to, but not the same as, _CLKFREQ. CLKFREQ is command that returns the current System Clock frequency whereas _CLKFREQ is an application-defined constant that contains the application's System Clock frequency at startup. In other words, CLKFREQ is the current clock frequency and _CLKFREQ is the original clock frequency; they both may happen to be the same value but they certainly can be different.

_CLKFREQ

Pre-defined, one-time settable constant for specifying the System Clock frequency.

```
CON
  _CLKFREQ = Expression
```

- **Expression** is an integer expression that indicates the System Clock frequency upon application start-up.

Explanation

_CLKFREQ specifies the System Clock frequency for start-up. It is a pre-defined constant symbol whose value is determined by the top object file of an application. _CLKFREQ is either set directly by the application itself, or is set indirectly as the result of the _CLKMODE and _XINFREQ settings.

The top object file in an application (the one where compilation starts from) can specify a setting for _CLKFREQ in its CON block. This defines the initial System Clock frequency for the application and is the frequency that the System Clock will switch to as soon as the application is booted up and execution begins.

The application can specify either _CLKFREQ or _XINFREQ in the CON block; they are mutually exclusive and the non-specified one is automatically calculated and set as a result of specifying the other.

The following examples assume that they are contained within the top object file. Any _CLKFREQ settings in child objects are simply ignored by the compiler.

For example:

```
CON
  _CLKMODE = XTAL1 + PLL8X
  _CLKFREQ = 32_000_000
```

The first declaration in the above CON block sets the clock mode for an external low-speed crystal and a Clock PLL multiplier of 8. The second declaration sets the System Clock frequency to 32 MHz, which means the external crystal's frequency must be 4 MHz because 4 MHz * 8 = 32 MHz. The _XINFREQ value is automatically set to 4 MHz because of these declarations.

```
CON
  _CLKMODE = XTAL2
  _CLKFREQ = 10_000_000
```

These two declarations set the clock mode for an external medium-speed crystal, no Clock PLL multiplier, and a System Clock frequency of 10 MHz. The **_XINFREQ** value is automatically set to 10 MHz, as well, because of these declarations.

_CLKFREQ vs CLKFREQ

_CLKFREQ is related to, but not the same as, **CLKFREQ**. **_CLKFREQ** contains the application's System Clock frequency at startup whereas **CLKFREQ** is a command that returns the current System Clock frequency. In other words, **_CLKFREQ** is the original System Clock frequency and **CLKFREQ** is the current System Clock frequency; they both may happen to be the same value but they certainly can be different.

CLKMODE

Current clock mode setting.

```
((PUB ┊ PRI))
   CLKMODE
```

Returns: Current clock mode.

Explanation

The clock mode setting is the byte-sized value, determined by the application at compile time, from the CLK register. See CLK Register, page 28, for explanation of the possible settings. For example:

```
Mode := clkmode
```

This statement can be used to set a variable, Mode, to the current clock mode setting. Many applications maintain a static clock mode setting; however, some applications will change the clock mode setting during run time for clock speed adjustments, low-power modes, etc. It may be necessary for some objects to pay attention to the potential for dynamic clock modes in order to maintain proper timing and functionality.

CLKMODE vs _CLKMODE

CLKMODE is related to, but not the same as, _CLKMODE. CLKMODE is a command that returns the current clock mode (in the form of the CLK register's bit pattern) whereas _CLKMODE is an application-defined constant containing the requested clock mode at startup (in the form of clock setting constants that are OR'd together). Both may describe the same logical clock mode but their values are not equivalent.

_CLKMODE

Pre-defined, one-time settable constant for specifying application-level clock mode settings.

CON
  _CLKMODE = *Expression*

- *Expression* is an integer expression made up of one or two Clock Mode Setting Constants shown in table Table 4-3. This will be the clock mode upon application start-up.

Explanation

_CLKMODE is used to specify the desired nature of the System Clock. It is a pre-defined constant symbol whose value is determined by the top object file of an application. The clock mode setting is a byte whose value is described by a combination of the RCxxxx, XINPUT, XTALx and PLLxx constants at compile time. Table 4-3 illustrates the clock mode setting constants. Note that not every combination is valid; Table 4-4 shows all valid combinations.

Table 4-3: Clock Mode Setting Constants			
Clock Mode Setting Constant[1]	XO Resistance[2]	XI/XO Capacitance[2]	Description
RCFAST	Infinite	n/a	Internal fast oscillator (~12 MHz). May be 8 MHz to 20 MHz. (Default)
RCSLOW	Infinite	n/a	Internal slow oscillator (~20 KHz). May be 13 KHz to 33 KHz.
XINPUT	Infinite	6 pF (pad only)	External clock-oscillator (DC to 80 MHz); XI pin only, XO disconnected
XTAL1	2 kΩ	36 pF	External low-speed crystal (4 MHz to 16 MHz)
XTAL2	1 kΩ	26 pF	External medium-speed crystal (8 MHz to 32 MHz)
XTAL3	500 Ω	16 pF	External high-speed crystal (20 MHz to 80 MHz)
PLL1X	n/a	n/a	Multiply external frequency times 1
PLL2X	n/a	n/a	Multiply external frequency times 2
PLL4X	n/a	n/a	Multiply external frequency times 4
PLL8X	n/a	n/a	Multiply external frequency times 8
PLL16X	n/a	n/a	Multiply external frequency times 16

1. All constants are also available in Propeller Assembly.
2. All necessary resistors/capacitors are included in Propeller chip.

Table 4-4: Valid Clock Mode Expressions and CLK Register Values			
Valid Expression	**CLK Register Value**	**Valid Expression**	**CLK Register Value**
RCFAST	0_0_0_00_000	XTAL1 + PLL1X	0_1_1_01_011
		XTAL1 + PLL2X	0_1_1_01_100
RCSLOW	0_0_0_00_001	XTAL1 + PLL4X	0_1_1_01_101
		XTAL1 + PLL8X	0_1_1_01_110
XINPUT	0_0_0_00_010	XTAL1 + PLL16X	0_1_1_01_111
		XTAL2 + PLL1X	0_1_1_10_011
XTAL1	0_0_1_01_010	XTAL2 + PLL2X	0_1_1_10_100
XTAL2	0_0_1_10_010	XTAL2 + PLL4X	0_1_1_10_101
XTAL3	0_0_1_11_010	XTAL2 + PLL8X	0_1_1_10_110
		XTAL2 + PLL16X	0_1_1_10_111
XINPUT + PLL1X	0_1_1_00_011	XTAL3 + PLL1X	0_1_1_11_011
XINPUT + PLL2X	0_1_1_00_100	XTAL3 + PLL2X	0_1_1_11_100
XINPUT + PLL4X	0_1_1_00_101	XTAL3 + PLL4X	0_1_1_11_101
XINPUT + PLL8X	0_1_1_00_110	XTAL3 + PLL8X	0_1_1_11_110
XINPUT + PLL16X	0_1_1_00_111	XTAL3 + PLL16X	0_1_1_11_111

The top object file in an application (the one where compilation starts from) can specify a setting for **_CLKMODE** in its CON block. This defines the initial clock mode setting for the application and is the mode that the System Clock will switch to as soon as the application is booted up and execution begins. The following examples assume that they are contained within the top object file. Any **_CLKMODE** settings in child objects are simply ignored by the compiler. For example:

```
CON
  _CLKMODE = RCFAST
```

This sets the clock mode for the internal, fast RC Clock/Oscillator circuit. The System Clock would run at approximately 12 MHz with this setting. The **RCFAST** setting is the default setting, so if no **_CLKMODE** was actually defined, this is the setting that would be used. Note that the Clock PLL can not be used with the internal RC Clock/Oscillator. Here's an example with an external clock:

```
CON
  _CLKMODE = XTAL1 + PLL8X
```

This sets the clock mode for an external low-speed crystal (**XTAL1**), enables the Clock PLL circuit and sets the System Clock to use the 8x tap from the Clock PLL (**PLL8X**). If an external 4 MHz crystal was attached to XI and XO, for example, its signal would be multiplied by 16 (the Clock PLL always multiplies by 16) but the 8x result would be used; the System Clock would be 4 MHz * 8 = 32 MHz.

```
CON
  _CLKMODE = XINPUT + PLL2X
```

This sets the clock mode for an external clock-oscillator, connected to XI only, and enables the Clock PLL circuit and sets the System Clock to use the 2x result. If an external clock-oscillator pack of 8 MHz was attached to XI, the System clock would run at 16 MHz; that's 8 MHz * 2.

Note that the Clock PLL is not required and can be disabled by simply not specifying any multiplier setting, for example:

```
CON
  _CLKMODE = XTAL1
```

This sets the clock mode for an external low-speed crystal but leaves the Clock PLL disabled; the System Clock will be equal to the external crystal's frequency.

The _CLKFREQ and _XINFREQ Settings

For simplicity, the examples above only show **_CLKMODE** settings, but either a **_CLKFREQ** or **_XINFREQ** setting is required to follow it so that objects can determine their actual System Clock's frequency. The following is the second example with an external crystal frequency (**_XINFREQ**) of 4 MHz.

```
CON
  _CLKMODE = XTAL1 + PLL8X    'low-speed crystal x 8
  _XINFREQ = 4_000_000        'external crystal of 4 MHz
```

This example is exactly like the second example above, but **_XINFREQ** indicates that the frequency of the external crystal is 4 MHz. The Propeller chip uses this value along with the **_CLKMODE** setting to determine the System Clock frequency (as reported by the **CLKFREQ** command) so that objects can properly adjust their timing. See **_XINFREQ**, page 337.

_CLKMODE vs CLKMODE

_CLKMODE is related to, but not the same as, **CLKMODE**. **_CLKMODE** is an application-defined constant containing the requested clock mode at startup (in the form of clock setting constants that are OR'd together) whereas **CLKMODE** is a command that returns the current clock mode (in the form of the CLK register's bit pattern). Both may describe the same logical clock mode but their values are not equivalent.

CLKSET

Set both the clock mode and System Clock frequency at run time.

((PUB ¦ PRI))
   CLKSET (*Mode*, *Frequency*)

- *Mode* is an integer expression that will be written to the CLK register to change the clock mode.
- *Frequency* is an integer expression that indicates the resulting System Clock frequency.

Explanation

One of the most powerful features of the Propeller chip is the ability to change the clock behavior at run time. An application can choose to toggle back and forth between a slow clock speed (for low-power consumption) and a fast clock speed (for high-bandwidth operations), for example. CLKSET is used to change the clock mode and frequency during run time. It is the run-time equivalent of the _CLKMODE and _CLKFREQ constants defined by the application at compile time. For example:

```
clkset(%01101100, 4_000_000)              'Set to XTAL1 + PLL2x
```

This sets the clock mode to a low-speed external crystal and a Clock PLL multiplier of 2, and indicates the resulting System Clock frequency (CLKFREQ) is 4 MHz. After executing this command, the CLKMODE and CLKFREQ commands will report the updated settings for objects that use them.

When switching from the internal clock to an external crystal, it is important to perform it as a three-stage process:

1) First set the PLLENA, OSCENA, OSCM1 and OSCM2 bits as necessary,
2) Wait for 10 ms to give the crystal time to stabilize,
3) Set the CLKSELx bits as necessary to switch the System Clock to the new source.

It takes approximately 75 μs for the Propeller Chip to perform the clock source switching action.

CNT

System Counter register.

```
((PUB ¦ PRI))
   CNT
```

Returns: Current 32-bit System Counter value.

Explanation

The CNT register contains the current value in the global 32-bit System Counter. The System Counter serves as the central time reference for all cogs; it increments its 32-bit value once every System Clock cycle.

Upon power-up/reset, the System Counter starts with an arbitrary value and counts upwards from there, incrementing with every System Clock cycle. Since the System Counter is a read-only resource, every cog can read it simultaneously and can use the returned value to synchronize events, count cycles and measure time.

Using CNT

Read CNT to get the current System Counter value. The actual value itself does not matter for any particular purpose, but the difference in successive reads is very important. Most often, the CNT register is used to delay execution for a specific period or to synchronize an event to the start of a window of time. The next examples use the WAITCNT instruction to achieve this.

```
waitcnt(3_000_000 + cnt)    'Wait for 3 million clock cycles
```

The above code is an example of a "fixed delay." It delays the cog's execution for 3 million system clock cycles (about ¼ second when running with the internal fast oscillator).

The next is an example of a "synchronized delay." It notes the current count at one place and performs an action (toggles a pin) every millisecond thereafter with accuracy as good as that of the oscillator driving the Propeller chip.

```
PUB Toggle | TimeBase, OneMS
  dira[0]~~                     'Set P0 to output
  OneMS := clkfreq / 1000       'Calculate cycles per 1 millisecond
  TimeBase := cnt               'Get current count
  repeat                        'Loop endlessly
    waitcnt(TimeBase += OneMS)  '  Wait to start of next millisecond
    !outa[0]                    '  Toggle P0
```

Here, I/O pin 0 is set to output. Then the local variable OneMS is set equal to the current System Clock frequency divided by 1000; i.e.: the number of System Clock cycles per 1 millisecond of time. Next, the local variable TimeBase is set to the current System Counter value. Finally, the last two lines of code repeat endlessly; each time waiting until the start of the next millisecond and then toggling the state of P0.

For more information, see the WAITCNT sections's Fixed Delays on page 322 and Synchronized Delays on page 323.

COGID

Current cog's ID number (0-7).

```
((PUB ¦ PRI))
   COGID
```

Returns: The current cog's ID (0-7).

Explanation

The value returned by **COGID** is the ID of the cog that executed the command. Normally, the actual cog that code is running in does not matter, however, for some objects it might be important to keep track of it. For example:

```
PUB StopMyself
  'Stop cog this code is running in
  cogstop(cogid)
```

This example method, StopMyself, has one line of code that simply calls **COGSTOP** with **COGID** as the parameter. Since **COGID** returns the ID of the cog running that code, this routine causes the cog to terminate itself.

COGINIT

Start or restart a cog by ID to run the Spin code or Propeller Assembly code.

((PUB ┊ PRI))
    COGINIT *(CogID, SpinMethod ⟨ (ParameterList) ⟩, StackPointer)*

((PUB ┊ PRI))
    COGINIT *(CogID, AsmAddress, Parameter)*

- ***CogID*** is the ID $(0 - 7)$ of the cog to start, or restart. A *CogID* above 7 results in the next available cog being started (if possible).
- ***SpinMethod*** is the PUB or PRI Spin method that the affected cog should run. Optionally, it can be followed by a parameter list enclosed in parentheses.
- ***ParameterList*** is an optional, comma-delimited list of one or more parameters for *SpinMethod*. It must be included only if *SpinMethod* requires parameters.
- ***StackPointer*** is a pointer to memory, such as a long array, reserved for stack space for the affected cog. The affected cog uses this space to store temporary data during further calls and expression evaluations. If insufficient space is allocated, either the application will fail to run or it will run with strange results.
- ***AsmAddress*** is the address of a Propeller Assembly routine from a DAT block.
- ***Parameter*** is used to optionally pass a value to the new cog. This value ends up in the affected cog's read-only Cog Boot Parameter (PAR) register. *Parameter* can be used to pass a either a single 14-bit value or the address of a block of memory to be used by the assembly routine. *Parameter* is required by COGINIT, but if not needed for your routine simply set it to an innocuous value like zero (0).

Explanation

COGINIT works exactly like COGNEW with two exceptions: 1) it launches code into a specific cog whose ID is *CogID*, and 2) it does not return a value. Since COGINIT operates on a specific cog, as directed by the *CogID* parameter, it can be used to stop and restart an active cog in one step. This includes the current cog; i.e.: a cog can use COGINIT to stop and restart itself to run, perhaps, completely different code.

Spin Code (Syntax 1)

To run a Spin method in a specific cog, the COGINIT command needs the cog ID, the method name, its parameters, and a pointer to some stack space. For example:

```
coginit(1, Square(@X) , @SqStack)   'Launch Square in Cog 1
```

This example launches the Square method into Cog 1, passing the address of X into Square and the address of SqStack as COGINIT's stack pointer. See COGNEW, page 189, for more information.

Propeller Assembly Code (Syntax 2)

To run Propeller Assembly code in a specific cog, the COGINIT command needs the cog ID, the address of the assembly routine, and a value that can optionally be used by the assembly routine. For example:

```
coginit(2, @Update, Pos)
```

This example launches the Propeller Assembly routine, Update, into Cog 2 with the address of Pos in Cog 2's PAR parameter. See COGNEW, page 189, for more information.

COGNEW

Start the next available cog to run Spin code or Propeller Assembly code.

((PUB ┊ PRI))
    COGNEW (*SpinMethod* ⟨ *(ParameterList)* ⟩, *StackPointer*)

((PUB ┊ PRI))
    COGNEW (*AsmAddress*, *Parameter*)

Returns: The ID of the newly started cog (0-7) if successful, or -1 otherwise.

- *SpinMethod* is the PUB or PRI Spin method that the new cog should run. Optionally, it can be followed by a parameter list enclosed in parentheses.
- *ParameterList* is an optional, comma-delimited list of one or more parameters for *SpinMethod*. It must be included only if *SpinMethod* requires parameters.
- *StackPointer* is a pointer to memory, such as a long array, reserved for stack space for the new cog. The new cog uses this space to store temporary data during further calls and expression evaluations. If insufficient space is allocated, either the application will fail to run or it will run with strange results.
- *AsmAddress* is the address of a Propeller Assembly routine, usually from a DAT block.
- *Parameter* is used to optionally pass a value to the new cog. This value ends up in the new cog's read-only Cog Boot Parameter (PAR) register. *Parameter* can be used to pass a either a single 14-bit value or the address of a block of memory to be used by the assembly routine. *Parameter* is required by COGNEW, but if not needed for your routine, simply set it to an innocuous value like zero (0).

Explanation

COGNEW starts a new cog and runs either a Spin method or a Propeller Assembly routine within it. If successful, COGNEW returns the ID of the newly started cog. If there were no more cogs available, COGNEW returns -1.

Spin Code (Syntax 1)

To run a Spin method in another cog, the COGNEW command needs the method name, its parameters, and a pointer to some stack space. For example:

```
VAR
    long SqStack[6]                    'Stack space for Square cog


PUB Main | X
    X := 2                             'Initialize X
    cognew(Square(@X), @SqStack)       'Launch square cog
    <check X here>                     'Loop here and check X


PUB Square(XAddr)
    'Square the value at XAddr
    repeat                             'Repeat the following endlessly
        long[XAddr] *= long[XAddr]     '   Square value, store back
        waitcnt(2_000_000 + cnt)       '   Wait 2 million cycles
```

This example shows two methods, Main and Square. Main starts another cog that runs Square endlessly, then Main can monitor the results in the X variable. Square, being run by another cog, takes the value of XAddr, squares it and stores the result back into XAddr, then waits for 2 million cycles before it does it again. More explanation follows, but the result is that X starts out as 2, and the second cog, running Square, iteratively sets X to 4, 16, 256, 65536 and then finally to 0 (it overflowed 32 bits), all independent of the first cog which may be checking the value of X or performing some other task.

The Main method declares a local variable, X, that is set to 2 in its first line. Then Main starts a new cog, with COGNEW, to run the Square method in a separate cog. COGNEW's first parameter, Square(@X), is the Spin method to run and its required parameter; in this case we pass it the address of the X variable. The second parameter of COGNEW, @SqStack, is the address of stack space reserved for the new cog. When a cog is started to run Spin code, it needs some stack space where it can store temporary data such as call stacks, parameters and intermediate expression results. This example only requires 6 longs of stack space for proper operation (see the "Stack Length" object in the Propeller Library for more information).

After the COGNEW command is executed, two cogs are running; the first is still running the Main method and the second is starting to run the Square method. Despite the fact that they are using code from the same Spin object, they are running independently. The "<check X here>" line can be replaced with code that uses the value of X in some way.

Propeller Assembly Code (Syntax 2)

To run Propeller Assembly code in another cog, the COGNEW command needs the address of the assembly routine and a value that can optionally be used by the assembly routine. For example:

```
VAR
   byte Cog      'Used to store ID of newly started cog


PUB Start(Pos) : Pass
   'Start a new cog to run Update with Pos,
   'return TRUE if successful
   Pass := (Cog := cognew(@Update, Pos) + 1) > 0


PUB Stop
   'Stop the cog we started earlier, if any.
   if Cog
     cogstop(Cog~ - 1)
```

This example shows two methods, Start and Stop, within a hypothetical object. The design of that object is such that it needs to launch another cog to run an assembly routine, called Update (not shown), and pass it a parameter, Pos. Later it may need to stop that new cog.

The Start method takes a single parameter, Pos, and returns TRUE or FALSE to indicate whether or not a new cog was successfully started. First, it calls COGNEW, "cognew(@Update, Pos)" with the address of the Update routine as the first parameter and Pos as the second parameter. Additionally, it takes the value returned by COGNEW, which is the ID of the new cog, or -1 if none available, adds 1 and stores the result in the Cog variable; "Cog := cognew(@Update, Pos) + 1". Lastly, if Cog is greater than zero (0) it sets its return value, Pass, to TRUE; otherwise Pass is set to FALSE. At this point, if a new cog was successfully started, that new cog begins loading up the Propeller Assembly code called Update, and runs it. Meanwhile this object's Cog variable (in the original cog) will be in the range 1 to 8, representing the new cog's ID, 0 through 7. If no cog was started, Cog will be 0.

Later, if the Stop method is called, it first checks the condition, "if Cog". This condition is true only if Cog is non-zero. If true (i.e.: a cog was successfully started by the Start routine) then the following line, "cogstop(Cog~ - 1)", is executed and is passed the ID of the cog to stop, "Cog~ - 1". The expression Cog~ - 1 returns the result of Cog - 1 for the COGSTOP parameter, then clears the Cog variable to zero (0). Because the Cog variable is cleared to zero after its value is used to stop the new cog, any future calls to Stop will not inadvertently stop cogs that this object didn't start.

This example can be improved by making the Start method call the Stop method, first, just in case the calling object called Start two times in a row. For example:

```
PUB Start(Pos) : Pass
  'Start a new cog to run Update with Pos,
  'return TRUE if successful
  Stop
  Pass := (Cog := cognew(@Update, Pos) + 1) > 0
```

It's important to note that the *Parameter* field is intended to pass a long address, so only 14-bits (bits 2 through 15) are passed into the cog's PAR register.

COGSTOP

Stop cog by its ID.

((PUB ⋮ PRI))
   COGSTOP (*CogID*)

- *CogID* is the ID (0 – 7) of the cog to stop.

Explanation

COGSTOP stops a cog whose ID is *CogID* and places that cog into a dormant state. In the dormant state, the cog ceases to receive System Clock pulses so that power consumption is greatly reduced.

To stop a cog, issue the COGSTOP command with the ID of the cog to stop. For example:

```
VAR
  byte Cog      'Used to store ID of newly started cog


PUB Start(Pos) : Pass
  'Start a new cog to run Update with Pos,
  'return TRUE if successful
  Pass := (Cog := cognew(@Update, Pos) + 1) > 0


PUB Stop
  'Stop the cog we started earlier, if any.
  if Cog
    cogstop(Cog~ - 1)
```

This example, from the COGNEW description, uses COGSTOP in the public Stop method to stop the cog that was previously started by the Start method. See COGNEW, page 189, for more information about this example.

CON

Declare a Constant Block.

CON
    Symbol **=** *Expression* ⟨((**,** ┆ ↵)) *Symbol* **=** *Expression*⟩...

CON
    #*Expression* ((**,** ┆ ↵)) *Symbol* ⟨((**,** ┆ ↵)) *Symbol*⟩...

CON
    Symbol ⟨((**,** ┆ ↵)) *Symbol*⟩...

- *Symbol* is the desired name for the constant.
- *Expression* is any valid integer, or floating-point, constant algebraic expression. Expression can include other constant symbols as long as they were defined previously.

Explanation

The Constant Block is a section of source code that declares global constant symbols and global Propeller configuration settings. This is one of six special declarations (CON, VAR, OBJ, PUB, PRI, and DAT) that provide inherent structure to the Spin language.

Constants are numerical values that can not change during run time. They can be defined in terms of single values (1, $F, 65000, %1010, %%2310, "A", etc.) or as expressions, called constant expressions, (25 + 16 / 2, 1000 * 5, etc.) that always resolve to a specific number.

The Constant Block is an area of code specifically used for assigning symbols (useful names) to constants so that the symbols can be used anywhere in code where that constant value is needed. This makes code more readable and easier to maintain should you later have to change the value of a constant that appears in many places. These constants are global to the object so that any method within it can use them. There are many ways to define constants, described below.

Common Constant Declarations (Syntax 1)

The most common forms of constant declarations begin with CON on a line by itself followed by one or more declarations. CON must start in column 1 (the leftmost column) of the line it is on and we recommend the lines following be indented by at least one space. The expressions can be combinations of numbers, operators, parentheses, and single quoted characters. See Operators, page 249, for examples of expressions.

Example:

```
CON
  Delay = 500
  Baud = 9600
  AChar = "A"
```

—or—

```
CON
  Delay = 500, Baud = 9600, AChar = "A"
```

Both of these examples create a symbol called Delay that is equal to 500, a symbol called Baud that is equal to 9600, and a symbol called AChar that is equal to the character "A". For the Delay declaration, for example, we could also have used an algebraic expression, such as:

```
  Delay = 250 * 2
```

The above statement results in Delay equaling 500, like before, but the expression may make the code easier to understand if the resulting number were not just an arbitrary value.

The CON block is also used for specifying global settings, such as system clock settings. The example below shows how to set the Clock Mode to low-speed crystal, the Clock PLL to 8x, and specify that the XIN pin frequency is 4 MHz.

```
CON
  _CLKMODE = XTAL1 + PLL8X
  _XINFREQ = 4_000_000
```

See **_CLKMODE**, page 180, and **_XINFREQ**, page 337, for detailed descriptions of these settings.

Floating-point values can also be defined as constants. Floating-point values are real numbers (with fractional components) and are encoded within 32 bits differently than integer constants. To specify a floating-point constant, you must give a clear indication that the value is a floating-point value; the expression must either be a single floating-point value or be made up entirely of floating-point values (no integers).

Floating-point values must be written as:

1) decimal digits followed by a decimal point and at least one more decimal digit,
2) decimal digits followed by "e" (for exponent) and an integer exponent value, or,
3) a combination of 1 and 2.

The following are examples of valid constants:

`0.5`	floating-point value
`1.0`	floating-point value
`3.14`	floating-point value
`1e16`	floating-point value
`51.025e5`	floating-point value
`3 + 4`	integer expression
`3.0 + 4.0`	floating-point expression
`3.0 + 4`	invalid expression; causes compile error
`3.0 + FLOAT(4)`	floating-point expression

Here is an example declaring an integer constant and two floating-point constants.

```
CON
  Num1 = 20
  Num2 = 127.38
  Num3 = 32.05 * 18.1 - Num2 / float(Num1)
```

The above code sets `Num1`, `Num2` and `Num3` to 20, 127.38 and 573.736, respectively. Notice that the last expression required `Num1` to be enclosed in the `FLOAT` declaration so that the compiler treats it as a floating-point value.

The Propeller compiler handles floating-point constants as a single-precision real number as described by the IEEE-754 standard. Single-precision real numbers are stored in 32 bits, with a 1-bit sign, an 8-bit exponent, and a 23-bit mantissa (the fractional part). This provides approximately 7.2 significant decimal digits.

For run-time floating-point operations, the FloatMath and FloatString objects provide math functions compatible with single-precision numbers.

See `FLOAT` on page 216, `ROUND` on page 303, `TRUNC` on page 314, and the FloatMath and FloatString objects for more information.

Enumerations (Syntax 2 and 3)

Constant Blocks can also declare enumerated constant symbols. Enumerations are logically grouped symbols which have incrementing integer constant values assigned to them that are each unique for the group. For example, an object may have the need for certain modes of operation. Each of these modes can be identified by a number, 0, 1, 2 and 3, for example. The numbers themselves don't really matter for our purposes; they just need to be unique within the context of the operation mode. Since the numbers themselves are not descriptive, it may be difficult to remember what mode 3 does, but it is a lot easier to remember what the mode means if it had a descriptive name instead. Look at the following example.

```
CON
  'Declare modes of operation
  RunTest    = 0
  RunVerbose = 1
  RunBrief   = 2
  RunFull    = 3
```

The above example would suffice for our purposes; now users of our object can indicate "RunFull" instead of "3" to specify the desired mode of operation. The problem is, defining a logical group of items this way may cause bugs and maintenance problems because if any value was changed (on purpose or by accident) without changing the rest accordingly, it may cause the program to fail. Also, imagine a case where there were 20 modes of operation. That would be a much longer set of constants and even more opportunities for maintenance issues.

Enumerations solve these problems by automatically incrementing values for symbols. We can rewrite the above example with enumeration syntax as follows:

```
CON    'Declare modes of operation
  #0, RunTest, RunVerbose, RunBrief, RunFull
```

Here, #0, tells the compiler to start counting from the number 0 and it sets the next symbol equal to that value. Then, any additional symbols that do not specify their own value (via an '= expression') are automatically assigned the previous value plus 1. The result is that RunTest equals 0, RunVerbose equals 1, RunBrief equals 2 and RunFull equals 3. For most cases, the values themselves don't usually matter; all that matters is that they are each assigned a unique number. Defining enumerated values like this has the advantages of insuring that the assigned values are unique and contiguous within the group.

Using the example above, the methods that use them can do things like the following (assume Mode is a symbol set by a calling object):

```
case Mode
  RunTest     : <test code here>
  RunVerbose  : <verbose code here>
  RunBrief    : <brief code here>
  RunFull     : <full code here>
```
—or—
```
if Mode > RunVerbose
  <brief and run mode code here>
```

Notice that these routines do not rely on the exact value of the mode, but rather they rely on the enumerated mode symbol itself for comparisons as well as the position of the symbol in relation to other symbols in the same enumeration. It is important to write code this way to decrease potentials for bugs introduced by future changes.

Enumerations don't have to consist of comma-separated items either. The following also works and leaves room for right-side comments about each mode.

```
CON       'Declare modes of operation
  #0
  RunTest              'Run in test mode
  RunVerbose           'Run in verbose mode
  RunBrief             'Run with brief prompts
  RunFull              'Run in full production mode
```

The above example does the same thing as the previous in-line example, but now we have convenient room to describe the purpose of each mode without losing the automatic incrementing advantage. Later on, if there's a need to add a fifth mode, simply add it to the list in whatever position is necessary. If there is a need for the list to begin at a certain value, simply change the #0 to whatever you need: #1, #20, etc.

It is even possible to modify the enumerated value in the middle of the list.

```
CON
  'Declare modes of operation
  #1, RunTest, RunVerbose, #5, RunBrief, RunFull
```

Here, RunTest and RunVerbose are 1 and 2, respectively, and RunBrief and RunFull are 5 and 6, respectively. While this feature may be handy, to maintain good programming practices it should only be used in rare cases.

Syntax 3 is a variation of the enumeration syntax. It doesn't specify any starting value. Anything defined this way will always start with the first symbol equal to either 0 (for new CON blocks) or to the last enumerated value plus 1 (within the same CON block).

Scope of Constants

Symbolic constants defined in Constant Blocks are global to the object in which they are defined but not outside of that object. This means that constants can be accessed directly from anywhere within the object but their name will not conflict with symbols defined in other parent or child objects.

Symbolic constants can be indirectly accessed by parent objects, however, by using the constant reference syntax. Example:

```
OBJ
  Num : "Numbers"

PUB SomeRoutine
  Format := Num#DEC      'Set Format to Number's Decimal constant
```

Here an object, "Numbers," is declared as the symbol Num. Later, a method refers to numbers' DEC constant with Num#DEC. Num is the object reference, # indicates we need to access that object's constants, and DEC is the constant within the object we need. This feature allows objects to define constants for use with themselves and for parent objects to access those constants freely without interfering with any symbols they created themselves.

CONSTANT

Declare in-line constant expression to be completely resolved at compile time.

```
((PUB ┆ PRI))
    CONSTANT (ConstantExpression )
```

Returns: Resolved value of constant expression.

- *ConstantExpression* is the desired constant expression.

Explanation

The CON block may be used to create constants from expressions that are referenced from multiple places in code, but there are occasions when a constant expression is needed for temporary, one-time purposes. The CONSTANT directive is used to fully resolve a method's in-line, constant expression at compile time. Without the use of the CONSTANT directive, a method's in-line expressions are always resolved at run time, even if the expression is always a constant value.

Using CONSTANT

The CONSTANT directive can create one-time-use constant expressions that save code space and speed up run-time execution. Note the two examples below:

Example 1, using standard run-time expressions:

```
CON
  X = 500
  Y = 2500

PUB Blink
  !outa[0]
  waitcnt(X+200 + cnt)              'Standard run-time expression
  !outa[0]
  waitcnt((X+Y)/2 + cnt)            'Standard run-time expression
```

Example 2, same as above, but with CONSTANT directive around constant, run-time expressions:

```
CON
  X = 500
  Y = 2500

PUB Blink
  !outa[0]
  waitcnt(constant(X+200) + cnt)    'exp w/compile & run-time parts
  !outa[0]
  waitcnt(constant((X+Y)/2) + cnt)'exp w/compile & run-time parts
```

The above two examples do exactly the same thing: their Blink methods toggle P0, wait for X+200 cycles, toggle P0 again and wait for (X+Y)/2 cycles before returning. While the CON block's X and Y symbols may need to be used in multiple places within the object, the WAITCNT expressions used in each example's Blink method might only need to be used in that one place. For this reason, it may not make sense to define additional constants in the CON block for things like X+200 and (X+Y)/2. There is nothing wrong with putting the expressions right in the run-time code, as in Example 1, but that entire expression is unfortunately evaluated at run time, requiring extra time and code space.

The CONSTANT directive is perfect for this situation, because it completely resolves each one-time-use constant expression to a single, static value, saving code space and speeding up execution. In Example 1, the Blink method consumes 33 bytes of code space while Example 2's Blink method, with the addition of the CONSTANT directives, only requires 23 bytes of space. Note that the "+ cnt" portion of the expressions are not included within the CONSTANT directive's parentheses; this is because cnt is a variable (the System Counter variable; see CNT, page 184) so its value cannot be resolved at compile time.

If a constant needs to be used in more than one place in code, it is better to define it in the CON block so it is defined only once and the symbol representing it can be used multiple times.

Constants (pre-defined)

The following constants are pre-defined by the compiler:

TRUE	Logical true:	-1	($FFFFFFFF)
FALSE	Logical false:	0	($00000000)
POSX	Maximum positive integer:	2,147,483,647	($7FFFFFFF)
NEGX	Maximum negative integer:	-2,147,483,648	($80000000)
PI	Floating-point value for PI:	≈ 3.141593	($40490FDB)
RCFAST	Internal fast oscillator:	$00000001	(%00000000001)
RCSLOW	Internal slow oscillator:	$00000002	(%00000000010)
XINPUT	External clock/oscillator:	$00000004	(%00000000100)
XTAL1	External low-speed crystal:	$00000008	(%00000001000)
XTAL2	External medium-speed crystal:	$00000010	(%00000010000)
XTAL3	External high-speed crystal:	$00000020	(%00000100000)
PLL1X	External frequency times 1:	$00000040	(%00001000000)
PLL2X	External frequency times 2:	$00000080	(%00010000000)
PLL4X	External frequency times 4:	$00000100	(%00100000000)
PLL8X	External frequency times 8:	$00000200	(%01000000000)
PLL16X	External frequency times 16:	$00000400	(%10000000000)

(All of these constants are also available in Propeller Assembly.)

TRUE and FALSE

TRUE and FALSE are usually used for Boolean comparison purposes:

```
if (X = TRUE) or (Y = FALSE)
   <code to execute if total condition is true>
```

POSX and NEGX

POSX and NEGX are typically used for comparison purposes or as a flag for a specific event:

```
if Z > NEGX
  <code to execute if Z hasn't reached smallest negative>
```

—or—

```
PUB FindListItem(Item) : Index
  Index := NEGX                    'Default to "not found" response
  <code to find Item in list>
  if <item found>
    Index := <items index>
```

PI

PI can be used for floating-point calculations, either floating-point constants or floating-point variable values using the FloatMath and FloatString object.

RCFAST through PLL16X

RCFAST through PLL16X are Clock Mode Setting constants. They are explained in further detail in the _CLKMODE section beginning on page 180.

CTRA, CTRB
Counter A and Counter B Control Registers.

((PUB ┊ PRI))
   CTRA

((PUB ┊ PRI))
   CTRB

Returns: Current value of Counter A or Counter B Control Register, if used as a source variable.

Explanation

CTRA and CTRB are two of six registers (CTRA, CTRB, FRQA, FRQB, PHSA, and PHSB) that affect the behavior of a cog's Counter Modules. Each cog has two identical counter modules (A and B) that can perform many repetitive tasks. The CTRA and CTRB registers contain the configuration settings of the Counter A and Counter B Modules, respectively.

The following discussion uses CTRx, FRQx and PHSx to refer to both the A and B pairs of each register.

Each of the two counter modules can control or monitor up to two I/O pins and perform conditional 32-bit accumulation of the value in the FRQx register into the PHSx register on every clock cycle. Each Counter Module has its own phase-locked loop (PLLx) which can be used to synthesize frequencies from 64 MHz to 128 MHz.

With just a little configuration and in some cases a little maintenance from the cog, the counter modules can be used for:

- Frequency synthesis
- Frequency measurement
- Pulse counting
- Pulse measurement
- Multi-pin state measurement

- Pulse-width modulation (PWM)
- Duty-cycle measurement
- Digital-to-analog conversion (DAC)
- Analog-to-digital conversion (ADC)
- And more.

For some of these operations the cog can set the counter's configuration, via CTRA or CTRB, and it will perform its task completely independently. For others, the cog may use WAITCNT to time-align the counter's reads and writes within a loop; creating the effect of a more complex

---

state machine. Since the counter's update period may be brief (12.5 ns at 80 MHz), very dynamic signal generation and measurement is possible.

Control Register Fields

The CTRA and CTRB registers each contain four fields shown in the table below.

Table 4-5: CTRA and CTRB Registers						
31	30..26	25..23	22..15	14..9	8..6	5..0
-	CTRMODE	PLLDIV	-	BPIN	-	APIN

APIN

The APIN field of CTRA selects a primary I/O pin for that counter. May be ignored if not used. %0xxxxx = Port A, %1xxxxx = Port B (reserved for future use). In Propeller Assembly, the APIN field can conveniently be written using the MOVS instruction.

Note that writing a zero to CTRA will immediately disable the Counter A and stop all related pin output and PHSA accumulation.

BPIN

The BPIN field of CTRx selects a secondary I/O pin for that counter. This field may be ignored if not used. %0xxxxx = Port A, %1xxxxx = Port B (reserved for future use). In Propeller Assembly, the BPIN field can conveniently be written using the MOVD instruction.

PLLDIV

The PLLDIV field of CTRx selects a PLLx output tap, see table below. This determines which power-of-two division of the VCO frequency will be used as the final PLLx output (a range of 500 KHz to 128 MHz). This field may be ignored if not used. In Propeller Assembly, the PLLDIV field can conveniently be written, along with CTRMODE, using the MOVI instruction.

Table 4-6: PLLDIV Field							
PLLDIV	%000	%001	%010	%011	%100	%101	%110	%111
Output	VCO ÷ 128	VCO ÷ 64	VCO ÷ 32	VCO ÷ 16	VCO ÷ 8	VCO ÷ 4	VCO ÷ 2	VCO ÷ 1

CTRMODE

The CTRMODE field of CTRA and CTRB selects one of 32 operating modes, shown in Table 4-7, for the corresponding Counter A or Counter B. In Propeller Assembly, the CTRMODE field can conveniently be written, along with PLLDIV, using the MOVI instruction.

The modes %00001 through %00011 cause FRQx-to-PHSx, accumulation to occur every clock cycle. This creates a numerically-controlled oscillator (NCO) in PHSx[31], which feeds the PLLx's reference input. The PLLx will multiply this frequency by 16 using its voltage-controlled oscillator (VCO).

For stable operation, it is recommended that the VCO frequency be kept within 64 MHz to 128 MHz. This translates to an NCO frequency of 4 MHz to 8 MHz.

Using CTRA and CTRB

In Spin, CTRx can be read/written just like any other register or pre-defined variable. As soon as this register is written, the new operating mode goes into effect for the counter. For example:

```
CTRA := %00100 << 26
```

The above code sets CTRA's CTRMODE field to the NCO mode (%00100) and all other bits to zero.

Table 4-7: Counter Modes (CTRMODE Field Values)				
CTRMODE	Description	Accumulate FRQx to PHSx	APIN Output*	BPIN Output*
%00000	Counter disabled (off)	0 (never)	0 (none)	0 (none)
%00001	PLL internal (video mode)	1 (always)	0	0
%00010	PLL single-ended	1	PLLx	0
%00011	PLL differential	1	PLLx	!PLLx
%00100	NCO/PWM single-ended	1	PHSx[31]	0
%00101	NCO/PWM differential	1	PHSx[31]	!PHSx[31]
%00110	DUTY single-ended	1	PHSx-Carry	0
%00111	DUTY differential	1	PHSx-Carry	!PHSx-Carry
%01000	POS detector	A^1	0	0
%01001	POS detector with feedback	A^1	0	$!A^1$
%01010	POSEDGE detector	A^1 & $!A^2$	0	0
%01011	POSEDGE detector w/ feedback	A^1 & $!A^2$	0	$!A^1$
%01100	NEG detector	$!A^1$	0	0
%01101	NEG detector with feedback	$!A^1$	0	$!A^1$
%01110	NEGEDGE detector	$!A^1$ & A^2	0	0
%01111	NEGEDGE detector w/ feedback	$!A^1$ & A^2	0	$!A^1$
%10000	LOGIC never	0	0	0
%10001	LOGIC !A & !B	$!A^1$ & $!B^1$	0	0
%10010	LOGIC A & !B	A^1 & $!B^1$	0	0
%10011	LOGIC !B	$!B^1$	0	0
%10100	LOGIC !A & B	$!A^1$ & B^1	0	0
%10101	LOGIC !A	$!A^1$	0	0
%10110	LOGIC A <> B	A^1 <> B^1	0	0
%10111	LOGIC !A | !B	$!A^1$ | $!B^1$	0	0
%11000	LOGIC A & B	A^1 & B^1	0	0
%11001	LOGIC A == B	$!A^1$ == B^1	0	0
%11010	LOGIC A	A^1	0	0
%11011	LOGIC A | !B	A^1 | $!B^1$	0	0
%11100	LOGIC B	B^1	0	0
%11101	LOGIC !A | B	$!A^1$ | B^1	0	0
%11110	LOGIC A | B	A^1 | B^1	0	0
%11111	LOGIC always	1	0	0

*Must set corresponding DIR bit to affect pin
A^1 = APIN input delayed by 1 clock
A^2 = APIN input delayed by 2 clocks
B^1 = BPIN input delayed by 1 clock

DAT

Declare a Data Block.

DAT
⟨**Symbol**⟩ **Alignment** ⟨**Size**⟩ ⟨**Data**⟩ ⟨, ⟨**Size**⟩ **Data**⟩...

DAT
⟨**Symbol**⟩ ⟨**Condition**⟩ **Instruction** ⟨**Effect(s)**⟩

- **Symbol** is an optional name for the data, reserved space, or instruction that follows.
- Alignment is the desired alignment and default size (BYTE, WORD, or LONG) of the data elements that follow.
- **Size** is the desired size (BYTE, WORD, or LONG) of the following data element immediately following it; alignment is unchanged.
- **Data** is a constant expression or comma-separated list of constant expressions. Quoted strings of characters are also allowed; they are treated as a comma-separated list of characters.
- **Condition** is an assembly language condition, IF_C, IF_NC, IF_Z, etc.
- **Instruction** is an assembly language instruction, ADD, SUB, MOV, etc., and all its operands.
- **Effect(s)** is/are one, two or three assembly language effects that cause the result of the instruction to be written or not, NR, WR, WC, or WZ.

Explanation

A Data Block is a section of source code that contains pre-defined data, memory reserved for run-time use and Propeller Assembly code. This is one of six special declarations (CON, VAR, OBJ, PUB, PRI, and DAT) that provide inherent structure to the Spin language.

Data blocks are multi-purpose sections of source code that are used for data tables, run-time workspace, and Propeller Assembly code. Assembly code and data can be intermixed, if necessary, so that data is loaded into a cog along with the assembly code.

Declaring Data (Syntax 1)

Data is declared with a specific alignment and size (BYTE, WORD, or LONG) to indicate how it should be stored in memory. The location where data is actually stored depends on the structure of the object and the application it is compiled into since data is included as part of the compiled code.

For example:

```
DAT
  byte 64, "A", "String", 0
  word $FFC2, 75000
  long $44332211, 32
```

The first thing on line two of this example, BYTE, indicates the data following it should be byte-aligned and byte-sized. At compile time, the data following BYTE, 64, "A", etc., is stored in program memory a byte at a time starting at the next available location. Line three specifies word-aligned and word-sized data. Its data, $FFC2 and 75000, will begin at the next word boundary position following the data that appeared before it; with any unused bytes from the previous data filled with zeros to pad up to the next word boundary. The fourth line specifies long-aligned and long-sized data; its data will be stored at the next long boundary following the word-aligned data that appeared before it, with zero-padded words leading up to that boundary. Table 4-8 shows what this looks like in memory (shown in hexadecimal).

Table 4-8: Example Data in Memory																							
L	0				2				3				4				5				6			
W	0		1		2		3		4		5		6		7		8		9		10		11	
B	0	1	2	3	4	5	6	7	8	9	10	11	12	13	14	15	16	17	18	19	20	21	22	23
D	40	41	53	74	72	69	6E	67	00	00	C2	FF	F8	24	00	00	11	22	33	44	20	00	00	00

L = longs, W = words, B = bytes, D = data

The first nine bytes (0 – 8) are the byte data from line one; $40 = 64 (decimal), $41 = "A", $53 = "S", etc. Byte 9 is padded with zero to align the first word of word-aligned data, $FFC2, at byte 10. Bytes 10 and 11 (word 5) contain the first word-sized value, $FFC2, stored in low-byte-first format as $C2 and $FF. Bytes 12 and 13 (word 6) is the lowest word of 75000; more on this later. Bytes 14 and 15 (word 7) are zero padded to align the first long of long-aligned data, $44332211. Bytes 16 through 19 (long 5) contain that value in low-byte-first format. Finally, bytes 20 through 23 (long 6) contains the second long of data, 32, in low-byte-first format.

You may have noticed that the value 75000 was specified as a word-sized one. The number 75000 in hexadecimal is $124F8, but since that's larger than a word, only the lowest word ($24F8) of the value was stored. This resulted in word 6 (bytes 12 and 13) containing $F8 and $24, and word 7 (bytes 14 and 15) containing $00 and $00 due to the padding for the following long-aligned values.

This phenomenon, whether or not it is intentional, occurs for byte-aligned/byte-sized data as well, for example:

```
DAT
  byte $FFAA, $BB995511
```

...results in only the low bytes of each value, $AA and $11 being stored in consecutive locations.

Occasionally, however, it is desirable to store an entire large value as smaller elemental units that are not necessarily aligned according to the size of the value itself. To do this, specify the value's size just before the value itself.

```
DAT
  byte word $FFAA, long $BB995511
```

This example specifies byte-aligned data, but a word-sized value followed by a long-sized value. The result is that the memory contains $AA and $FF, consecutively, and following it, $11, $55, $99 and $BB.

If we modify line three of the first example above as follows:

```
  word $FFC2, long 75000
```

...then we'd end up with $F8, $24, $01, and $00 occupying bytes 12 through 15. Byte 15 is the upper byte of the value and it just happens to be immediately left of the next long boundary so no additional zero-padded bytes are needed for the next long-aligned data.

Optionally, the *Symbol* field of syntax 1 can be included to "name" the data. This makes referencing the data from a PUB or PRI block easy. For example:

```
DAT
  MyData    byte $FF, 25, %1010

PUB GetData | Temp
  Temp := MyData[0]                'Get first byte of data table
```

This example creates a data table called MyData that consists of bytes $FF, 25 and %1010. The public method, GetData, reads the first byte of MyData from main memory and stores it in its local variable, Temp.

You can also use the BYTE, WORD, and LONG declarations to read main memory locations. For example:

```
DAT
  MyData     byte $FF, 25, %1010

PUB GetData | Temp
  Temp := BYTE[@MyData][0]          'Get first byte of data table
```

This example is similar to the previous one except that it uses the BYTE declaration to read the value stored at the address of MyData. Refer to BYTE, page 165; WORD, page 331; and LONG, page 236, for more information on reading and writing main memory.

Writing Propeller Assembly Code (Syntax 2)

In addition to numerical and string data, the Data Block is used for Propeller Assembly code. For example,

```
DAT
              org                        'reset address pointer
Loop          rdlong    t1, par    WZ    'wait for command
       if_z   jmp       #Loop            'jump of zero
              movd      :arg, #arg0      'get 8 arguments
:arg          mov       t2, t1
```

This example contains optional symbols, "Loop" and ":arg", an optional conditional, "IF_Z", the required instruction field, ORG, RDLONG, etc, followed by operands and an effect statement, "WZ."

Note that any dual commands (those available in both Spin and Propeller Assembly) that are used in a DAT block are treated as assembly instructions. Conversely, any dual commands that are used outside of a DAT block are treated as Spin commands.

DIRA, DIRB

Direction Register for 32-bit Ports A and B.

((PUB ¦ PRI))

   DIRA ⟨[*Pin(s)*]⟩

((PUB ¦ PRI))

   DIRB ⟨[*Pin(s)*]⟩ (Reserved for future use)

Returns: Current value of direction bits for I/O *Pin(s)* in Ports A or B, if used as a source variable.

- *Pin(s)* is an optional expression, or a range-expression, that specifies the I/O pin, or pins, to access in Port A (0-31) or Port B (32-63). If given as a single expression, only the pin specified is accessed. If given as a range-expression (two expressions in a range format; x..y) the contiguous pins from the start to end expressions are accessed.

Explanation

DIRA and DIRB are one of six registers (DIRA, DIRB, INA, INB, OUTA and OUTB) that directly affect the I/O pins. The DIRA register holds the direction states for each of the 32 I/O pins in Port A; bits 0 through 31 correspond to P0 through P31. The DIRB register holds the direction states for each of the 32 I/O pins in Port B; bits 0 through 31 correspond to P32 through P63.

NOTE: DIRB is reserved for future use; the Propeller P8X32A does not include Port B I/O pins so only DIRA is discussed below.

DIRA is used to both set and get the current direction states of one or more I/O pins in Port A. A low (0) bit sets the corresponding I/O pin to an input direction. A high (1) bit sets the corresponding I/O pin to an output direction. The DIRA register defaults zero, all 0 bits, upon cog startup; all I/O pins are specified as inputs by that cog until the code instructs otherwise.

Each cog has access to all I/O pins at any given time. Essentially, all I/O pins are directly connected to each cog so that there is no hub-related mutually-exclusive access involved. Each cog maintains its own DIRA register that gives it the ability to set any I/O pin's direction. Each cog's DIRA register is OR'd with that of the other cogs' DIRA registers and the resulting 32-bit value becomes the I/O directions of Port A pins P0 through P31. The result is that each I/O pin's direction state is the "wired-OR" of the entire cog collective. See I/O Pins on page 26 for more information.

This configuration can easily be described in the following simple rules:

A. A pin is an input <u>only</u> of no active cog sets it to an output.
B. A pin is an output <u>if any</u> active cog sets it to an output.

If a cog is disabled, its direction register is treated as if were cleared to 0, causing it to exert no influence on I/O pin directions and states.

Note that because of the "wired-OR" nature of the I/O pins, no electrical contention between cogs is possible, yet they can all still access I/O pins simultaneously. It is up to the application developer to ensure that no two cogs cause logical contention on the same I/O pin during run time.

Using DIRA

Set or clear bits in **DIRA** to affect the direction of I/O pins as desired. For example:

```
DIRA := %00000000_00000000_10110000_11110011
```

The above code sets the entire **DIRA** register (all 32 bits at once) to a value that makes I/O pins 15, 13, 12, 7, 6, 5, 4, 1 and 0 to outputs and the rest to inputs.

Using the post-clear (~) and post-set (~~) unary operators, the cog can set all I/O pins to inputs, or outputs, respectively; it's not usually desirable to set all I/O pins to outputs, however. For example:

```
DIRA~                   'Clear DIRA register (all I/Os are inputs)
```

—and—

```
DIRA~~                  'Set DIRA register (all I/Os are outputs)
```

The first example above clears the entire **DIRA** register (all 32 bits at once) to zero; all I/Os P0 through P31 to inputs. The second example above sets the entire **DIRA** register (all 32 bits at once) to ones; all I/Os P0 through P31 to outputs.

To affect only one I/O pin (one bit), include the optional *Pin(s)* field. This treats the **DIRA** register as an array of 32 bits.

```
DIRA[5]~~               'Set DIRA bit 5 (P5 to output)
```

This sets P5 to an output. All other bits of **DIRA** (and thus all other corresponding I/O pins) remain in their previous state.

The **DIRA** register supports a special form of expression, called a range-expression, which allows you to affect a group of I/O pins at once, without affecting others outside the specified range. To affect multiple, contiguous I/O pins at once, use a range expression (like x..y) in the *Pin(s)* field.

```
DIRA[5..3]~~          'Set DIRA bits 5 through 3 (P5-P3 to output)
```

This sets P5, P4 and P3 to outputs; all other bits of **DIRA** remain in their previous state. Here's another example:

```
DIRA[5..3] := %110    'Set P5 and P4 to output, P3 to input
```

The above example sets **DIRA** bits 5, 4 and 3 equal to 1, 1, and 0, respectively, leaving all other bits in their previous state. Consequently, P5 and P4 are now outputs and P3 is an input.

IMPORTANT: The order of the values in a range-expression affects how it is used. For example, the following swaps the order of the range-expression of the previous example.

```
DIRA[3..5] := %110    'Set P3 and P4 to output, P5 to input
```

Here, **DIRA** bits 3, 4 and 5 are set equal to 1, 1, and 0, respectively, making P3 and P4 outputs and P5 an input.

This is a powerful feature of range-expressions, but if care is not taken, it can also cause strange, unintentional results.

Normally **DIRA** is only written to but it can also be read from to retrieve the current I/O pin directions. The following assumes Temp is a variable created elsewhere:

```
Temp := DIRA[7..4]    'Get direction of P7 through P4
```

The above sets Temp equal to **DIRA** bits 7, 6, 5, and 4; i.e.: the lower 4 bits of Temp are now equal to DIRA7:4 and the other bits of Temp are cleared to zero.

FILE

Import external file as data.

```
DAT
    FILE "FileName"
```

- *FileName* is the name, without extension, of the desired data file. Upon compile, a file with this name is searched for in the editor tabs, the working directory and the library directory. *FileName* can contain any valid filename characters; disallowed characters are \, /, :, *, ?, ", <, >, and |.

Explanation

The FILE directive is used to import an external data file (usually a binary file) into the DAT block of an object. The data can then be accessed by the object just like any regular DAT block data.

Using FILE

FILE is used in DAT blocks similar to how BYTE would be used, except that following it is a filename in quotes instead of data values. For example:

```
DAT
    Str     byte    "This is a data string.", 0
    Data    file    "Datafile.dat"
```

In this example, the DAT block is made up of a byte string followed by the data from a file called Datafile.dat. Upon compile, the Propeller Tool will search through the editor tabs, the working directory or the library directory for a file called Datafile.dat and will load its data into the first byte following the zero-terminated string, Str. Methods can access the imported data using the BYTE, WORD or LONG declarations as they would normal data. For example:

```
PUB GetData | Index, Temp
  Index := 0
  repeat
    Temp := byte[Data][Index++]  'Read data into Temp 1 byte at a time
    <do something with Temp>      'Perform task with value in Temp
  while Temp > 0                   'Loop until end found
```

This example will read the imported data, one byte at a time, until it finds a byte equal to 0.

FLOAT

Convert an integer constant expression to a compile-time floating-point value.

((CON ¦ VAR ¦ OBJ ¦ PUB ¦ PRI ¦ DAT))
   FLOAT (*IntegerConstant*)

Returns: Resolved value of integer constant expression as a floating-point number.

- *IntegerConstant* is the desired integer constant expression to be used as a constant floating-point value.

Explanation

FLOAT is one of three directives (FLOAT, ROUND and TRUNC) used for floating-point constant expressions. The FLOAT directive converts a constant integer value to a constant floating-point value.

Using FLOAT

While most constants are 32-bit integer values, the Propeller compiler supports 32-bit floating-point values and constant expressions for compile-time use. Note that this is for constant expressions only, not run-time variable expressions.

For typical floating-point constant declarations, the expression must be shown as a floating-point value in one of three ways: 1) as an integer value followed by a decimal point and at least one digit, 2) as an integer with an E followed by an exponent value, or 3) both 1 and 2. For example:

```
CON
   OneHalf = 0.5
   Ratio   = 2.0 / 5.0
   Miles   = 10e5
```

The above code creates three floating-point constants. OneHalf is equal to 0.5, Ratio is equal to 0.4 and Miles is equal to 1,000,000.

Notice that in the above example, every component of every expression is shown as a floating-point value. Now take a look at the following example:

```
CON
   Two     = 2
   Ratio   = Two / 5.0
```

Here, Two is defined as an integer constant and Ratio appears to be defined as a floating-point constant. This causes an error on the Ratio line because, for floating-point constant expressions, every value within the expression must be a floating-point value; you cannot mix integer and floating-point values like Ratio = 2 / 5.0.

You can, however, use the FLOAT directive to convert an integer value to a floating-point value, such as in the following:

```
CON
  Two    = 2
  Ratio  = float(Two) / 5.0
```

The FLOAT directive in this example converts the integer constant, Two, into the floating-point form of that value so that it can be used in the floating-point expression.

About Floating Point

The Propeller compiler handles floating-point constants as a single-precision real number as described by the IEEE-754 standard. Single-precision real numbers are stored in 32 bits, with a 1-bit sign, an 8-bit exponent, and a 23-bit mantissa (the fractional part). This provides approximately 7.2 significant decimal digits.

Floating-point constant expressions can be defined and used for many compile-time purposes, but for run-time floating-point operations, the FloatMath and FloatString objects provide math functions compatible with single-precision numbers.

See Constant Assignment '=' in the Operators section on page 254, ROUND on page 303, and TRUNC on page 314, as well as the the FloatMath and FloatString objects for more information.

_FREE

Pre-defined, one-time settable constant for specifying the size of an application's free space.

CON
    _FREE = *Expression*

- *Expression* is an integer expression that indicates the number of longs to reserve for free space.

Explanation

_FREE is a pre-defined, one-time settable optional constant that specifies the required free memory space of an application. This value is added to _STACK, if specified, to determine the total amount of free/stack memory space to reserve for a Propeller Application. Use _FREE if an application requires a minimum amount of free memory in order to run properly. If the resulting compiled application is too large to allow the specified free memory, an error message will be displayed. For example:

```
CON
    _FREE   = 1000
```

The _FREE declaration in the above CON block indicates that the application needs to have at least 1,000 longs of free memory left over after compilation. If the resulting compiled application does not have that much room left over, an error message will indicate by how much it was exceeded. This is a good way to prevent successful compiles of an application that will fail to run properly due to lack of memory.

Note that only the top object file can set the value of _FREE. Any child object's _FREE declarations will be ignored.

FRQA, FRQB

Counter A and Counter B frequency registers.

((PUB ¦ PRI))
    FRQA

((PUB ¦ PRI))
    FRQB

Returns: Current value of Counter A or Counter B Frequency Register, if used as a source variable.

Explanation

FRQA and FRQB are two of six registers (CTRA, CTRB, FRQA, FRQB, PHSA, and PHSB) that affect the behavior of a cog's Counter Modules. Each cog has two identical counter modules (A and B) that can perform many repetitive tasks. The FRQA register contains the value that is accumulated into the PHSA register. The FRQB register contains the value that is accumulated into the PHSB register. See CTRA, CTRB on page 204 for more information.

Using FRQA and FRQB

FRQA and FRQB can be read/written just like any other register or pre-defined variable. For example:

```
FRQA := $00001AFF
```

The above code sets FRQA to $00001AFF. Depending on the CTRMODE field of the CTRA register, this value in FRQA may be added into the PHSA register at a frequency determined by the System Clock and the primary and/or secondary I/O pins. See CTRA, CTRB on page 204 for more information.

IF

Test condition(s) and execute a block of code if valid (positive logic).

```
((PUB ¦ PRI))
    IF Condition(s)
    →┃ IfStatement(s)
    ⟨ ELSEIF Condition(s)
    →┃ ElseIfStatement(s) ⟩...
    ⟨ ELSEIFNOT Condition(s)
    →┃ ElseIfNotStatement(s) ⟩...
    ⟨ ELSE
    →┃ ElseStatement(s) ⟩
```

- **Condition(s)** is one or more Boolean expressions to test.
- **IfStatement(s)** is a block of one or more lines of code to execute when the IF's *Condition(s)* is true.
- **ElseIfStatement(s)** is an optional block of one or more lines of code to execute when all the previous *Condition(s)* are invalid and the ELSEIF's *Condition(s)* is true.
- **ElseIfNotStatement(s)** is an optional block of one or more lines of code to execute when all the previous *Condition(s)* are invalid and the ELSEIFNOT's *Condition(s)* is false.
- **ElseStatement(s)** is an optional block of one or more lines of code to execute when all the previous *Condition(s)* are invalid.

Explanation

IF is one of the three major conditional commands (IF, IFNOT, and CASE) that conditionally executes a block of code. IF can optionally be combined with one or more ELSEIF commands, one or more ELSEIFNOT commands, and/or an ELSE command to form sophisticated conditional structures.

IF tests *Condition(s)* and, if true, executes *IfStatement(s)*. If *Condition(s)* is false, the following optional ELSEIF *Condition(s)*, and/or ELSEIFNOT *Condition(s),* are tested, in order, until a valid condition line is found, then the associated *ElseIfStatement(s)*, or *ElseIfNotStatement(s)*, block is executed. The optional *ElseStatement(s)* block is executed if no previous valid condition lines are found.

A "valid" condition is one that evaluates to TRUE for a positive conditional statement (IF or ELSEIF) or evaluates to FALSE for a negative conditional statement (ELSEIFNOT).

Indention is Critical

IMPORTANT: Indention is critical. The Spin language relies on indention (of one space or more) on lines following conditional commands to determine if they belong to that command or not. To have the Propeller Tool indicate these logically grouped blocks of code on-screen, you can press Ctrl + I to turn on block-group indicators. Pressing Ctrl + I again will disable that feature. See Indenting and Outdenting, page 69, and Block-Group Indicators, page 74.

Simple IF Statement

The most common form of the **IF** conditional command performs an action if, and only if, a condition is true. This is written as an **IF** statement followed by one or more indented lines of code. For example:

```
if X > 10            'If X is greater than 10
  !outa[0]           'Toggle P0
!outa[1]             'Toggle P1
```

This example tests if X is greater than 10; if it is, I/O pin 0 is toggled. Whether or not the **IF** condition was true, I/O pin P1 is toggled next.

Since the `!outa[0]` line is indented from the **IF** line, it belongs to the *IfStatement(s)* block and is executed only if the **IF** condition is true. The next line, `!outa[1]`, is not indented from the **IF** line, so it is executed next whether or not the **IF**'s *Condition(s)* was true. Here's another version of the same example:

```
if X > 10            'If X is greater than 10
  !outa[0]           'Toggle P0
  !outa[1]           'Toggle P1
waitcnt(2_000 + cnt) 'Wait for 2,000 cycles
```

This example is very similar to the first, except there are now two lines of code indented from the **IF** statement. In this case, if X is greater than 10, P0 is toggled then P1 is toggled and finally the `waitcnt` line is executed. If, however, X was not greater than 10, the `!outa[0]` and `!outa[1]` lines are skipped (since they are indented and part of the *IfStatement(s)* block) and the `waitcnt` line is executed (since it is not indented; it is not part of the *IfStatement(s)* block).

Combining Conditions

The *Condition(s)* field is evaluated as one single Boolean condition, but it can be made up of more than one Boolean expression by combining them with the **AND** and **OR** operators; see pages 272-273. For example:

```
if X > 10 AND X < 100    'If X greater than 10 and less than 100
```

This **IF** statement would be true if, and only if, X is greater than 10 and X is also less than 100. In other words, it's true if X is in the range 11 to 99. Sometimes statements like these can be a little difficult to read. To make it easier to read, parentheses can be used to group each sub-condition, such as with the following.

```
if (X > 10) AND (X < 100)'If X greater than 10 and less than 100
```

Using IF with ELSE

The second most common form of the **IF** conditional command performs an action if a condition is true or a different action if that condition is false. This is written as an **IF** statement followed by its *IfStatement(s)* block, then an **ELSE** followed by its *ElseStatement(s)* block, as shown below:

```
if X > 100           'If X is greater than 100
   !outa[0]          'Toggle P0
else                 'Else, X <= 100
   !outa[1]          'Toggle P1
```

Here, if X is greater than 100, I/O pin 0 is toggled, otherwise, X must be less than or equal to 100, and I/O pin 1 is toggled. This **IF...ELSE** construct, as written, always performs either a toggle on P0 or a toggle on P1; never both, and never neither.

Remember, the code that logically belongs to the *IfStatement(s)* or the *ElseStatement(s)* must be indented from the **IF** or the **ELSE**, respectively, by at least one space. Also note that the **ELSE** must be lined up horizontally with the **IF** statement; they must both begin on the same column or the compiler will not know that the **ELSE** goes with that **IF**.

For every **IF** statement, there can be zero or one **ELSE** component. **ELSE** must be the last component in an **IF** statement, appearing after any potential **ELSEIF**s.

Using IF with ELSEIF

The third form of the **IF** conditional command performs an action if a condition is true or a different action if that condition is false but another condition is true, etc. This is written as an **IF** statement followed by its *IfStatement(s)* block, then one or more **ELSEIF** statements followed by their respective *ElseIfStatement(s)* blocks. Here's an example:

```
if X > 100           'If X is greater than 100
   !outa[0]          'Toggle P0
elseif X == 90       'Else If X = 90
```

```
!outa[1]                    'Toggle P1
```

Here, if X is greater than 100, I/O pin 0 is toggled, otherwise, if X equals 90, I/O pin 1 is toggled, and if neither of those conditions were true, neither P0 nor P1 is toggled. This is a slightly shorter way of writing the following code:

```
if X > 100                  'If X is greater than 100
  !outa[0]                  'Toggle P0
else                        'Otherwise,
  if X == 90                'If X = 90
    !outa[1]                'Toggle P1
```

Both of these examples perform the same actions, but the first is shorter and is usually considered easier to read. Note that the ELSEIF, just like the ELSE, must be lined up (start in the same column) as the IF that it is associated with.

Each IF conditional statement can have zero or more ELSEIF statements associated with it. Look at the following:

```
if X > 100                  'If X is greater than 100
  !outa[0]                  'Toggle P0
elseif X == 90              'Else If X = 90
  !outa[1]                  'Toggle P1
elseif X > 50               'Else If X > 50
  !outa[2]                  'Toggle P2
```

We have three conditions and three possible actions here. Just like the previous example, if X is greater than 100, P0 is toggled, otherwise, if X equals 90, P1 is toggled, but if neither of those conditions were true and X is greater than 50, P2 is toggled. If none of those conditions were true, then none of those actions would occur.

There is an important concept to note about this example. If X is 101 or higher, P0 is toggled, or if X is 90, P1 is toggled, or if X is 51 to 89, or 91 to 100, P2 is toggled. This is because the IF and ELSEIF conditions are tested, one at a time, in the order they are listed and only the first condition that is true has its block of code executed; no further conditions are tested after that. This means that if we had rearranged the two ELSEIFs so that the "X > 50" were checked first, we'd have a bug in our code.

We did this below:

```
if X > 100           'If X is greater than 100
   !outa[0]          'Toggle P0
elseif X > 50        'Else If X > 50
   !outa[2]          'Toggle P2
elseif X == 90       'Else If X = 90 <-- ERROR, ABOVE COND.
   !outa[1]          'Toggle P1      <-- SUPERSEDES THIS AND
                     '                       THIS CODE NEVER RUNS
```

The above example contains an error because, while X could be equal to 90, the elseif X == 90 statement would never be tested because the previous one, elseif X > 50, would be tested first, and since it is true, its block is executed and no further conditions of that IF structure are tested. If X were 50 or less, the last ELSEIF condition is tested, but of course, it will never be true.

Using IF with ELSEIF and ELSE

Another form of the IF conditional command performs one of many different actions if one of many different conditions is true, or an alternate action if none of the previous conditions were true. This is written as with an IF, one or more ELSEIFs, and finally an ELSE. Here's an example:

```
if X > 100           'If X is greater than 100
   !outa[0]          'Toggle P0
elseif X == 90       'Else If X = 90
   !outa[1]          'Toggle P1
elseif X > 50        'Else If X > 50
   !outa[2]          'Toggle P2
else                 'Otherwise,
   !outa[3]          'Toggle P3
```

This is just like the example above, except that if none of the IF or ELSEIF conditions are true, P3 is toggled.

The ELSEIFNOT Condition

The ELSEIFNOT condition behaves exactly like ELSEIF except that it uses negative logic; it executes its *ElseIfNotStatement(s)* block only if its *Condition(s)* expression evaluates to FALSE. Multiple ELSEIFNOT and ELSEIF conditions can be combined in a single IF conditional command, in any order, between the IF and the optional ELSE.

IFNOT

Test condition(s) and execute a block of code if valid (negative logic).

```
((PUB ¦ PRI))
    IFNOT Condition(s)
    ⇥ IfNotStatement(s)
    〈 ELSEIF Condition(s)
    ⇥ ElseIfStatement(s) 〉...
    〈 ELSEIFNOT Condition(s)
    ⇥ ElseIfNotStatement(s) 〉...
    〈 ELSE
    ⇥ ElseStatement(s) 〉
```

- *Condition(s)* is one or more Boolean expressions to test.
- *IfNotStatement(s)* is a block of one or more lines of code to execute when the IFNOT's *Condition(s)* is false.
- *ElseIfStatement(s)* is an optional block of one or more lines of code to execute when all the previous *Condition(s)* are invalid and the ELSEIF's *Condition(s)* is true.
- *ElseIfNotStatement(s)* is an optional block of one or more lines of code to execute when all the previous *Condition(s)* are invalid and the ELSEIFNOT's *Condition(s)* is false.
- *ElseStatement(s)* is an optional block of one or more lines of code to execute when all the previous *Condition(s)* are invalid.

Explanation

IFNOT is one of the three major conditional commands (IF, IFNOT, and CASE) that conditionally executes a block of code. IFNOT is the complementary (negative) form of IF.

IFNOT tests *Condition(s)* and, if false, executes *IfNotStatement(s)*. If *Condition(s)* is true, the following optional ELSEIF *Condition(s)*, and/or ELSEIFNOT *Condition(s),* are tested, in order, until a valid condition line is found, then the associated *ElseIfStatement(s)*, or *ElseIfNotStatement(s)*, block is executed. The optional *ElseStatement(s)* block is executed if no previous valid condition lines are found.

A "valid" condition is one that evaluates to FALSE for a negative conditional statement (IFNOT, or ELSEIFNOT) or evaluates to TRUE for a positive conditional statement (ELSEIF).

See IF on page 220 for information on the optional components of IFNOT.

INA, INB

Input Registers for 32-bit Ports A and B.

((PUB ¦ PRI))

    INA ⟨[*Pin(s)*]⟩

((PUB ¦ PRI))

    INB ⟨[*Pin(s)*]⟩ (Reserved for future use)

Returns: Current state of I/O *Pin(s)* for Port A or B.

- *Pin(s)* is an optional expression, or a range-expression, that specifies the I/O pin, or pins, to access in Port A (0-31) or Port B (32-63). If given as a single expression, only the pin specified is accessed. If given as a range-expression (two expressions in a range format; x..y) the contiguous pins from the start to end expressions are accessed.

Explanation

INA and INB are two of six registers (DIRA, DIRB, INA, INB, OUTA and OUTB) that directly affect the I/O pins. The INA register contains the current states for each of the 32 I/O pins in Port A; bits 0 through 31 correspond to P0 through P31. The INB register contains the current states for each of the 32 I/O pins in Port B; bits 0 through 31 correspond to P32 through P63.

NOTE: INB is reserved for future use; the Propeller P8X32A does not include Port B I/O pins so only INA is discussed below.

INA is read-only and is not really implemented as a register but rather is just an address that, when accessed as a source item in an expression, reads the Port A I/O pins directly at that moment. In the result, a low (0) bit indicates the corresponding I/O pin senses ground, and a high (1) bit indicates the corresponding I/O pin senses VDD (3.3 volts). Since the Propeller is a CMOS device, the I/O pins sense anything above ½ VDD to be high, so a high means the pin senses approximately 1.65 volts or higher.

Each cog has access to all I/O pins at any given time. Essentially, all I/O pins are directly connected to each cog so that there is no hub-related mutually-exclusive access involved. Each cog has its own INA pseudo-register that gives it the ability to read the I/O pins states (low or high) at any time. The actual I/O pins' values are read, regardless of their designated input or output direction.

Note because of the "wired-OR" nature of the I/O pins, no electrical contention between cogs is possible, yet they can all still access I/O pins simultaneously. It is up to the application developer to ensure that no two cogs cause logical contention on the same I/O pin during run time. Since all cogs share all I/O pins, a cog could use INA to read pins it is using as well as the pins that are in use by one or more other cogs.

Using INA

Read INA to get the state of I/O pins at that moment. The following example assumes Temp was created elsewhere.

```
Temp := INA              'Get state of P0 through P31
```

This example reads the states of all 32 I/O pins of Port A into Temp.

Using the optional *Pin(s)* field, the cog can read one I/O pin (one bit) at a time. For example:

```
Temp := INA[16]          'Get state of P16
```

The above line reads I/O pin 16 and stores its state (0 or 1) in the lowest bit of Temp; all other bits of Temp are cleared.

In Spin, the INA register supports a special form of expression, called a range-expression, which allows you to read a group of I/O pins at once, without reading others outside the specified range. To read multiple, contiguous I/O pins at once, use a range expression (like x..y) in the *Pin(s)* field.

```
Temp := INA[18..15]      'Get states of P18:P15
```

Here, the lowest four bits of Temp (3, 2, 1, and 0) are set to the states of I/O pins 18, 17, 16, and 15, respectively, and all other bits of Temp are cleared to 0.

IMPORTANT: The order of the values in a range-expression affects how it is used. For example, the following swaps the order of the range from the previous example.

```
Temp := INA[15..18]      'Get states of P15:P18
```

Here, Temp bits 3, 2, 1, and 0 are set to the states of I/O pins 15, 16, 17, and 18, respectively.

This is a powerful feature of range-expressions, but if care is not taken it can also cause strange, unintentional results.

LOCKCLR
Clear lock to false and get its previous state.

```
((PUB ┆ PRI))
   LOCKCLR ( ID )
```

Returns: Previous state of lock (TRUE or FALSE).

- *ID* is the ID (0 – 7) of the lock to clear to false.

Explanation
LOCKCLR is one of four lock commands (LOCKNEW, LOCKRET, LOCKSET, and LOCKCLR) used to manage resources that are user-defined and deemed mutually-exclusive. LOCKCLR clears lock ID to FALSE and retrieves the previous state of that lock (TRUE or FALSE).

See About Locks, page 230, and Suggested Rules for Locks, page 231 for information on the typical use of locks and the LOCKxxx commands.

The following assumes that a cog (either this one or another) has already checked out a lock using LOCKNEW and shared the ID with this cog, which saved it as SemID. It also assumes this cog has an array of longs called LocalData.

```
PUB ReadResource | Idx
  repeat until not lockset(SemID)    'wait until we lock the resource
  repeat Idx from 0 to 9            'read all 10 longs of resource
    LocalData[Idx] := long[Idx]
  lockclr(SemID)                    'unlock the resource

PUB WriteResource | Idx
  repeat until not lockset(SemID)    'wait until we lock the resource
  repeat Idx from 0 to 9            'write all 10 longs to resource
    long[Idx] := LocalData[Idx]
  lockclr(SemID)                    'unlock the resource
```

Both of these methods, ReadResource and WriteResource, follow the same rules before and after accessing the resource. First, they wait indefinitely at the first repeat loop until it has locked the resource; i.e.: it has successfully "set" the associated lock. If LOCKSET returns TRUE, the condition "until not lockset..." is FALSE, meaning that some other cog is currently accessing the resource, so that first repeat loop tries again. If LOCKSET returns FALSE, the condition "until not lockset..." is true, meaning we have "locked the resource" and the first repeat loop ends. The second repeat loop in each method reads or writes the resource, via the `long[Idx]` and `LocalData[Idx]` statements. The last line of each method, `lockclr(SemID)`, clears the resource's associated lock to FALSE, logically unlocking or releasing the resource for others to use.

See LOCKNEW, page 230; LOCKRET, page 233; and LOCKSET, page 234 for more information.

LOCKNEW
Check out a new lock and get its ID.

```
((PUB ┆ PRI))
    LOCKNEW
```

Returns: ID (0-7) of the lock checked out, or -1 if none were available.

Explanation
LOCKNEW is one of four lock commands (LOCKNEW, LOCKRET, LOCKSET, and LOCKCLR) used to manage resources that are user-defined and deemed mutually-exclusive. LOCKNEW checks out a unique lock, from the hub, and retrieves the ID of that lock. If no locks were available, LOCKNEW returns -1.

About Locks
A lock is a semaphore mechanism that is used to communicate between to two or more entities. In the Propeller chip, a lock is simply one of eight global bits in a protected register within the Hub. The Hub maintains an inventory of which locks are in use and their current states. Cogs can check out, set, clear, and return locks as needed during run time to indicate whether a custom shared item, such as a block of memory, is available or not. Since locks are managed by the Hub only one cog can affect them at a time, making this an effective control mechanism.

In applications where two or more cogs are sharing the same memory, a tool such as a lock may be required to prevent catastrophic collisions from occurring. The Hub prevents such collisions from occurring on elemental data (such a byte, word or long) at every moment in time, but it can not prevent "logical" collisions on blocks of multiple elements (such as a block of bytes, words, longs or any combination of these). For example, if two or more cogs are sharing a single byte of main memory, each one is guaranteed exclusive access to that byte by nature of the Hub. But if those two cogs share multiple bytes of main memory, the Hub can not prevent one cog from writing a few of those bytes while another cog is reading all of them; all cogs' interactions with those bytes may be interleaved in time. In this case, the developer should design each process (in each cog that shares this memory) so that they cooperatively share the memory block in a non-destructive way. Locks serve as flags that notify each cog when a memory block is safe to manipulate or not.

Using LOCKNEW

A user-defined, mutually-exclusive resource should be initially set up by a cog, then that same cog should use **LOCKNEW** to check out a unique lock in which to manage that resource and pass the ID of that lock to any other cogs that require it. For example:

```
VAR
  byte SemID

PUB SetupSharedResource
  <code to set up user-defined, shared resource here>
  if (SemID := locknew) == -1
    <error, no locks available>
  else
    <share SemID's value with other cogs>
```

The example above calls **LOCKNEW** and stores the result in SemID. If that result is -1, an error occurs. If the SemID is not -1, then a valid lock was checked out and that SemID needs to be shared with other cogs along with the address of the resource that SemID is used for. The method used to communicate the SemID and resource address depends on the application, but typically they are both passed as parameters to the Spin method that is launched into a cog, or as the **PAR** parameter when launching an assembly routine into a cog. See **COGNEW**, page 189.

Suggested Rules for Locks

The following are the suggested rules for using locks.

- Objects needing a lock to manage a user-defined, mutually-exclusive resource should check out a lock using **LOCKNEW** and save the ID returned, we'll call it SemID here. Only one cog should check out this lock. The cog that checked out the lock must communicate SemID to all other cogs that will use the resource.

- Any cog that needs to access the resource must first successfully set the lock SemID. A successful "set" is when LOCKSET(SemID) returns **FALSE**; ie: the lock was not already set. If **LOCKSET** returned **TRUE**, then another cog must be accessing the resource; you must wait and try again later to get a successful "set".

- The cog that has achieved a successful "set" can manipulate the resource as necessary. When done, it must clear the lock via LOCKCLR(SemID) so another cog can have access to the resource. In a well-behaved system, the result of LOCKCLR can be ignored here since this cog is the only one with the logical right to clear it.

- If a resource is no longer needed, or becomes non-exclusive, the associated lock should be returned to the lock pool via LOCKRET (SemID). Usually this is done by the same cog that checked out the lock originally.

Applications should be written such that locks are not accessed with LOCKSET or LOCKCLR unless they are currently checked out.

Note that user-defined resources are not actually locked by either the Hub or the checked-out lock. The lock feature only provides a means for objects to cooperatively lock those resources. It's up to the objects themselves to decide on, and abide by, the rules of lock use and what resource(s) will be governed by them. Additionally, the Hub does not directly assign a lock to the cog that called LOCKNEW, rather it simply marks it as being "checked out" by a cog; any other cog can "return" locks to the pool of available locks. Also, any cog can access any lock through the LOCKCLR and LOCKSET commands even if those locks were never checked out. Doing such things is generally not recommended because of the havoc it can cause with other, well-behaved objects in the application.

See LOCKRET, page 233; LOCKCLR, page 228; and LOCKSET, page 234 for more information.

LOCKRET

Release lock back to lock pool, making it available for future LOCKNEW requests.

((PUB ┊ PRI))
    LOCKRET (*ID*)

- *ID* is the ID (0 – 7) of the lock to return to the lock pool.

Explanation

LOCKRET is one of four lock commands (LOCKNEW, LOCKRET, LOCKSET, and LOCKCLR) used to manage resources that are user-defined and deemed mutually-exclusive. LOCKRET returns a lock, by *ID*, back to the Hub's lock pool so that it may be reused by other cogs at a later time. For example:

    LOCKRET (2)

This example returns Lock 2 back to the Hub. This doesn't prevent cogs from accessing Lock 2 afterwards, it only allows the Hub to reassign it to cogs that call LOCKNEW in the future. Applications should be written such that locks are not accessed with LOCKSET or LOCKCLR unless they are currently checked out.

See About Locks, page 230, and Suggested Rules for Locks, page 231 for information on the typical use of locks and the LOCKxxx commands.

Note that user-defined resources are not actually locked by either the Hub or the checked-out lock. The lock feature only provides a means for objects to cooperatively lock those resources. It's up to the objects themselves to decide on, and abide by, the rules of lock use and what resource(s) will be governed by them. Additionally, the Hub does not directly assign a lock to the cog that called LOCKNEW, rather it simply marks it as being "checked out" by a cog; any other cog can "return" locks to the pool of available locks. Also, any cog can access any lock through the LOCKCLR and LOCKSET commands even if those locks were never checked out. Doing such things is generally not recommended because of the havoc it can cause with other, well-behaved objects in the application.

See LOCKNEW, page 230; LOCKCLR, page 228; and LOCKSET, page234 for more information.

LOCKSET

Set lock to true and get its previous state.

```
((PUB ¦ PRI))
  LOCKSET ( ID )
```

Returns: Previous state of lock (TRUE or FALSE).

- *ID* is the ID (0 – 7) of the lock to set to TRUE.

Explanation

LOCKSET is one of four lock commands (LOCKNEW, LOCKRET, LOCKSET, and LOCKCLR) used to manage resources that are user-defined and deemed mutually-exclusive. LOCKSET sets lock *ID* to TRUE and retrieves the previous state of that lock (TRUE or FALSE).

See About Locks, page 230, and Suggested Rules for Locks, page 231 for information on the typical use of locks and the LOCKxxx commands.

The following assumes that a cog (either this one or another) has already checked out a lock using LOCKNEW and shared the *ID* with this cog, which saved it as SemID. It also assumes this cog has an array of longs called LocalData.

```
PUB ReadResource | Idx
  repeat until not lockset(SemID)    'wait until we lock the resource
  repeat Idx from 0 to 9             'read all 10 longs of resource
    LocalData[Idx] := long[Idx]
  lockclr(SemID)                     'unlock the resource

PUB WriteResource | Idx
  repeat until not lockset(SemID)    'wait until we lock the resource
  repeat Idx from 0 to 9             'write all 10 longs to resource
    long[Idx] := LocalData[Idx]
  lockclr(SemID)                     'unlock the resource
```

Both of these methods, ReadResource and WriteResource, follow the same rules before and after accessing the resource. First, they wait indefinitely at the first repeat loop until it has locked the resource; i.e.: it has successfully "set" the associated lock. If LOCKSET returns TRUE, the condition "until not lockset…" is false, meaning that some other cog is currently accessing the resource, so that first repeat loop tries again. If LOCKSET returns FALSE, the condition "until not lockset…" is true, meaning we have "locked the resource" and the first repeat loop ends. The second repeat loop in each method reads or writes the resource, via the `long[Idx]` and `LocalData[Idx]` statements. The last line of each method, `lockclr(SemID)`, clears the resource's associated lock to FALSE, logically unlocking or releasing the resource for others to use.

See LOCKNEW, page 230; LOCKRET, page 233; and LOCKCLR, page 228 for more information.

LONG

Declare long-sized symbol, long aligned/sized data, or read/write a long of main memory.

VAR
 LONG *Symbol* 〈[*Count*]〉

DAT
 LONG *Data*

((PUB ┊ PRI))
 LONG [*BaseAddress*] 〈[*Offset*]〉

- *Symbol* is the desired name for the variable.
- *Count* is an optional expression indicating the number of long-sized elements for *Symbol*, arranged in an array from element 0 to element *Count*-1.
- *Data* is a constant expression or comma-separated list of constant expressions.
- *BaseAddress* is an expression describing the address of main memory to read or write. If *Offset* is omitted, *BaseAddress* is the actual address to operate on. If *Offset* is specified, *BaseAddress* + *Offset* is the actual address to operate on.
- *Offset* is an optional expression indicating the offset from *BaseAddress* to operate on.

Explanation

LONG is one of three multi-purpose declarations (BYTE, WORD, and LONG) that declares or operates on memory. LONG can be used to:

 1) declare a long-sized (32-bit) symbol or a multi-long symbolic array in a VAR block, or
 2) declare long-aligned, and/or long-sized, data in a DAT block, or
 3) read or write a long of main memory at a base address with an optional offset.

Long Variable Declaration (Syntax 1)

In VAR blocks, syntax 1 of LONG is used to declare global, symbolic variables that are either long-sized, or are any array of longs. For example:

```
VAR
  long  Temp              'Temp is a long (2 words, 4 bytes)
  long  List[25]          'List is a long array
```

The above example declares two variables (symbols), Temp and List. Temp is simply a single, long-sized variable. The line under the Temp declaration uses the optional *Count* field to create an array of 25 long-sized variable elements called List. Both Temp and List can be accessed from any PUB or PRI method within the same object that this VAR block was declared; they are global to the object. An example of this is below.

```
PUB SomeMethod
  Temp := 25_000_000        'Set Temp to 25,000,000
  List[0] := 500_000        'Set first element of List to 500,000
  List[1] := 9_000          'Set second element of List to 9,000
  List[24] := 60            'Set last element of List to 60
```

For more information about using LONG in this way, refer to the VAR section's Variable Declarations (Syntax 1) on page 315, and keep in mind that LONG is used for the *Size* field in that description.

Long Data Declaration (Syntax 2)

In DAT blocks, syntax 2 of LONG is used to declare long-aligned, and/or long-sized data that is compiled as constant values in main memory. DAT blocks allow this declaration to have an optional symbol preceding it which can be used for later reference (see DAT, page 208). For example:

```
DAT
  MyData  long  640_000, $BB50           'Long-aligned/sized data
  MyList  byte  long $FF995544, long 1_000  'Byte-aligned/long-sized
```

The above example declares two data symbols, MyData and MyList. MyData points to the start of long-aligned and long-sized data in main memory. MyData's values, in main memory, are 640,000 and $0000BB50, respectively. MyList uses a special DAT block syntax of LONG that creates a byte-aligned but long-sized set of data in main memory. MyList's values, in main memory, are $FF995544 and 1,000, respectively. When accessed a byte at a time, MyList contains $44, $55, $99, $FF, 232 and 3, 0 and 0 since the data is stored in little-endian format.

Note: MyList could have been defined as word-aligned, long-sized data if the "byte" reference were replaced with "word".

This data is compiled into the object and resulting application as part of the executable code section and may be accessed using the read/write form, syntax 3, of LONG (see below). For more information about using LONG in this way, refer to the DAT section's Declaring Data (Syntax 1) on page 208, and keep in mind that LONG is used for the *Size* field in that description.

Reading/Writing Longs of Main Memory (Syntax 3)

In PUB and PRI blocks, syntax 3 of LONG is used to read or write long-sized values of main memory. In the following two examples, we'll assume our object contained the DAT block from the example above, and we will demonstrate two different ways to access that data.

First, let's try accessing the data directly using the labels we provided in our data block.

```
PUB GetData | Index, Temp
  Temp := MyData                  'Read first long of MyData into Temp
  <do something with Temp>        'Perform task with Temp

  repeat Index from 0 to 1        'Repeat two times
    Temp := MyList[Index]         'Read data into Temp 1 long at a time
    <do something with Temp>      'Perform task with value in Temp
```

The first line inside of the GetData method, Temp := MyData, reads the first value in the MyData list (the long-sized value 640,000) and stores it in Temp. Further down, in the REPEAT loop, the Temp := MyList[Index] line reads a byte of main memory from the location of MyList + Index. The first time through the loop (Index = 0) the value $44 ($FF995544's byte 0) is read from MyList and the second time through the loop (Index = 1) the next byte is read, $55 ($FF995544's byte 1). Why were bytes read instead of longs? MyList points at the start of our desired data and our data was specified as long-sized data but the symbol MyList is treated as a byte pointer since that data was specified to be byte-aligned.

Perhaps you intended to read long-sized data from MyList just like we did from MyData. Coincidentally, even though MyList is declared as byte-aligned long data, it is also happens to be long-aligned as well because the previous declaration finished on a long boundary. This fact allows us to use the LONG declaration to achieve our goal.

```
PUB GetData | Index, Temp
  Temp := LONG[@MyData]             'Read first long of MyData into Temp
  <do something with Temp>          'Perform task with Temp

  repeat Index from 0 to 1          'Repeat two times
    Temp := LONG[@MyList][Index]    'Read data to Temp 1 long at a time
    <do something with Temp>        'Perform task with value in Temp
```

In this example, the first line inside of the GetData method uses the LONG declaration to read a long of main memory from the address of MyData and stores it in Temp, in this case, the value 640,000. Further down, in the REPEAT loop, the LONG declaration reads a long of main memory from the address of MyList + Index and stores it in Temp. Since the first iteration of the loop has Index set to 0, the first long of MyList is read, $FF995544. The next time through the loop it reads the next long, effectively @MyList + 1 (the 1,000).

Note that if the data was not long-aligned, either intentionally or coincidentally, we'd have different results from the REPEAT loop just described. For example, if MyList happened to be shifted forward by one byte, the first value read by the loop would be $995544xx; where xx is an unknown byte-sized value. Similarly, the second value read would be 256255; made up of the $FF from the upper byte of MyList's first value, and the 3 and 232 from the lower two bytes of MyList's second value. Make sure to pay close attention to data value alignments in memory to avoid this likely unintentional result.

Using a similar syntax, longs of main memory can be written to as well, as long as they are RAM locations. For example:

```
LONG[@MyList][0] := 2_000_000_000     'Write 2 billion to first word
                                      'of MyList
```

This line writes the value 2,000,000,000 to the first long of data at MyList.

LONGFILL

Fill longs of main memory with a value.

((PUB ┆ PRI))
   LONGFILL (*StartAddress*, *Value*, *Count*)

- *StartAddress* is an expression indicating the location of the first long of memory to fill with *Value*.
- *Value* is an expression indicating the value to fill longs with.
- *Count* is an expression indicating the number of longs to fill, starting with *StartAddress*.

Explanation

LONGFILL is one of three commands (BYTEFILL, WORDFILL, and LONGFILL) used to fill blocks of main memory with a specific value. WORDFILL fills *Count* longs of main memory with *Value*, starting at location *StartAddress*.

Using LONGFILL

LONGFILL is a great way to clear large blocks of long-sized memory. For example:

```
VAR
  long    Buff[100]

PUB Main
  longfill(@Buff, 0, 100)     'Clear Buff to 0
```

The first line of the Main method, above, clears the entire 100-long (400-byte) Buff array to all zeros. LONGFILL is faster at this task than a dedicated REPEAT loop is.

LONGMOVE

Copy longs from one region to another in main memory.

((PUB ¦ PRI))
    LONGMOVE (*DestAddress, SrcAddress, Count*)

- *DestAddress* is an expression specifying the main memory location to copy the first long of source to.
- *SrcAddress* is an expression specifying the main memory location of the first long of source to copy.
- *Count* is an expression indicating the number of longs of the source to copy to the destination.

Explanation

LONGMOVE is one of three commands (BYTEMOVE, WORDMOVE, and LONGMOVE) used to copy blocks of main memory from one area to another. LONGMOVE copies *Count* longs of main memory starting from *SrcAddress* to main memory starting at *DestAddress*.

Using LONGMOVE

LONGMOVE is a great way to copy large blocks of long-sized memory. For example:

```
VAR
    long    Buff1[100]
    long    Buff2[100]

PUB Main
    longmove(@Buff2, @Buff1, 100)      'Copy Buff1 to Buff2
```

The first line of the Main method, above, copies the entire 100-long (400-byte) Buff1 array to the Buff2 array. LONGMOVE is faster at this task than a dedicated REPEAT loop is.

LOOKDOWN, LOOKDOWNZ – Spin Language Reference

LOOKDOWN, LOOKDOWNZ

Get the index of a value in a list.

((PUB ┊ PRI))
    LOOKDOWN (*Value* : *ExpressionList*)

((PUB ┊ PRI))
    LOOKDOWNZ (*Value* : *ExpressionList*)

Returns: One-based index position (LOOKDOWN) or a zero-based index position (LOOKDOWNZ) of *Value* in *ExpressionList*, or 0 if *Value* not found.

- *Value* is an expression indicating the value to find in *ExpressionList*.
- *ExpressionList* is a comma-separated list of expressions. Quoted strings of characters are also allowed; they are treated as a comma-separated list of characters.

Explanation

LOOKDOWN and LOOKDOWNZ are commands that retrieve indexes of values from a list of values. LOOKDOWN returns the one-based index position (1..N) of *Value* from *ExpressionList*. LOOKDOWNZ is just like LOOKDOWN except it returns the zero-based index position (0..N−1). For both commands, if *Value* is not found in *ExpressionList* then 0 is returned.

Using LOOKDOWN or LOOKDOWNZ

LOOKDOWN and LOOKDOWNZ are useful for mapping a set of non-contiguous numbers (25, -103, 18, etc.) to a set of contiguous numbers (1, 2, 3, etc. –or– 0, 1, 2, etc.) where no algebraic expression can be found to do so concisely. The following example assumes Print is a method created elsewhere.

```
PUB ShowList | Index
  Print(GetIndex(25))
  Print(GetIndex(300))
  Print(GetIndex(2510))
  Print(GetIndex(163))
  Print(GetIndex(17))
  Print(GetIndex(8000))
  Print(GetIndex(3))

PUB GetIndex(Value): Index
  Index := lookdown(Value: 25, 300, 2_510, 163, 17, 8_000, 3)
```

The GetIndex method in this example uses LOOKDOWN to find Value and returns the index where it was found in the *ExpressionList*, or 0 if not found. The ShowList method calls GetIndex repeatedly with different values and prints the resulting index on a display. Assuming Print is a method that displays a value, this example will print 1, 2, 3, 4, 5, 6 and 7 on a display.

If LOOKDOWNZ were used instead of LOOKDOWN this example would print 0, 1, 2, 3, 4, 5, and 6 on a display.

If *Value* is not found, LOOKDOWN, or LOOKDOWNZ, returns 0. So if one of the lines of the ShowList method was, Print(GetIndex(50)), the display would show 0 at the time it was executed.

If using LOOKDOWNZ, keep in mind that it may return 0 if either *Value* was not found or *Value* is at index 0. Make sure this will not cause an error in your code or use LOOKDOWN instead.

LOOKUP, LOOKUPZ

Get value from an indexed position within a list.

((PUB ⦙ PRI))
   LOOKUP (*Index* : *ExpressionList*)

((PUB ⦙ PRI))
   LOOKUPZ (*Index* : *ExpressionList*)

Returns: Value at the one-based *Index* position (LOOKUP) or zero-based *Index* position (LOOKUPZ) of *ExpressionList*, or 0 if out-of-range.

- *Index* is an expression indicating the position of the desired value in *ExpressionList*. For LOOKUP, *Index* is one-based (1..N). For LOOKUPZ, *Index* is zero-based (0..N-1).
- *ExpressionList* is a comma-separated list of expressions. Quoted strings of characters are also allowed; they are treated as a comma-separated list of characters.

Explanation

LOOKUP and LOOKUPZ are commands that retrieve entries from a list of values. LOOKUP returns the value from *ExpressionList* that is located in the one-based position (1..N) given by *Index*. LOOKUPZ is just like LOOKUP except it uses a zero-based *Index* (0..N-1). For both commands, if *Index* is out of range then 0 is returned.

Using LOOKUP or LOOKUPZ

LOOKUP and LOOKUPZ are useful for mapping a contiguous set of numbers (1, 2, 3, etc. –or– 0, 1, 2, etc.) to a set of non-contiguous numbers (45, -103, 18, etc.) where no algebraic expression can be found to do so concisely. The following example assumes Print is a method created elsewhere.

```
PUB ShowList | Index, Temp
  repeat Index from 1 to 7
    Temp := lookup(Index: 25, 300, 2_510, 163, 17, 8_000, 3)
    Print(Temp)
```

This example looks up all the values in LOOKUP's *ExpressionList* and displays them. The REPEAT loop counts with Index from 1 to 7. Each iteration of the loop, LOOKUP uses Index to retrieve a value from its list. If Index equals 1, the value 25 is returned. If Index equals 2, the value 300 is returned. Assuming Print is a method that displays the value of Temp, this example will print 25, 300, 2510, 163, 17, 8000 and 3 on a display.

If LOOKUPZ is used, the list is zero-based (0..N-1) instead of one-based; an Index of 0 returns 25, Index of 1 returns 300, etc.

If *Index* is out of range 0 is returned. So, for LOOKUP, if the REPEAT statement went from 0 to 8, instead of 1 to 7, this example would print 0, 25, 300, 2510, 163, 17, 8000, 3 and 0 on a display.

NEXT

Skip remaining statements of REPEAT loop and continue with the next loop iteration.

((PUB ┊ PRI))
   NEXT

Explanation

NEXT is one of two commands (NEXT and QUIT) that affect REPEAT loops. NEXT causes any further statements in the REPEAT loop to be skipped and the next iteration of the loop to be started thereafter.

Using NEXT

NEXT is typically used as an exception case, in a conditional statement, in REPEAT loops to move immediately to the next iteration of the loop. For example, assume that X is a variable created earlier and Print () is a method created elsewhere that prints a value on a display:

```
repeat X from 0 to 9        'Repeat 10 times
  if X == 4
    next                    'Skip if X = 4
  byte[$7000][X] := 0       'Clear RAM locations
  Print(X)                  'Print X on screen
```

The above code iteratively clears RAM locations and prints the value of X on a display, but with one exception. If X equals 4, the IF statement executes the NEXT command which causes the loop to skip remaining lines and go right to the next iteration. This has the effect of clearing RAM locations $7000 through $7003 and locations $7005 through $7009 and printing 0, 1, 2, 3, 5, 6, 7, 8, 9 on the display.

The NEXT command can only be used within a REPEAT loop; an error will occur otherwise.

OBJ

Declare an Object Block.

OBJ
    Symbol ⟨*[Count]*⟩: *"ObjectName"* ⟨ ↪ *Symbol* ⟨*[Count]*⟩: *"ObjectName"*⟩...

- **Symbol** is the desired name for the object symbol.
- **Count** is an optional expression, enclosed in brackets, that indicates this is an array of objects, with *Count* number of elements. When later referencing these elements, they begin with element 0 and end with element *Count*-1.
- **ObjectName** is the filename, without extension, of the desired object. Upon compile, an object with this filename is searched for in the editor tabs, the working directory and the library directory. The object name can contain any valid filename characters; disallowed characters are \, /, :, *, ?, ", <, >, and |.

Explanation

The Object Block is a section of source code that declares which objects are used and the object symbols that represent them. This is one of six special declarations (CON, VAR, OBJ, PUB, PRI, and DAT) that provide inherent structure to the Spin language.

Object declarations begin with OBJ on a line by itself followed by one or more declarations. OBJ must start in column 1 (the leftmost column) of the line it is on and we recommend the lines following be indented by at least one space. For example:

```
OBJ
  Num  : "Numbers"
  Term : "TV_Terminal"
```

This example defines Num as an object symbol of type "Numbers" and Term as an object symbol of type "TV_Terminal". Public and Private methods can then refer to these objects using the object symbols as in the following example.

```
PUB Print | S
  S := Num.ToStr (LongVal, Num#DEC)
  Term.Str (@S)
```

This public method, Print, calls the Numbers' ToStr method and also the TV_Terminal's Str method. It does this by using the Num and Term object symbols followed by the Object-

Method reference symbol (a period '.') and finally the name of the method to call. Num.ToStr, for instance, calls the Numbers object's public ToStr method. Term.Str calls the TV_Terminal's public Str method. In this case the Num.ToStr has two parameters, in parentheses, and Term.Str has one parameter.

Also notice that the second parameter of the Num.ToStr call is Num#DEC. The # symbol is the Object-Constant reference symbol; it gives access to an object's constants. In this case, Num#DEC refers to the DEC (decimal format) constant in the Numbers object.

See Object-Method Reference '.' and Object-Constant Reference '#'> in Table 4-16: Symbols on page 312 for more information.

Multiple instances of an object can be declared with the same object symbol using array syntax and can be accessed similar to arrays as well. For example:

```
OBJ
  PWM[2] : "PWM"
PUB GenPWM
  PWM[0].Start
  PWM[1].Start
```

This example declares PWM as an array of two objects (two instances of the same object). The object itself just happens to be called "PWM" as well. The public method, GenPWM, calls the Start method of each instance using indexes 0 and 1 with the object symbol array, PWM.

Both instances of the PWM object are compiled into the application such that there is one copy of its program code (PUBs, PRIs, and DATs) and two copies of its variable blocks (VARs). This is because, for each instance, the code is the same but each instance needs its own variable space so it can operate independent of the other.

An important point to consider with multiple instances of an object is that there is only one copy of its DAT block because it may contain Propeller Assembly code. DAT blocks can also contain initialized data and regions set aside for workspace purposes, all with symbolic names. Since there is only one copy of it for multiple instances of an object, that area is shared among all instances. This provides a convenient way to create shared memory between multiple instances of a particular object.

Scope of Object Symbols

Object symbols defined in Object Blocks are global to the object in which they are defined but are not available outside of that object. This means that these object symbols can be accessed directly from anywhere within the object but their name will not conflict with symbols defined in other parent or child objects.

Operators

The Propeller chip features a powerful set of math and logic operators. A subset of these operators is supported by the Propeller Assembly language; however, since the Spin language has a use for every form of operator supported by the Propeller, this section describes every operator in detail. Please see the Operators section on page 390 for a list of operators available in Propeller Assembly.

Expression Workspace

The Propeller is a 32-bit device and, unless otherwise noted, expressions are always evaluated using 32-bit, signed integer math. This includes intermediate results as well. If any intermediate result overflows or underflows a 32-bit signed integer (above 2,147,483,647 or below -2,147,483,648), the final result of the expression will not be as expected. A workspace of 32 bits provides lots of room for intermediate results but it is still wise to keep overflow/underflow possibilities in mind.

If fractional underflow is an issue, or if real numbers rather than integers are desired in an expression, floating-point support can help. The compiler supports 32-bit floating-point values and constant expressions with many of the same math operators as it does for integer constant expressions. Note that this is for constant expressions only, not run time variable expressions. For floating-point run-time expressions, the Propeller chip provides support through the FloatMath object supplied with the software installation. See Constant Assignment '=', page 254; FLOAT, page 216; ROUND, page 303; and TRUNC, page 314, as well as the FloatMath and FloatString objects for more information

Operator Attributes

The operators have the following important attributes, each of which is shown in the following two tables and further explained afterwards:

- Unary / Binary
- Normal / Assignment
- Constant and/or Variable Expression
- Level of Precedence

Normal Operator	Assignment Operator	Constant Expressions[1]		Is Unary	Description, Page Number
		Integer	Float		
=	always	n/a[1]	n/a[1]		Constant assignment (CON blocks), 254
:=	always	n/a[1]	n/a[1]		Variable assignment (PUB/PRI blocks), 255
+	+=	✓	✓		Add, 255
+	never	✓	✓	✓	Positive (+X); unary form of Add, 256
-	-=	✓	✓		Subtract, 256
-	if solo	✓	✓	✓	Negate (-X); unary form of Subtract, 256
--	always			✓	Pre-decrement (--X) or post-decrement (X--), 257
++	always			✓	Pre-increment (++X) or post-increment (X++), 257
*	*=	✓	✓		Multiply and return lower 32 bits (signed), 258
**	**=	✓			Multiply and return upper 32 bits (signed), 259
/	/=	✓	✓		Divide (signed), 259
//	//=	✓			Modulus (signed), 260
#>	#>=	✓	✓		Limit minimum (signed), 260
<#	<#=	✓	✓		Limit maximum (signed), 261
^^	if solo	✓	✓	✓	Square root, 261
||	if solo	✓	✓	✓	Absolute value, 261
~	always			✓	Sign-extend from bit 7 (~X) or post-clear to 0 (X~); all bits low, 262
~~	always			✓	Sign-extend from bit 15 (~~X) or post-set to -1 (X~~); all bits high, 263
~>	~>=	✓			Shift arithmetic right, 264
?	always			✓	Random number forward (?X) or reverse (X?), 264
|<	if solo	✓		✓	Bitwise: Decode value (0 - 31) into single-high-bit long, 265
>|	if solo	✓		✓	Bitwise: Encode long into value (0 - 32) as high-bit priority, 266
<<	<<=	✓			Bitwise: Shift left, 266
>>	>>=	✓			Bitwise: Shift right, 267
<-	<-=	✓			Bitwise: Rotate left, 267
->	->=	✓			Bitwise: Rotate right, 268
><	><=	✓			Bitwise: Reverse, 268
&	&=	✓			Bitwise: AND, 269
		|=	✓			Bitwise: OR, 270
^	^=	✓			Bitwise: XOR, 271
!	if solo	✓		✓	Bitwise: NOT, 272
AND	AND=	✓	✓		Boolean: AND (promotes non-0 to -1), 272
OR	OR=	✓	✓		Boolean: OR (promotes non-0 to -1), 273
NOT	if solo	✓	✓	✓	Boolean: NOT (promotes non-0 to -1), 274
==	===	✓	✓		Boolean: Is equal, 275
<>	<>=	✓	✓		Boolean: Is not equal, 275
<	<=	✓	✓		Boolean: Is less than (signed), 276
>	>=	✓	✓		Boolean: Is greater than (signed), 277
=<	=<=	✓	✓		Boolean: Is equal or less (signed), 277
=>	=>=	✓	✓		Boolean: Is equal or greater (signed), 277
@	never	✓		✓	Symbol address, 278
@@	never			✓	Object address plus symbol, 278

Table 4-9: Math and Logic Operators

[1] Assignment forms of operators are not allowed in constant expressions.

Table 4-10: Operator Precedence Levels			
Level	Notes	Operators	Operator Names
Highest (0)	Unary	`--, ++, ~, ~~, ?, @, @@`	Inc/Decrement, Clear, Set, Random, Symbol/Object Address
1	Unary	`+, -, ^^, ||, |<, >|, !`	Positive, Negate, Square Root, Absolute, Decode, Encode, Bitwise NOT
2		`->, <-, >>, <<, ~>, ><`	Rotate Right/Left, Shift Right/Left, Shift Arithmetic Right, Reverse
3		`&`	Bitwise AND
4		`|, ^`	Bitwise OR, Bitwise XOR
5		`*, **, /, //`	Multiply-Low, Multiply-High, Divide, Modulus
6		`+, -`	Add, Subtract
7		`#>, <#`	Limit Minimum/Maximum
8		`<, >, <>, ==, =<, =>`	Boolean: Less/Greater Than, Not Equal, Equal, Equal or Less/Greater
9	Unary	`NOT`	Boolean NOT
10		`AND`	Boolean AND
11		`OR`	Boolean OR
Lowest (12)		`=, :=,  all other assignments`	Constant/Variable Assignment, assignment forms of Binary Operators

Unary / Binary

Each operator is either unary or binary in nature. Unary operators are those that operate on only one operand. For example:

```
!Flag      ' bitwise NOT of Flag
^^Total    ' square root of Total
```

Binary operators are those that operate on two operands. For example:

```
X + Y      ' add X and Y
Num << 4 ' shift Num left 4 bits
```

Note that the term "binary operator" means "two operands," and has nothing to do with binary digits. To distinguish operators whose function relates to binary digits, we'll use the term "bitwise" instead.

Normal / Assignment

Normal operators, like Add '+' and Shift Left '<<', operate on their operand(s) and provide the result for use by the rest of the expression, without affecting the operand or operands themselves. Those that are assignment operators, however, write their result to either the variable they operated on (unary), or to the variable to their immediate left (binary), in addition to providing the result for use by the rest of the expression.

Here are assignment operator examples:

```
Count++      ' (Unary) evaluate Count + 1
             ' and write result to Count
Data >>= 3   ' (Binary) shift Data right 3 bits
             ' and write result to Data
```

Binary operators have special forms that end in equal '=' to make them assignment operators. Unary operators do not have a special assignment form; some always assign while others assign only in special situations. See Table 4-9 below and the operator's explanation, for more information.

Constant and/or Variable Expression

Operators which have the integer-constant-expression attribute can be used both at run time in variable expressions, and at compile time in constant expressions. Operators which have the float-constant-expression attribute can be used in compile-time constant expressions. Operators without either of the constant-expression attributes can only be used at run time in variable expressions. Most operators have a normal, non-assignment form that allows them to be used in both constant and variable expressions.

Level of Precedence

Each operator has an assigned level of precedence that determines when it will take action in relation to other operators within the same expression. For example, it is commonly known that Algebraic rules require multiply and divide operations to be performed before add and subtract operations. The multiply and divide operators are said to have a "higher level of precedence" than add and subtract. Additionally, multiply and divide are commutable; both are on the same precedence level, so their operations result in the same value regardless of the order it is performed (multiply first, then divide, or vice versa). Commutative operators are always evaluated left to right except where parentheses override that rule.

The Propeller chip applies the order-of-operations rules as does Algebra: expressions are evaluated left-to-right, except where parentheses and differing levels of precedence exist.

Following these rules, the Propeller will evaluate:

$$X = 20 + 8 * 4 - 6 / 2$$

...to be equal to 49; that is, $8 * 4 = 32$, $6 / 2 = 3$, and $20 + 32 - 3 = 49$. If you wish the expression to be evaluated differently, use parentheses to enclose the necessary portions of the expression.

For example:

X = (20 + 8) * 4 – 6 / 2

This will evaluate the expression in parentheses first, the 20 + 8, causing the expression to now result in 109, instead of 49.

Table 4-10 indicates each operator's level of precedence from highest (level 0) to lowest (level 12). Operators with a higher precedence are performed before operators of a lower precedence; multiply before add, absolute before multiply, etc. The only exception is if parentheses are included; they override every precedence level.

Intermediate Assignments

The Propeller chip's expression engine allows for, and processes, assignment operators at intermediate stages. This is called "intermediate assignments" and it can be used to perform complex calculations in less code. For example, the following equation relies heavily on X, and X + 1.

```
X := X - 3 * (X + 1) / ||(X + 1)
```

The same statement could be rewritten, taking advantage of the intermediate assignment property of the increment operator:

```
X := X++ - 3 * X / ||X
```

Assuming X started out at -5, both of these statements evaluate to -2, and both store that value in X when done. The second statement, however, does it by relying on an intermediate assignment (the X++ part) in order to simplify the rest of the statement. The Increment operator '++' is evaluated first (highest precedence) and increments X's -5 to -4. Since this is a "post increment" (see Increment, pre- or post- '++', page 257) it first returns X's original value, -5, to the expression and then writes the new value, -4, to X. So, the "X++ - 3..." part of the expression becomes "-5 – 3..." Then the absolute, multiply, and divide operators are evaluated, but the value of X has been changed, so they use the new value, -4, for their operations:

-5 – 3 * -4 / ||-4 → -5 – 3 * -4 / 4 → -5 – 3 * -1 → -5 – -3 = -2

Occasionally, the use of intermediate assignments can compress multiple lines of expressions into a single expression, resulting in slightly smaller code size and slighter faster execution.

The remaining pages of this section further explain each math and logic operator shown in Table 4-9 in the same order shown.

Constant Assignment '='

The Constant Assignment operator is used within CON blocks to declare compile-time constants. For example,

```
CON
  _xinfreq = 4096000
  WakeUp   = %00110000
```

This code sets the symbol _xinfreq to 4,096,000 and the symbol WakeUp to %00110000. Throughout the rest of the program the compiler will use these numbers in place of their respective symbols. See CON, page 194.

These declarations are constant expressions, so many of the normal operators can be used to calculate a final constant value at compile time. For example, it may be clearer to rewrite the above example as follows:

```
CON
  _xinfreq   = 4096000
  Reset      = %00100000
  Initialize = %00010000
  WakeUp     = Reset & Initialize
```

Here, WakeUp is still set to %00110000 at compile time, but it is now more obvious to future readers that the WakeUp symbol contains the binary codes for a Reset and an Initialize sequence for that particular application.

The above examples create 32-bit signed integer constants; however, it is also possible to create 32-bit floating-point constants. To do so, the expression must be expressed as a floating-point value in one of three ways: 1) as an integer value followed by a decimal point and at least one digit, 2) as an integer with an E followed by an exponent value, or 3) both 1 and 2 For example:

```
CON
  OneHalf = 0.5
  Ratio   = 2.0 / 5.0
  Miles   = 10e5
```

The above code creates three floating-point constants. OneHalf is equal to 0.5, Ratio is equal to 0.4 and Miles is equal to 1,000,000. Note that if Ratio were defined as 2 / 5 instead of 2.0 / 5.0, the expression would be treated as an integer constant and the result would be an integer constant equal to 0. For floating-point constant expressions, every value within the expression must be a floating-point value; you cannot mix integer and floating-point values like Ratio = 2 / 5.0. You can, however, use the `FLOAT` declaration to convert an integer value to a floating-point value, such as `Ratio` = FLOAT(2) / 5.0.

The Propeller compiler handles floating-point constants as a single-precision real number as described by the IEEE-754 standard. Single-precision real numbers are stored in 32 bits, with a 1-bit sign, an 8-bit exponent, and a 23-bit mantissa (the fractional part). This provides approximately 7.2 significant decimal digits.

For run-time floating-point operations, the FloatMath and FloatString objects provide math functions compatible with single-precision numbers.

See `FLOAT`, page 216; `ROUND`, page 303; `TRUNC`, page 314, as well as the FloatMath and FloatString objects for more information.

Variable Assignment ':='

The Variable Assignment operator is used within methods (`PUB` and `PRI` blocks) to assign a value to a variable. For example,

```
Temp := 21
Triple := Temp * 3
```

At run time this code would set the `Temp` variable equal to 21 and set `Triple` to 21 * 3, which is 63.

As with other assignment operators, the Variable Assignment operator can be used within expressions to assign intermediate results, such as:

```
Triple := 1 + (Temp := 21) * 3
```

This example first sets `Temp` to 21, then multiplies `Temp` by 3 and adds 1, finally assigning the result, 64, to `Triple`.

Add '+', '+='

The Add operator adds two values together. Add can be used in both variable and constant expressions. Example:

```
X := Y + 5
```

Add has an assignment form, `+=`, that uses the variable to its left as both the first operand and the result destination.

For example,

```
X += 10   'Short form of X := X + 10
```

Here, the value of X is added to 10 and the result is stored back in X. The assignment form of Add may also be used within expressions for intermediate results; see Intermediate Assignments, page 253.

Positive '+' (unary form of Add)

Positive is the unary form of Add and can be used similar to Negate except that it is never an assignment operator. Positive is essentially ignored by the compiler, but is handy when the sign of operands is important to emphasize. For example:

```
Val := +2 - A
```

Subtract '–', '–='

The Subtract operator subtracts two values. Subtract can be used in both variable and constant expressions. Example:

```
X := Y - 5
```

Subtract has an assignment form, –=, that uses the variable to its left as both the first operand and the result destination. For example,

```
X -= 10   'Short form of X := X - 10
```

Here, 10 is subtracted from the value of X and the result is stored back in X. The assignment form of subtract may also be used within expressions for intermediate results; see Intermediate Assignments, page 253.

Negate '–' (unary form of Subtract)

Negate is the unary form of Subtract. Negate toggles the sign of the value on its right; a positive value becomes negative and a negative value becomes positive. For example:

```
Val := -2 + A
```

Negate becomes an assignment operator when it is the sole operator to the left of a variable on a line by itself. For example:

```
-A
```

This would negate the value of A and store the result back to A.

Decrement, pre- or post- '--'

The Decrement operator is a special, immediate operator that decrements a variable by one and assigns the new value to that same variable. It can only be used in run-time variable expressions. Decrement has two forms, pre-decrement and post-decrement, depending on which side of the variable it appears on. The pre-decrement form appears to the left of a variable and the post-decrement form appears to the right of a variable. This is extremely useful in programming since there are many situations that call for the decrementing of a variable right before or right after the use of that variable's value. For example:

```
Y := --X + 2
```

The above shows the pre-decrement form; it means "decrement before providing the value for the next operation". It decrements the value of X by one, writes that result to X and provides that result to the rest of the expression. If X started out as 5 in this example, --X would store 4 in X, then the expression, 4 + 2 is evaluated, finally writing the result, 6, into Y. After this statement, X equals 4 and Y equals 6.

```
Y := X-- + 2
```

The above shows the post-decrement form; it means "decrement after providing the value for the next operation". It provides the current value of X for the next operation in the expression, then decrements the value of X by one and writes that result to X. If X began as 5 in this example, X-- would provide the current value for the expression (5 + 2) to be evaluated later, then would store 4 in X. The expression 5 + 2 is then evaluated and the result, 7, is stored into Y. After this statement, X equals 4 and Y equals 7.

Since Decrement is always an assignment operator, the rules of Intermediate Assignments (see page 253) apply here. Assume X started out as 5 for the following examples.

```
Y := --X + X
```

Here, X would first be set to 4, then 4 + 4 is evaluated and Y is set to 8.

```
Y := X-- + X
```

Here, X's current value, 5, is saved for the next operation (the Add) and X itself is decremented to 4, then 5 + 4 is evaluated and Y is set to 9.

Increment, pre- or post- '++'

The Increment operator is a special, immediate operator that increments a variable by one and assigns the new value to that same variable. It can only be used in run-time variable expressions. Increment has two forms, pre-increment and post-increment, depending on which side of the variable it appears on. The pre-increment form appears to the left of a variable and the post-increment form appears to the right of a variable. This is extremely useful in programming since there are many situations that call for the incrementing of a variable right before or right after the use of that variable's value. For example:

```
Y := ++X - 4
```

The above shows the pre-increment form; it means "increment before providing the value for the next operation". It increments the value of X by one, writes that result to X and provides that result to the rest of the expression. If X started out as 5 in this example, ++X would store 6 in X, then the expression, 6 - 4 is evaluated, finally writing the result, 2, into Y. After this statement, X equals 6 and Y equals 2.

```
Y := X++ - 4
```

The above shows the post-increment form; it means "increment after providing the value for the next operation". It provides the current value of X for the next operation in the expression, then increments the value of X by one and writes that result to X. If X started out as 5 in this example, X++ would provide the current value for the expression (5 - 4) to be evaluated later, then would store 6 in X. The expression 5 - 4 is then evaluated and the result, 1, is stored into Y. After this statement, X equals 6 and Y equals 1.

Since Increment is always an assignment operator, the rules of Intermediate Assignments (see page 253) apply here. Assume X started out as 5 for the following examples.

```
Y := ++X + X
```

Here, X would first be set to 6, then 6 + 6 is evaluated and Y is set to 12.

```
Y := X++ + X
```

Here, X's current value, 5, is saved for the next operation (the Add) and X itself is incremented to 6, then 5 + 6 is evaluated and Y is set to 11.

Multiply, Return Low '*', '*='

This operator is also called Multiply-Low, or simply Multiply. It can be used in both variable and constant expressions. When used with variable expressions or integer constant expressions, Multiply Low multiplies two values together and returns the lower 32 bits of the 64-bit result. When used with floating-point constant expressions, Multiply Low multiplies two values together and returns the 32-bit single-precision floating-point result. Example:

```
X := Y * 8
```

Multiply-Low has an assignment form, *=, that uses the variable to its left as both the first operand and the result destination. For example,

```
X *= 20   'Short form of X := X * 20
```

Here, the value of X is multiplied by 20 and the lowest 32 bits of the result is stored back in X. The assignment form of Multiply-Low may also be used within expressions for intermediate results; see Intermediate Assignments, page 253.

Multiply, Return High '**', '**='

This operator is also called Multiply-High. It can be used in both variable and integer constant expressions, but not in floating-point constant expressions. Multiply High multiplies two values together and returns the upper 32 bits of the 64-bit result. Example:

```
X := Y ** 8
```

If Y started out as 536,870,912 (2^{29}) then Y ** 8 equals 1; the value in the upper 32 bits of the result.

Multiply-High has an assignment form, **=, that uses the variable to its left as both the first operand and the result destination. For example,

```
X **= 20  'Short form of X := X ** 20
```

Here, the value of X is multiplied by 20 and the upper 32 bits of the result is stored back in X. The assignment form of Multiply-High may also be used within expressions for intermediate results; see Intermediate Assignments, page 253.

Divide '/', '/='

Divide can be used in both variable and constant expressions. When used with variable expressions or integer constant expressions, it divides one value by another and returns the 32-bit integer result. When used with floating-point constant expressions, it divides one value by another and returns the 32-bit single-precision floating-point result. Example:

```
X := Y / 4
```

Divide has an assignment form, /=, that uses the variable to its left as both the first operand and the result destination. For example,

```
X /= 20   'Short form of X := X / 20
```

Here, the value of X is divided by 20 and the integer result is stored back in X. The assignment form of Divide may also be used within expressions for intermediate results; see Intermediate Assignments, page 253.

Modulus '//', '//='

Modulus can be used in both variable and integer constant expressions, but not in floating-point constant expressions. Modulus divides one value by another and returns the 32-bit integer remainder. Example:

```
X := Y // 4
```

If Y started out as 5 then Y // 4 equals 1, meaning the division of 5 by 4 results in a real number whose fractional component equals ¼, or .25.

Modulus has an assignment form, //=, that uses the variable to its left as both the first operand and the result destination. For example,

```
X //= 20 'Short form of X := X // 20
```

Here, the value of X is divided by 20 and the 32-bit integer remainder is stored back in X. The assignment form of Modulus may also be used within expressions for intermediate results; see Intermediate Assignments, page 253.

Limit Minimum '#>', '#>='

The Limit Minimum operator compares two values and returns the highest value. Limit Minimum can be used in both variable and constant expressions. Example:

```
X := Y - 5 #> 100
```

The above example subtracts 5 from Y and limits the result to a minimum value to 100. If Y is 120 then 120 − 5 = 115; it is greater than 100 so X is set to 115. If Y is 102 then 102 − 5 = 97; it is less than 100 so X is set to 100 instead.

Limit Minimum has an assignment form, #>=, that uses the variable to its left as both the first operand and the result destination. For example,

```
X #>= 50 'Short form of X := X #> 50
```

Here, the value of X is limited to a minimum value of 50 and the result is stored back in X. The assignment form of Limit Minimum may also be used within expressions for intermediate results; see Intermediate Assignments, page 253.

Limit Maximum '<#', '<#='

The Limit Maximum operator compares two values and returns the lowest value. Limit Maximum can be used in both variable and constant expressions. Example:

```
X := Y + 21 <# 250
```

The above example adds 21 to Y and limits the result to a maximum value to 250. If Y is 200 then $200 + 21 = 221$; it is less than 250 so X is set to 221. If Y is 240 then $240 + 21 = 261$; it is greater than 250 so X is set to 250 instead.

Limit Maximum has an assignment form, <#=, that uses the variable to its left as both the first operand and the result destination. For example,

```
X <#= 50  'Short form of X := X <# 50
```

Here, the value of X is limited to a maximum value of 50 and the result is stored back in X. The assignment form of Limit Minimum may also be used within expressions for intermediate results; see Intermediate Assignments, page 253.

Square Root '^^'

The Square Root operator returns the square root of a value. Square Root can be used in both variable and constant expressions. When used with variable expressions or integer constant expressions, Square Root returns the 32-bit truncated integer result. When used with floating-point constant expressions, Square Root returns the 32-bit single-precision floating-point result. Example:

```
X := ^^Y
```

Square Root becomes an assignment operator when it is the sole operator to the left of a variable on a line by itself. For example:

```
^^Y
```

This would store the square root of the value of Y back into Y.

Absolute Value '||'

The Absolute Value operator, also called Absolute, returns the absolute value (the positive form) of a number. Absolute Value can be used in both variable and constant expressions. When used with variable expressions or integer constant expressions, Absolute Value returns the 32-bit integer result. When used with floating-point constant expressions, Absolute Value returns the 32-bit single-precision floating-point result. Example:

```
X := ||Y
```

If Y is -15, the absolute value, 15, would be stored into X.

Absolute Value becomes an assignment operator when it is the sole operator to the left of a variable on a line by itself. For example:

```
||Y
```

This would store the absolute value of Y back into Y.

Sign–Extend 7 or Post–Clear '~'

This operator is a special, immediate operator that has a dual purpose depending on which side of the variable it appears on. It can only be used in run-time variable expressions. The Sign-Extend 7 form of the operator appears to the left of a variable and the Post-Clear form appears to the right of a variable.

The following is an example of the Sign-Extend 7 operator form:

```
Y := ~X + 25
```

The Sign-Extend 7 operator in this example extends the sign of the value, X in this case, from bit 7 up to bit 31. A 32-bit signed integer is stored in twos-complement form and the most significant bit (31) indicates the sign of the value (positive or negative). There may be times where calculations on simple data result in byte-sized values that should be treated as a signed integer in the range of -128 to +127. When you need to perform further calculations with those byte-sized values, use the Sign-Extend 7 operator to convert the number into the proper 32-bit signed integer form. In the above example, assume X represents the value -20, which in 8-bit twos-complement form is actually the value 236 (%11101100). The ~X portion of the expression extends the sign bit from bit 7 all the way up to bit 31, converting the number to the proper 32-bit twos-complement form of -20 (%11111111 11111111 11111111 11101100). Adding that sign-extended value to 25 results in 5, the intended result, whereas it would have resulted in 261 without the proper sign extension.

The following is an example of the Post-Clear operator form.

```
Y := X~ + 2
```

The Post-Clear operator in this example clears the variable to 0 (all bits low) after providing its current value for the next operation. In this example if X started out as 5, X~ would provide the current value for the expression (5 + 2) to be evaluated later, then would store 0 in X. The expression 5 + 2 is then evaluated and the result, 7, is stored into X. After this statement, X equals 0 and Y equals 7.

Since Sign-Extend 7 and Post-Clear are always assignment operators, the rules of Intermediate Assignments apply to them (see page 253).

Sign–Extend 15 or Post–Set '~~'

This operator is a special, immediate operator that has a dual purpose depending on which side of the variable it appears on. It can only be used in run-time variable expressions. The Sign-Extend 15 form of the operator appears to the left of a variable and the Post-Set form appears to the right of a variable.

The following is an example of the Sign-Extend 15 operator form:

```
Y := ~~X + 50
```

The Sign-Extend 15 operator in this example extends the sign of the value, X in this case, from bit 15 up to bit 31. A 32-bit signed integer is stored in twos-complement form and the most significant bit (31) indicates the sign of the value (positive or negative). There may be times where calculations on simple data result in word-sized values that should be treated as a signed integer in the range of -32768 to +32767. When you need to perform further calculations with those word-sized values, use the Sign-Extend 15 operator to convert the number into the proper 32-bit signed integer form. In the above example, assume X represents the value -300, which in 16-bit twos-complement form is actually the value 65,236 (%11111110 11010100). The ~~X portion of the expression extends the sign bit from bit 15 all the way up to bit 31, converting the number to the proper 32-bit twos-complement form of -300 (%11111111 11111111 11111110 11010100). Adding that sign-extended value to 50 results in -250, the intended result, whereas it would have resulted in 65,286 without the proper sign extension.

The following is an example of the Post-Set operator form.

```
Y := X~~ + 2
```

The Post-Set operator in this example sets the variable to -1 (all bits high) after providing its current value for the next operation. In this example if X started out as 6, X~~ would provide the current value for the expression (6 + 2) to be evaluated later, then would store -1 in X. The expression 6 + 2 is then evaluated and the result, 8, is stored into Y. After this statement, X equals -1 and Y equals 8.

Since Sign-Extend 15 and Post-Set are always assignment operators, the rules of Intermediate Assignments apply to them (see page 253).

Shift Arithmetic Right '~>', '~>='

The Shift Arithmetic Right operator is just like the Shift Right operator except that it maintains the sign, like a divide by 2, 4, 8, etc on a signed value. Shift Arithmetic Right can be used in variable and integer constant expressions, but not in floating-point constant expressions. Example:

```
X := Y ~> 4
```

The above example shifts Y right by 4 bits, maintaining the sign. If Y is -3200 (%11111111 11111111 11110011 10000000) then -3200 ~> 4 = -200 (%11111111 11111111 11111111 00111000). If the same operation had been done with the Shift Right operator instead, the result would have been 268,435,256 (%00001111 11111111 11111111 00111000).

Shift Arithmetic Right has an assignment form, ~>=, that uses the variable to its left as both the first operand and the result destination. For example,

```
X ~>= 2    'Short form of X := X ~> 2
```

Here, the value of X is shifted right 2 bits, maintaining the sign, and the result is stored back in X. The assignment form of Shift Arithmetic Right may also be used within expressions for intermediate results; see Intermediate Assignments, page 253.

Random '?'

The Random operator is a special, immediate operator that uses a variable's value as a seed to create a pseudo random number and assigns that number to the same variable. It can only be used in run-time variable expressions. Random has two forms, forward and reverse, depending on which side of the variable it appears on. The forward form appears to the left of a variable and the reverse form appears to the right of a variable.

Random generates pseudo-random numbers ranging from -2,147,483,648 to +2,147,483,647. It's called "pseudo-random" because the numbers appear random, but are really generated by a logic operation that uses a "seed" value as a tap into a sequence of over 4 billion essentially random numbers. If the same seed value is used again, the same sequence of numbers is generated. The Propeller chip's Random output is reversible; in fact, specifically it is a 32-bit maximum-length, four-tap LFSR (Linear Feedback Shift Register) with taps in both the LSB (Least Significant Bit, rightmost bit) and the MSB (Most Significant Bit, leftmost bit) allowing for bi-directional operation.

Think of the pseudo-random sequence it generates as simply a static list of over 4 billion numbers. Starting with a particular seed value and moving forward results in a list of a specific set of numbers. If, however, you took that last number generated and used it as the first seed value moving backward, you would end up with a list of the same numbers as before, but in the reverse order. This is handy in many applications.

Here's an example:

```
?X
```

The above shows the Random forward form; it uses X's current value to retrieve the next pseudo-random number in the forward direction and stores that number back in X. Executing ?X again results in yet a different number, again stored back into X.

```
X?
```

The above shows the Random reverse form; it uses X's current value to retrieve the next pseudo-random number in the reverse direction and stores that number back in X. Executing X? again results in yet a different number, again stored back into X.

Since Random is always an assignment operator, the rules of Intermediate Assignments apply to it (see page 253).

Bitwise Decode '|<'

The Bitwise Decode operator decodes a value (0 – 31) into a 32-bit long value with a single bit set high corresponding to the bit position of the original value. Bitwise Decode can be used in variable and integer constant expressions, but not in floating-point constant expressions. Example:

```
Pin := |<PinNum
```

The above example sets Pin equal to the 32-bit value whose single high-bit corresponds to the position indicated by PinNum.

If PinNum is 3, Pin is set equal to %00000000 00000000 00000000 00001000.

If PinNum is 31, Pin is set equal to %10000000 00000000 00000000 00000000.

There are many uses for Bitwise Decode, but one of the most useful is to convert from an I/O pin number to the 32-bit pattern that describes that pin number in relation to the I/O registers. For example, Bitwise Decode is very handy for the mask parameter of the WAITPEQ and WAITPNE commands.

Bitwise Decode becomes an assignment operator when it is the sole operator to the left of a variable on a line by itself. For example:

```
|<PinNum
```

This would store the decoded value of PinNum back into PinNum.

Bitwise Encode '>|'

The Bitwise Encode operator encodes a 32-bit long value into the value (0 – 32) that represents the highest bit set, plus 1. Bitwise Encode can be used in variable and integer constant expressions, but not in floating-point constant expressions. Example:

```
PinNum := >|Pin
```

The above example sets PinNum equal to the number of the highest bit set in Pin, plus 1.

If Pin is %00000000 00000000 00000000 00000000, PinNum is set equal to 0; no bits are set.

If Pin is %00000000 00000000 00000000 10000000, PinNum is set equal to 8; bit 7 is set.

If Pin is %10000000 00000000 00000000 00000000, PinNum is set equal to 32; bit 31 is set.

If Pin is %00000000 00010011 00010010 00100000, PinNum is set equal to 21; bit 20 is the highest bit set.

Bitwise Shift Left '<<', '<<='

The Bitwise Shift Left operator shifts the bits of the first operand left by the number of bits indicated in the second operand. The original MSBs (leftmost bits) drop off and the new LSBs (rightmost bits) are set to zero. Bitwise Shift Left can be used in both variable and integer constant expressions, but not in floating-point constant expressions. Example:

```
X := Y << 2
```

If Y started out as:

%10000000 01110000 11111111 00110101

...the Bitwise Shift Left operator would shift that value left by two bits, setting X to:

%00000001 11000011 11111100 11010100

Since the nature of binary is base-2, shifting a value left is like multiplying that value by powers of two, 2^b, where b is the number of bits shifted.

Bitwise Shift Left has an assignment form, <<=, that uses the variable to its left as both the first operand and the result destination. For example,

```
X <<= 4     'Short form of X := X << 4
```

Here, the value of X is shifted left four bits and is stored back in X. The assignment form of Bitwise Shift Left may also be used within expressions for intermediate results; see Intermediate Assignments, page 253.

Bitwise Shift Right '>>', '>>='

The Bitwise Shift Right operator shifts the bits of the first operand right by the number of bits indicated in the second operand. The original LSBs (rightmost bits) drop off and the new MSBs (leftmost bits) are set to zero. Bitwise Shift Right can be used in both variable and integer constant expressions, but not in floating-point constant expressions. Example:

```
X := Y >> 3
```

If Y started out as:

%10000000 01110000 11111111 00110101

...the Bitwise Shift Right operator would shift that value right by three bits, setting X to:

%00010000 00001110 00011111 11100110

Since the nature of binary is base-2, shifting a value right is like performing an integer divide of that value by powers of two, 2^b, where b is the number of bits shifted.

Bitwise Shift Right has an assignment form, >>=, that uses the variable to its left as both the first operand and the result destination. For example,

```
X >>= 2   'Short form of X := X >> 2
```

Here, the value of X is shifted right two bits and is stored back in X. The assignment form of Bitwise Shift Right may also be used within expressions for intermediate results; see Intermediate Assignments, page 253.

Bitwise Rotate Left '<-', '<-='

The Bitwise Rotate Left operator is similar to the Bitwise Shift Left operator, except that the MSBs (leftmost bits) are rotated back around to the LSBs (rightmost bits). Bitwise Rotate Left can be used in both variable and integer constant expressions, but not in floating-point constant expressions. Example:

```
X := Y <- 4
```

If Y started out as:

%10000000 01110000 11111111 00110101

the Bitwise Rotate Left operator would rotate that value left by four bits, moving the original four MSBs to the four new LSBs, and setting X to:

%00000111 00001111 11110011 01011000

Bitwise Rotate Left has an assignment form, `<-=`, that uses the variable to its left as both the first operand and the result destination. For example,

```
X <-= 1   'Short form of X := X <- 1
```

Here, the value of X is rotated left one bit and is stored back in X. The assignment form of Bitwise Rotate Left may also be used within expressions for intermediate results; see Intermediate Assignments, page 253.

Bitwise Rotate Right '->', '->='

The Bitwise Rotate Right operator is similar to the Bitwise Shift Right operator, except that the LSBs (rightmost bits) are rotated back around to the MSBs (leftmost bits). Bitwise Rotate Right can be used in both variable and integer constant expressions, but not in floating-point constant expressions. Example:

```
X := Y -> 5
```

If Y started out as:

%10000000 01110000 11111111 00110101

...the Bitwise Rotate Right operator would rotate that value right by five bits, moving the original five LSBs to the five new MSBs, and setting X to:

%10101100 00000011 10000111 11111001

Bitwise Rotate Right has an assignment form, `->=`, that uses the variable to its left as both the first operand and the result destination. For example,

```
X ->= 3   'Short form of X := X -> 3
```

Here, the value of X is rotated right three bits and is stored back in X. The assignment form of Bitwise Rotate Right may also be used within expressions for intermediate results; see Intermediate Assignments, page 253.

Bitwise Reverse '><', '><='

The Bitwise Reverse operator returns bits from the first operand in their reverse order, the total number of which is indicated by the second operand. All other bits to the left of the reversed bits are zeros in the result. Bitwise Reverse can be used in both variable and integer constant expressions, but not in floating-point constant expressions. Example:

```
X := Y >< 6
```

If Y started out as:

%10000000 01110000 11111111 00110101

...the Bitwise Reverse operator would return the six LSBs in reverse order with all other bits zero, setting X to:

%00000000 00000000 00000000 00101011

Bitwise Reverse has an assignment form, ><=, that uses the variable to its left as both the first operand and the result destination. For example,

```
X ><= 8   'Short form of X := X >< 8
```

Here, the eight LSBs of the value of X are reversed, all other bits are set to zero and the result is stored back in X. The assignment form of Bitwise Reverse may also be used within expressions for intermediate results; see Intermediate Assignments, page 253.

Bitwise AND '&', '&='

The Bitwise AND operator performs a bitwise AND of the bits of the first operand with the bits of the second operand. Bitwise AND can be used in both variable and integer constant expressions, but not in floating-point constant expressions.

Each bit of the two operands is subject to the following logic:

Table 4-11: Bitwise AND Truth Table		
Bit States		Result
0	0	0
0	1	0
1	0	0
1	1	1

Example:

```
X := %00101100 & %00001111
```

The above example ANDs %00101100 with %00001111 and writes the result, %00001100, to X.

Bitwise AND has an assignment form, &=, that uses the variable to its left as both the first operand and the result destination. For example,

```
X &= $F    'Short form of X := X & $F
```

Here, the value of X is ANDed with $F and the result is stored back in X. The assignment form of Bitwise AND may also be used within expressions for intermediate results; see Intermediate Assignments, page 253.

Be careful not to get Bitwise AND '&' confused with Boolean AND 'AND'. Bitwise AND is for bit manipulation while Boolean AND is for comparison purposes (see page 272).

Bitwise OR '|', '|='

The Bitwise OR operator performs a bitwise OR of the bits of the first operand with the bits of the second operand. Bitwise OR can be used in both variable and integer constant expressions, but not in floating-point constant expressions.

Each bit of the two operands is subject to the following logic:

Table 4-12: Bitwise OR Truth Table		
Bit States		Result
0	0	0
0	1	1
1	0	1
1	1	1

Example:
```
X := %00101100 | %00001111
```

The above example ORs %00101100 with %00001111 and writes the result, %00101111, to X.

Bitwise OR has an assignment form, |=, that uses the variable to its left as both the first operand and the result destination. For example,

```
X |= $F    'Short form of X := X | $F
```

Here, the value of X is ORed with $F and the result is stored back in X. The assignment form of Bitwise OR may also be used within expressions for intermediate results; see Intermediate Assignments, page 253.

Be careful not to get Bitwise OR '|'confused with Boolean OR 'OR'. Bitwise OR is for bit manipulation while Boolean OR is for comparison purposes (see page 273).

Bitwise XOR '∧', '∧='

The Bitwise XOR operator performs a bitwise XOR of the bits of the first operand with the bits of the second operand. Bitwise XOR can be used in both variable and integer constant expressions, but not in floating-point constant expressions.

Each bit of the two operands is subject to the following logic:

Table 4-13: Bitwise XOR Truth Table		
Bit States		Result
0	0	0
0	1	1
1	0	1
1	1	0

Example:

```
X := %00101100 | %00001111
```

The above example XORs %00101100 with %00001111 and writes the result, %00100011, to X.

Bitwise XOR has an assignment form, ∧=, that uses the variable to its left as both the first operand and the result destination. For example,

```
X ∧= $F    'Short form of X := X ∧ $F
```

Here, the value of X is XORed with $F and the result is stored back in X. The assignment form of Bitwise XOR may also be used within expressions for intermediate results; see Intermediate Assignments, page 253.

Bitwise NOT '!'

The Bitwise NOT '!' operator performs a bitwise NOT (inverse, or one's-complement) of the bits of the operand that follows it. Bitwise NOT can be used in both variable and integer constant expressions, but not in floating-point constant expressions.

Each bit of the two operands is subject to the following logic:

Table 4-14: Bitwise NOT Truth Table	
Bit State	Result
0	1
1	0

Example:

```
X := !%00101100
```

The above example NOTs %00101100 and writes the result, %11010011, to X.

Bitwise NOT becomes an assignment operator when it is the sole operator to the left of a variable on a line by itself. For example:

```
!Flag
```

This would store the inverted value Flag back into Flag.

Be careful not to get Bitwise NOT '!' confused with Boolean NOT 'NOT'. Bitwise NOT is for bit manipulation while Boolean NOT is for comparison purposes (see page 274).

Boolean AND 'AND', 'AND='

The Boolean AND 'AND' operator compares two operands and returns TRUE (-1) if both values are TRUE (non-zero), or returns FALSE (0) if one or both operands are FALSE (0). Boolean AND can be used in both variable and constant expressions. Example:

```
X := Y AND Z
```

The above example compares the value of Y with the value of Z and sets X to either: TRUE (-1) if both Y and Z are non-zero, or FALSE (0) if either Y or Z are zero. During the comparison, it promotes each of the two values to -1 if they are non-zero, making any value, other than 0, a -1, so that the comparison becomes: "If Y is true and Z is true…"

Quite often this operator is used in combination with other comparison operators, such as in the following example.

```
IF (Y == 20) AND (Z == 100)
```

This example evaluates the result of Y == 20 against that of Z == 100, and if both are true, the Boolean AND operator returns TRUE (-1).

Boolean AND has an assignment form, AND=, that uses the variable to its left as both the first operand and the result destination. For example,

```
X AND= True      'Short form of X := X AND True
```

Here, the value of X is promoted to TRUE if it is non-zero, then is compared with TRUE and the Boolean result (TRUE / FALSE, -1 / 0) is stored back in X. The assignment form of Boolean AND may also be used within expressions for intermediate results; see Intermediate Assignments, page 253.

Be careful not to get Boolean AND 'AND' confused with Bitwise AND '&'. Boolean AND is for comparison purposes while Bitwise AND is for bit manipulation (see page 269).

Boolean OR 'OR', 'OR='

The Boolean OR 'OR' operator compares two operands and returns TRUE (-1) if either value is TRUE (non-zero), or returns FALSE (0) if both operands are FALSE (0). Boolean OR can be used in both variable and constant expressions. Example:

```
X := Y OR Z
```

The above example compares the value of Y with the value of Z and sets X to either: TRUE (-1) if either Y or Z are non-zero, or FALSE (0) if both Y and Z are zero. During the comparison, it promotes each of the two values to -1 if they are non-zero, making any value, other than 0, a -1, so that the comparison becomes: "If Y is true or Z is true…"

Quite often this operator is used in combination with other comparison operators, such as in the following example.

```
IF (Y == 1) OR (Z > 50)
```

This example evaluates the result of Y == 1 against that of Z > 50, and if either are true, the Boolean OR operator returns TRUE (-1).

Boolean OR has an assignment form, OR=, that uses the variable to its left as both the first operand and the result destination. For example,

```
X OR= Y        'Short form of X := X OR Y
```

Here, the value of X is promoted to TRUE if it is non-zero, then is compared with Y (also promoted to TRUE if non-zero) and the Boolean result (TRUE / FALSE, -1 / 0) is stored back in X. The assignment form of Boolean OR may also be used within expressions for intermediate results; see Intermediate Assignments, page 253.

Be careful not to get Boolean OR 'OR' confused with Bitwise OR'|'. Boolean OR is for comparison purposes while Bitwise OR is for bit manipulation (see page 270).

Boolean NOT 'NOT'

The Boolean NOT 'NOT' operator returns TRUE (-1) if the operand is FALSE (0), or returns FALSE (0) if the operand is TRUE (non-zero). Boolean NOT can be used in both variable and constant expressions. Example:

```
X := NOT Y
```

The above example returns the Boolean opposite of Y; TRUE (-1) if Y is zero, or FALSE (0) if Y is non-zero. During the comparison, it promotes the value of Y to -1 if it is non-zero, making any value, other than 0, a -1, so that the comparison becomes: "If NOT true" or "If NOT false"

Quite often this operator is used in combination with other comparison operators, such as in the following example.

```
IF NOT ( (Y > 9) AND (Y < 21) )
```

This example evaluates the result of (Y > 9 AND Y < 21), and returns the Boolean opposite of the result; TRUE (-1) if Y is in the range 10 to 20, in this case.

Boolean NOT becomes an assignment operator when it is the sole operator to the left of a variable on a line by itself. For example:

```
NOT Flag
```

This would store the Boolean opposite of Flag back into Flag.

Be careful not to get Boolean NOT 'NOT' confused with Bitwise NOT'!'. Boolean NOT is for comparison purposes while Bitwise NOT is for bit manipulation (see page 272).

Boolean Is Equal '==', '==='

The Boolean operator Is Equal compares two operands and returns TRUE (-1) if both values are the same, or returns FALSE (0), otherwise. Is Equal can be used in both variable and constant expressions. Example:

```
X := Y == Z
```

The above example compares the value of Y with the value of Z and sets X to either: TRUE (-1) if Y is the same value as Z, or FALSE (0) if Y is not the same value as Z.

This operator is often used in conditional expressions, such as in the following example.

```
IF (Y == 1)
```

Here, the Is Equal operator returns TRUE if Y equals 1.

Is Equal has an assignment form, ===, that uses the variable to its left as both the first operand and the result destination. For example,

```
X === Y        'Short form of X := X == Y
```

Here, X is compared with Y, and if they are equal, X is set to TRUE (-1), otherwise X is set to FALSE (0). The assignment form of Is Equal may also be used within expressions for intermediate results; see Intermediate Assignments, page 253.

Boolean Is Not Equal '<>', '<>='

The Boolean operator Is Not Equal compares two operands and returns True (-1) if the values are not the same, or returns FALSE (0), otherwise. Is Not Equal can be used in both variable and constant expressions. Example:

```
X := Y <> Z
```

The above example compares the value of Y with the value of Z and sets X to either: TRUE (-1) if Y is not the same value as Z, or FALSE (0) if Y is the same value as Z.

This operator is often used in conditional expressions, such as in the following example.

```
IF (Y <> 25)
```

Here, the Is Not Equal operator returns TRUE if Y is not 25.

Is Not Equal has an assignment form, <>=, that uses the variable to its left as both the first operand and the result destination. For example,

```
X <>= Y        'Short form of X := X <> Y
```

Here, X is compared with Y, and if they are not equal, X is set to TRUE (-1), otherwise X is set to FALSE (0). The assignment form of Is Not Equal may also be used within expressions for intermediate results; see Intermediate Assignments, page 253.

Boolean Is Less Than '<', '<='

The Boolean operator Is Less Than compares two operands and returns TRUE (-1) if the first value is less than the second value, or returns FALSE (0), otherwise. Is Less Than can be used in both variable and constant expressions. Example:

```
X := Y < Z
```

The above example compares the value of Y with the value of Z and sets X to either: TRUE (-1) if Y is less than the value of Z, or FALSE (0) if Y is equal to or greater than the value of Z.

This operator is often used in conditional expressions, such as in the following example.

```
IF (Y < 32)
```

Here, the Is Less Than operator returns TRUE if Y is less than 32.

Is Less Than has an assignment form, <=, that uses the variable to its left as both the first operand and the result destination. For example,

```
X <= Y         'Short form of X := X < Y
```

Here, X is compared with Y, and if X is less than Y, X is set to TRUE (-1), otherwise X is set to FALSE (0). The assignment form of Is Less Than may also be used within expressions for intermediate results; see Intermediate Assignments, page 253.

Boolean Is Greater Than '>', '>='

The Boolean operator Is Greater Than compares two operands and returns TRUE (-1) if the first value is greater than the second value, or returns FALSE (0), otherwise. Is Greater Than can be used in both variable and constant expressions. Example:

```
X := Y > Z
```

The above example compares the value of Y with the value of Z and sets X to either: TRUE (-1) if Y is greater than the value of Z, or FALSE (0) if Y is equal to or less than the value of Z.

This operator is often used in conditional expressions, such as in the following example.

```
IF (Y > 50)
```

Here, the Is Greater Than operator returns TRUE if Y is greater than 50.

Is Greater Than has an assignment form, >=, that uses the variable to its left as both the first operand and the result destination. For example,

```
X >= Y        'Short form of X := X > Y
```

Here, X is compared with Y, and if X is greater than Y, X is set to TRUE (-1), otherwise X is set to FALSE (0). The assignment form of Is Greater Than may also be used within expressions for intermediate results; see Intermediate Assignments, page 253.

Boolean Is Equal or Less '=<', '=<='

The Boolean operator Is Equal or Less compares two operands and returns TRUE (-1) if the first value is equal to or less than the second value, or returns FALSE (0), otherwise. Is Equal or Less can be used in both variable and constant expressions. Example:

```
X := Y =< Z
```

The above example compares the value of Y with the value of Z and sets X to either: TRUE (-1) if Y is equal to or less than the value of Z, or FALSE (0) if Y is greater than the value of Z.

This operator is often used in conditional expressions, such as in the following example.

```
IF (Y =< 75)
```

Here, the Is Equal or Less operator returns TRUE if Y is equal to or less than 75.

Is Equal or Less has an assignment form, =<=, that uses the variable to its left as both the first operand and the result destination. For example,

```
X =<= Y        'Short form of X := X =< Y
```

Here, X is compared with Y, and if X is equal to or less than Y, X is set to TRUE (-1), otherwise X is set to FALSE (0). The assignment form of Is Equal or Less may also be used within expressions for intermediate results; see Intermediate Assignments, page 253.

Boolean Is Equal or Greater '=>', '=>='

The Boolean operator Is Equal or Greater compares two operands and returns TRUE (-1) if the first value is equal to greater than the second value, or returns FALSE (0), otherwise. Is Equal or Greater can be used in both variable and constant expressions. Example:

```
X := Y => Z
```

The above example compares the value of Y with the value of Z and sets X to either: TRUE (-1) if Y is equal to or greater than the value of Z, or FALSE (0) if Y is less than the value of Z.

This operator is often used in conditional expressions, such as in the following example.

```
IF (Y => 100)
```

Here, the Is Equal or Greater operator returns TRUE if Y is equal to or greater than 100.

Is Equal or Greater has an assignment form, =>=, that uses the variable to its left as both the first operand and the result destination. For example,

```
X =>= Y        'Short form of X := X => Y
```

Here, X is compared with Y, and if X is equal to or greater than Y, X is set to TRUE (-1), otherwise X is set to FALSE (0). The assignment form of Is Equal or Greater may also be used within expressions for intermediate results; see Intermediate Assignments, page 253.

Symbol Address '@'

The Symbol Address operator returns the address of the symbol following it. Symbol Address can be used in variable and integer constant expressions, but not in floating-point constant expressions. Example:

```
BYTE[@Str] := "A"
```

In the above example, the Symbol Address operator returns the address of the Str symbol, which is then used by the BYTE memory array reference to store the character "A" at that address.

Symbol Address is often used to pass the address of strings and data structures, defined in a DAT block, to methods that operate on them.

It is important to note that this is a special operator that behaves differently in variable expressions than it does in constant expressions. At run time, like our example above shows, it returns the absolute address of the symbol following it. This run-time, absolute address consists of the object's program base address plus the symbol's offset address.

In constant expressions, it only returns the symbol's offset within the object. It can not return the absolute address, effective at run time, because that address changes depending on the object's actual address at run time. To properly use the Symbol Address in a constant, such as a table of data, see the Object Address Plus Symbol operator, below.

Object Address Plus Symbol '@@'

The Object Address Plus Symbol operator returns the value of the symbol following it plus the current object's program base address. Object Address Plus Symbol can only be used in variable expressions.

This operator is useful when creating a table of offset addresses, then at run time, using those offsets to reference the absolute run-time addresses they represent. For example, a DAT block may contain a number of strings to which you want both direct and indirect access. Here's an example DAT block containing strings.

```
DAT
   Str1   byte   "Hello.", 0
   Str2   byte   "This is an example", 0
   Str3   byte   "of strings in a DAT block.",0
```

At run time we can access those strings directly, using @Str1, @Str2, and @Str3, but accessing them indirectly is troublesome because each string is of a different length; making it difficult to use any of them as a base for indirect address calculations.

The solution might seem to be within reach by simply making another table of the addresses themselves, as in:

```
DAT
   StrAddr   word   @Str1, @Str2, @Str3
```

This creates a table of words, starting at StrAddr, where each word contains the address of a unique string. Unfortunately, for compile-time constants (like those of the StrAddr table), the address returned by @ is only the compile-time offset address, rather than the run-time absolute address, of the symbol. To get the true, run-time address, we need to add the object's program base address to the symbol's offset address. That is what the Object Address Plus Symbol operator does. Example:

```
REPEAT Idx FROM 0 TO 2
   PrintStr (@@StrAddr[Idx])
```

The above example increments Idx from 0 through 2. The StrAddr[Idx] statement retrieves the compile-time offset of the string stored in element Idx of the StrAddr table. The @@ operator in front of the StrAddr[Idx] statement adds the object's base address to the compile-time offset value that was retrieved, resulting in a valid run-time address of the string. The PrintStr method, whose code is not shown in this example, can use that address to process each character of the string.

OUTA, OUTB

Output registers for 32-bit Ports A and B.

((PUB ⁝ PRI))
    OUTA ⟨[*Pin(s)*]⟩

((PUB ⁝ PRI))
    OUTB ⟨[*Pin(s)*]⟩ (Reserved for future use)

Returns: Current value of output *Pin(s)* for Port A or B, if used as a source variable.

- *Pin(s)* is an optional expression, or a range-expression, that specifies the I/O pin, or pins, to access in Port A (0-31) or Port B (32-63). If given as a single expression, only the pin specified is accessed. If given as a range-expression (two expressions in a range format; x..y) the contiguous pins from the start to end expressions are accessed.

Explanation

OUTA and OUTB are two of six registers (DIRA, DIRB, INA, INB, OUTA and OUTB) that directly affect the I/O pins. The OUTA register holds the output states for each of the 32 I/O pins in Port A; bits 0 through 31 correspond to P0 through P31. The OUTB register holds the output states for each of the 32 I/O pins in Port B; bits 0 through 31 correspond to P32 through P63.

NOTE: OUTB is reserved for future use; the Propeller P8X32A does not include Port B I/O pins so only OUTA is discussed below.

OUTA is used to both set and get the current output states of one or more I/O pins in Port A. A low (0) bit sets the corresponding I/O pin to ground. A high (1) bit sets the corresponding I/O pin VDD (3.3 volts). The OUTA register defaults zero, all 0 bits, upon cog startup.

Each cog has access to all I/O pins at any given time. Essentially, all I/O pins are directly connected to each cog so that there is no hub-related mutually-exclusive access involved. Each cog maintains its own OUTA register that gives it the ability to set any I/O pin's output state (low or high). Each cog's output states is OR'd with that of the other cogs' output states and the resulting 32-bit value becomes the output states of Port A pins P0 through P31. The result is that each I/O pin's output state is the "wired-OR" of the entire cog collective. See I/O Pins on page 26 for more information.

Note that each cog's output states are made up of the OR'd states of its internal I/O hardware (Output Register, Video Generator, etc.) and that is all AND'd with its Direction Register's states.

An I/O pin actually outputs low or high, as specified by the cog's output states, if, and only if, that pin's bit in that same cog's direction register (DIRA) is high (1). Otherwise, that cog specifies the pin to be an input and its output state is ignored.

This configuration can easily be described in the following simple rules:

    A. A pin outputs low <u>only</u> if all active cogs that set it to output also set it to low.
    B. A pin outputs high <u>if any</u> active cog sets it to an output and also sets it high.

If a cog is disabled, its direction register is treated as if were cleared to 0, causing it to exert no influence on I/O pin directions and states.

Note because of the "wired-OR" nature of the I/O pins, no electrical contention between cogs is possible, yet they can all still access I/O pins simultaneously. It is up to the application developer to ensure that no two cogs cause logical contention on the same I/O pin during run time.

Using OUTA

Set or clear bits in OUTA to affect the output state of I/O pins as desired. Make sure to also set the corresponding bits of DIRA to make that pin an output. For example:

```
DIRA := %00000100_00110000_00000001_11110000
OUTA := %01000100_00110000_00000001_10010000
```

The DIRA line above sets the I/O pins 25, 21, 20, 8, 7, 6, 5 and 4 to outputs and the rest to inputs. The OUTA line sets I/O pins 30, 25, 21, 20, 8, 7, and 4 to high, the rest to low. The result is that I/O pins 25, 21, 20, 8, 7, and 4 output high and I/O pins 6 and 5 output low. I/O pin 30 is set to an input direction (according to DIRA) so the high in bit 30 of OUTA is ignored and the pin remains an input according to this cog.

Using the optional *Pin(s)* field, and the post-clear (~) and post-set (~~) unary operators, the cog can affect one I/O pin (one bit) at a time. The *Pin(s)* field treats the I/O pin registers as an array of 32 bits. For example:

```
DIRA[10]~~          'Set P10 to output
OUTA[10]~           'Make P10 low
OUTA[10]~~          'Make P10 high
```

The first line in the code above sets I/O pin 10 to output. The second line clears P10's output latch bit, making P10 output low (ground). The third line sets P10's output latch bit, making P10 output high (VDD).

In Spin, the OUTA register supports a special form of expression, called a range-expression, which allows you to affect a group of I/O pins at once, without affecting others outside the specified range. To affect multiple, contiguous I/O pins at once, use a range expression (like x..y) in the *Pin(s)* field.

```
DIRA[12..8]~~            'Set DIRA12:8 (P12-P8 to output)
OUTA[12..8] := %11001    'Set P12:8 to 1, 1, 0, 0, and 1
```

The first line, "DIRA...," sets P12, P11, P10, P9 and P8 to outputs; all other pins remain in their previous state. The second line, "OUTA...," sets P12, P11, and P8 to output high, and P10 and P9 to output low.

IMPORTANT: The order of the values in a range-expression affects how it is used. For example, the following swaps the order of the range from the previous example.

```
DIRA[8..12]~~            'Set DIRA8:12 (P8-P12 to output)
OUTA[8..12] := %11001    'Set OUTA8:12 to 1, 1, 0, 0, and 1
```

Here, DIRA bits 8 through 12 are set to high (like before) but OUTA bits 8, 9, 10, 11 and 12 are set equal to 1, 1, 0, 0, and 1, respectively, making P8, P9 and P12 output high and P10 and P11 output low.

This is a powerful feature of range-expressions, but if care is not taken it can also cause strange, unintentional results.

Normally OUTA is only written to but it can also be read from to retrieve the current I/O pin output latch states. This is ONLY the cog's output latch states, not necessarily the actual output states of the Propeller chip's I/O pins, as they can be further affected by other cogs or even this cog's other I/O hardware (Video Generator, Count A, etc.). The following assumes Temp is a variable created elsewhere:

```
Temp := OUTA[15..13]     'Get output latch state of P15 to P13
```

The above sets Temp equal to OUTA bits 15, 14, and 13; i.e.: the lower 3 bits of Temp are now equal to OUTA15:13 and the other bits of Temp are cleared to zero.

PAR

Cog Boot Parameter register.

```
((PUB ¦ PRI))
    PAR
```

Returns: Address value passed during boot-up with `COGINIT` or `COGNEW`.

Explanation

The `PAR` register contains the address value passed into the *Parameter* field of a `COGINIT` or `COGNEW` command; see `COGINIT`, page 187 and `COGNEW`, page 189. The `PAR` register's contents are used by Propeller Assembly code to locate and operate on memory shared between Spin code and assembly code.

Since the `PAR` register is intended to contain an address upon cog boot-up, the value stored into it via `COGINIT` and `COGNEW` is limited to 14-bits; a 16-bit word with lower two bits cleared to zero.

Using PAR

`PAR` is affected by Spin code and is used by assembly code as a memory pointer mechanism to point to shared main memory between the two. Either the `COGINIT` or `COGNEW` command, when launching Propeller Assembly into a cog, affects the `PAR` register. For example:

```
VAR
  long    Shared                     'Shared variable (Spin & Assy)

PUB Main | Temp
  cognew(@Process, @Shared)          'Launch assy, pass Shared addr
  repeat
    <do something with Shared vars>

DAT
                  org 0
Process           mov Mem, PAR        'Retrieve shared memory addr
:loop             <do something>
                  wrlong ValReg, Mem  'Move ValReg value to Shared
                  jmp :loop
                  jmp :loop
```

```
Mem        res   1
ValReg     res   1
```

In the example above, the Main method launches the Process assembly routine into a new cog with COGNEW. The second parameter of COGNEW is used by Main to pass the address of a variable, Shared. The assembly routine, Process, retrieves that address value from its PAR register and stores it locally in Mem. Then it performs some task, updating its local ValReg register (created at the end of the DAT block) and finally updates the Shared variable via wrlong ValReg, Mem.

PHSA, PHSB
Counter A and Counter B Phase-Locked Loop (PLL) Registers.

((PUB ¦ PRI))
   PHSA
___
((PUB ¦ PRI))
   PHSB
___
Returns: Current value of Counter A or Counter B Phase Lock Loop Register, if used as a source variable.

Explanation
PHSA and PHSB are two of six registers (CTRA, CTRB, FRQA, FRQB, PHSA, and PHSB) that affect the behavior of a cog's Counter Modules. Each cog has two identical counter modules (A and B) that can perform many repetitive tasks. The PHSA and PHSB registers contain values that can be directly read or written by the cog, but may also be accumulating with the value of FRQA and FRQB, respectively, on potentially every System Clock cycle. See CTRA on page 204 for more information.

Using PHSA and PHSB
PHSA and PHSB can be read/written like other registers or pre-defined variables. For example:

   PHSA := $1FFFFFFF

The above code sets PHSA to $1FFFFFFF. Depending on the CTRMODE field of the CTRA register, this value may remain the same, or may automatically increment by the value in FRQA at a frequency determined by the System Clock and the primary and/or secondary I/O pins. See CTRA, CTRB on page 204 for more information.

Keep in mind that writing to PHSA or PHSB directly overrides both the current accumulated value and any potential accumulation scheduled for the same moment the write is performed.

PRI

Declare a Private Method Block.

((PUB ¦ PRI))
    PRI *Name* ⟨ *(Param* ⟨, *Param*⟩...) ⟩ ⟨: *RValue*⟩ ⟨| *LocalVar* ⟨[*Count*]⟩⟩ ⟨, *LocalVar* ⟨[*Count*]⟩⟩...
    SourceCodeStatements

- *Name* is the desired name for the private method.
- *Param* is a parameter name (optional). Methods can contain zero or more comma-delimited parameters, enclosed in parentheses. *Param* must be globally unique, but other methods may also use the same symbol name. Each parameter is essentially a long variable and can be treated as such.
- *RValue* is a name for the return value of the method (optional). This becomes an alias to the method's built-in RESULT variable. *RValue* must be globally unique, but other methods may also use the same symbol name. The *RValue* (and/or RESULT variable) is initialized to zero (0) upon each call to the method.
- *LocalVar* is a name for a local variable (optional). *LocalVar* must be globally unique, but other methods may also use the same symbol name. All local variables are of size long (four bytes) and are left uninitialized upon each call to the method. Methods can contain zero or more comma-delimited local variables.
- *Count* is an optional expression, enclosed in brackets, that indicates this is a local array variable, with *Count* number of elements; each being a long in size. When later referencing these elements, they begin with element 0 and end with element *Count*-1.
- *SourceCodeStatements* is one or more lines of executable source code, indented by at least one space, that perform the function of the method.

Explanation

PRI is the Private Method Block declaration. A Private Method is a section of source code that performs a specific function then returns a result value. This is one of six special declarations (CON, VAR, OBJ, PUB, PRI, and DAT) that provide inherent structure to the Spin language.

Every object can contain a number of private (PRI) and public (PUB) methods. Private methods can only be accessed from inside of the object and serve to perform vital, protected functions, for the object. Private methods are like Public methods in every way except that they are declared with PRI, instead of PUB, and are not accessible from outside the object. Please see PUB, Page 287, for more information.

PUB

Declare a Public Method Block.

((PUB ¦ PRI))
    PUB *Name* ⟨ *(Param* ⟨ *, Param*⟩...*)* ⟩ ⟨ *: RValue*⟩ ⟨ *| LocalVar* ⟨ *[Count]*⟩⟩ ⟨ *, LocalVar* ⟨ *[Count]*⟩⟩...
    SourceCodeStatements

- *Name* is the desired name for the public method.
- *Param* is a parameter name (optional). Methods can contain zero or more comma-delimited parameters, enclosed in parentheses. *Param* must be globally unique, but other methods may also use the same symbol name. Each parameter is essentially a long variable and can be treated as such.
- *RValue* is a name for the return value of the method (optional). This becomes an alias to the method's built-in RESULT variable. *RValue* must be globally unique, but other methods may also use the same symbol name. The *RValue* (and/or RESULT variable) is initialized to zero (0) upon each call to the method.
- *LocalVar* is a name for a local variable (optional). *LocalVar* must be globally unique, but other methods may also use the same symbol name. All local variables are of size long (four bytes) and are left uninitialized upon each call to the method. Methods can contain zero or more comma-delimited local variables.
- *Count* is an optional expression, enclosed in brackets, that indicates this is a local array variable, with *Count* number of elements; each being a long in size. When later referencing these elements, they begin with element 0 and end with element *Count*-1.
- *SourceCodeStatements* is one or more lines of executable source code, indented by at least one space, that perform the function of the method.

Explanation

PUB is the Public Method Block declaration. A Public Method is a section of source code that performs a specific function then returns a result value. This is one of six special declarations (CON, VAR, OBJ, PUB, PRI, and DAT) that provide inherent structure to the Spin language.

Every object can contain a number of public (PUB) and private (PRI) methods. Public methods can be accessed outside of the object itself and serve to make up the interface to the object.

The PUB and PRI declarations don't return a value themselves, but the public and private methods they represent always return a value when called from elsewhere in the code.

PUB – Spin Language Reference

Public Method Declaration

Public Method declarations begin with `PUB`, in column 1 of a line, followed a unique name and an optional set of parameters, a result variable, and local variables.

Example:

```
PUB Init
  <initialization code>

PUB MotorPos : Position
  Position := <code to retrieve motor position>

PUB MoveMotor(Position, Speed) : Success | PosIndex
  <code that moves motor to Position at Speed and returns True/False>
```

This example contains three public methods, `Init`, `MotorPos` and `MoveMotor`. The `Init` method has no parameters and declares no return value or local variables. The `MotorPos` method has no parameters but declares a return value called `Position`. The `MoveMotor` method has two parameters, `Position` and `Speed`, a return value, `Success`, and a local variable, `PosIndex`.

All executable statements that belong to a `PUB` method appear underneath its declaration, indented by at least one space.

The Return Value

Whether or not a `PUB` declaration specifies a *RValue* , there is always an implied return value that defaults to zero (0). There is a pre-defined name for this return value within every `PUB` method, called `RESULT`. At any time within a method, `RESULT` can be updated like any other variable and, upon exiting the method, the current value of `RESULT` will be passed back to the caller. In addition, if a `RESULT` is declared for the method, that name can be used interchangeably with the built-in `RESULT` variable. For instance, the `MotorPos` method above sets "`Position := ...`" and could also have used "`Result := ...`" for the same effect. Despite this, it is considered good practice to give a descriptive name to the return value (in the `PUB` declaration) for any method whose return value is significant. Likewise, it is good practice to leave the return value unnamed (in the `PUB` declaration) for any method whose return value is unimportant and unused.

Parameters and Local Variables

Parameters and local variables are all longs (four bytes). In fact, parameters are really just variables that are initialized to the corresponding values specified by the caller of the method. Local variables, however, are not initialized; they contain random data whenever the method is called.

All parameters are passed into a method by value, not by reference, so any changes to the parameters themselves are not reflected outside of the method. For example, if we called MoveMotor using a variable called Pos for the first parameter, it may look something like this:

```
Pos := 250
MoveMotor(Pos, 100)
```

When the MoveMotor method is executed, it receives the value of Pos in its Position parameter, and the value 100 in its Speed parameter. Inside the MoveMotor method, it can change Position and Speed at any time, but the value of Pos (the caller's variable) remains at 250.

If a variable must be altered by a routine, the caller must pass the variable by reference; meaning it must pass the address of the variable instead of the value of the variable, and the routine must treat that parameter as the address of a memory location in which to operate on. The address of a variable, or other register-based symbol, can be retrieved by using the Symbol Address operator, '@'. For example,

```
Pos := 250
MoveMotor(@Pos, 100)
```

The caller passed the address of Pos for the first parameter to MoveMotor. What MoveMotor receives in its Position parameter is the address of the caller's Pos variable. The address is just a number, like any other, so the MoveMotor method must be designed to treat it as an address, rather than a value. The MoveMotor method then must use something like:

```
PosIndex := LONG[Position]
```

...to retrieve the value of the caller's Pos variable, and something like:

```
LONG[Position] := <some expression>
```

...to modify the caller's Pos variable, if necessary.

Passing a value by reference with the Symbol Address operator is commonly used when providing a string variable to a method. Since string variables are really just byte arrays, there is no way to pass them to a method by value; doing so would result in the method receiving only the first character. Even if a method does not need to modify a string, or other logical array, the array in question still needs to be passed by reference because there are multiple elements to be accessed.

Exiting a Method

A method is exited either when execution reaches the last statement within the method or when it reaches a RETURN or ABORT command. A method may have only one exit point (the last executable statement), or may have many exit points (any number of RETURN or ABORT commands in addition to the last executable statement). The RETURN and ABORT commands can also be used to set the RESULT variable upon exit; see RETURN, page 301, and ABORT, page 161.

QUIT

Exit from REPEAT loop immediately.

((PUB ┆ PRI))
    QUIT

Explanation

QUIT is one of two commands (NEXT and QUIT) that affect REPEAT loops. QUIT causes a REPEAT loop to terminate immediately.

Using QUIT

QUIT is typically used as an exception case, in a conditional statement, in REPEAT loops to terminate the loop prematurely. For example, assume that DoMore and SystemOkay are methods created elsewhere that each return Boolean values:

```
repeat while DoMore          'Repeat while more to do
  !outa[0]                   'Toggle status light
  <do something>             'Perform some task
  if !SystemOkay
    quit                     'If system failure, exit
  <more code here>           'Perform other tasks
```

The above code toggles a status light on P0 and performs other tasks while the DoMore method returns TRUE. However, if the SystemOkay method returns FALSE part-way through the loop, the IF statement executes the QUIT command which causes the loop to terminate immediately.

The QUIT command can only be used within a REPEAT loop; an error will occur otherwise.

REBOOT

Reset the Propeller chip.

```
((PUB ¦ PRI))
    REBOOT
```

Explanation

This is a software controlled reset, but acts like just like a hardware reset via the RESn pin.

Use REBOOT if you want to reset the Propeller chip to its power-up state. All the same hardware-based, power-up/reset delays, as well as the boot-up processes, are applied as if the Propeller had been reset via the RESn pin or a power cycle.

REPEAT

Execute code block repetitively.

((PUB ┊ PRI))
  REPEAT ⟨*Count*⟩
  →┤ *Statement(s)*

((PUB ┊ PRI))
  REPEAT *Variable* FROM *Start* TO *Finish* ⟨STEP *Delta*⟩
  →┤ *Statement(s)*

((PUB ┊ PRI))
  REPEAT ((UNTIL ┊ WHILE)) *Condition(s)*
  →┤ *Statement(s)*

((PUB ┊ PRI))
  REPEAT
  →┤ *Statement(s)*
  ((UNTIL ┊ WHILE)) *Condition(s)*

- **Count** is an optional expression indicating the finite number of times to execute *Statement(s)*. If *Count* is omitted, syntax 1 creates an infinite loop made up of *Statement(s)*.
- **Statement(s)** is an optional block of one or more lines of code to execute repeatedly. Omitting *Statement(s)* is rare, but may be useful in syntax 3 and 4 if *Condition(s)* achieves the needed effects.
- **Variable** is a variable, usually user-defined, that will be iterated from *Start* to *Finish*, optionally by *Delta* units per iteration. *Variable* can be used in *Statement(s)* to determine or utilize the iteration count.
- **Start** is an expression that determines the starting value of *Variable* in syntax 2. If *Start* is less than *Finish*, *Variable* will be incremented each iteration; it will be decremented otherwise.
- **Finish** is an expression that determines the ending value of *Variable* in syntax 2. If *Finish* is greater than *Start*, *Variable* will be incremented each iteration; it will be decremented otherwise.
- **Delta** is an optional expression that determines the units in which to increment/decrement *Variable* each iteration (syntax 2). If omitted, *Variable* is incremented/decremented by 1 each iteration.

- *Condition(s)* is one or more Boolean expression(s) used by syntax 3 and 4 to continue or terminate the loop. When preceded by UNTIL, *Condition(s)* terminates the loop when true. When preceded by WHILE, *Conditions(s)* terminates the loop when FALSE.

Explanation

REPEAT is the very flexible looping structure for Spin code. It can be used to create any type of loop, including: infinite, finite, with/without loop counter, and conditional zero-to-many/one-to-many loops.

Indention is Critical

IMPORTANT: Indention is critical. The Spin language relies on indention (of one space or more) on lines following conditional commands to determine if they belong to that command or not. To have the Propeller Tool indicate these logically grouped blocks of code on-screen, you can press Ctrl + I to turn on block-group indicators. Pressing Ctrl + I again will disable that feature. See Indenting and Outdenting, page 69, and Block-Group Indicators, page 74.

Infinite Loops (Syntax 1)

Truthfully, any of the four forms of REPEAT can be made into infinite loops, but the form used most often for this purpose is syntax 1 without the *Count* field. For example:

```
repeat                  'Repeat endlessly
  !outa[25]             'Toggle P25
  waitcnt(2_000 + cnt)  'Pause for 2,000 cycles
```

This code repeats the !outa[25] and waitcnt(2_000 + cnt) lines endlessly. Both lines are indented from the REPEAT so they belong to the REPEAT loop.

Since *Statement(s)* is really an optional part of REPEAT, the REPEAT command by itself can be used as an endless loop that does nothing but keep the cog active. This can be intentional, but sometimes is unintentional due to improper indention. For example:

```
repeat              'Repeat endlessly
!outa[25]           'Toggle P25        <-- This is never run
```

The above example is erroneous; the last line is never executed because the REPEAT above it is an endless loop that has no *Statement(s)*; there is nothing indented immediately below it, so the cog simply sits in an endless loop at the REPEAT line that does nothing but keep the cog active and consuming power.

Simple Finite Loops (Syntax 1)

Most loops are finite in nature; they execute a limited number of iterations only. The simplest form is syntax 1 with the *Count* field included.

For example:

```
repeat 10            'Repeat 10 times
  !outa[25]          'Toggle P25
  byte[$7000]++      'Increment RAM location $7000
```

The above code toggles P25 ten times, then increments the value in RAM location $7000.

Counted Finite Loops (Syntax 2)

Quite often it is necessary to count the loop iterations so the loop's code can perform differently based on that count. The REPEAT command makes it easy to do this with syntax 2. The next example assumes the variable Index was created previously.

```
repeat Index from 0 to 9    'Repeat 10 times
  byte[$7000][Index]++      'Increment RAM locations $7000 to $7009
```

Like the previous example, the code above loops 10 times, but each time it adjusts the variable Index. The first time through the loop, Index will be 0 (as indicated by the "from 0") and each upon each iteration afterwards Index will be 1 higher than the previous (as indicated by the "to 9"): ..1, 2, 3...9. After the tenth iteration, Index will be incremented to 10 and the loop will terminate, causing the next code following the REPEAT loop structure to execute, if any exists. The code in the loop uses Index as an offset to affect memory, byte[$7000][Index]++; in this case it is incrementing each of the byte-sized values in RAM locations $7000 to $7009 by 1, one at a time.

The REPEAT command automatically determines whether the range suggested by *Start* and *Finish* is increasing or decreasing. Since the above example used 0 to 9, the range is an increasing range; adjusting Index by +1 every time. To get the count to go backwards, simply reverse the *Start* and *Finish* values, as in:

```
repeat Index from 9 to 0    'Repeat 10 times
  byte[$7000][Index]++      'Increment RAM $7009 down through $7000
```

This example also loops 10 times, but counts with Index from 9 down to 0; adjusting Index by -1 each time. The contents of the loop still increments the values in RAM, but from locations $7009 down to $7000. After the tenth iteration, Index will equal -1.

Since the *Start* and *Finish* fields can be expressions, they can contain variables. The next example assumes that S and F are variables created previously.

```
S := 0
F := 9
repeat 2                          'Repeat twice
  repeat Index from S to F        'Repeat 10 times
    byte[$7000][Index]++          'Increment RAM locations 7000..$7009
  S := 9
  F := 0
```

The above example uses a nested loop. The outer loop (the first one) repeats 2 times. The inner loop repeats with Index from S to F, which were previously set to 0 and 9, respectively. The inner loop increments the values in RAM locations $7000 to $7009, in that order, because the inner loop is counting iterations from 0 to 9. Then, the inner loop terminates (with Index being set to 10) and the last two lines set S to 9 and F to 0, effectively swapping the *Start* and *Finish* values. Since this is still inside the outer loop, the outer loop then executes its contents again (for the second time) causing the inner loop to repeat with Index from 9 down to 0. The inner loop increments the values in RAM locations $7009 to $7000, in that order (reverse of the previous time) and terminates with Index equaling -1. The last two lines set S and F again, but the outer loop does not repeat a third time.

REPEAT loops don't have to be limited to incrementing or decrementing by 1 either. If the REPEAT command uses the optional STEP *Delta* syntax, it will increment or decrement the *Variable* by the *Delta* amount. In the syntax 2 form, REPEAT is actually always using a *Delta* value, but when the "STEP *Delta*" component is omitted, it uses either +1 or -1 by default, depending on the range of *Start* and *Finish*. The following example includes the optional *Delta* value to increment by 2.

```
repeat Index from 0 to 8 step 2  'Repeat 5 times
  byte[$7000][Index]++           'Increment even RAM $7000 to $7008
```

Here, REPEAT loops five times, with Index set to 0, 2, 4, 6, and 8, respectively. This code effectively increments every other RAM location (the even numbered locations) from $7000 to $7008 and terminates with Index equaling 10.

The *Delta* field can be positive or negative, regardless of the natural ascending/descending range of the *Start* and *Finish* values, and can even be adjusted within the loop to achieve interesting effects. For example, assuming Index and D are previously defined variables, the following code sets Index to the following sequence: 5, 6, 6, 5, 3.

```
D := 2
repeat Index from 5 to 10 step D
  --D
```

This loop started out with Index at 5 and a *Delta* (D) of +2. But each iteration of the loop decrements D by one, so at the end of iteration 1, Index = 5 and D = +1. Iteration 2 has Index = 6 and D = 0. Iteration 3 has Index = 6 and D = -1. Iteration 4 has Index = 5 and D = -2. Iteration 5 has Index = 3 and D = -3. The loop then terminates because Index plus *Delta* (3 + -3) is outside the range of *Start* to *Finish* (5 to 10).

Conditional Loops (Syntax 3 and 4)

The final forms of REPEAT, syntax 3 and 4, are finite loops with conditional exits and have flexible options allowing for the use of either positive or negative logic and the creation of zero-to-many or one-to-many iteration loops. These two forms of REPEAT are usually referred to as "repeat while" or "repeat until" loops.

Let's look at the REPEAT form described by syntax 3. It consists of the REPEAT command followed immediately by either WHILE or UNTIL then *Condition(s)* and finally, on the lines below it, optional *Statement(s)*. Since this form tests *Condition(s)* at the start of every iteration, it creates a zero-to-many loop; the *Statement(s)* block will execute zero or more times, depending on the *Condition(s)*. For example, assume that X is a variable created earlier:

```
X := 0
repeat while X < 10          'Repeat while X is less than 10
  byte[$7000][X] := 0        'Increment RAM value
  X++                        'Increment X
```

This example first sets X to 0, then repeats the loop while X is less than 10. The code inside the loop clears RAM locations based on X (starting at location $7000) and increments X. After the 10th iteration of the loop, X equals 10, making the condition while X < 10 false and the loop terminates.

This loop is said to use "positive" logic because it continues "WHILE" a condition is true. It could also be written with "negative" logic using UNTIL, instead. Such as:

```
X := 0
repeat until X > 9           'Repeat until X is greater than 9
  byte[$7000][X] := 0        'Increment RAM value
  X++                        'Increment X
```

The above example performs the same way as the previous, but the repeat loop uses negative logic because it continues "UNTIL" a condition is true; i.e: it continues while a condition is false.

In either example, if X was equal to 10 or higher before the first iteration of the REPEAT loop, the condition would cause the loop to never execute at all, which is why we call it a zero-to-many loop.

The REPEAT form described by syntax 4 is very similar to syntax 3, but the condition is tested at the end of every iteration, making it a one-to-many loop. For example:

```
X := 0
repeat
  byte[$7000][X] := 0        'Increment RAM value
  X++                        'Increment X
while X < 10                 'Repeat while X is less than 10
```

This works the same as the previous examples, looping 10 times, except that the condition is not tested until the end of each iteration. However, unlike the previous examples, even if X was equal to 10 or higher before the first iteration, the loop would run once then terminate, which is why we call it a one-to-many loop.

Other REPEAT Options

There are two other commands that affect the behavior or REPEAT loops: NEXT and QUIT. See the NEXT (page 246) and QUIT (page 291) commands for more information.

RESULT

The return value variable for methods.

```
((PUB ┊ PRI))
  RESULT
```

Explanation

The **RESULT** variable is a pre-defined local variable for each **PUB** and **PRI** method. **RESULT** holds the method's return value; the value passed back to the caller of the method, when the method is terminated.

When a public or private method is called, its built-in **RESULT** variable is cleared to zero (0). If that method does not alter **RESULT**, or does not call **RETURN** or **ABORT** with a value specified, then zero will be the return value upon that method's termination.

Using RESULT

In the example below, the DoSomething method sets **RESULT** equal to 100 at its end. The Main method calls DoSomething and sets its local variable, Temp, equal to the result; so that when DoSomething exits, Temp will be set to 100

```
PUB Main | Temp
  Temp := DoSomething      'Call DoSomething, set Temp to return value

PUB DoSomething
  <do something here>
  result := 100            'Set result to 100
```

You can also provide an alias name for a method's **RESULT** variable in order to make it more clear what the method returns. This is highly recommended since it makes a method's intent more easily discerned. For example:

```
PUB GetChar : Char
  <do something>
  Char := <retrieved character>   'Set Char (result) to the character
```

The above method, GetChar, declares Char as an alias for its built-in **RESULT** variable; see **PUB**, page 287 or **PRI**, page 286, for more information. The GetChar method then performs some task to get a character then it sets Char to the value of the retrieved character. It could have also used "`result := ...`" to set the return value since either statement affects the method's return value.

Either the RESULT variable, or the alias provided for it, may be modified multiple times within the method before exiting since they both affect RESULT and only the last value of RESULT will be used upon exiting.

RETURN

Exit from PUB/PRI method with optional return *Value*.

```
((PUB ¦ PRI))
    RETURN ⟨Value⟩
```

Returns: Either the current RESULT value, or *Value* if provided.

- **Value** is an optional expression whose value is to be returned from the PUB or PRI method.

Explanation

RETURN is one of two commands (ABORT and RETURN) that terminate a PUB or PRI method's execution. RETURN causes a return from a PUB or PRI method with normal status; meaning it pops the call stack once and returns to the caller of this method, delivering a value in the process.

Every PUB or PRI method has an implied RETURN at its end, but RETURN can also be manually entered in one or more places within the method to create multiple exit points.

When RETURN appears without the optional *Value*, it returns the current value of the PUB/PRI's built-in RESULT variable. If the *Value* field was entered, however, the PUB or PRI returns with that *Value* instead.

About the Call Stack

When methods are called, simply by referring to them from other methods, there must be some mechanism in place to store where to return to once the called method is completed. This mechanism is a called a "stack" but we'll use the term "call stack" here. It is simply RAM memory used to store return addresses, return values, parameters and intermediate results. As more and more methods are called, the call stack logically gets longer. As more and more methods are returned from (via RETURN or by reaching the end of the method) the call stack gets shorter. This is called "pushing" onto the stack and "popping" off of the stack, respectively.

The RETURN command pops the most recent data off the call stack to facilitate returning to the immediate caller; the one who directly called the method that just returned.

Using RETURN

The following example demonstrates two uses of RETURN. Assume that DisplayDivByZeroError is a method defined elsewhere.

```
PUB Add (Num1, Num2)
  Result := Num1 + Num2          'Add Num1 + Num2
  return

PUB Divide (Dividend, Divisor)
  if Divisor == 0                'Check if Divisor = 0
    DisplayDivByZeroError        'If so, display error
    return 0                     'and return with 0
  return Dividend / Divisor      'Otherwise return quotient
```

The Add method sets its built-in RESULT variable equal to Num1 plus Num2, then executes RETURN. The RETURN causes Add to return the value of RESULT to the caller. Note that this RETURN was not really required because the Propeller Tool Compiler will automatically put it in at the end of any methods that don't have one.

The Divide method checks the Divisor value. If Divisor equals zero, it calls a DisplayDivByZeroError method and then executes return 0, which immediately causes the method to return with the value 0. If, however, the Divisor was not equal to zero, it executes return Dividend / Divisor, which causes the method to return with the result of the division. This is an example where the last RETURN was used to perform the calculation and return the result all in one step rather than separately affecting the built-in RESULT variable beforehand.

ROUND

Round a floating-point constant to the nearest integer.

```
((CON ┊ VAR ┊ OBJ ┊ PUB ┊ PRI ┊ DAT))
   ROUND ( FloatConstant )
```

Returns: Nearest integer to original floating-point constant value.

- *FloatConstant* is the floating-point constant expression to be rounded to the nearest integer.

Explanation

ROUND is one of three directives (FLOAT, ROUND and TRUNC) used for floating-point constant expressions. ROUND returns an integer constant that is the closest integer value to the given floating-point constant expression. Fractional values of ½ (.5) or higher are rounded up to the nearest whole number while lower fractions are rounded down.

Using ROUND

ROUND can be used to round floating-point constants up or down to the nearest integer value. Note that this is for compile-time constant expressions only, not run-time variable expressions. For example:

```
CON
   OneHalf = 0.5
   Smaller = 0.4999
   Rnd1    = round(OneHalf)
   Rnd2    = round(Smaller)
   Rnd3    = round(Smaller * 10.0) + 4
```

The above code creates two floating-point constants, OneHalf and Smaller, equal to 0.5 and 0.4999, respectively. The next three constants, Rnd1, Rnd2 and Rnd3, are integer constants that are based on OneHalf and Smaller using the ROUND directive. Rnd1 = 1, Rnd2 = 0, and Rnd3 = 9.

About Floating–Point Constants

The Propeller compiler handles floating-point constants as a single-precision real number as described by the IEEE-754 standard. Single-precision real numbers are stored in 32 bits, with a 1-bit sign, an 8-bit exponent, and a 23-bit mantissa (the fractional part). This provides approximately 7.2 significant decimal digits.

Floating-point constant expressions can be defined and used for many compile-time purposes, but for run-time floating-point operations, the FloatMath and FloatString objects provide math functions compatible with single-precision numbers.

See the Constant Assignment '=' in the Operators section on page 254, FLOAT on page 216, and TRUNC on page 314, as well as the FloatMath and FloatString objects for more information.

SPR

Special Purpose Register array; provides indirect access to cog's special registers.

((PUB ┊ PRI))
   SPR [*Index*]

Returns: Value in special purpose register at *Index*.

- *Index* is an expression that specifies the index (0-15) of the special purpose register to access (PAR through VSCL).

Explanation

SPRis an array of the 16 special purpose registers in the cog. Element 0 is the PAR register and element 15 is the VSCL register. See Table 4-15 below. SPR provides an indirect method of accessing the cog's special purpose registers.

Table 4-15: Cog RAM Special Purpose Registers			
Name	**Index**	**Type**	**Description**
PAR	0	Read-Only	Boot Parameter
CNT	1	Read-Only	System Counter
INA	2	Read-Only	Input States for P31 - P0
INB	3	Read-Only	Input States for P63- P32[1]
OUTA	4	Read/Write	Output States for P31 - P0
OUTB	5	Read/Write	Output States for P63 – P32[1]
DIRA	6	Read/Write	Direction States for P31 - P0
DIRB	7	Read/Write	Direction States for P63 - P32[1]
CTRA	8	Read/Write	Counter A Control
CTRB	9	Read/Write	Counter B Control
FRQA	10	Read/Write	Counter A Frequency
FRQB	11	Read/Write	Counter B Frequency
PHSA	12	Read/Write	Counter A Phase
PHSB	13	Read/Write	Counter B Phase
VCFG	14	Read/Write	Video Configuration
VSCL	15	Read/Write	Video Scale

Note 1: Reserved for future use

Using SPR

SPR can be used like any other long-sized array. The following assumes `Temp` is a variable defined elsewhere.

```
spr[4] := %11001010          'Set outa register
Temp := spr[2]               'Get ina value
```

This example sets the OUTA register (index 4 of SPR) to %11001010 and then sets Temp equal to the INA register (index 2 of SPR).

_STACK

Pre-defined, one-time settable constant for specifying the size of an application's stack space.

```
CON
  _STACK = Expression
```

- *Expression* is an integer expression that indicates the number of longs to reserve for stack space.

Explanation

_STACK is a pre-defined, one-time settable optional constant that specifies the required stack space of an application. This value is added to _FREE if specified, to determine the total amount of stack/free memory space to reserve for a Propeller application. Use _STACK if an application requires a minimum amount of stack space in order to run properly. If the resulting compiled application is too large to allow the specified stack space, an error message will be displayed. For example:

```
CON
  _STACK    = 3000
```

The _STACK declaration in the above CON block indicates that the application needs to have at least 3,000 longs of stack space left over after compilation. If the resulting compiled application does not have that much room left over, an error message will indicate by how much it was exceeded. This is a good way to prevent successful compiles of an application that will fail to run properly due to lack of memory.

Note that only the top object file can set the value of _STACK. Any child object's _STACK declarations will be ignored. The stack space reserved by this constant is used by the application's main cog to store temporary data such as call stacks, parameters, and intermediate expression results.

STRCOMP

Compare two strings for equality.

((PUB ┊ PRI))
    STRCOMP (*StringAddress1*, *StringAddress2*)

Returns: TRUE if both strings are equal, FALSE otherwise.

- *StringAddress1* is an expression specifying the starting address of the first string to compare.
- *StringAddress2* is an expression specifying the starting address of the second string to compare.

Explanation

STRCOMP is one of two commands (STRCOMP and STRSIZE) that retrieve information about a string. STRCOMP compares the contents of the string at *StringAddress1* to the contents of the string at *StringAddress2*, up to the zero-terminator of each string, and returns TRUE if both strings are equivalent, FALSE otherwise. This comparison is case-sensitive.

Using STRCOMP

The following example assumes PrintStr is a method created elsewhere.

```
PUB Main
  if strcomp(@Str1, @Str2)
    PrintStr(string("Str1 and Str2 are equal"))
  else
    PrintStr(string("Str1 and Str2 are different"))

DAT
  Str1  byte  "Hello World", 0
  Str2  byte  "Testing.", 0
```

The above example has two zero-terminated strings in the DAT block, Str1 and Str2. The Main method calls STRCOMP to compare the contents of each string. Assuming PrintStr is a method that displays a string, this example prints "Str1 and Str2 are different" on the display.

Zero-Terminated Strings

The STRCOMP command requires the strings being compared to be zero-terminated; a byte equal to 0 must immediately follow each string. This practice is quite common and is recommended since most string-handling methods rely on zero terminators.

STRING

Declare in-line string constant and get its address.

```
((PUB ┊ PRI))
    STRING (StringExpression )
```

Returns: Address of in-line string constant.

- *StringExpression* is the desired string expression to be used for temporary, in-line purposes.

Explanation

The DAT block is used often to create strings or string buffers that are reusable for various purposes, but there are occasions when a string is needed for temporary purposes like debugging or one-time uses in an object. The STRING directive is meant for those one-time uses; it compiles an in-line, zero-terminated string into memory and returns the address of that string.

Using STRING

The STRING directive is very good for creating one-time-use strings and passing the address of that string to other methods. For example, assuming PrintStr is a method created elsewhere.

```
PrintStr(string("This is a test string."))
```

The above example uses the STRING directive to compile a string, "This is a test string.", into memory and return the address of that string as the parameter for the fictitious PrintStr method.

If a string needs to be used in more than one place in code, it is better to define it in the DAT block so the address can be used multiple times.

STRSIZE

Get size of string.

((PUB ┊ PRI))
   STRSIZE (*StringAddress*)

Returns: Size (in bytes) of zero-terminated string.

- *StringAddress* is an expression specifying the starting address of the string to measure.

Explanation

STRSIZE is one of two commands (STRCOMP and STRSIZE) that retrieve information about a string. STRSIZE measures the length of a string at *StringAddress*, in bytes, up to, but not including, a zero-termination byte.

Using STRSIZE

The following example assumes Print is a method created elsewhere.

```
PUB Main
  Print(strsize(@Str1))
  Print(strsize(@Str2))

DAT
  Str1  byte  "Hello World", 0
  Str2  byte  "Testing.", 0
```

The above example has two zero-terminated strings in the DAT block, Str1 and Str2. The Main method calls STRSIZE to get the length of each string. Assuming Print is a method that displays a value, this example prints 11 and 8 on the display.

Zero-Terminated Strings

The STRSIZE command requires the string being measured to be zero-terminated; a byte equal to 0 must immediately follow the string. This practice is quite common and is recommended since most string-handling methods rely on zero terminators.

Symbols

The symbols in Table 4-16 below serve one or more special purposes in Spin code. Each symbol's purpose is described briefly with references to other sections that describe it directly or use it in examples.

Table 4-16: Symbols	
Symbol	**Purpose(s)**
%	Binary indicator: used to indicate that a value is being expressed in binary (base-2). See Value Representations on page 159.
%%	Quaternary indicator: used to indicate a value is being expressed in quaternary (base-4). See Value Representations on page 159.
$	Hexadecimal indicator: used to indicate a value is being expressed in hexadecimal (base-16). See Value Representations on page 159.
" "	String designator: used to begin and end a string of text characters. Usually used in Object blocks (page 247), Data blocks (page 208), or in Public/Private blocks with the STRING directive (page 310).
_	1) Delimiter: used as a group delimiter in constant values (where a comma ',' or period '.' may normally be used as a number group delimiter). See See Value Representations on page 159. 2) Underscore: used as part of a symbol. See Symbol Rules on page 159.
#	1) Object-Constant reference: used to reference a sub-object's constants. See the CON section's Scope of Constants, page 199, and OBJ, page 247. 2) Enumeration Set: used in a CON block to set the start of an enumerated set of symbols. See the CON section's Enumerations (Syntax 2 and 3) on page 197. 3) Assembly Literal: used to indicate an expression or symbol is a literal value rather than a register address.
.	1) Object-Method reference: used to reference a sub-object's methods. See OBJ, page 247. 2) Decimal point: used in floating-point constant expressions. See CON, page 194.
..	Range indicator: indicates a range from one expression to another for CASE statements or an I/O register index. See OUTA, OUTB on page 280, INA, INB on page 226, and DIRA, DIRB on page 212.

	Table 4-16: Symbols (continued)
Symbol	**Purpose(s)**
:	1) Return value separator: appears immediately before a symbolic return value on a PUB or PRI declaration. See PUB on page 287, PRI on page 286, and RESULT on page 299. 2) Object assignment: appears in an object reference declaration in an OBJ block. See OBJ, page 247. 3) Case statement separator: appears immediately after the match expressions in a CASE structure. See CASE, page 171.
|	1) Local variable separator: appears immediately before a list of local variables on a PUB or PRI declaration. See PUB, page 287 and PRI, page 286. 2) Bitwise OR: used in expressions. See Bitwise OR '|', '|=' on page 270.
****	Abort trap: appears immediately before a method call that could potentially abort. See ABORT on page 161.
,	List delimiter: used to separate items in lists. See LOOKUP, LOOKUPZ on page 244, LOOKDOWN, LOOKDOWNZ on page 242, and the DAT section's Declaring Data (Syntax 1) on page 208.
( )	Parameter list designators: used to surround method parameters. See PUB, page 287 and PRI, page 286.
[ ]	Array index designators: used to surround indexes on variable arrays or main memory references. See VAR, page 315; BYTE, page 165; WORD, page 331; and LONG, page 236.
'	Code comment designator: used to enter single-line code comments (non-compiled text) for code viewing purposes. See Exercise 3: Output.spin - Comments on page 100.
' '	Document comment designator: used to enter single-line document comments (non-compiled text) for documentation viewing purposes. See Exercise 3: Output.spin - Comments on page 100.
{ }	In-line/multi-line code comment designators: used to enter multi-line code comments (non-compiled text) for code viewing purposes.
{{ }}	In-line/multi-line document comment designators: used to enter multi-line document comments (non-compiled text) for documentation viewing purposes. See Exercise 3: Output.spin - Comments on page 100.

TRUNC

Remove, "truncate," the fractional portion from a floating-point constant.

```
((CON ┆ VAR ┆ OBJ ┆ PUB ┆ PRI ┆ DAT))
    TRUNC ( FloatConstant )
```

Returns: Integer that is the given floating-point constant value truncated at the decimal point.

- *FloatConstant* is the floating-point constant expression to be truncated to an integer.

Explanation

TRUNC is one of three directives (FLOAT, ROUND and TRUNC) used for floating-point constant expressions. TRUNC returns an integer constant that is the given floating-point constant expression with the fractional portion removed.

Using TRUNC

TRUNC can be used to retrieve the integer portion of a floating-point constant. For example:

```
CON
    OneHalf = 0.5
    Bigger  = 1.4999
    Int1    = trunc (OneHalf)
    Int2    = trunc (Bigger)
    Int3    = trunc (Bigger * 10.0) + 4
```

The above code creates two floating-point constants, OneHalf and Bigger, equal to 0.5 and 1.4999, respectively. The next three constants, Int1, Int2 and Int3, are integer constants that are based on OneHalf and Bigger using the TRUNC directive. Int1 = 0, Int2 = 1, and Int3 = 18.

About Floating–Point Constants

The Propeller compiler handles floating-point constants as a single-precision real number as described by the IEEE-754 standard. Single-precision real numbers are stored in 32 bits, with a 1-bit sign, an 8-bit exponent, and a 23-bit mantissa (the fractional part). This provides approximately 7.2 significant decimal digits.

Floating-point constant expressions can be defined and used for many compile-time purposes, but for run-time floating-point operations, the FloatMath and FloatString objects provide math functions compatible with single-precision numbers. See the Constant Assignment '=' in the Operators section on page 254, FLOAT on page 216, and ROUND on page 303, as well the FloatMath and FloatString objects for more information.

VAR

Declare a Variable Block.

VAR

Size Symbol ⟨[**Count**]⟩ ⟨ ↪ **Size Symbol** ⟨ [**Count**]⟩⟩...

VAR

Size Symbol ⟨[**Count**]⟩ ⟨ , **Symbol** ⟨ [**Count**]⟩⟩...

- **Size** is the desired size of the variable, BYTE, WORD or LONG.
- **Symbol** is the desired name for the variable.
- **Count** is an optional expression, enclosed in brackets, that indicates this is an array variable, with *Count* number of elements; each being of size byte, word or long. When later referencing these elements, they begin with element 0 and end with element *Count*-1.

Explanation

VAR is the Variable Block declaration. The Variable Block is a section of source code that declares global variable symbols. This is one of six special declarations (CON, VAR, OBJ, PUB, PRI, and DAT) that provide inherent structure to the Spin language.

Variable Declarations (Syntax 1)

The most common form of variable declarations begins with VAR on a line by itself followed by one or more declarations. VAR must start in column 1 (the leftmost column) of the line it is on and the lines following it must be indented by at least one space.

```
VAR
  byte  Str[10]
  word  Code
  long  LargeNumber
```

This example defines Str as a byte array of 10 elements, Code as a word (two bytes) and LargeNumber as a long (four bytes). Public and Private methods can refer to these variables in ways similar to the following:

```
PUB SomeMethod
  Code := 60000
  LargeNumber := Code * 250
  GetString(@Str)
  if Str[0] == "A"
    <more code here>
```

Notice that Code and LargeNumber are used directly by expressions. The Str reference in the GetString method's parameter list looks different; it has an @, the Symbol Address operator, preceding it. This is because our fictitious GetString method needs to write back to the Str variable. If we had said GetString(Str), then the first byte of Str, element 0, would have been passed to GetString. By using the Symbol Address operator, @, we caused the address of Str to be passed to GetString instead; GetString can use that address to write to Str's elements. Lastly, we use Str[0] in the condition of an IF statement to see if the first byte is equal to the character "A". Remember, the first element of an array is always zero (0).

Variable Declarations (Syntax 2)

A variation on Syntax 1 allows for comma delimited variables of the same size. The following is, similar to the above example, but we declare two words, Code and Index.

```
VAR
  byte  Str[10]
  word  Code, Index
  long  LargeNumber
```

Scope of Variables

Symbolic variables defined in Variable Blocks are global to the object in which they are defined but not outside of that object. This means that these variables can be accessed directly from anywhere within the object but their name will not conflict with symbols defined in other parent or child objects.

Public and Private methods have the ability to declare their own local variables. See PUB, page 287, and PRI, page 286.

Global variables are not accessible outside of an object unless the address of that variable is passed into, or back to, another object through a method call.

VCFG

Video Configuration Register.

((PUB ¦ PRI))
    VCFG

Returns: Current value of cog's Video Configuration Register, if used as a source variable.

Explanation

VCFG is one of two registers (VCFG and VSCL) that affect the behavior of a cog's Video Generator. Each cog has a video generator module that facilitates transmitting video image data at a constant rate. The VCFG register contains the configuration settings of the video generator, as shown in Table 4-17.

Table 4-17: VCFG Register									
VCFG Bits									
31	30..29	28	27	26	25..23	22..12	11..9	8	7..0
-	VMode	CMode	Chroma1	Chroma0	AuralSub	-	VGroup	-	VPins

In Propeller Assembly, the VMode field through AuralSub fields can conveniently be written using the MOVI instruction, the VGroup field can be written with the MOVD instruction, and the VPins field can be written with the MOVS instruction.

VMode

The 2-bit VMode (video mode) field selects the type and orientation of video output, if any, according to Table 4-18.

Table 4-18: The Video Mode Field	
VMode	**Video Mode**
00	Disabled, no video generated.
01	VGA mode; 8-bit parallel output on VPins7:0
10	Composite Mode 1; broadcast on VPins 7:4, baseband on VPins 3:0
11	Composite Mode 2; baseband on VPins 7:4, broadcast on VPins 3:0

CMode

The CMode (color mode) field selects two or four color mode. 0 = two-color mode; pixel data is 32 bits by 1 bit and only colors 0 or 1 are used. 1 = four-color mode; pixel data is 16 bits by 2 bits, and colors 0 through 3 are used.

Chroma1

The Chroma1 (broadcast chroma) bit enables or disables chroma (color) on the broadcast signal. 0 = disabled, 1 = enabled.

Chroma0

The Chroma0 (baseband chroma) bit enables or disables chroma (color) on the baseband signal. 0 = disabled, 1 = enabled.

AuralSub

The AuralSub (aural sub-carrier) field selects the source of the FM aural (audio) sub-carrier frequency to be modulated on. The source is the PLLA of one of the cogs, identified by AuralSub's value.

| Table 4-19: The AuralSub Field ||
AuralSub	Sub-Carrier Frequency Source
000	Cog 0's PLLA
001	Cog 1's PLLA
010	Cog 2's PLLA
011	Cog 3's PLLA
100	Cog 4's PLLA
101	Cog 5's PLLA
110	Cog 6's PLLA
111	Cog 7's PLLA

VGroup

The VGroup (video output pin group) field selects which group of 8 I/O pins to output video on.

Table 4-20: The VGroup Field	
VGroup	**Pin Group**
000	Group 0: P7..P0
001	Group 1: P15..P8
010	Group 2: P23..P16
011	Group 3: P31..P24
100-111	<reserved for future use>

VPins

The VPins (video output pins) field is a mask applied to the pins of VGroup that indicates which pins to output video signals on.

Table 4-21: The VPins Field	
VPins	**Effect**
00001111	Drive Video on lower 4 pins only; composite
11110000	Drive Video on upper 4 pins only; composite
11111111	Drive video on all 8 pins; VGA

Using VCFG

VCFG can be read/written like other registers or pre-defined variables. For example:

```
VCFG := %0_10_1_0_1_000_00000000000_001_0_00001111
```

This sets the video configuration register to enable video in composite mode 1 with 4 colors, baseband chroma (color) enabled, on pin group 1, lower 4 pins (which is pins P11:8).

VSCL

Video Scale Register.

```
((PUB ¦ PRI))
    VSCL
```

Returns: Current value of cog's Video Scale Register, if used as a source variable.

Explanation

VSCL is one of two registers (VCFG and VSCL) that affect the behavior of a cog's Video Generator. Each cog has a video generator module that facilitates transmitting video image data at a constant rate. The VSCL register sets the rate at which video data is generated.

Table 4-22: VSCL Register		
VSCL Bits		
31..20	**19..12**	**11..0**
–	PixelClocks	FrameClocks

PixelClocks

The 8-bit PixelClocks field indicates the number of clocks per pixel; the number of clocks that should elapse before each pixel is shifted out by the video generator module. These clocks are the PLLA clocks, not the System Clock.

FrameClocks

The 12-bit FrameClocks field indicates the number of clocks per frame; the number of clocks that should elapse before each frame is shifted out by the video generator module. These clocks are the PLLA clocks, not the System Clock. A frame is one long of pixel data (delivered via the WAITVID command). Since the pixel data is either 16 bits by 2 bits, or 32 bits by 1 bit (meaning 16 pixels wide with 4 colors, or 32 pixels wide with 2 colors, respectively), the FrameClocks is typically 16 or 32 times that of the PixelClocks value.

Using VSCL

VSCL can be read/written like other registers or pre-defined variables. For example:

```
VSCL := %000000000000_10100000_101000000000
```

This sets the video scale register for 160 PixelClocks and 2,560 FrameClocks (for a 16-pixel by 2-bit color frame). Of course, the actual rate at which pixels clock out depends on the frequency of PLLA in combination with this scale factor.

WAITCNT

Pause a cog's execution temporarily.

```
((PUB ¦ PRI))
  WAITCNT ( Value )
```

- *Value* is the desired 32-bit System Counter value to wait for.

Explanation

WAITCNT, "Wait for System Counter," is one of four wait commands (WAITCNT, WAITPEQ, WAITPNE, and WAITVID) used to pause execution of a cog until a condition is met. WAITCNT pauses the cog until the global System Counter equals *Value*.

When executed, WAITCNT activates special "wait" hardware in the cog that prevents the System Clock from causing further code execution within the cog until the moment the System Counter equals *Value*. The wait hardware checks the System Counter every System Clock cycle and the cog's power consumption is reduced by approximately $7/8^{ths}$ during this time. In normal applications, WAITCNT may be used strategically to reduce power consumption anywhere in the program where time is wasted waiting for low-bandwidth events.

There are two types of delays WAITCNT can be used for: fixed delays and synchronized delays. Both are explained below.

Fixed Delays

Fixed delays are those that are all unrelated to one specific point in time and only serve the purpose of pausing execution for a fixed amount of time. A fixed delay, for example, may be used to wait for 10 milliseconds after an event occurs, before proceeding with another action. For example:

```
CON
  _clkfreq = xtal1              'Set for slow crystal
  _xinfreq = 5_000_000          'Use 5 MHz accurate crystal

  repeat
   !outa[0]                     'Toggle pin 0
   waitcnt(50_000 + cnt)        'Wait for 10 ms
```

This code toggles the state of I/O pin P0 and waits for 50,000 system clock cycles before repeating the loop again. Remember, the *Value* parameter must be the desired 32-bit value to match against the System Clock's value. Since the System Clock is a global resource that changes every clock cycle, to delay for a certain number of cycles from "now" we need a value that is added to the current System Counter value. The cnt in "50_000 + cnt" is the System Counter Register variable; it returns the value of the System Counter at that moment in time. So our code says to wait for 50,000 cycles plus the current value of the System Counter; i.e: wait 50,000 cycles from now. Assuming that an external 5 MHz crystal is being used, 50,000 cycles is about 10 ms (1/100th second) of time.

IMPORTANT: Since WAITCNT pauses the cog until the System Counter matches the given value, care must be taken to ensure that the given value was not already surpassed by the System Counter. If the System Counter already passed the given value before the wait hardware activated then the cog will appear to have halted permanently when, in fact, it is waiting for the counter to exceed 32 bits and wrap around to the given value. Even at 80 MHz, it takes over 53 seconds for the 32-bit System Counter to wrap around!

Related to this, when using WAITCNT in Spin code as shown above, make sure to write the *Value* expression the same way we did: in the form "offset + cnt" as opposed to "cnt + offset." This is because the Spin interpreter will evaluate this expression from left to right, and each intermediate evaluation within an expression takes time to perform. If cnt were at the start of the expression, the System Counter would be read first then the rest of the expression would be evaluated, taking an unknown amount of cycles and making our cnt value quite old by the time the final result is calculated. However, having cnt as the last value in the WAITCNT expression ensures a fixed amount of overhead (cycles) between reading the System Counter and activating the wait hardware. In fact, the interpreter takes 381 cycles of final overhead when the command is written in the form waitcnt(offset + cnt). **This means the value of offset must always be at least 381 to avoid unexpectedly long delays.**

Synchronized Delays

Synchronized delays are those that are all directly related to one specific point in time, a "base" time, and serve the purpose of "time-aligning" future events relative to that point. A synchronized delay, for example, may be used to output or input a signal at a specific interval, despite the unknown amounts of overhead associated with the code itself. To understand how this is different than the Fixed Delay example, let's look at that example's timing diagram.

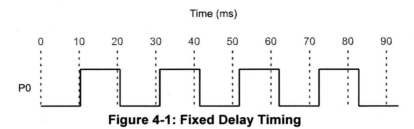

Figure 4-1: Fixed Delay Timing

Figure 4-1 shows the output of our previous example, the fixed delay example. Notice how the I/O pin P0 toggles roughly every 10 milliseconds, but not exactly? In fact, there's a cumulative error that makes successive state changes further and further out-of-sync in relation to our start time, 0 ms. The delay is 10 ms in length, but the error occurs because that delay doesn't compensate for the length of the rest of the loop. The repeat, !outa[0] and WAITCNT statements each take a little time to execute, and all that extra time is in addition to the 10 ms delay that WAITCNT specified.

Using WAITCNT a slightly different way, for a synchronized delay, will eliminate this timing error. The following example assumes we're using a 5 MHz external crystal.

```
CON
  _clkfreq = xtal1              'Set for slow crystal
  _xinfreq = 5_000_000          'Use 5 MHz accurate crystal

PUB Toggle | Time
  Time := cnt                   'Get current system counter value
  repeat
    waitcnt(Time += 50_000)     'Wait for 10 ms
    !outa[0]                    'Toggle pin 0
```

This code first retrieves the value of the System Counter, Time := cnt, then starts the repeat loop where it waits for the System Counter to reach Time + 50,000, toggles the state of I/O pin P0 and repeats the loop again. The statement Time += 50_000 is actually an assignment statement; it adds the value of Time to 50,000, stores that result back into Time and then executes the WAITCNT command using that result. Notice that we retrieved the System Counter's value only once, at the start of the example; that is our base time. Then we wait for the System Counter to equal that original base time plus 50,000 and perform the actions in the loop. Each successive iteration through the loop, we wait for the System Counter to equal another multiple of 50,000 from the base time. This method automatically compensates for

---

the overhead time consumed by the loop statements: `repeat`, `!outa[0]` and `waitcnt`. The resulting output looks like Figure 4-2.

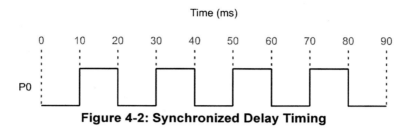

Figure 4-2: Synchronized Delay Timing

Using the synchronized delay method, our output signal is always perfectly aligned to the time base plus a multiple of our interval. This will work as long as the time base (an external crystal) is accurate and the overhead in the loop does not exceed the time interval itself. Note that we waited, with WAITCNT, before the first toggle so that the time between the very first toggle and the second matches that of all the rest.

Calculating Time

An object can delay a specific amount of time even if the application changes the System Clock frequency occasionally. To do this, use WAITCNT combined with an expression that includes the current System Clock frequency (CLKFREQ). For example, without you knowing what the actual clock frequency will be for applications using your object, the following line can be used to delay the cog for 1 millisecond; as long as the clock frequency is fast enough.

```
waitcnt(clkfreq / 1000 + cnt)        'delay cog 1 millisecond
```

For more information, see CLKFREQ on page 175.

WAITPEQ

Pause a cog's execution until I/O pin(s) match designated state(s).

((PUB ┆ PRI))
  WAITPEQ (*State*, *Mask*, *Port*)

- **_State_** is the logic state(s) to compare the pin(s) against. It is a 32-bit value that indicates the high or low states of up to 32 I/O pins. *State* is compared against either (INA & *Mask*), or (INB & *Mask*), depending on *Port*.
- **_Mask_** is the desired pin(s) to monitor. *Mask* is a 32-bit value that contains high (1) bits for every I/O pin that should be monitored; low (0) bits indicate pins that should be ignored. Mask is bitwised-ANDed with the 32-bit port's input states and the resulting value is compared against the entire *State* value.
- **_Port_** is a 1-bit value indicating the I/O port to monitor; 0 = Port A, 1 = Port B. Only Port A exists on current (P8X32A) Propeller chips.

Explanation

WAITPEQ, "Wait for Pin(s) to Equal," is one of four wait commands (WAITCNT, WAITPEQ, WAITPNE, and WAITVID) used to pause execution of a cog until a condition is met. WAITPEQ pauses the cog until the value of *Port's* I/O pin states, bitwised-ANDed with *Mask*, matches that of *State*.

When executed, WAITPEQ activates special "wait" hardware in the cog that prevents the System Clock from causing further code execution within the cog until the moment the designated pin, or group of pins, equals the indicated state(s). The wait hardware checks the I/O pins every System Clock cycle and the cog's power consumption is reduced by approximately 7/8^{ths} during this time.

Using WAITPEQ

WAITPEQ is a great way to synchronize code to external events. For example:

```
waitpeq(%0100, %1100, 0)      'Wait for P3 & P2 to be low & high
outa[0] := 1                  'Set P0 high
```

The above code pauses the cog until I/O pin 3 is low and I/O pin 2 is high, then sets I/O pin 0 high.

Using Variable Pin Numbers

For Propeller objects, quite often it is necessary to monitor a single pin whose pin number is specified outside the object itself. An easy way to translate that pin number into the proper 32-bit *State* and *Mask* value is by using the Bitwise Decode operator "|<" (See 265 for more information). For example, if the pin number was specified by the variable Pin, and we needed to wait until that pin is high, we could use the following code:

```
waitpeq(|< Pin, |< Pin, 0)   'Wait for Pin to go high
```

The *Mask* parameter, |< Pin, evaluates to a long value where only one bit is high; the bit that corresponds to the pin number given by Pin.

Waiting for Transitions

If we needed to wait for a transition from one state to another (high-to-low, for example) we could use the following code:

```
waitpeq(%100000, 5, 0)        'Wait for Pin 5 to go high
waitpeq(%000000, 5, 0)        'Then wait for Pin 5 to go low
```

This example first waits for P5 to go high, then waits for it to go low; a high-to-low transition. If we had used the second line of code without the first, the cog would not have paused at all if P5 had been low to start with.

WAITPNE

Pause a cog's execution until I/O pin(s) do not match designated state(s).

((PUB ⦙ PRI))
  WAITPNE (*State*, *Mask*, *Port*)

- **State** is the logic state(s) to compare the pins against. It is a 32-bit value that indicates the high or low states of up to 32 I/O pins. *State* is compared against either (INA & *Mask*), or (INB & *Mask*), depending on *Port*.
- **Mask** is the desired pin(s) to monitor. *Mask* is a 32-bit value that contains high (1) bits for every I/O pin that should be monitored; low (0) bits indicate pins that should be ignored. Mask is bitwised-ANDed with the 32-bit port's input states and the resulting value is compared against the entire *State* value.
- **Port** is a 1-bit value indicating the I/O port to monitor; 0 = Port A, 1 = Port B. Only Port A exists on current (P8X32A) Propeller chips.

Explanation

WAITPNE, "Wait for Pin(s) to Not Equal," is one of four wait commands (WAITCNT, WAITPEQ, WAITPNE, and WAITVID) used to pause execution of a cog until a condition is met. WAITPNE is the complimentary form of WAITPEQ; it pauses the cog until the value of *Port's* I/O pin states, bitwised-ANDed with *Mask*, does not match that of *State*.

When executed, WAITPNE activates special "wait" hardware in the cog that prevents the System Clock from causing further code execution within the cog until the moment the designated pin, or group of pins, does not equal the designated state(s). The wait hardware checks the I/O pins every System Clock cycle and the cog's power consumption is reduced by approximately $7/8^{ths}$ during this time.

Using WAITPNE

WAITPNE is a great way to synchronize code to external events. For example:

```
waitpeq(%0100, %1100, 0) 'Wait for P3 & P2 to be low & and high
waitpne(%0100, %1100, 0) 'Wait for P3 & P2 to not match prev. state
outa[0] := 1             'Set P0 high
```

The above code pauses the cog until P3 is low and P2 is high, then pauses the cog again until one or both of those pins changes states, then it sets P0 high.

WAITVID

Pause a cog's execution until its Video Generator is available to take pixel data.

((PUB ¦ PRI))
    WAITVID (*Colors*, *Pixels*)

-    *Colors* is a long containing four byte-sized color values, each describing the four possible colors of the pixel patterns in *Pixels*.
-    *Pixels* is the next 16-pixel by 2-bit (or 32-pixel by 1-bit) pixel pattern to display.

Explanation

WAITVID, "Wait for Video Generator," is one of four wait commands (WAITCNT, WAITPEQ, WAITPNE, and WAITVID) used to pause execution of a cog until a condition is met. WAITVID pauses the cog until its Video Generator hardware is ready for the next pixel data, then the Video Generator accepts that data and the cog continues execution with the next line of code.

When executed, WAITVID activates special "wait" hardware in the cog that prevents the System Clock from causing further code execution within the cog until the moment the Video Generator is ready. The wait hardware checks the Video Generator's status every System Clock cycle and the cog's power consumption is reduced significantly during this time.

Using WAITVID

WAITVID is simply a delivery mechanism for data to the cog's Video Generator hardware. Since the Video Generator works independently from the cog itself, the two must synchronize each time data is needed for the display device. The frequency at which this occurs depends on the display device and the corresponding settings for the Video Generator, but in every case, the cog must have new data available the moment the Video Generator is ready for it. The cog uses the WAITVID command to wait for the right time and then "hand off" this data to the Video Generator.

The *Colors* parameter is a 32-bit value containing either four 8-bit color values (for 4-color mode) or two 8-bit color values in the lower 16 bits (for 2-color mode). For VGA, each color value's upper 6-bits is the 2-bit red, 2-bit green, and 2-bit blue color components describing the desired color; the lower 2-bits are "don't care" bits. Each of the color values corresponds to one of the four possible colors per 2-bit pixel (when *Pixels* is used as a 16x2 bit pixel pattern) or as one of the two possible colors per 1-bit pixel (when *Pixels* is used at a 32x1 bit pixel pattern).

Pixels describes the pixel pattern to display, either 16 pixels or 32 pixels depending on the color-depth configuration of the Video Generator.

Review the TV and VGA objects for examples of how WAITVID is used.

Make sure to start the cog's Video Generator and Counter A before executing the WAITVID command or it will wait forever.

WORD

Declare word-sized symbol, word aligned/sized data, or read/write a word of main memory.

VAR
>   WORD *Symbol* ⟨[*Count*]⟩

DAT
>   WORD *Data*

((PUB ¦ PRI))
>   WORD [*BaseAddress*] ⟨[*Offset*]⟩

((PUB ¦ PRI))
>   *Symbol*. WORD ⟨[*Offset*]⟩

- *Symbol* is the desired name for the variable (Syntax 1) or the existing name of the variable (Syntax 4).
- *Count* is an optional expression indicating the number of word-sized elements for *Symbol*, arranged in an array from element 0 to element *Count*-1.
- *Data* is a constant expression or comma-separated list of constant expressions.
- *BaseAddress* is an expression describing the address of main memory to read or write. If *Offset* is omitted, *BaseAddress* is the actual address to operate on. If *Offset* is specified, *BaseAddress* + *Offset* is the actual address to operate on.
- *Offset* is an optional expression indicating the offset from *BaseAddress* to operate on, or the offset from word 0 of Symbol.

Explanation

WORD is one of three multi-purpose declarations (BYTE, WORD, and LONG) that declare or operate on memory. WORD can be used to:

1) declare a word-sized (16-bit) symbol or a multi-word symbolic array in a VAR block, or
2) declare word-aligned, and/or word-sized, data in a DAT block, or
3) read or write a word of main memory at a base address with an optional offset, or
4) access a word within a long-sized variable.

Word Variable Declaration (Syntax 1)

In VAR blocks, syntax 1 of WORD is used to declare global, symbolic variables that are either word-sized, or are any array of words. For example:

```
VAR
  word  Temp            'Temp is a word (2 bytes)
  word  List[25]        'List is a word array
```

The above example declares two variables (symbols), Temp and List. Temp is simply a single, word-sized variable. The line under the Temp declaration uses the optional *Count* field to create an array of 25 word-sized variable elements called List. Both Temp and List can be accessed from any PUB or PRI method within the same object that this VAR block was declared; they are global to the object. An example of this is below.

```
PUB SomeMethod
  Temp := 25_000        'Set Temp to 25,000
  List[0] := 500        'Set first element of List to 500
  List[1] := 9_000      'Set second element of List to 9,000
  List[24] := 60_000    'Set last element of List to 60,000
```

For more information about using WORD in this way, refer to the VAR section's Variable Declarations (Syntax 1) on page 315, and keep in mind that WORD is used for the *Size* field in that description.

Word Data Declaration (Syntax 2)

In DAT blocks, syntax 2 of WORD is used to declare word-aligned, and/or word-sized data that is compiled as constant values in main memory. DAT blocks allow this declaration to have an optional symbol preceding it, which can be used for later reference. See DAT, page 208. For example:

```
DAT
  MyData  word  640, $AAAA, 5_500        'Word-aligned/word-sized data
  MyList  byte  word $FF99, word 1_000   'Byte-aligned/word-sized data
```

The above example declares two data symbols, MyData and MyList. MyData points to the start of word-aligned and word-sized data in main memory. MyData's values, in main memory, are 640, $AAAA and 5,500, respectively. MyList uses a special DAT block syntax of WORD that creates a byte-aligned but word-sized set of data in main memory. MyList's values, in main memory, are $FF99 and 1,000, respectively. When accessed a byte at a time, MyList contains $99, $FF, 232 and 3 since the data is stored in little-endian format.

This data is compiled into the object and resulting application as part of the executable code section and may be accessed using the read/write form, syntax 3, of WORD (see below). For more information about using WORD in this way, refer to the DAT section's Declaring Data

(Syntax 1) on page 208 and keep in mind that WORD is used for the *Size* field in that description.

Reading/Writing Words of Main Memory (Syntax 3)

In PUB and PRI blocks, syntax 3 of WORD is used to read or write word-sized values of main memory. In the following two examples, we'll assume our object contained the DAT block from the example above, and we will demonstrate two different ways to access that data.

First, let's try accessing the data directly using the labels we provided in our data block.

```
PUB GetData | Index, Temp
    Temp := MyData                  'Read first word of MyData into Temp
    <do something with Temp>        'Perform task with Temp

    repeat Index from 0 to 1        'Repeat two times
        Temp := MyList[Index]       'Read data to Temp, 1 byte at a time
        <do something with Temp>    'Perform task with value in Temp
```

The first line inside of the GetData method, Temp := MyData, reads the first value in the MyData list (the word-sized value 640) and stores it in Temp. Further down, in the REPEAT loop, the Temp := MyList[Index] line reads a byte of main memory from the location of MyList + Index. The first time through the loop (Index = 0) the value $99 ($FF99's low-byte) is read from MyList and the second time through the loop (Index = 1) the next byte is read, $FF ($FF99's high-byte). Why were bytes read instead of words? MyList points at the start of our desired data and our data was specified as word-sized data but the symbol MyList is treated as a byte pointer since that data was specified to be byte-aligned.

Perhaps you intended to read word-sized data from MyList just like we did from MyData. Coincidentally, even though MyList is declared as byte-aligned word data, it is also happens to be word-aligned as well because the previous declaration finished on a word boundary. This fact allows us to use the WORD declaration to achieve our goal.

```
PUB GetData | Index, Temp
    Temp := WORD[@MyData]                   'Read first word of MyData into Temp
    <do something with Temp>                'Perform task with Temp

    repeat Index from 0 to 1                'Repeat two times
        Temp := WORD[@MyList][Index]        'Read data to Temp 1 word at a time
        <do something with Temp>            'Perform task with value in Temp
```

In this example, the first line inside of the GetData method uses the WORD declaration to read a word of main memory from the address of MyData and stores it in Temp, in this case, the value 640. Further down, in the REPEAT loop, the WORD declaration reads a word of main memory from the address of MyList + Index and stores it in Temp. Since the first iteration of the loop has Index set to 0, the first word of MyList is read, $FF99. The next time through the loop it reads the next word, effectively @MyList + 1 (the 1,000).

Note that if the data was not word-aligned, either intentionally or coincidentally, we'd have different results from the REPEAT loop just described. For example, if MyList happened to be shifted forward by one byte, the first value read by the loop would be $99xx; where xx is an unknown byte-sized value. Similarly, the second value read would be 59647; made up of the $FF from the upper byte of MyList's first value, and the 232 from the lower byte of MyList's second value. Make sure to pay close attention to data value alignments in memory to avoid this likely unintentional result.

Using a similar syntax, words of main memory can be written to as well, as long as they are RAM locations. For example:

```
WORD[@MyList][0] := 8_192        'Write 8,192 to first word of MyList
```

This line writes the value 8,192 to the first word of data at MyList.

Accessing Words of Long-Sized Variables (Syntax 4)

In PUB and PRI blocks, syntax 4 of WORD is used to read or write word-sized components of long-sized variables. For example:

```
VAR
  long  LongVar

PUB Main
  LongVar.word := 65000        'Set first word of LongVar to 65000
  LongVar.word[0] := 65000     'Same as above
  LongVar.word[1] := 1         'Set second word of LongVar to 1
```

This example accesses the word-sized components of LongVar, individually. The comments indicate what each line is doing. At the end of the Main method LongVar will equal 130,536.

WORDFILL

Fill words of main memory with a value.

```
((PUB ┊ PRI))
   WORDFILL (StartAddress, Value, Count )
```

- **StartAddress** is an expression indicating the location of the first word of memory to fill with *Value*.
- **Value** is an expression indicating the value to fill words with.
- **Count** is an expression indicating the number of words to fill, starting with *StartAddress*.

Explanation

WORDFILL is one of three commands (BYTEFILL, WORDFILL, and LONGFILL) used to fill blocks of main memory with a specific value. WORDFILL fills *Count* words of main memory with *Value*, starting at location *StartAddress*.

Using WORDFILL

WORDFILL is a great way to clear large blocks of word-sized memory. For example:

```
VAR
  word    Buff[100]

PUB Main
  wordfill(@Buff, 0, 100)     'Clear Buff to 0
```

The first line of the Main method, above, clears the entire 100-word (200-byte) Buff array to all zeros. WORDFILL is faster at this task than a dedicated REPEAT loop is.

WORDMOVE

Copy words from one region to another in main memory.

((PUB ┆ PRI))
   WORDMOVE (*DestAddress, SrcAddress, Count*)

- *DestAddress* is an expression specifying the main memory location to copy the first word of source to.
- *SrcAddress* is an expression specifying the main memory location of the first word of source to copy.
- *Count* is an expression indicating the number of words of the source to copy to the destination.

Explanation

WORDMOVE is one of three commands (BYTEMOVE, WORDMOVE, and LONGMOVE) used to copy blocks of main memory from one area to another. WORDMOVE copies *Count* words of main memory starting from *SrcAddress* to main memory starting at *DestAddress*.

Using WORDMOVE

WORDMOVE is a great way to copy large blocks of word-sized memory. For example:

```
VAR
   word    Buff1[100]
   word    Buff2[100]

PUB Main
   wordmove(@Buff2, @Buff1, 100)     'Copy Buff1 to Buff2
```

The first line of the Main method, above, copies the entire 100-word (200-byte) Buff1 array to the Buff2 array. WORDMOVE is faster at this task than a dedicated REPEAT loop.

_XINFREQ

Pre-defined, one-time settable constant for specifying the external crystal frequency.

```
CON
  _XINFREQ = Expression
```

- **Expression** is an integer expression that indicates the external crystal frequency; the frequency on the XI pin. This value is used for application start-up.

Explanation

_XINFREQ specifies the external crystal frequency, which is used along with the clock mode to determine the System Clock frequency at start-up. It is a pre-defined constant symbol whose value is determined by the top object file of an application. _XINFREQ is either set directly by the application itself, or is set indirectly as the result of the _CLKMODE and _CLKFREQ settings.

The top object file in an application (the one where compilation starts from) can specify a setting for _XINFREQ in its CON block. This, along with the clock mode, defines the frequency that the System Clock will switch to as soon as the application is booted up and execution begins.

The application can specify either _XINFREQ or _CLKFREQ in the CON block; they are mutually exclusive and the non-specified one is automatically calculated and set as a result of specifying the other.

The following examples assume that they are contained within the top object file. Any _XINFREQ settings in child objects are simply ignored by the compiler.

For example:

```
CON
    _CLKMODE = XTAL1 + PLL8X
    _XINFREQ = 4_000_000
```

The first declaration in the above CON block sets the clock mode for an external low-speed crystal and a Clock PLL multiplier of 8. The second declaration indicates the external crystal frequency is 4 MHz, which means the System Clock's frequency will be 32 MHz because 4 MHz * 8 = 32 MHz. The _CLKFREQ value is automatically set to 32 MHz because of these declarations.

```
CON
  _CLKMODE = XTAL2
  _XINFREQ = 10_000_000
```

These two declarations set the clock mode for an external medium-speed crystal, no Clock PLL multiplier, and an external crystal frequency of 10 MHz. The **_CLKFREQ** value, and thus the System Clock frequency, is automatically set to 10 MHz, as well, because of these declarations.

Chapter 5: Assembly Language Reference

This chapter describes all elements of the Propeller chip's Assembly language and is best used as a reference for individual elements of the assembly language. Many instructions have corresponding Spin commands so referring to the Spin Language Reference is recommended for further information.

The Assembly Language Reference is divided into two main sections:

1) **The Structure of Propeller Assembly**. Propeller Assembly code is an optional part of Propeller Objects. This section describes the general structure of Propeller Assembly code and how it fits within objects.

2) **The Categorical Listing of the Propeller Assembly Language.** All elements, including operators, are grouped by related function. This is a great way to quickly realize the breadth of the language and what features are available for specific uses. Each listed element has a page reference for more information. Some elements are marked with a superscript "s" indicating that they are also available in Propeller Spin, though syntax may vary. Such marked elements are also included in Chapter 4: Spin Language Reference.

3) **The Assembly Language Elements.** All instructions are listed in a Master Table at the start, and most elements have their own dedicated sub-section, alphabetically arranged to ease searching for them. Those individual elements without a dedicated sub-section, such as Operators, are grouped within other related sub-sections but can be easily located by following their page references from the Categorical Listing.

The Structure of Propeller Assembly

Every Propeller Object consists of Spin code plus optional assembly code and data. An object's Spin code provides it with structure, consisting of special-purpose blocks. Data and Propeller Assembly code, if included, are located in the special-purpose block called DAT (data block). See DAT, page 208.

Spin code is executed by a cog running the Spin Interpreter, however, Propeller Assembly code is executed by a cog in its pure form. Because of this nature, Propeller Assembly code and any data belonging to it must be loaded (in its entirety) into a cog in order to execute it. In this way, both Propeller Assembly code and data are treated the same during the cog loading process. The following example shows an object whose Spin code in the `Main` method launches another cog to run the Propeller Assembly routine `Toggle`.

```
{{ AssemblyToggle.spin }}

CON
  _clkmode = xtal1 + pll16x
  _xinfreq = 5_000_000


PUB Main
{Launch cog to toggle P16 endlessly}

  cognew(@Toggle, 0)                      'Launch new cog


DAT
{Toggle P16}
                    ORG     0             'Begin at Cog RAM addr 0
Toggle              mov     dira, Pin     'Set Pin to output
                    mov     Time, cnt     'Calculate delay time
                    add     Time, #9      'Set minimum delay here
:loop               waitcnt Time, Delay   'Wait
                    xor     outa, Pin     'Toggle Pin
                    jmp     #:loop        'Loop endlessly

Pin       long      |< 16                 'Pin number
Delay     long      6_000_000             'Clock cycles to delay
Time      res  1                          'System Counter Workspace
```

Both assembly and data may be intermixed within the **DAT** block but care should be taken to arrange it such that all critical elements are loaded into the cog in the proper order for execution. The **COGNEW** and **COGINIT** commands, when used to launch Propeller Assembly code, cause the cog to be loaded with 496 consecutive long values starting from the specified address. Whether or not it is required by the code, any data intermixed with this 496 longs of space will be loaded as well.

Each Propeller assembly instruction has common syntax elements consisting of an optional label, optional condition, instruction, and optional effects. See Common Syntax Elements, page 348, for more information.

Categorical Listing of Propeller Assembly Language

Directives

ORG	Adjust compile-time cog address pointer; p 392.
FIT	Validate that previous instructions/data fit entirely in cog; p 372.
RES	Reserve next long(s) for symbol; p 397.

Configuration

CLKSET[s]	Set clock mode at run time; p 361.

Cog Control

COGID[s]	Get current cog's ID; p 365.
COGINIT[s]	Start, or restart, a cog by ID; p 366.
COGSTOP[s]	Stop a cog by ID; p 367.

Process Control

LOCKNEW[s]	Check out a new lock; p 376.
LOCKRET[s]	Return a lock; p 376.
LOCKCLR[s]	Clear a lock by ID; p 375.
LOCKSET[s]	Set a lock by ID; p 377.
WAITCNT[s]	Pause execution temporarily; p 411.
WAITPEQ[s]	Pause execution until pin(s) match designated state(s); p 412.
WAITPNE[s]	Pause execution until pin(s) do not match designated state(s); p 413.
WAITVID[s]	Pause execution until Video Generator is available for pixel data; p 414.

Conditions

IF_ALWAYS	Always; p 369.
IF_NEVER	Never; p 369.
IF_E	If equal (Z = 1); p 369.
IF_NE	If not equal (Z = 0); p 369.
IF_A	If above (!C & !Z = 1); p 369.

IF_B	If below (C = 1); p 369.
IF_AE	If above or equal (C = 0); p 369.
IF_BE	If below or equal (C | Z = 1); p 369.
IF_C	If C set; p 369.
IF_NC	If C clear; p 369.
IF_Z	If Z set; p369.
IF_NZ	If Z clear; p 369.
IF_C_EQ_Z	If C equal to Z; p 369.
IF_C_NE_Z	If C not equal to Z; p 369.
IF_C_AND_Z	If C set and Z set; p 369.
IF_C_AND_NZ	If C set and Z clear; p 369.
IF_NC_AND_Z	If C clear and Z set; p 369.
IF_NC_AND_NZ	If C clear and Z clear; p 369.
IF_C_OR_Z	If C set or Z set; p 369.
IF_C_OR_NZ	If C set or Z clear; p 369.
IF_NC_OR_Z	If C clear or Z set; p 369.
IF_NC_OR_NZ	If C clear or Z clear; p 369.
IF_Z_EQ_C	If Z equal to C; p 369.
IF_Z_NE_C	If Z not equal to C; p 369.
IF_Z_AND_C	If Z set and C set; p 369.
IF_Z_AND_NC	If Z set and C clear; p 369.
IF_NZ_AND_C	If Z clear and C set; p 369.
IF_NZ_AND_NC	If Z clear and C clear; p 369.
IF_Z_OR_C	If Z set or C set; p 369.
IF_Z_OR_NC	If Z set or C clear; p 369.
IF_NZ_OR_C	If Z clear or C set; p 369.
IF_NZ_OR_NC	If Z clear or C clear; p 369.

Flow Control

CALL	Jump to address with intention to return to next instruction; p 360.
DJNZ	Decrement value and jump to address if not zero; p 370.
JMP	Jump to address unconditionally; p 374.
JMPRET	Jump to address with intention to "return" to another address; p 374.
TJNZ	Test value and jump to address if not zero; p 409.
TJZ	Test value and jump to address if zero; p 410.
RET	Return to stored address; p 399.

Effects

NR	No result (don't write result); p 371.
WR	Write result; p 371.
WC	Write C status; p 371.
WZ	Write Z status; p 371.

Main Memory Access

RDBYTE	Read byte of main memory; p 394.
RDWORD	Read word of main memory; p 396.
RDLONG	Read long of main memory; p 395.
WRBYTE	Write a byte to main memory; p 414.
WRWORD	Write a word to main memory; p 416.
WRLONG	Write a long to main memory; p 415.

Common Operations

ABS	Get absolute value of a number; p 353.
ABSNEG	Get negative of number's absolute value; p 354.
NEG	Get negative of a number; p 386.
NEGC	Get a value, or its additive inverse, based on C; p 386.
NEGNC	Get a value or its additive inverse, based on !C; p 387.
NEGZ	Get a value, or its additive inverse, based on Z; p 389.

Assembly Language Reference

NEGNZ	Get a value, or its additive inverse, based on !Z; p 388.
MIN	Limit minimum of unsigned value to another unsigned value; p 379.
MINS	Limit minimum of signed value to another signed value; p 380.
MAX	Limit maximum of unsigned value to another unsigned value; p 378.
MAXS	Limit maximum of signed value to another signed value; p 378.
ADD	Add two unsigned values; p 354.
ADDABS	Add absolute value to another value; p 355.
ADDS	Add two signed values; p 356.
ADDX	Add two unsigned values plus C; p 357.
ADDSX	Add two signed values plus C; p 356.
SUB	Subtract two unsigned values; p 403.
SUBABS	Subtract an absolute value from another value; p 404.
SUBS	Subtract two signed values; p 404.
SUBX	Subtract unsigned value plus C from another unsigned value; p 406.
SUBSX	Subtract signed value plus C from another signed value; p 405.
SUMC	Sum signed value with another of C-affected sign; p 406.
SUMNC	Sum signed vaule with another of !C-affected sign; p 407.
SUMZ	Sum signed value with another Z-affected sign; p 408.
SUMNZ	Sum signed value with another of !Z-afected sign; p 408.
MUL	<reserved for future use>
MULS	<reserved for future use>
AND	Bitwise AND two values; p 358.
ANDN	Bitwise AND value with NOT of another; p 359.
OR	Bitwise OR two values; p 392.
XOR	Bitwise XOR two values; p 417.
ONES	<reserved for future use>
ENC	<reserved for future use>
RCL	Rotate C left into value by specified number of bits; p 393.
RCR	Rotate C right into value by specified number of bits; p 394.
REV	Reverse LSBs of value and zero-extend; p 399.
ROL	Rotate value left by specified number of bits; p 400.

ROR	Rotate value right by specified number of bits; p 400.
SHL	Shift value left by specified number of bits; p 402.
SHR	Shift value right by specified number of bits; p 402.
SAR	Shift value arithmetically right by specified number of bits; p 401.
CMP	Compare two unsigned values; p 362.
CMPS	Compare two signed values; p 362.
CMPX	Compare two unsigned values plus C; p 364.
CMPSX	Compare two signed values plus C; p 364.
CMPSUB	Compare unsigned values, subtract second if lesser or equal; p 363.
TEST	Bitwise AND two values to affect flags only; p 409.
MOV	Set a register to a value; p 380.
MOVS	Set a register's source field to a value; p 382.
MOVD	Set a register's destination field to a value; p 381.
MOVI	Set a register's instruction field to a value; p 381.
MUXC	Set discrete bits of a value to the state of C; p 383.
MUXNC	Set discrete bits of a value to the state of !C; p 384.
MUXZ	Set discrete bits of a value to the state of Z; p 385.
MUXNZ	Set discrete bits of a value to the state of !Z; p 384.
HUBOP	Perform a hub operation; p 373.
NOP	No operation, just elapse four cycles; p 389.

Registers

DIRA[s]	Direction Register for 32-bit port A; p 397.
DIRB[s]	Direction Register for 32-bit port B (future use); p 397.
INA[s]	Input Register for 32-bit port A (read only); p 397.
INB[s]	Input Register for 32-bit port B (read only) (future use); p 397.
OUTA[s]	Output Register for 32-bit port A; p 397.
OUTB[s]	Output Register for 32-bit port B (future use); p 397.
CNT[s]	32-bit System Counter Register (read only); p 397.
CTRA[s]	Counter A Control Register; p 397.
CTRB[s]	Counter B Control Register; p 397.

Assembly Language Reference

FRQA[s]	Counter A Frequency Register; p 397.
FRQB[s]	Counter B Frequency Register; p 397.
PHSA[s]	Counter A Phase Lock Loop (PLL) Register; p 397.
PHSB[s]	Counter B Phase Lock Loop (PLL) Register; p 397.
VCFG[s]	Video Configuration Register; p 397.
VSCL[s]	Video Scale Register; p 397.
PAR[s]	Cog Boot Parameter Register (read only); p 397.

Constants
NOTE: Refer to Constants (pre-defined) in Chapter 4: Spin Language Reference.

TRUE[s]	Logical true: -1 ($FFFFFFFF); p 202.
FALSE[s]	Logical false: 0 ($00000000); p 202.
POSX[s]	Maximum positive integer: 2,147,483,647 ($7FFFFFFF); p 203.
NEGX[s]	Maximum negative integer: -2,147,483,648 ($80000000); p 203.
PI[s]	Floating-point value for PI: ~3.141593 ($40490FDB); p 203.

Unary Operators
NOTE: All operators shown are constant-expression operators.

+	Positive (+X) unary form of Add; p 391.
−	Negate (−X); unary form of Subtract; p 391.
^^	Square root; p 391.
||	Absolute Value; p 391.
|<	Decode value (0-31) into single-high-bit long; p 391.
>|	Encode long into value (0 - 32) as high-bit priority; p 391.
!	Bitwise: NOT; p 391.
@	Address of symbol; p 391.

Binary Operators

NOTE: All operators shown are constant expression operators.

+	Add; p 391.
–	Subtract; p 391.
*	Multiply and return lower 32 bits (signed); p 391.
**	Multiply and return upper 32 bits (signed); p 391.
/	Divide and return quotient (signed); p 391.
//	Divide and return remainder (signed); p 391.
#>	Limit minimum (signed); p 391.
<#	Limit maximum (signed); p 391.
~>	Shift arithmetic right; p 391.
<<	Bitwise: Shift left; p 391.
>>	Bitwise: Shift right; p 391.
<–	Bitwise: Rotate left; p 391.
–>	Bitwise: Rotate right; p 391.
><	Bitwise: Reverse; p 391.
&	Bitwise: AND; p 391.
|	Bitwise: OR; p 391.
^	Bitwise: XOR; p 391.
AND	Boolean: AND (promotes non-0 to -1); p 391.
OR	Boolean: OR (promotes non-0 to -1); p 391.
==	Boolean: Is equal; p 391.
<>	Boolean: Is not equal; p 391.
<	Boolean: Is less than (signed); p 391.
>	Boolean: Is greater than (signed); p 391.
=<	Boolean: Is equal or less (signed); p 391.
=>	Boolean: Is equal or greater (signed); p 391.

Assembly Language Elements

Syntax Definitions

In addition to detailed descriptions, the following pages contain syntax definitions for many elements that describe, in short terms, all the options of that element. The syntax definitions use special symbols to indicate when and how certain element features are to be used.

BOLDCAPS	Items in bold uppercase should be typed in exactly as shown.
Bold Italics	Items in bold italics should be replaced by user text; symbols, operators, expressions, etc.
. : , #	Periods, colons, commas, and pound signs should be typed in where shown.
⟨ ⟩	Angle bracket symbols enclose optional items. Enter the enclosed item if desired. Do not enter the angle brackets.
Double line	Separates instruction from the result value.

Common Syntax Elements

When reading the syntax definitions in this chapter, keep in mind that all Propeller Assembly instructions have three common, optional elements; a label, a condition, and effects. Each Propeller Assembly instruction has the following basic syntax:

⟨*Label*⟩ ⟨*Condition*⟩ *Instruction* ⟨*Effects*⟩

- *Label* is an optional statement label. *Label* can be global (starting with an underscore '_' or a letter) or can be local (starting with a colon ':'). Local *Labels* must be separated from other same-named local labels by at least one global label. *Label* is used by instructions like JMP, CALL and COGINIT to designate the target destination.
- *Condition* is an optional execution condition (IF_C, IF_Z, etc.) that causes *Instruction* to be executed or not. See Conditions on page 368 for more information.
- *Instruction* is a Propeller Assembly instruction (MOV, ADD, COGINIT, etc.) and its operands.
- *Effects* is an optional list of one to three execution effects (WZ, WC, WR, and NR) to apply to the instruction, if executed. They cause the *Instruction* to modify the Z flag, C flag, and to write, or not write, the instruction's result value to the destination register, respectively. See Effects on page 371 for more information.

Since every instruction can include these three optional fields (*Label*, *Condition*, and *Effects*), for simplicity those common fields are intentionally left out of the instruction's syntax description.

So, when you read a syntax description such as this:

WAITCNT *Target*, ⟨#⟩ *Delta*

...remember that the true syntax is this:

⟨*Label*⟩ ⟨*Condition*⟩ WAITCNT *Target*, ⟨#⟩ *Delta* ⟨*Effects*⟩

This rule applies only to Propeller Assembly instructions; it does not apply to Propeller Assembly directives.

Many syntax definitions end with a table similar to the one below. This table lists the instruction's 32-bit opcode, outputs and number of clock cycles. The opcode consists of the instruction bits (–INSTR–), the "effect" status for the Z flag, C flag, result and indirect/immediate status (ZCRI), the conditional execution bits (–CON–), and the destination and source bits (–DEST- and –SRC–). The meaning of the Z and C flags, if any, is shown in the Z Result and C Result fields; indicating the meaning of a 1 in those flags. The Result field shows the instruction's default behavior for writing or not writing the instruction's result value. The Clocks field shows the number of clocks the instruction requires for execution.

0 1	Zeros (0) and ones (1) mean binary 0 and 1.
i	Lower case "i" denotes a bit that is affected by immediate status.
d s	Lower case "d" and "s" indicate destination and source bits.
?	Question marks denote bits that are dynamically set by the compiler.
---	Hyphens indicate items that are not applicable or not important.
..	Double-periods represent a range of contiguous values.

–INSTR–	ZCRI	–CON–	–DEST–	–SRC–	Z Result	C Result	Result	Clocks
000011	0001	1111	ddddddddd	------000	---	---	Not Written	7..22

Propeller Assembly Instruction Master Table

A master table for all Propeller Assembly instructions is provided on the next two pages. In this table, D and S refer to the instructions' destination and source fields, also known as d-field and s-field, respectively. For entries with asterisks in the Clocks column, be sure to read the Notes for Master Table on page 352.

Assembly Language Reference

Instruction	-INSTR- ZCRI -CON- -DEST- -SRC-	Z Result	C Result	Result	Clocks
ABS D, S	101010 001i 1111 dddddddd ssssssss	Result = 0	S[31]	Written	4
ABSNEG D, S	101011 001i 1111 dddddddd ssssssss	Result = 0	S[31]	Written	4
ADD D, S	100000 001i 1111 dddddddd ssssssss	Result = 0	Unsigned Carry	Written	4
ADDABS D, S	100010 001i 1111 dddddddd ssssssss	Result = 0	Unsigned Carry	Written	4
ADDS D, S	110100 001i 1111 dddddddd ssssssss	Result = 0	Signed Overflow	Written	4
ADDSX D, S	110110 001i 1111 dddddddd ssssssss	Z & (Result = 0)	Signed Overflow	Written	4
ADDX D, S	110010 001i 1111 dddddddd ssssssss	Z & (Result = 0)	Unsigned Carry	Written	4
AND D, S	011000 001i 1111 dddddddd ssssssss	Result = 0	Parity of Result	Written	4
ANDN D, S	011001 001i 1111 dddddddd ssssssss	Result = 0	Parity of Result	Written	4
CALL #S	010111 0011 1111 ???????? ssssssss	Result = 0	---	Written	4
CLKSET D	000011 0001 1111 dddddddd ------000	---	---	Not Written	7..22 *
CMP D, S	100001 000i 1111 dddddddd ssssssss	Result = 0	Unsigned Borrow	Not Written	4
CMPS D, S	110000 000i 1111 dddddddd ssssssss	Result = 0	Signed Borrow	Not Written	4
CMPSUB D, S	111000 000i 1111 dddddddd ssssssss	D = S	Unsigned (D => S)	Not Written	4
CMPSX D, S	110001 000i 1111 dddddddd ssssssss	Z & (Result = 0)	Signed Borrow	Not Written	4
CMPX D, S	110011 000i 1111 dddddddd ssssssss	Z & (Result = 0)	Unsigned Borrow	Not Written	4
COGID D	000011 0011 1111 dddddddd ------001	Result = 0	---	Written	7..22 *
COGINIT D	000011 0001 1111 dddddddd ------010	Result = 0	No Cog Free	Not Written	7..22 *
COGSTOP D	000011 0001 1111 dddddddd ------011	---	---	Not Written	7..22 *
DJNZ D, S	111001 001i 1111 dddddddd ssssssss	Result = 0	Unsigned Borrow	Written	4 or 8 **
HUBOP D, S	000011 000i 1111 dddddddd ssssssss	Result = 0	---	Not Written	7..22 *
JMP S	010111 000i 1111 --------- ssssssss	Result = 0	---	Not Written	4
JMPRET D, S	010111 001i 1111 dddddddd ssssssss	Result = 0	---	Written	4
LOCKCLR D	000011 0001 1111 dddddddd ------111	---	Prior Lock State	Not Written	7..22 *
LOCKNEW D	000011 0011 1111 dddddddd ------100	Result = 0	No Lock Free	Written	7..22 *
LOCKRET D	000011 0001 1111 dddddddd ------101	---	---	Not Written	7..22 *
LOCKSET D	000011 0001 1111 dddddddd ------110	---	Prior Lock State	Not Written	7..22 *
MAX D, S	010011 001i 1111 dddddddd ssssssss	D = S	Unsigned (D < S)	Written	4
MAXS D, S	010001 001i 1111 dddddddd ssssssss	D = S	Signed (D < S)	Written	4
MIN D, S	010010 001i 1111 dddddddd ssssssss	D = S	Unsigned (D < S)	Written	4
MINS D, S	010000 001i 1111 dddddddd ssssssss	D = S	Signed (D < S)	Written	4
MOV D, S	101000 001i 1111 dddddddd ssssssss	Result = 0	S[31]	Written	4
MOVD D, S	010101 001i 1111 dddddddd ssssssss	Result = 0	---	Written	4
MOVI D, S	010110 001i 1111 dddddddd ssssssss	Result = 0	---	Written	4
MOVS D, S	010100 001i 1111 dddddddd ssssssss	Result = 0	---	Written	4
MUXC D, S	011100 001i 1111 dddddddd ssssssss	Result = 0	Parity of Result	Written	4
MUXNC D, S	011101 001i 1111 dddddddd ssssssss	Result = 0	Parity of Result	Written	4
MUXNZ D, S	011111 001i 1111 dddddddd ssssssss	Result = 0	Parity of Result	Written	4
MUXZ D, S	011110 001i 1111 dddddddd ssssssss	Result = 0	Parity of Result	Written	4

Instruction	-INSTR- ZCRI -CON- -DEST- -SRC-	Z Result	C Result	Result	Clocks
NEG D, S	101001 001i 1111 ddddddddd sssssssss	Result = 0	S[31]	Written	4
NEGC D, S	101100 001i 1111 ddddddddd sssssssss	Result = 0	S[31]	Written	4
NEGNC D, S	101101 001i 1111 ddddddddd sssssssss	Result = 0	S[31]	Written	4
NEGNZ D, S	101111 001i 1111 ddddddddd sssssssss	Result = 0	S[31]	Written	4
NEGZ D, S	101110 001i 1111 ddddddddd sssssssss	Result = 0	S[31]	Written	4
NOP	------ ---- 0000 --------- ---------	---	---	---	4
OR D, S	011010 001i 1111 ddddddddd sssssssss	Result = 0	Parity of Result	Written	4
RDBYTE D, S	000000 001i 1111 ddddddddd sssssssss	Result = 0	---	Written	7..22 *
RDLONG D, S	000010 001i 1111 ddddddddd sssssssss	Result = 0	---	Written	7..22 *
RDWORD D, S	000001 001i 1111 ddddddddd sssssssss	Result = 0	---	Written	7..22 *
RCL D, S	001101 001i 1111 ddddddddd sssssssss	Result = 0	D[31]	Written	4
RCR D, S	001100 001i 1111 ddddddddd sssssssss	Result = 0	D[0]	Written	4
RET	010111 0001 1111 --------- ---------	Result = 0	---	Not Written	4
REV D, S	001111 001i 1111 ddddddddd sssssssss	Result = 0	D[0]	Written	4
ROL D, S	001001 001i 1111 ddddddddd sssssssss	Result = 0	D[31]	Written	4
ROR D, S	001000 001i 1111 ddddddddd sssssssss	Result = 0	D[0]	Written	4
SAR D, S	001110 001i 1111 ddddddddd sssssssss	Result = 0	D[0]	Written	4
SHL D, S	001011 001i 1111 ddddddddd sssssssss	Result = 0	D[31]	Written	4
SHR D, S	001010 001i 1111 ddddddddd sssssssss	Result = 0	D[0]	Written	4
SUB D, S	100001 001i 1111 ddddddddd sssssssss	Result = 0	Unsigned Borrow	Written	4
SUBABS D, S	100011 001i 1111 ddddddddd sssssssss	Result = 0	Unsigned Borrow	Written	4
SUBS D, S	110101 001i 1111 ddddddddd sssssssss	Result = 0	Signed Underflow	Written	4
SUBSX D, S	110111 001i 1111 ddddddddd sssssssss	Z & (Result = 0)	Signed Underflow	Written	4
SUBX D, S	110011 001i 1111 ddddddddd sssssssss	Z & (Result = 0)	Unsigned Borrow	Written	4
SUMC D, S	100100 001i 1111 ddddddddd sssssssss	Result = 0	Signed Overflow	Written	4
SUMNC D, S	100101 001i 1111 ddddddddd sssssssss	Result = 0	Signed Overflow	Written	4
SUMNZ D, S	100111 001i 1111 ddddddddd sssssssss	Result = 0	Signed Overflow	Written	4
SUMZ D, S	100110 001i 1111 ddddddddd sssssssss	Result = 0	Signed Overflow	Written	4
TEST D, S	011000 000i 1111 ddddddddd sssssssss	Result = 0	Parity of Result	Not Written	4
TJNZ D, S	111010 000i 1111 ddddddddd sssssssss	Result = 0	0	Not Written	4 or 8 **
TJZ D, S	111011 000i 1111 ddddddddd sssssssss	Result = 0	0	Not Written	4 or 8 **
WAITCNT D, S	111110 001i 1111 ddddddddd sssssssss	Result = 0	Unsigned Carry	Written	5+
WAITPEQ D, S	111100 000i 1111 ddddddddd sssssssss	Result = 0	---	Not Written	5+
WAITPNE D, S	111101 000i 1111 ddddddddd sssssssss	Result = 0	---	Not Written	5+
WAITVID D, S	111111 000i 1111 ddddddddd sssssssss	Result = 0	---	Not Written	5+
WRBYTE D, S	000000 000i 1111 ddddddddd sssssssss	---	---	Not Written	7..22 *
WRLONG D, S	000010 000i 1111 ddddddddd sssssssss	---	---	Not Written	7..22 *
WRWORD D, S	000001 000i 1111 ddddddddd sssssssss	---	---	Not Written	7..22 *
XOR D, S	011011 001i 1111 ddddddddd sssssssss	Result = 0	Parity of Result	Written	4

Notes for Master Table

*Clock Cycles for Hub Instructions

Hub instructions require 7 to 22 clock cycles to execute depending on the relation between the cog's hub access window and the instruction's moment of execution. The Hub provides a "hub access window" to each cog every 16 clocks. Because each cog runs independently of the hub, it must sync to the hub when executing a hub instruction. The first hub instruction in a sequence will take from 0 to 15 clocks to sync up to the hub access window, and 7 clocks afterwards to execute; thus the 7 to 22 (15 + 7) clock cycles to execute. After the first hub instruction, there will be 9 (16 − 7) free clocks before a subsequent hub access window arrives for that cog; enough time to execute two 4-clock instructions without missing the next hub access window. To minimize clock waste, you can insert two normal instructions between any two otherwise-contiguous hub instructions without any increase in execution time. Beware that hub instructions can cause execution timing to appear indeterminate; particularly the first hub instruction in a sequence.

** Clock Cycles for Modify-Branch Instructions

Instructions that modify a value and possibly jump, based on the result, require a different amount of clock cycles depending on whether or not a jump is required. These instructions take 4 clock cycles if a jump is required and 8 clock cycles if no jump is required. Since loops utilizing these instructions typically need to be fast, they are optimized in this way for speed.

ABS

Instruction: Get the absolute value of a number.

ABS AValue, ⟨#⟩ SValue

Result: Absolute *SValue* is stored in *AValue*.

- **AValue** (d-field) is the register in which to write the absolute of *SValue*.
- **SValue** (s-field) is a register or a 9-bit literal whose absolute value will be written to *AValue*.

–INSTR– ZCRI –CON– –DEST– –SRC–	Z Result	C Result	Result	Clocks
101010 001i 1111 ddddddddd sssssssss	Result = 0	SValue[31]	Written	4

Explanation

ABS takes the absolute value of *SValue* and writes the result into *AValue*.

If the WZ effect is specified, the Z flag is set (1) if *SValue* is zero. If the WC effect is specified, the C flag is set (1) if *SValue* is negative, or cleared (0) if *SValue* is positive. The result is written to *AValue* unless the NR effect is specified.

Literal *SValues* are zero-extended, so ABS is really best used with register *SValues*.

ABSNEG

Instruction: Get the negative of a number's absolute value.

ABSNEG *NValue*, ⟨#⟩ *SValue*

Result: Absolute negative of *SValue* is stored in *NValue*.

- **NValue** (d-field) is the register in which to write the negative of *SValue*'s absolute value.
- **SValue** (s-field) is a register or a 9-bit literal whose absolute negative value will be written to *NValue*.

–INSTR–	ZCRI	–CON–	–DEST–	–SRC–	Z Result	C Result	Result	Clocks
101011	001i	1111	ddddddddd	sssssssss	Result = 0	S[31]	Written	4

Explanation

ABSNEG negates the absolute value of *SValue* and writes the result into *NValue*.

If the WZ effect is specified, the Z flag is set (1) if *SValue* is zero. If the WC effect is specified, the C flag is set (1) if *SValue* is negative, or cleared (0) if *SValue* is positive. The result is written to *NValue* unless the NR effect is specified.

Literal *SValues* are zero-extended, so ABS is really best used with register *SValues*.

ADD

Instruction: Add two unsigned values.

ADD *Value1*, ⟨#⟩ *Value2*

Result: Sum of unsigned *Value1* and unsigned *Value2* is stored in *Value1*.

- **Value1** (d-field) is the register containing the value to add to *Value2* and is the destination in which to write the result.
- **Value2** (s-field) is a register or a 9-bit literal whose value is added into *Value1*.

–INSTR–	ZCRI	–CON–	–DEST–	–SRC–	Z Result	C Result	Result	Clocks
100000	001i	1111	ddddddddd	sssssssss	Result = 0	Unsigned Carry	Written	4

Explanation

ADD sums the two unsigned values of *Value1* and *Value2* together and stores the result into the *Value1* register.

If the WZ effect is specified, the Z flag is set (1) if *Value1* + *Value2* equals zero. If the WC effect is specified, the C flag is set (1) if the summation resulted in an unsigned carry (32-bit overflow). The result is written to *Value1* unless the NR effect is specified.

ADDABS

Instruction: Add an absolute value to another value.

ADDABS Value, ⟨#⟩ SValue

Result: Sum of *Value* and absolute of signed *SValue* is stored in *Value*.

- **Value** (d-field) is the register containing the value to add to the absolute of *SValue* and is the destination in which to write the result.
- **SValue** (s-field) is a register or a 9-bit literal whose absolute value is added into *Value*.

–INSTR– ZCRI –CON– –DEST– –SRC–	Z Result	C Result	Result	Clocks
100010 001i 1111 ddddddddd sssssssss	Result = 0	Unsigned Carry	Written	4

Explanation

ADDABS sums *Value* and the absolute of *SValue* together and stores the result into the *Value* register.

If the WZ effect is specified, the Z flag is set (1) if *Value* + |*SValue*| equals zero. If the WC effect is specified, the C flag is set (1) if the summation resulted in an unsigned carry (32-bit overflow). The result is written to *Value* unless the NR effect is specified.

ADDS

Instruction: Add two signed values.

ADDS SValue1, ⟨#⟩ SValue2

Result: Sum of signed *SValue1* and signed *SValue2* is stored in *SValue1*.

- **SValue1** (d-field) is the register containing the value to add to *SValue2* and is the destination in which to write the result.
- **SValue2** (s-field) is a register or a 9-bit literal whose value is added into *SValue1*.

–INSTR– ZCRI –CON– –DEST– –SRC–	Z Result	C Result	Result	Clocks
110100 001i 1111 ddddddddd sssssssss	Result = 0	Signed Overflow	Written	4

Explanation

ADDS sums the two signed values of *SValue1* and *SValue2* together and stores the result into the *SValue1* register.

If the WZ effect is specified, the Z flag is set (1) if *SValue1* + *SValue2* equals zero. If the WC effect is specified, the C flag is set (1) if the summation resulted in a signed overflow. The result is written to *SValue1* unless the NR effect is specified.

ADDSX

Instruction: Add two signed values plus C.

ADDSX SValue1, ⟨#⟩ SValue2

Result: Sum of signed *SValue1* and signed *SValue2* plus C flag is stored in *SValue1*.

- **SValue1** (d-field) is the register containing the value to add to *SValue2* plus C, and is the destination in which to write the result.
- **SValue2** (s-field) is a register or a 9-bit literal whose value plus C is added into *SValue1*.

–INSTR– ZCRI –CON– –DEST– –SRC–	Z Result	C Result	Result	Clocks
110110 001i 1111 ddddddddd sssssssss	Z & (Result = 0)	Signed Overflow	Written	4

Explanation

ADDSX (Add Signed, Extended) sums the two signed values of *SValue1* and *SValue2* plus C, and stores the result into the *SValue1* register. Use the ADDSX instruction after an ADD or ADDX (with the WC, and optionally WZ, effect) to perform multi-long, signed additions; 64-bit additions, for example.

If the WZ effect is specified, the Z flag is set (1) if Z was previously set and *SValue1* + *SValue2* + C equals zero (use WC and WZ on preceding ADD or ADDX instruction). If the WC effect is specified, the C flag is set (1) if the summation resulted in a signed overflow. The result is written to *SValue1* unless the NR effect is specified.

Note that in a multi-long signed operation, the first instruction is unsigned (ex: ADD), any middle instructions are unsigned, extended (ex: ADDX), and the last instruction is signed, extended (ex: ADDSX).

ADDX

Instruction: Add two unsigned values plus C.

ADDX *Value1*, ⟨#⟩ *Value2*

Result: Sum of unsigned *Value1* and unsigned *Value2* plus C flag is stored in *Value1*.

- **Value1** (d-field) is the register containing the value to add to *Value2* plus C, and is the destination in which to write the result.
- **Value2** (s-field) is a register or a 9-bit literal whose value plus C is added into *Value1*.

–INSTR–	ZCRI	–CON–	–DEST–	–SRC–	Z Result	C Result	Result	Clocks
110010	001i	1111	dddddddddd	ssssssss	Z & (Result = 0)	Unsigned Carry	Written	4

Explanation

ADDX (Add Extended) sums the two unsigned values of *Value1* and *Value2* plus C, and stores the result into the *Value1* register. Use the ADDX instruction after an ADD or ADDX (with the WC, and optionally WZ, effect) to perform multi-long additions; 64-bit additions, for example.

If the WZ effect is specified, the Z flag is set (1) if Z was previously set and *Value1* + *Value2* + C equals zero (use WC and WZ on preceding ADD or ADDX instruction). If the WC effect is specified, the C flag is set (1) if the summation resulted in an unsigned carry (32-bit overflow). The result is written to *Value1* unless the NR effect is specified.

AND

Instruction: Bitwise AND two values.

AND *Value1*, ⟨#⟩ *Value2*

Result: *Value1* AND *Value2* is stored in *Value1*.

- **Value1** (d-field) is the register containing the value to bitwise AND with *Value2* and is the destination in which to write the result.
- **Value2** (s-field) is a register or a 9-bit literal whose value is bitwise ANDed with *Value1*.

–INSTR– ZCRI –CON– –DEST– –SRC–	Z Result	C Result	Result	Clocks
011000 001i 1111 ddddddddd sssssssss	Result = 0	Parity of Result	Written	4

Explanation

AND (bitwise AND) performs a bitwise AND of the value in *Value2* into that of *Value1*.

If the **WZ** effect is specified, the Z flag is set (1) if *Value1* AND *Value2* equals zero. If the **WC** effect is specified, the C flag is set (1) if the result contains an odd number of high (1) bits. The result is written to *Value1* unless the **NR** effect is specified.

ANDN

Instruction: Bitwise AND a value with the NOT of another.

ANDN *Value1*, ⟨#⟩ *Value2*

Result: *Value1* AND !*Value2* is stored in *Value1*.

- **Value1** (d-field) is the register containing the value to bitwise AND with !*Value2* and is the destination in which to write the result.
- **Value2** (s-field) is a register or a 9-bit literal whose value is inverted (bitwise NOT) and bitwise ANDed with *Value1*.

–INSTR– ZCRI –CON– –DEST– –SRC–	Z Result	C Result	Result	Clocks
011001 001i 1111 ddddddddd sssssssss	Result = 0	Parity of Result	Written	4

Explanation

ANDN (bitwise AND NOT) performs a bitwise AND of the inverted value (bitwise NOT) of *Value2* into that of *Value1*.

If the WZ effect is specified, the Z flag is set (1) if *Value1* AND !*Value2* equals zero. If the WC effect is specified, the C flag is set (1) if the result contains an odd number of high (1) bits. The result is written to *Value1* unless the NR effect is specified.

CALL

Instruction: Jump to address with intention to return to next instruction.

CALL #*Address*

Result: PC + 1 is written to the s-field of the register indicated by the d-field.

- *Address* (s-field) is the register or 9-bit literal whose value is the address to jump to.

–INSTR– ZCRI –CON– –DEST– –SRC–	Z Result	C Result	Result	Clocks
010111 0011 1111 ????????? sssssssss	Result = 0	---	Written	4

Explanation

CALL records the address of the next instruction (PC + 1) then jumps to *Address*. The routine at *Address* should eventually execute a RET instruction to return to the recorded address (the instruction following the CALL).

The Propeller does not use a call stack, so the return address is stored in a different manner; it is recorded at the location of the routine's RET command itself. For the CALL instruction, the assembler searches for a label that is *Address* with "_ret" appended to it. It then encodes the address of the label *Address*_ret into the CALL instruction as well as the *Address* you specified to jump to. At run time, when executing the CALL instruction, the cog first stores the return address (PC + 1) into the source field of the "RET" instruction at *Address*_ret and then jumps to *Address*. See the example below:

```
                call    Routine
                <other code here>

Routine         <more code>
                  .
                  .
                  .
Routine_ret     ret
```

In this example, the first instruction is a call to Routine. The assembler searches for another label called Routine_ret and encodes its address as well as Routine's address into the CALL instruction. At run time, when executing the CALL instruction, the cog first writes the address of <other code here> into the source field of the instruction at Routine_ret, then jumps to

Routine. The RET instruction at Routine_ret essentially becomes a JMP instruction with a destination of the <other code here> line.

CALL is a really a subset of the JMPRET instruction; in fact, it is the same opcode as JMPRET but with the i-field set (since CALL uses an immediate value only) and the d-field set to the address of a label named *Address*_ret.

The return address is written to the *Address*_ret register unless the NR effect is specified.

CLKSET

Instruction: Set the clock mode at run time.

CLKSET *Mode*

- *Mode* (d-field) is the register containing the 8-bit pattern to write to the CLK register.

–INSTR– ZCRI –CON– –DEST– –SRC–	Z Result	C Result	Result	Clocks
000011 0001 1111 dddddddd ------000	---	---	Not Written	7..22

Explanation

CLKSET changes the System Clock mode during run time. The CLKSET instruction behaves similar to the Spin command of the same name (see CLKSET on page 183) except that it only sets the clock mode, not the frequency.

After issuing a CLKSET instruction, it is important to update the System Clock Frequency value by writing to its location in Main RAM (long 0): WRLONG freqaddr, #0. If the System Clock Frequency value is not updated, other objects will misbehave due to invalid clock frequency data.

CLKSET is a Hub instruction. Hub instructions require 7 to 22 clock cycles to execute depending on the relation between the cog's hub access window and the instruction's moment of execution. See Hub on page 24 for more information.

CMP, CMPS – Assembly Language Reference

CMP

Instruction: Compare two unsigned values.

CMP Value1, ⟨#⟩ Value2

Result: Optionally, equality and greater/lesser status is written to the Z and C flags.

- **Value1** (d-field) is the register containing the value to compare with that of *Value2*.
- **Value2** (s-field) is a register or a 9-bit literal whose value is compared with *Value1*.

–INSTR– ZCRI –CON– –DEST– –SRC–	Z Result	C Result	Result	Clocks
100001 000i 1111 ddddddddd sssssssss	Result = 0	Unsigned Borrow	Not Written	4

Explanation

CMP (Compare Unsigned) compares the unsigned values of *Value1* and *Value2*. The Z and C flags, if written, indicate the relative equal, and greater or lesser relationship between the two.

If the WZ effect is specified, the Z flag is set (1) if *Value1* equals *Value2*. If the WC effect is specified, the C flag is set (1) if *Value1* is less than *Value2*.

CMPS

Instruction: Compare two signed values.

CMPS SValue1, ⟨#⟩ SValue2

Result: Optionally, equality and greater/lesser status is written to the Z and C flags.

- **SValue1** (d-field) is the register containing the value to compare with that of *SValue2*.
- **SValue2** (s-field) is a register or a 9-bit literal whose value is compared with *SValue1*.

–INSTR– ZCRI –CON– –DEST– –SRC–	Z Result	C Result	Result	Clocks
110000 000i 1111 ddddddddd sssssssss	Result = 0	Signed Borrow	Not Written	4

Explanation

CMPS (Compare Signed) compares the signed values of *SValue1* and *SValue2*. The Z and C flags, if written, indicate the relative equal, and greater or lesser relationship between the two.

If the WZ effect is specified, the Z flag is set (1) if *SValue1* equals *SValue2*. If the WC effect is specified, the C flag is set (1) if *SValue1* is less than or equal to *SValue2*.

CMPSUB

Instruction: Compare two unsigned values and subtract the second if it is lesser or equal.

CMPSUB Value1, ⟨#⟩ Value2

Result: Optionally, *Value1* = *Value1* – *Value2*, and Z and C flags = comparison results.

- **Value1** (d-field) is the register containing the value to compare with that of *Value2* and is the destination in which to write the result if a subtraction is performed.
- **Value2** (s-field) is a register or a 9-bit literal whose value is compared with and possibly subtracted from *Value1*.

–INSTR– ZCRI –CON– –DEST– –SRC–	Z Result	C Result	Result	Clocks
111000 000i 1111 ddddddddd sssssssss	D = S	Unsigned (D => S)	Not Written	4

Explanation

CMPSUB compares the unsigned values of *Value1* and *Value2*, and if *Value2* is equal to or greater than *Value1* then it is subtracted from *Value1* (if the WR effect is specified). The Z and C flags, if written, indicate the relative equal, and greater or lesser relationship between the two.

If the WZ effect is specified, the Z flag is set (1) if *Value1* equals *Value2*. If the WC effect is specified, the C flag is set (1) if *Value1* is equal to or greater than *Value2*. If the WR effect is specified, the result, if any, is written to *Value1*.

CMPSX, CMPX – Assembly Language Reference

CMPSX

Instruction: Compare two signed values plus C.

CMPSX *SValue1*, ⟨#⟩ *SValue2*

Result: Optionally, equality and greater/lesser status is written to the Z and C flags.

- *SValue1* (d-field) is the register containing the value to compare with that of *SValue2*.
- *SValue2* (s-field) is a register or a 9-bit literal whose value is compared with *SValue1*.

–INSTR– ZCRI –CON– –DEST– –SRC–	Z Result	C Result	Result	Clocks
110001 000i 1111 ddddddddd sssssssss	Z & (Result = 0)	Signed Borrow	Not Written	4

Explanation

CMPSX (Compare Signed, Extended) compares the signed values of *SValue1* and *SValue2* plus C. Use the CMPSX instruction after a CMP or CMPX (with the WC, and optionally WZ, effect) to perform multi-long, signed comparisons; 64-bit signed comparisons, for example. The Z and C flags, if written, indicate the relative equal, and greater or lesser relationship between the two.

If the WZ effect is specified, the Z flag is set (1) if Z was previously set and *SValue1* equals *SValue2* + C (use WC and WZ on preceding CMP or CMPX instruction). If the WC effect is specified, the C flag is set (1) if *SValue1* is less than *SValue2* (as multi-long values).

Note that in a multi-long signed operation, the first instruction is unsigned (ex: CMP), any middle instructions are unsigned, extended (ex: CMPX), and the last instruction is signed, extended (ex: CMPSX).

CMPX

Instruction: Compare two unsigned values plus C.

CMPX *Value1*, ⟨#⟩ *Value2*

Result: Optionally, equality and greater/lesser status is written to the Z and C flags.

- *Value1* (d-field) is the register containing the value to compare with that of *Value2*.
- *Value2* (s-field) is a register or a 9-bit literal whose value is compared with *Value1*.

–INSTR– ZCRI –CON– –DEST– –SRC–	Z Result	C Result	Result	Clocks
110011 000i 1111 ddddddddd sssssssss	Z & (Result = 0)	Unsigned Borrow	Not Written	4

Explanation

CMPX (Compare Extended) compares the unsigned values of *Value1* and *Value2* plus C. Use the CMPX instruction after a CMP or CMPX (with the WC, and optionally WZ, effect) to perform multi-long comparisons; 64-bit unsigned comparisons, for example. The Z and C flags, if written, indicate the relative equal, and greater or lesser relationship between the two.

If the WZ effect is specified, the Z flag is set (1) if Z was previously set and *Value1* equals *Value2* + C (use WC and WZ on preceding CMP or CMPX instruction). If the WC effect is specified, the C flag is set (1) if *Value1* is less than *Value2* (as multi-long values).

COGID

Instruction: Get current cog's ID.

COGID *Destination*

Result: The current cog's ID (0-7) is written to *Destination*.

- *Destination* (d-field) is the register to write the cog's ID into.

–INSTR– ZCRI –CON– –DEST– –SRC–	Z Result	C Result	Result	Clocks
000011 0011 1111 ddddddddd ------001	Result = 0	---	Written	7..22

Explanation

COGID returns the ID of the cog that executed the command. The COGID instruction behaves similar to the Spin command of the same name; see COGID on page 186.

If the WZ effect is specified, the Z flag is set if the cog ID is zero. The result is written to *Destination* unless the NR effect is specified.

COGID is a Hub instruction. Hub instructions require 7 to 22 clock cycles to execute depending on the relation between the cog's hub access window and the instruction's moment of execution. See Hub on page 24 for more information.

COGINIT

Instruction: Start or restart a cog, optionally by ID, to run Propeller Assembly or Spin code.

COGINIT *Destination*

Result: Optionally, the started/restarted cog's ID (0-7) is written to *Destination*.

- *Destination* (d-field) is the register containing startup information for the target cog and optionally becomes the destination of the started cog's ID if a new cog is started.

–INSTR–	ZCRI	–CON–	–DEST–	–SRC–	Z Result	C Result	Result	Clocks
000011	0001	1111	dddddddd	------010	Result = 0	No Cog Free	Not Written	7..22

Explanation

The COGINIT instruction behaves similar to two Spin commands, COGNEW and COGINIT, put together. Propeller Assembly's COGINIT instruction can be used to start a new cog or restart an active cog. The *Destination* register has four fields that determine which cog is started, where its program begins in main memory, and what its PAR register will contain. The table below describes these fields.

Table 5-1: Destination Register Fields			
31:18	**17:4**	**3**	**2:0**
14-bit Long address for PAR Register	14-bit Long address of code to load	New	Cog ID

The first field, bits 31:18, will be written to the started cog's PAR register bits 15:2. This is 14-bits total that are intended to be the upper bits of a 16-bit long address. Similar to the *Parameter* field of Spin's version of COGINIT, this first field of *Destination* is used to pass the 14-bit address of an agreed-upon memory location or structure to the started cog.

The second field, bits 17:4, holds the upper 14-bits of a 16-bit long address pointing to the desired assembly program to load into the cog. Cog registers $000 through $1EF will be loaded sequentially starting at this address, the special purpose registers will be cleared to zero (0), and the cog will start executing the code at register $000.

The third field, bit 3, should be set (1) if a new cog should be started, or cleared (0) if a specific cog should be started or restarted.

If the third field bit is set (1), the Hub will start the next available (lowest-numbered inactive) cog and return that cog's ID in *Destination* (if the WR effect is specified).

If the third field bit is clear (0), the Hub will start or restart the cog identified by *Destination*'s fourth field, bits 2:0.

If the WZ effect is specified, the Z flag will be set (1) if the cog ID returned is 0. If the WC effect is specified, the C flag will be set (1) if no cog was available. If the WR effect is specified, *Destination* is written with the ID of the cog that the hub started, or would have started, if you let it pick one.

Make sure to follow the COGINIT instruction with WC, WZ, and/or WR if you wish the flags or *Destination* to be updated with the results.

It is not practical to launch Spin code from user's Propeller Assembly code; we recommend launching only assembly code with this instruction.

COGINIT is a Hub instruction. Hub instructions require 7 to 22 clock cycles to execute depending on the relation between the cog's hub access window and the instruction's moment of execution. See Hub on page 24 for more information.

COGSTOP

Instruction: Stop a cog by its ID.

COGSTOP *CogID*

- *CogID* (d-field) is the register containing the ID (0 – 7) of the cog to stop.

–INSTR– ZCRI –CON– –DEST– –SRC–	Z Result	C Result	Result	Clocks
000011 0001 1111 dddddddd ------011	---	---	Not Written	7..22

Explanation

The COGSTOP instruction stops a cog whose ID is in the register *CogID*; placing that cog into a dormant state. In the dormant state, the cog ceases to receive System Clock pulses so that power consumption is greatly reduced.

COGSTOP is a Hub instruction. Hub instructions require 7 to 22 clock cycles to execute depending on the relation between the cog's hub access window and the instruction's moment of execution. See Hub on page 24 for more information.

Conditions (IF_x)

Every Propeller Assembly instruction has an optional "condition" field that is used to dynamically determine whether or not it executes when it is reached at run time. The basic syntax for Propeller Assembly instructions is:

⟨*Label*⟩ ⟨*Condition*⟩ *Instruction* ⟨*Effects*⟩

The optional *Condition* field can contain one of 32 conditions (see Table 5-2) and defaults to IF_ALWAYS when no condition is specified. The 4-bit **Value** shown for each condition is the value used for the **–CON–** field in the instruction's opcode.

This feature, along with proper use of instructions' optional *Effects* field, makes Propeller Assembly very powerful. Flags can be affected at will and later instructions can be conditionally executed based on the results. Here's an example:

```
          test    _pins, #$20        wc
          and     _pins, #$38
          shl     t1, _pins
          shr     _pins, #3
          movd    vcfg, _pins
if_nc     mov     dira, t1
if_nc     mov     dirb, #0
if_c      mov     dira, #0
if_c      mov     dirb, t1
```

The first instruction, test _pins, #$20 wc, performs its operation and adjusts the state of the C flag because the WC effect was specified. The next four instructions perform operations that could affect the C flag, but they do not affect it because no WC effect was specified. This means that the state of the C flag is preserved since it was last modified by the first instruction. The last four instructions are conditionally executed based on the state of the C flag that was set five instructions prior. Among the last for instructions, the first two mov instructions have if_nc conditions, causing them to execute only "if not C" (if C = 0). The last two mov instructions have if_c conditions, causing them to execute only "if C" (if C = 1). In this case, the two pairs of mov instructions are executed in a mutually-exclusive fashion.

When an instruction's condition evaluates to FALSE, the instruction dynamically becomes a NOP, elapsing 4 clock cycles but affecting no flags or registers. This makes multi-decision code such as this example very deterministically timed.

Table 5-2: Conditions			
Condition	**Instruction Executes**	**Value**	**Synonyms**
IF_ALWAYS	always	1111	
IF_NEVER	never	0000	
IF_E	if equal (Z = 1)	1010	IF_Z
IF_NE	if not equal (Z = 0)	0101	IF_NZ
IF_A	if above (!C & !Z = 1)	0001	IF_NC_AND_NZ –and– IF_NZ_AND_NC
IF_B	if below (C = 1)	1100	IF_C
IF_AE	if above or equal (C = 0)	0011	IF_NC
IF_BE	if below or equal (C | Z = 1)	1110	IF_C_OR_Z –and– IF_Z_OR_C
IF_C	if C set	1100	IF_B
IF_NC	if C clear	0011	IF_AE
IF_Z	if Z set	1010	IF_E
IF_NZ	if Z clear	0101	IF_NE
IF_C_EQ_Z	if C equal to Z	1001	IF_Z_EQ_C
IF_C_NE_Z	if C not equal to Z	0110	IF_Z_NE_C
IF_C_AND_Z	if C set and Z set	1000	IF_Z_AND_C
IF_C_AND_NZ	if C set and Z clear	0100	IF_NZ_AND_C
IF_NC_AND_Z	if C clear and Z set	0010	IF_Z_AND_NC
IF_NC_AND_NZ	if C clear and Z clear	0001	IF_A –and– IF_NZ_AND_NC
IF_C_OR_Z	if C set or Z set	1110	IF_BE –and– IF_Z_OR_C
IF_C_OR_NZ	if C set or Z clear	1101	IF_NZ_OR_C
IF_NC_OR_Z	if C clear or Z set	1011	IF_Z_OR_NC
IF_NC_OR_NZ	if C clear or Z clear	0111	IF_NZ_OR_NC
IF_Z_EQ_C	if Z equal to C	1001	IF_C_EQ_Z
IF_Z_NE_C	if Z not equal to C	0110	IF_C_NE_Z
IF_Z_AND_C	if Z set and C set	1000	IF_C_AND_Z
IF_Z_AND_NC	if Z set and C clear	0010	IF_NC_AND_Z
IF_NZ_AND_C	if Z clear and C set	0100	IF_C_AND_NZ
IF_NZ_AND_NC	if Z clear and C clear	0001	IF_A –and– IF_NC_AND_NZ
IF_Z_OR_C	if Z set or C set	1110	IF_BE –and– IF_C_OR_Z
IF_Z_OR_NC	if Z set or C clear	1011	IF_NC_OR_Z
IF_NZ_OR_C	if Z clear or C set	1101	IF_C_OR_NZ
IF_NZ_OR_NC	if Z clear or C clear	0111	IF_NC_OR_NZ

DJNZ

Instruction: Decrement value and jump to address if not zero.

DJNZ *Value*, ⟨#⟩ *Address*

Result: *Value*-1 is written to *Value*.

- **Value** (d-field) is the register to decrement and test.
- **Address** (s-field) is the register or a 9-bit literal whose value is the address to jump to when the decremented *Value* is not zero.

–INSTR– ZCRI –CON– –DEST– –SRC–	Z Result	C Result	Result	Clocks
111001 001i 1111 ddddddddd sssssssss	Result = 0	Unsigned Borrow	Written	4 or 8

Explanation

DJNZ decrements the *Value* register and jumps to *Address* if the result is not zero.

When the WZ effect is specified, the Z flag is set (1) if the decremented *Value* is zero. When the WC effect is specified, the C flag is set (1) if the decrement results in an underflow. The decremented result is written to *Value* unless the NR effect is specified.

DJNZ requires a different amount of clock cycles depending on whether or not it has to jump. If it must jump it takes 4 clock cycles, if no jump occurs it takes 8 clock cycles. Since loops utilizing DJNZ need to be fast, it is optimized in this way for speed.

Effects

Every Propeller Assembly instruction has an optional "effects" field that causes it to modify a flag or register when it executes. The basic syntax for Propeller Assembly instructions is:

⟨*Label*⟩ ⟨*Condition*⟩ *Instruction* ⟨*Effects*⟩

The optional *Effects* field can contain one of four conditions, shown below. For any effect not specified, the default behavior remains as indicated by the corresponding bit (Z, C, or R) in the **ZCRI** field of the instruction's opcode.

Table 5-3: Effects	
Effect	**Results In**
WC	C Flag modified
WZ	Z Flag modified
WR	Destination Register modified
NR	Destination Register not modified

Follow an instruction with one to three space-delimited *Effects* to cause that instruction to affect the indicated item. For example:

```
and     temp1, #$20     wc
andn    temp2, #$38     wz, nr
```

The first instruction performs a bitwise AND of the value in the temp1 register with $20, stores the result in temp1 and modifies with C flag with the parity of the result. The second instruction performs a bitwise AND NOT of the value in the temp2 register with $38, modifies the Z flag according to whether or not the result is zero, and does not write the result to temp2. During the execution of the first instruction, the Z flag is not altered. During the execution of the second instruction, the C flag is not altered. If these instructions did not include the WC and WZ effects, those flags would not be altered at all.

Using *Effects* on instructions, along with *Conditions* on later instructions, enables code to be much more powerful than what is possible with typical assembly languages. See Conditions on page 368 for more information.

FIT

Directive: Validate that previous instructions/data fit entirely below a specific address.

FIT ⟨*Address*⟩

Result: Compile-time error if previous instructions/data exceed *Address*-1.

- *Address* is an optional Cog RAM address (0-$1F0) for which prior assembly code should not reach. If *Address* is not given, the value $1F0 is used (the address of the first special purpose register).

Explanation

The FIT directive checks the current compile-time cog address pointer and generates an error if it is beyond *Address*-1 or if it is beyond $1EF (the end of general purpose Cog RAM). This directive can be used to ensure that the previous instructions and data fit within Cog RAM, or a limited region of Cog RAM. Note: any instructions that do not fit in Cog RAM will be left out when the assembly code is launched into the cog. Consider the following example:

```
DAT
                ORG     492
Toggle          mov     dira, Pin
:Loop           mov     outa, Pin
                mov     outa, #0
                jmp     #:Loop

Pin     long    $1000

                FIT
```

This code was artificially pushed into upper Cog RAM space by the ORG statement, causing the code to overlap the first special purpose register ($1F0) and causing the FIT directive to cause a compile-time error when the code is compiled.

HUBOP

Instruction: Perform a hub operation.

HUBOP *Destination*, ⟨#⟩ *Operation*

Result: Varies depending on the operation performed.

- *Destination* (d-field) is the register containing a value to use in the *Operation*.
- *Operation* (s-field) is a register or a 3-bit literal that indicates the hub operation to perform.

–INSTR– ZCRI –CON– –DEST– –SRC–	Z Result	C Result	Result	Clocks
000011 000i 1111 ddddddddd ssssssss	Result = 0	---	Not Written	7..22

Explanation

HUBOP is the template for every hub operation instruction in the Propeller chip: CLKSET, COGID, COGINIT, COGSTOP, LOCKNEW, LOCKRET, LOCKSET, and LOCKCLR. The instructions that perform hub operations set the *Operation* field (s-field of the opcode) to the 3-bit immediate value that represents the desired operation (see the opcode of the hub instruction's syntax description for more information). The HUBOP instruction itself should rarely be used, but may be handy for special situations.

HUBOP is a Hub instruction. Hub instructions require 7 to 22 clock cycles to execute depending on the relation between the cog's hub access window and the instruction's moment of execution. See Hub on page 24 for more information.

IF_x

See Conditions on page 368.

JMP

Instruction: Jump to address unconditionally.

JMP ⟨#⟩ *Address*

- *Address* (s-field) is the register or a 9-bit literal whose value is the address to jump to.

–INSTR– ZCRI –CON– –DEST– –SRC–	Z Result	C Result	Result	Clocks
010111 000i 1111 --------- sssssssss	Result = 0	---	Not Written	4

Explanation

JMP sets the Program Counter (PC) to *Address* causing execution to jump that location in Cog RAM.

JMPRET

Instruction: Jump to address with intention to "return" to another address.

JMPRET *RetInstAddr*, ⟨#⟩ *DestAddress*

Result: PC + 1 is written to the s-field of the register indicated by the d-field.

- *RetInstAddr* (d-field) is the register in which to store the return address (PC + 1); it should be the address of an appropriate RET or JMP instruction for *DestAddress*.
- *DestAddress* (s-field) is the register or 9-bit literal whose value is the address to jump to.

–INSTR– ZCRI –CON– –DEST– –SRC–	Z Result	C Result	Result	Clocks
010111 001i 1111 ddddddddd sssssssss	Result = 0	---	Written	4

Explanation

JMPRET stores the address of the next instruction (PC + 1) into the source field of the instruction at *RetInstAddr*, then jumps to *DestAddress*. The routine at *DestAddress* should eventually execute the RET or JMP instruction at the *RetInstAddr* to return to the stored address (the instruction following the JMPRET).

The Propeller does not use a call stack, so the return address must be stored at the location of the routine's RET, or returning JMP, command itself. JMPRET is a superset of the CALL instruction; in fact, it is the same opcode as CALL but the i-field and d-field configured by the developer, rather than the assembler. See CALL on page 360 for more information.

The return address is written to the *RetInstAddr* register unless the NR effect is specified.

LOCKCLR

Instruction: Clear lock to false and get its previous state.

LOCKCLR *ID*

Result: Optionally, previous state of lock is written to C flag.

- *ID* (d-field) is the register containing the ID (0 – 7) of the lock to clear.

–INSTR– ZCRI –CON– –DEST– –SRC–	Z Result	C Result	Result	Clocks
000011 0001 1111 ddddddddd ------111	---	Prior Lock State	Not Written	7..22

Explanation

LOCKCLR is one of four lock instructions (LOCKNEW, LOCKRET, LOCKSET, and LOCKCLR) used to manage resources that are user-defined and deemed mutually-exclusive. LOCKCLR clears the lock described by the register *ID* to zero (0) and returns the previous state of that lock in the C flag; if the WC effect is specified. The LOCKCLR instruction behaves similar to Spin's LOCKCLR command; see LOCKCLR on page 228.

LOCKCLR is a Hub instruction. Hub instructions require 7 to 22 clock cycles to execute depending on the relation between the cog's hub access window and the instruction's moment of execution. See Hub on page 24 for more information.

LOCKNEW

Instruction: Check out a new lock and get its ID.

LOCKNEW *NewID*

Result: The new lock's ID (0-7) is written to *NewID*.

- *NewID* (d-field) is the register where the newly checked-out lock's ID is written.

–INSTR– ZCRI –CON– –DEST– –SRC–	Z Result	C Result	Result	Clocks
000011 0011 1111 ddddddddd ------100	Result = 0	No Lock Free	Written	7..22

Explanation

LOCKNEW is one of four lock instructions (LOCKNEW, LOCKRET, LOCKSET, and LOCKCLR) used to manage resources that are user-defined and deemed mutually-exclusive. LOCKNEW checks out a unique lock, from the hub, and retrieves the ID of that lock. The LOCKNEW instruction behaves similar to Spin's LOCKNEW command; see LOCKNEW on page 230.

If the WZ effect is specified, the Z flag is set (1) if the returned ID is zero (0). If the WC effect is specified, the C flag is set if no lock was available for checking out. The ID of the newly checked-out lock is written to *NewID* unless the NR effect is specified.

LOCKNEW is a Hub instruction. Hub instructions require 7 to 22 clock cycles to execute depending on the relation between the cog's hub access window and the instruction's moment of execution. See Hub on page 24 for more information.

LOCKRET

Instruction: Release lock back for future "new lock" requests.

LOCKRET *ID*

- *ID* (d-field) is the register containing the ID (0 – 7) of the lock to return to the lock pool.

–INSTR– ZCRI –CON– –DEST– –SRC–	Z Result	C Result	Result	Clocks
000011 0001 1111 ddddddddd ------101	---	---	Not Written	7..22

Explanation

LOCKRET is one of four lock instructions (LOCKNEW, LOCKRET, LOCKSET, and LOCKCLR) used to manage resources that are user-defined and deemed mutually-exclusive. LOCKRET returns a lock, by *ID*, back to the Hub's lock pool so that it may be reused by other cogs at a later time. The LOCKRET instruction behaves similar to Spin's LOCKRET command; see LOCKRET on page 233.

LOCKRET is a Hub instruction. Hub instructions require 7 to 22 clock cycles to execute depending on the relation between the cog's hub access window and the instruction's moment of execution. See Hub on page 24 for more information.

LOCKSET

Instruction: Set lock to true and get its previous state.

LOCKSET *ID*

Result: Optionally, previous state of lock is written to C flag.

- *ID* (d-field) is the register containing the ID (0 – 7) of the lock to set.

–INSTR–	ZCRI	–CON–	–DEST–	–SRC–	Z Result	C Result	Result	Clocks
000011	0001	1111	ddddddddd	------110	---	Prior Lock State	Not Written	7..22

Explanation

LOCKSET is one of four lock instructions (LOCKNEW, LOCKRET, LOCKSET, and LOCKCLR) used to manage resources that are user-defined and deemed mutually-exclusive. LOCKSET sets the lock described by the register *ID* to one (1) and returns the previous state of that lock in the C flag; if the WC effect is specified. The LOCKSET instruction behaves similar to Spin's LOCKSET command; see LOCKSET on page 234.

LOCKSET is a Hub instruction. Hub instructions require 7 to 22 clock cycles to execute depending on the relation between the cog's hub access window and the instruction's moment of execution. See Hub on page 24 for more information.

MAX

Instruction: Limit maximum of unsigned value to another unsigned value.

MAX *Value1*, ⟨#⟩ *Value2*

Result: Lesser of unsigned *Value1* and unsigned *Value2* is stored in *Value1*.

- **Value1** (d-field) is the register containing the value to compare against *Value2* and is the destination in which to write the lesser of the two.
- **Value2** (s-field) is a register or a 9-bit literal whose value is compared against *Value1*.

-INSTR- ZCRI -CON- -DEST- -SRC-	Z Result	C Result	Result	Clocks
010011 001i 1111 ddddddddd sssssssss	D = S	Unsigned (D < S)	Written	4

Explanation

MAX compares the unsigned values of *Value1* and *Value2* and stores the lesser of the two into the *Value1* register, effectively limiting *Value1* to a maximum of *Value2*.

If the WZ effect is specified, the Z flag is set (1) if *Value1* and *Value2* are equal. If the WC effect is specified, the C flag is set (1) if the unsigned *Value1* is less than the unsigned *Value2*. The lesser of the two values is written to *Value1* unless the NR effect is specified.

MAXS

Instruction: Limit maximum of signed value to another signed value.

MAXS *SValue1*, ⟨#⟩ *SValue2*

Result: Lesser of signed *SValue1* and signed *SValue2* is stored in *SValue1*.

- **SValue1** (d-field) is the register containing the value to compare against *SValue2* and is the destination in which to write the lesser of the two.
- **SValue2** (s-field) is a register or a 9-bit literal whose value is compared against *SValue1*.

-INSTR- ZCRI -CON- -DEST- -SRC-	Z Result	C Result	Result	Clocks
010001 001i 1111 ddddddddd sssssssss	D = S	Signed (D < S)	Written	4

Explanation

MAXS compares the signed values of *SValue1* and *SValue2* and stores the lesser of the two into the *SValue1* register, effectively limiting *SValue1* to a maximum of *SValue2*.

If the WZ effect is specified, the Z flag is set (1) if *SValue1* and *SValue2* are equal. If the WC effect is specified, the C flag is set (1) if the signed *SValue1* is less than the signed *SValue2*. The lesser of the two values is written to *SValue1* unless the NR effect is specified.

MIN

Instruction: Limit minimum of unsigned value to another unsigned value.

MIN *Value1*, ⟨#⟩ *Value2*

Result: Greater of unsigned *Value1* and unsigned *Value2* is stored in *Value1*.

- *Value1* (d-field) is the register containing the value to compare against *Value2* and is the destination in which to write the greater of the two.
- *Value2* (s-field) is a register or a 9-bit literal whose value is compared against *Value1*.

–INSTR– ZCRI –CON– –DEST– –SRC–	Z Result	C Result	Result	Clocks
010010 001i 1111 ddddddddd sssssssss	D = S	Unsigned (D < S)	Written	4

Explanation

MIN compares the unsigned values of *Value1* and *Value2* and stores the greater of the two into the *Value1* register, effectively limiting *Value1* to a minimum of *Value2*.

If the WZ effect is specified, the Z flag is set (1) if *Value1* and *Value2* are equal. If the WC effect is specified, the C flag is set (1) if the unsigned *Value1* is less than the unsigned *Value2*. The greater of the two values is written to *Value1* unless the NR effect is specified.

MINS

Instruction: Limit minimum of signed value to another signed value.

MINS SValue1, ⟨#⟩ SValue2

Result: Greater of signed *SValue1* and signed *SValue2* is stored in *SValue1*.

- **SValue1** (d-field) is the register containing the value to compare against *SValue2* and is the destination in which to write the greater of the two.
- **SValue2** (s-field) is a register or a 9-bit literal whose value is compared against *SValue1*.

–INSTR– ZCRI –CON– –DEST– –SRC–	Z Result	C Result	Result	Clocks
010000 001i 1111 ddddddddd sssssssss	D = S	Signed (D < S)	Written	4

Explanation

MINS compares the signed values of *SValue1* and *SValue2* and stores the greater of the two into the *SValue1* register, effectively limiting *SValue1* to a minimum of *SValue2*.

If the WZ effect is specified, the Z flag is set (1) if *SValue1* and *SValue2* are equal. If the WC effect is specified, the C flag is set (1) if the signed *SValue1* is less than the signed *SValue2*. The greater of the two values is written to *SValue1* unless the NR effect is specified.

MOV

Instruction: Set a register to a value.

MOV Destination, ⟨#⟩ Value

Result: *Value* is stored in *Destination*.

- **Destination** (d-field) is the register in which to store *Value*.
- **Value** (s-field) is a register or a 9-bit literal whose value is stored into *Destination*.

–INSTR– ZCRI –CON– –DEST– –SRC–	Z Result	C Result	Result	Clocks
101000 001i 1111 ddddddddd sssssssss	Result = 0	S[31]	Written	4

Explanation

MOV copies, or stores, the number in *Value* into *Destination*.

If the WZ effect is specified, the Z flag is set (1) if *Value* equals zero. If the WC effect is specified, the C flag is set to *Value's* MSB. The result is written to *Destination* unless the NR effect is specified.

MOVD

Instruction: Set a register's destination field to a value.

MOVD *Destination*, ⟨#⟩ *Value*

Result: *Value* is stored in *Destination's* d-field (bits 17..9).

- **Destination** (d-field) is the register whose destination field (bits 17..9) is set to *Value's* value.
- **Value** (s-field) is a register or a 9-bit literal whose value is stored into *Destination's* d-field.

–INSTR– ZCRI –CON– –DEST– –SRC–	Z Result	C Result	Result	Clocks
010101 001i 1111 ddddddddd sssssssss	Result = 0	---	Written	4

Explanation

MOVD copies the 9-bit value of *Value* into *Destination's* d-field (destination field) bits 17..9. *Destination's* other bits are left unchanged. This instruction is handy for setting certain registers like CTRA and VCFG, and for updating the destination field of instructions in self-modifying code.

If the WZ effect is specified, the Z flag is set (1) if *Value* equals zero. The result is written to *Destination* unless the NR effect is specified.

MOVI

Instruction: Set a register's instruction field to a value.

MOVI *Destination*, ⟨#⟩ *Value*

Result: *Value* is stored in *Destination's* i-field and effects-field (bits 31..23).

- **Destination** (d-field) is the register whose instruction and effects fields (bits 31..23) are set to *Value's* value.
- **Value** (s-field) is a register or a 9-bit literal whose value is stored into *Destination's* instruction and effects field.

–INSTR– ZCRI –CON– –DEST– –SRC–	Z Result	C Result	Result	Clocks
010110 001i 1111 ddddddddd sssssssss	Result = 0	---	Written	4

Explanation

MOVI copies the 9-bit value of *Value* into *Destination's* instruction and effects fields bits 31..23. *Destination's* other bits are left unchanged. This instruction is handy for setting certain registers like CTRA and VCFG, and for updating the instruction and effects fields of instructions in self-modifying code.

If the WZ effect is specified, the Z flag is set (1) if *Value* equals zero. The result is written to *Destination* unless the NR effect is specified.

MOVS

Instruction: Set a register's source field to a value.

MOVS *Destination*, ⟨#⟩ *Value*

Result: *Value* is stored in *Destination'* s-field (bits 8..0).

- **Destination** (d-field) is the register whose source field (bits 8..0) is set to *Value's* value.
- **Value** (s-field) is a register or a 9-bit literal whose value is stored into *Destination's* source field.

–INSTR– ZCRI –CON– –DEST– –SRC–	Z Result	C Result	Result	Clocks
010100 001i 1111 ddddddddd sssssssss	Result = 0	---	Written	4

Explanation

MOVS copies the 9-bit value of *Value* into *Destination's* source field (s-field) bits 8..0. *Destination's* other bits are left unchanged. This instruction is handy for setting certain registers like CTRA and VCFG, and for updating the source field of instructions in self-modifying code.

If the WZ effect is specified, the Z flag is set (1) if *Value* equals zero. The result is written to *Destination* unless the NR effect is specified.

MUXC

Instruction: Set discrete bits of a value to the state of C.

MUXC *Destination*, ⟨#⟩ *Mask*

Result: *Destination's* bits, indicated by *Mask*, are set to the state of C.

- **Destination** (d-field) is the register whose bits described by *Mask* are affected by C.
- **Mask** (s-field) is a register or a 9-bit literal whose value contains high (1) bits for every bit in *Destination* to set to the C flag's state.

–INSTR– ZCRI –CON– –DEST– –SRC–	Z Result	C Result	Result	Clocks
011100 001i 1111 ddddddddd sssssssss	Result = 0	Parity of Result	Written	4

Explanation

MUXC sets each bit of the value in *Destination*, which corresponds to *Mask's* high (1) bits, to the C state. All bits of *Destination* that are not targeted by high (1) bits of *Mask* are unaffected. This instruction is handy for setting or clearing discrete bits, or groups of bits, in an existing value.

If the WZ effect is specified, the Z flag is set (1) if *Destination's* final value is 0. If the WC effect is specified, the C flag is set (1) if the resulting *Destination* contains an odd number of high (1) bits. The result is written to *Destination* unless the NR effect is specified.

MUXNC

Instruction: Set discrete bits of a value to the state of !C.

MUXNC Destination, ⟨#⟩ Mask

Result: *Destination's* bits, indicated by *Mask*, are set to the state of !C.

- **Destination** (d-field) is the register whose bits described by *Mask* are affected by !C.
- **Mask** (s-field) is a register or a 9-bit literal whose value contains high (1) bits for every bit in *Destination* to set to the inverse of the C flag's state.

–INSTR– ZCRI –CON– –DEST– –SRC–	Z Result	C Result	Result	Clocks
011101 001i 1111 dddddddd ssssssss	Result = 0	Parity of Result	Written	4

Explanation

MUXNC sets each bit of the value in *Destination*, which corresponds to *Mask's* high (1) bits, to the !C state. All bits of *Destination* that are not targeted by high (1) bits of *Mask* are unaffected. This instruction is handy for setting or clearing discrete bits, or groups of bits, in an existing value.

If the WZ effect is specified, the Z flag is set (1) if *Destination's* final value is 0. If the WC effect is specified, the C flag is set (1) if the resulting *Destination* contains an odd number of high (1) bits. The result is written to *Destination* unless the NR effect is specified.

MUXNZ

Instruction: Set discrete bits of a value to the state of !Z.

MUXNZ Destination, ⟨#⟩ Mask

Result: *Destination's* bits, indicated by *Mask*, are set to the state of !Z.

- **Destination** (d-field) is the register whose bits described by *Mask* are affected by !Z.
- **Mask** (s-field) is a register or a 9-bit literal whose value contains high (1) bits for every bit in *Destination* to set to the inverse of the Z flag's state.

–INSTR– ZCRI –CON– –DEST– –SRC–	Z Result	C Result	Result	Clocks
011111 001i 1111 dddddddd ssssssss	Result = 0	Parity of Result	Written	4

Explanation

MUXNZ sets each bit of the value in *Destination*, which corresponds to *Mask's* high (1) bits, to the !Z state. All bits of *Destination* that are not targeted by high (1) bits of *Mask* are unaffected. This instruction is handy for setting or clearing discrete bits, or groups of bits, in an existing value.

If the WZ effect is specified, the Z flag is set (1) if *Destination's* final value is 0. If the WC effect is specified, the C flag is set (1) if the resulting *Destination* contains an odd number of high (1) bits. The result is written to *Destination* unless the NR effect is specified.

MUXZ

Instruction: Set discrete bits of a value to the state of Z.

MUXZ *Destination*, ⟨#⟩ *Mask*

Result: *Destination's* bits, indicated by *Mask*, are set to the state of Z.

- **Destination** (d-field) is the register whose bits described by *Mask* are affected by Z.
- **Mask** (s-field) is a register or a 9-bit literal whose value contains high (1) bits for every bit in *Destination* to set to the Z flag's state.

–INSTR– ZCRI –CON– –DEST– –SRC–	Z Result	C Result	Result	Clocks
011110 001i 1111 ddddddddd sssssssss	Result = 0	Parity of Result	Written	4

Explanation

MUXZ sets each bit of the value in *Destination*, which corresponds to *Mask's* high (1) bits, to the Z state. All bits of *Destination* that are not targeted by high (1) bits of *Mask* are unaffected. This instruction is handy for setting or clearing discrete bits, or groups of bits, in an existing value.

If the WZ effect is specified, the Z flag is set (1) if *Destination's* final value is 0. If the WC effect is specified, the C flag is set (1) if the resulting *Destination* contains an odd number of high (1) bits. The result is written to *Destination* unless the NR effect is specified.

NEG

Instruction: Get the negative of a number.

NEG *NValue*, ⟨#⟩ *SValue*

Result: *–SValue* is stored in *NValue*.

- **NValue** (d-field) is the register in which to write the negative of *SValue*.
- **SValue** (s-field) is a register or a 9-bit literal whose negative value will be written to *NValue*.

–INSTR– ZCRI –CON– –DEST– –SRC–	Z Result	C Result	Result	Clocks
101001 001i 1111 ddddddddd sssssssss	Result = 0	S[31]	Written	4

Explanation

NEG stores negative *SValue* into *NValue*.

If the WZ effect is specified, the Z flag is set (1) if *SValue* is zero. If the WC effect is specified, the C flag is set (1) if *SValue* is negative or cleared (0) if *SValue* is positive. The result is written to *NValue* unless the NR effect is specified.

NEGC

Instruction: Get a value, or its additive inverse, based on C.

NEGC *RValue*, ⟨#⟩ *Value*

Result: *Value* or *–Value* is stored in *RValue*.

- **RValue** (d-field) is the register in which to write *Value* or *–Value*.
- **Value** (s-field) is a register or a 9-bit literal whose value (if C = 0) or additive inverse value (if C = 1) will be written to *RValue*.

–INSTR– ZCRI –CON– –DEST– –SRC–	Z Result	C Result	Result	Clocks
101100 001i 1111 ddddddddd sssssssss	Result = 0	S[31]	Written	4

Explanation

NEGC stores *Value* (if C = 0) or *–Value* (if C = 1) into *RValue*.

If the WZ effect is specified, the Z flag is set (1) if *Value* is zero. If the WC effect is specified, the C flag is set (1) if *Value* is negative or cleared (0) if *Value* is positive. The result is written to *RValue* unless the NR effect is specified.

NEGNC

Instruction: Get a value, or its additive inverse, based on !C.

NEGNC RValue, ⟨#⟩ Value

Result: *–Value* or *Value* is stored in *RValue*.

- **RValue** (d-field) is the register in which to write *–Value* or Value.
- **Value** (s-field) is a register or a 9-bit literal whose additive inverse value (if C = 0) or value (if C = 1) will be written to *RValue*.

–INSTR– ZCRI –CON– –DEST– –SRC–	Z Result	C Result	Result	Clocks
101101 001i 1111 ddddddddd sssssssss	Result = 0	S[31]	Written	4

Explanation

NEGNC stores *–Value* (if C = 0) or *Value* (if C = 1) into *RValue*.

If the WZ effect is specified, the Z flag is set (1) if *Value* is zero. If the WC effect is specified, the C flag is set (1) if *Value* is negative or cleared (0) if *Value* is positive. The result is written to *RValue* unless the NR effect is specified.

NEGNZ

Instruction: Get a value, or its additive inverse, based on !Z.

NEGNZ *RValue*, ⟨#⟩ *Value*

Result: *–Value* or *Value* is stored in *RValue*.

- **RValue** (d-field) is the register in which to write *–Value* or *Value*.
- **Value** (s-field) is a register or a 9-bit literal whose additive inverse value (if Z = 0) or value (if Z = 1) will be written to *RValue*.

–INSTR– ZCRI –CON– –DEST– –SRC–	Z Result	C Result	Result	Clocks
101111 001i 1111 ddddddddd sssssssss	Result = 0	S[31]	Written	4

Explanation

NEGNZ stores *–Value* (if Z = 0) or *Value* (if Z = 1) into *RValue*.

If the WZ effect is specified, the Z flag is set (1) if *Value* is zero. If the WC effect is specified, the C flag is set (1) if *Value* is negative or cleared (0) if *Value* is positive. The result is written to *RValue* unless the NR effect is specified.

NEGZ

Instruction: Get a value, or its additive inverse, based on Z.

NEGZ *RValue,* ⟨#⟩ *Value*

Result: *Value* or *–Value* is stored in *RValue*.

- **RValue** (d-field) is the register in which to write *Value* or *–Value*.
- **Value** (s-field) is a register or a 9-bit literal whose value (if Z = 0) or additive inverse value (if Z = 1) will be written to *RValue*.

–INSTR– ZCRI –CON– –DEST– –SRC–	Z Result	C Result	Result	Clocks
101110 001i 1111 ddddddddd sssssssss	Result = 0	S[31]	Written	4

Explanation

NEGZ stores *Value* (if Z = 0) or *–Value* (if Z = 1) into *RValue*.

If the WZ effect is specified, the Z flag is set (1) if *Value* is zero. If the WC effect is specified, the C flag is set (1) if *Value* is negative or cleared (0) if *Value* is positive. The result is written to *RValue* unless the NR effect is specified.

NOP

Instruction: No operation, just elapse four clock cycles.

NOP

–INSTR– ZCRI –CON– –DEST– –SRC–	Z Result	C Result	Result	Clocks
------ ---- 0000 --------- ---------	---	---	---	4

Explanation

NOP performs no operation but consumes 4 clock cycles. NOP has its –CON– field set to all zeros, the NEVER condition; effectively, every instruction with a NEVER condition is a NOP instruction.

Operators

Propeller Assembly code can contain constant expressions, and those expressions may use any operators that are allowed in constant expressions. Table 5-4 summarizes all the operators allowed in Propeller Assembly code (all those allowed in constant expressions). Please refer to the Spin Language Reference Operators section for detailed descriptions of their functions; page numbers for each operator are given in Table 5-4

Table 5-4: Constant Expression Math/Logic Operators		
Normal Operator	**Is Unary**	**Description, Page Number**
+		Add, 255
+	✓	Positive (+X); unary form of Add, 256
–		Subtract, 256
–	✓	Negate (-X); unary form of Subtract, 256
*		Multiply and return lower 32 bits (signed), 258
**		Multiply and return upper 32 bits (signed), 259
/		Divide (signed), 259
//		Modulus (signed), 260
#>		Limit minimum (signed), 260
<#		Limit maximum (signed), 261
^^	✓	Square root, 261
||	✓	Absolute value, 261
~>		Shift arithmetic right, 264
|<	✓	Bitwise: Decode value (0-31) into single-high-bit long, 265
>|	✓	Bitwise: Encode long into value (0 - 32) as high-bit priority, 266
<<		Bitwise: Shift left, 266
>>		Bitwise: Shift right, 267
<-		Bitwise: Rotate left, 267
->		Bitwise: Rotate right, 268
><		Bitwise: Reverse, 268
&		Bitwise: AND, 269
|		Bitwise: OR, 270
^		Bitwise: XOR, 271
!	✓	Bitwise: NOT, 272
AND		Boolean: AND (promotes non-0 to -1), 272
OR		Boolean: OR (promotes non-0 to -1), 273
NOT	✓	Boolean: NOT (promotes non-0 to -1), 274
==		Boolean: Is equal, 275
<>		Boolean: Is not equal, 275
<		Boolean: Is less than (signed), 276
>		Boolean: Is greater than (signed), 276
=<		Boolean: Is equal or less (signed), 277
=>		Boolean: Is equal or greater (signed), 277
@	✓	Symbol address, 278

OR

Instruction: Bitwise OR two values.

OR *Value1*, ⟨#⟩ *Value2*

Result: *Value1* OR *Value2* is stored in *Value1*.

- **Value1** (d-field) is the register containing the value to bitwise OR with *Value2* and is the destination in which to write the result.
- **Value2** (s-field) is a register or a 9-bit literal whose value is bitwise ORed with *Value1*.

–INSTR– ZCRI –CON– –DEST– –SRC–	Z Result	C Result	Result	Clocks
011010 001i 1111 ddddddddd sssssssss	Result = 0	Parity of Result	Written	4

Explanation

OR (bitwise inclusive OR) performs a bitwise OR of the value in *Value2* into that of *Value1*.

If the WZ effect is specified, the Z flag is set (1) if *Value1* OR *Value2* equals zero. If the WC effect is specified, the C flag is set (1) if the result contains an odd number of high (1) bits. The result is written to *Value1* unless the NR effect is specified.

ORG

Directive: Adjust compile-time cog address pointer.

ORG ⟨*Address*⟩

- **Address** is an optional Cog RAM address (0-495) to assemble the following assembly code into. If *Address* is not given, the value 0 is used.

Explanation

The ORG (origin) directive sets the Propeller Tool's assembly pointer to a new value representing the Cog RAM position to use for the following assembly code. ORG typically appears at the start of any new assembly code intended for a cog.

When assembly code is launched into a cog, the cog begins execution at Cog RAM address 0 so it is critical to assemble at least one instruction for that position. Usually an entire assembly program begins at location 0. For example:

```
DAT
                ORG     0
Toggle          mov     dira, Pin
:Loop           mov     outa, Pin
                mov     outa, #0
                jmp     #:Loop
```

The ORG statement in this example sets the assembly pointer to zero (0), so the next instruction, mov dira, Pin, is assembled into Cog RAM location 0, the instruction after that is assembled into Cog RAM location 1, etc.

RCL

Instruction: Rotate C left into value by specified number of bits.

RCL *Value*, ⟨#⟩ *Bits*

Result: *Value* has *Bits* copies of C rotated left into it.

- **Value** (d-field) is the register in which to rotate C leftwards.
- **Bits** (s-field) is a register or a 5-bit literal whose value is the number of bits of *Value* to rotate C leftwards into.

–INSTR– ZCRI –CON– –DEST– –SRC–	Z Result	C Result	Result	Clocks
001101 001i 1111 ddddddddd ssssssss	Result = 0	D[31]	Written	4

Explanation

RCL (Rotate Carry Left) performs a rotate left of *Value*, *Bits* times, using the C flag's original value for each of the LSBs affected.

If the WZ effect is specified, the Z flag is set (1) if the resulting *Value* equals zero. If the WC effect is specified, at the end of the operation, the C flag is set equal to *Value's* original bit 31. The result is written to *Value* unless the NR effect is specified.

RCR

Instruction: Rotate C right into value by specified number of bits.

RCR Value, ⟨#⟩ Bits

Result: *Value* has *Bits* copies of C rotated right into it.

- **Value** (d-field) is the register in which to rotate C rightwards.
- **Bits** (s-field) is a register or a 5-bit literal whose value is the number of bits of *Value* to rotate C rightwards into.

–INSTR– ZCRI –CON– –DEST– –SRC–	Z Result	C Result	Result	Clocks
001100 001i 1111 ddddddddd sssssssss	Result = 0	D[0]	Written	4

Explanation

RCR (Rotate Carry Right) performs a rotate right of *Value*, *Bits* times, using the C flag's original value for each of the MSBs affected.

If the WZ effect is specified, the Z flag is set (1) if the resulting *Value* equals zero. If the WC effect is specified, at the end of the operation, the C flag is set equal to *Value's* original bit 0. The result is written to *Value* unless the NR effect is specified.

RDBYTE

Instruction: Read byte of main memory.

RDBYTE Value, ⟨#⟩ Address

Result: Zero-extended byte is stored in *Value*.

- **Value** (d-field) is the register to store the zero-extended byte value into.
- **Address** (s-field) is a register or a 9-bit literal whose value is the main memory address to read from.

–INSTR– ZCRI –CON– –DEST– –SRC–	Z Result	C Result	Result	Clocks
000000 001i 1111 ddddddddd sssssssss	Result = 0	---	Written	7..22

Explanation

RDBYTE syncs to the Hub, reads the byte of main memory at *Address*, zero-extends it, and stores it into the *Value* register.

If the WZ effect is specified, the Z flag will be set (1) if the value read from main memory is zero. The value from main memory will be written to *Value* unless the NR effect is specified.

RDBYTE is a Hub instruction. Hub instructions require 7 to 22 clock cycles to execute depending on the relation between the cog's hub access window and the instruction's moment of execution. See Hub on page 24 for more information.

RDLONG

Instruction: Read long of main memory.

RDLONG *Value*, ⟨#⟩ *Address*

Result: Long is stored in *Value*.

- **Value** (d-field) is the register to store the long value into.
- **Address** (s-field) is a register or a 9-bit literalwhose value is the main memory address to read from.

–INSTR– ZCRI –CON– –DEST– –SRC–	Z Result	C Result	Result	Clocks
000010 001i 1111 ddddddddd sssssssss	Result = 0	---	Written	7..22

Explanation

RDLONG syncs to the Hub, reads the long of main memory at *Address*, and stores it into the *Value* register.

If the WZ effect is specified, the Z flag will be set (1) if the value read from main memory is zero. The value from main memory will be written to *Value* unless the NR effect is specified.

RDLONG is a Hub instruction. Hub instructions require 7 to 22 clock cycles to execute depending on the relation between the cog's hub access window and the instruction's moment of execution. See Hub on page 24 for more information.

RDWORD

Instruction: Read word of main memory.

RDWORD *Value*, ⟨#⟩ *Address*

Result: Zero-extended word is stored in *Value*.

- *Value* (d-field) is the register to store the zero-extended word value into.
- *Address* (s-field) is a register or a 9-bit literalwhose value is the main memory address to read from.

–INSTR– ZCRI –CON– –DEST– –SRC–	Z Result	C Result	Result	Clocks
000001 001i 1111 ddddddddd sssssssss	Result = 0	---	Written	7..22

Explanation

RDWORD syncs to the Hub, reads the word of main memory at *Address*, zero-extends it, and stores it into the *Value* register.

If the WZ effect is specified, the Z flag will be set (1) if the value read from main memory is zero. The value from main memory will be written to *Value* unless the NR effect is specified.

RDWORD is a Hub instruction. Hub instructions require 7 to 22 clock cycles to execute depending on the relation between the cog's hub access window and the instruction's moment of execution. See Hub on page 24 for more information.

Registers

Each cog contains 16 special purpose registers for accessing I/O pins, the built-in counters and video generator, and the parameter passed at the moment the cog is launched. All of these registers are explained in the Spin Language Reference and most of the information applies to both Spin and Propeller Assembly. The following table illustrates the 16 special purpose registers, indicates where to find information and what details, if any, do not apply to Propeller Assembly.

Each of these registers can be accessed just like any other register in the Destination or Source fields of instructions, except for those that are designated "(Read-Only)." Read-only registers can only be used in the Source field of an instruction.

Table 5-5: Registers	
Register(s)	**Description**
DIRA, DIRB	Direction Registers for 32-bit port A and 32-bit port B. See the Explanation section of DIRA, DIRB on page 212. The optional "[*Pin(s)*]" parameter does not apply to Propeller Assembly; all bits of the entire register are read/written at once, unless using the MUXx instructions.
INA, INB	Input Registers for 32-bit port A and 32-bit port B. (Read-Only). See the Explanation section of INA, INB on page 226. The optional "[*Pin(s)*]" parameter does not apply to Propeller Assembly; all bits of the entire register are read at once.
OUTA, OUTB	Output Registers for 32-bit port A and 32-bit port B. See the Explanation section of OUTA, OUTB on page 280. The optional "[*Pin(s)*]" parameter does not apply to Propeller Assembly; all bits of the entire register are read/written at once, unless using the MUXx instructions.
CNT	32-bit System Counter Register. (Read-Only). See the Explanation section of CNT on page 184.
CTRA, CTRB	Counter A and Counter B Control Registers. See CTRA, CTRB on page 204.
FRQA, FRQB	Counter A and Counter B Frequency Registers. See FRQA, FRQB on page 219.
PHSA, PHSB	Counter A and Counter B Phase Lock Loop Registers. See PHSA, PHSB on page 285.
VCFG	Video Configuration Register. See VCFG on page 317.
VSCL	Video Scale Register. See VSCL on page 320.
PAR	Cog Boot Parameter Register. See PAR on page 283.

RES

Directive: Reserve next long(s) for symbol.

⟨*Symbol*⟩ RES ⟨*Count*⟩

- **Symbol** is an optional name for the reserved long in Cog RAM.
- **Count** is the optional number of longs to reserve for *Symbol*. If not specified, RES reserves one long.

Explanation

The RES (reserve) directive reserves one or more longs of Cog RAM by incrementing the compile-time cog address pointer by *Count*. Normally this is used to reserve memory for an assembly symbol. For example:

```
DAT
                ORG     0
                <some code here>
                mov       Time, cnt
                add       Time, Delay
                waitcnt Time, Delay
                <some code here>


Delay     long    6_000_000
Time      RES     1
```

The last line of the above example reserves one long of Cog RAM for the symbol Time. The assembly code uses that symbol as a long variable; to create a delay of 6 million clock cycles, in this case.

RET

Instruction: Return to address.

RET

–INSTR– ZCRI –CON– –DEST– –SRC–	Z Result	C Result	Result	Clocks
010111 0001 1111 --------- ---------	Result = 0	---	Not Written	4

Explanation

RET is a subset of the JMP instruction but with the i-field set and the s-field unspecified. The RET instruction is meant to be used along with a label in the form "label_ret" and a CALL instruction that targets RET's routine, "label." See CALL on page 360 for more information.

REV

Instruction: Reverse LSBs of value and zero-extend.

REV *Value*, ⟨#⟩ *Bits*

Result: *Value* has lower 32 - *Bits* of its LSBs reversed and upper bits cleared.

- **Value** (d-field) is the register containing the value whose bits are reversed.
- **Bits** (s-field) is a register or a 5-bit literal whose value subtracted from 32, (32 - *Bits*), is the number of *Value*'s LSBs to reverse. The upper *Bits* MSBs of *Value* are cleared.

–INSTR– ZCRI –CON– –DEST– –SRC–	Z Result	C Result	Result	Clocks
001111 001i 1111 ddddddddd sssssssss	Result = 0	D[0]	Written	4

Explanation

REV (Reverse) reverses the lower (32 - *Bits*) of *Value*'s LSB and clears the upper *Bits* of *Value*'s MSBs.

If the WZ effect is specified, the Z flag is set (1) if the resulting *Value* equals zero. If the WC effect is specified, the C flag is set equal to *Value*'s original bit 0. The result is written to *Value* unless the NR effect is specified.

ROL

Instruction: Rotate value left by specified number of bits.

ROL *Value*, ⟨#⟩ *Bits*

Result: *Value* is rotated left by *Bits*.

- **Value** (d-field) is the register to rotate left.
- **Bits** (s-field) is a register or a 5-bit literal whose value is the number of bits to rotate left.

–INSTR– ZCRI –CON– –DEST– –SRC–	Z Result	C Result	Result	Clocks
001001 001i 1111 ddddddddd sssssssss	Result = 0	D[31]	Written	4

Explanation

ROL (Rotate Left) rotates *Value* left, *Bits* times. The MSBs rotated out of *Value* are rotated into its LSBs.

If the WZ effect is specified, the Z flag is set (1) if the resulting *Value* equals zero. If the WC effect is specified, at the end of the operation, the C flag is set equal to *Value's* original bit 31. The result is written to *Value* unless the NR effect is specified.

ROR

Instruction: Rotate value right by specified number of bits.

ROR *Value*, ⟨#⟩ *Bits*

Result: *Value* is rotated right by *Bits*.

- **Value** (d-field) is the register to rotate right.
- **Bits** (s-field) is a register or a 5-bit literal whose value is the number of bits to rotate right.

–INSTR– ZCRI –CON– –DEST– –SRC–	Z Result	C Result	Result	Clocks
001000 001i 1111 ddddddddd sssssssss	Result = 0	D[0]	Written	4

Explanation

ROR (Rotate Right) rotates *Value* right, *Bits* times. The LSBs rotated out of *Value* are rotated into its MSBs.

If the WZ effect is specified, the Z flag is set (1) if the resulting *Value* equals zero. If the WC effect is specified, at the end of the operation, the C flag is set equal to *Value's* original bit 0. The result is written to *Value* unless the NR effect is specified.

SAR

Instruction: Shift value arithmetically right by specified number of bits.

SHR *Value*, ⟨#⟩ *Bits*

Result: *Value* is shifted arithmetically right by *Bits*.

- *Value* (d-field) is the register to shift arithmetically right.
- *Bits* (s-field) is a register or a 5-bit literal whose value is the number of bits to shift arithmetically right.

–INSTR– ZCRI –CON– –DEST– –SRC–	Z Result	C Result	Result	Clocks
001110 001i 1111 ddddddddd sssssssss	Result = 0	D[0]	Written	4

Explanation

SAR (Shift Arithmetic Right) shifts *Value* right by *Bits* places, extending the MSB along the way. This has the effect of preserving the sign in a signed value.

If the WZ effect is specified, the Z flag is set (1) if the resulting *Value* equals zero. If the WC effect is specified, the C flag is set equal to *Value's* original bit 0. The result is written to *Value* unless the NR effect is specified.

SHL

Instruction: Shift value left by specified number of bits.

SHL *Value*, ⟨#⟩ *Bits*

Result: *Value* is shifted left by *Bits*.

- **Value** (d-field) is the register to shift left.
- **Bits** (s-field) is a register or a 5-bit literal whose value is the number of bits to shift left.

–INSTR– ZCRI –CON– –DEST– –SRC–	Z Result	C Result	Result	Clocks
001011 001i 1111 ddddddddd ssssssss	Result = 0	D[31]	Written	4

Explanation

SHL (Shift Left) shifts *Value* left by *Bits* places.

If the WZ effect is specified, the Z flag is set (1) if the resulting *Value* equals zero. If the WC effect is specified, the C flag is set equal to *Value's* original bit 31. The result is written to *Value* unless the NR effect is specified.

SHR

Instruction: Shift value right by specified number of bits.

SHR *Value*, ⟨#⟩ *Bits*

Result: *Value* is shifted right by *Bits*.

- **Value** (d-field) is the register to shift right.
- **Bits** (s-field) is a register or a 5-bit literal whose value is the number of bits to shift right.

–INSTR– ZCRI –CON– –DEST– –SRC–	Z Result	C Result	Result	Clocks
001010 001i 1111 ddddddddd ssssssss	Result = 0	D[0]	Written	4

Explanation

SHR (Shift Right) shifts *Value* right by *Bits* places.

If the WZ effect is specified, the Z flag is set (1) if the resulting *Value* equals zero. If the WC effect is specified, the C flag is set equal to *Value's* original bit 0. The result is written to *Value* unless the NR effect is specified.

SUB

Instruction: Subtract two unsigned values.

SUB *Value1*, ⟨#⟩ *Value2*

Result: Difference of unsigned *Value1* and unsigned *Value2* is stored in *Value1*.

- **Value1** (d-field) is the register containing the value to subtract *Value2* from, and is the destination in which to write the result.
- **Value2** (s-field) is a register or a 9-bit literal whose value is subtracted from *Value1*.

–INSTR– ZCRI –CON– –DEST– –SRC–	Z Result	C Result	Result	Clocks
100001 001i 1111 ddddddddd sssssssss	Result = 0	Unsigned Borrow	Written	4

Explanation

SUB subtracts the unsigned *Value2* from the unsigned *Value1* and stores the result into the *Value1* register.

If the WZ effect is specified, the Z flag is set (1) if *Value1* − *Value2* equals zero. If the WC effect is specified, the C flag is set (1) if the subtraction resulted in an unsigned borrow (32-bit underflow). The result is written to *Value1* unless the NR effect is specified.

SUBABS

Instruction: Subtract an absolute value from another value.

SUBABS Value, ⟨#⟩ SValue

Result: Difference of *Value* and absolute of signed *SValue* is stored in *Value*.

- **Value** (d-field) is the register containing the value to subtract the absolute of *SValue* from, and is the destination in which to write the result.
- **SValue** (s-field) is a register or a 9-bit literal whose absolute value is subtracted from *Value*.

–INSTR– ZCRI –CON– –DEST– –SRC–	Z Result	C Result	Result	Clocks
100011 001i 1111 ddddddddd sssssssss	Result = 0	Unsigned Borrow	Written	4

Explanation

SUBABS subtracts the absolute of *SValue* from *Value* and stores the result into the *Value* register.

If the WZ effect is specified, the Z flag is set (1) if *Value* − |*SValue*| equals zero. If the WC effect is specified, the C flag is set (1) if the subtraction resulted in an unsigned borrow (32-bit underflow). The result is written to *Value* unless the NR effect is specified.

SUBS

Instruction: Subtract two signed values.

SUBS SValue1, ⟨#⟩ SValue2

Result: Difference of signed *SValue1* and signed *SValue2* is stored in *SValue1*.

- **SValue1** (d-field) is the register containing the value to subtract *SValue2* from, and is the destination in which to write the result.
- **SValue2** (s-field) is a register or a 9-bit literal whose value is subtracted from *SValue1*.

–INSTR– ZCRI –CON– –DEST– –SRC–	Z Result	C Result	Result	Clocks
110101 001i 1111 ddddddddd sssssssss	Result = 0	Signed Underflow	Written	4

Explanation

SUBS subtracts the signed *SValue2* from the signed *SValue1* and stores the result into the *SValue1* register.

If the WZ effect is specified, the Z flag is set (1) if *SValue1* − *SValue2* equals zero. If the WC effect is specified, the C flag is set (1) if the subtraction resulted in a signed underflow. The result is written to *SValue1* unless the NR effect is specified.

SUBSX

Instruction: Subtract signed value plus C from another signed value.

SUBSX *SValue1*, ⟨#⟩ *SValue2*

Result: Difference of signed *SValue1*, and signed *SValue2* plus C flag, is stored in *SValue1*.

- **SValue1** (d-field) is the register containing the value to subtract *SValue2* plus C from, and is the destination in which to write the result.
- **SValue2** (s-field) is a register or a 9-bit literal whose value plus C is subtracted from *SValue1*.

–INSTR– ZCRI –CON– –DEST– –SRC–	Z Result	C Result	Result	Clocks
110111 001i 1111 ddddddddd sssssssss	Z & (Result = 0)	Signed Underflow	Written	4

Explanation

SUBSX (Subtract Signed, Extended) subtracts the signed value of *SValue2* plus C from *SValue1*, and stores the result into the *SValue1* register. Use the SUBSX instruction after a SUB or SUBX (with the WC, and optionally WZ, effect) to perform multi-long, signed subtractions; 64-bit subtractions, for example.

If the WZ effect is specified, the Z flag is·set (1) if Z was previously set and *SValue1* − (*SValue2* + C) equals zero (use WC and WZ on preceding SUB or SUBX instruction). If the WC effect is specified, the C flag is set (1) if the subtraction resulted in a signed underflow. The result is written to *SValue1* unless the NR effect is specified.

Note that in a multi-long signed operation, the first instruction is unsigned (ex: SUB), any middle instructions are unsigned, extended (ex: SUBX), and the last instruction is signed, extended (ex: SUBSX).

SUBX

Instruction: Subtract unsigned value plus C from another unsigned value.

SUBX Value1, ⟨#⟩ Value2

Result: Difference of unsigned *Value1*, and unsigned *Value2* plus C flag, is stored in *Value1*.

- *Value1* (d-field) is the register containing the value to subtract *Value2* plus C from, and is the destination in which to write the result.
- *Value2* (s-field) is a register or a 9-bit literal whose value plus C is subtracted from *Value1*.

–INSTR– ZCRI –CON– –DEST– –SRC–	Z Result	C Result	Result	Clocks
110011 001i 1111 ddddddddd sssssssss	Z & (Result = 0)	Unsigned Borrow	Written	4

Explanation

SUBX (Subtract Extended) subtracts the unsigned value of *Value2* plus C from the unsigned *Value1* and stores the result into the *Value1* register. Use the SUBX instruction after a SUB or SUBX (with the WC, and optionally WZ, effect) to perform multi-long subtractions; 64-bit subtractions, for example.

If the WZ effect is specified, the Z flag is set (1) if Z was previously set and *Value1* − (*Value2* + C) equals zero (use WC and WZ on preceding SUB or SUBX instruction). If the WC effect is specified, the C flag is set (1) if the subtraction resulted in an unsigned borrow (32-bit underflow). The result is written to *Value1* unless the NR effect is specified.

SUMC

Instruction: Sum a signed value with another whose sign is inverted depending on C.

SUMC SValue1, ⟨#⟩ SValue2

Result: Sum of signed *SValue1* and ±*SValue2* is stored in *SValue1*.

- *SValue1* (d-field) is the register containing the value to sum with either –*SValue2* or *SValue2*, and is the destination in which to write the result.
- *SValue2* (s-field) is a register or a 9-bit literal whose value is sign-affected by C and summed into *SValue1*.

-INSTR- ZCRI -CON- -DEST- -SRC-	Z Result	C Result	Result	Clocks
100100 001i 1111 ddddddddd sssssssss	Result = 0	Signed Overflow	Written	4

Explanation

SUMC (Sum with C-affected sign) adds the signed value of *SValue1* to –*SValue2* (if C = 1) or to *SValue2* (if C = 0) and stores the result into the *SValue1* register.

If the WZ effect is specified, the Z flag is set (1) if *SValue1* ± *SValue2* equals zero. If the WC effect is specified, the C flag is set (1) if the summation resulted in a signed overflow. The result is written to *SValue1* unless the NR effect is specified.

SUMNC

Instruction: Sum a signed value with another whose sign is inverted depending on !C.

SUMNC *SValue1*, ⟨#⟩ *SValue2*

Result: Sum of signed *SValue1* and ±*SValue2* is stored in *SValue1*.

- **SValue1** (d-field) is the register containing the value to sum with either *SValue2* or -*SValue2*, and is the destination in which to write the result.
- **SValue2** (s-field) is a register or a 9-bit literal whose value is sign-affected by !C and summed into *SValue1*.

-INSTR- ZCRI -CON- -DEST- -SRC-	Z Result	C Result	Result	Clocks
100101 001i 1111 ddddddddd sssssssss	Result = 0	Signed Overflow	Written	4

Explanation

SUMNC (Sum with !C-affected sign) adds the signed value of *SValue1* to *SValue2* (if C = 1) or to –*SValue2* (if C = 0) and stores the result into the *SValue1* register.

If the WZ effect is specified, the Z flag is set (1) if *SValue1* ± *SValue2* equals zero. If the WC effect is specified, the C flag is set (1) if the summation resulted in a signed overflow. The result is written to *SValue1* unless the NR effect is specified.

SUMNZ

Instruction: Sum a signed value with another whose sign is inverted depending on !Z.

SUMNZ *SValue1*, ⟨#⟩ *SValue2*

Result: Sum of signed *SValue1* and ±*SValue2* is stored in *SValue1*.

- *SValue1* (d-field) is the register containing the value to sum with either *SValue2* or -*SValue2*, and is the destination in which to write the result.
- *SValue2* (s-field) is a register or a 9-bit literal whose value is sign-affected by !Z and summed into *SValue1*.

–INSTR– ZCRI –CON– –DEST– –SRC–	Z Result	C Result	Result	Clocks
100111 001i 1111 ddddddddd sssssssss	Result = 0	Signed Overflow	Written	4

Explanation

SUMNZ (Sum with !Z-affected sign) adds the signed value of *SValue1* to *SValue2* (if Z = 1) or to –*SValue2* (if Z = 0) and stores the result into the *SValue1* register.

If the WZ effect is specified, the Z flag is set (1) if *SValue1* ± *SValue2* equals zero. If the WC effect is specified, the C flag is set (1) if the summation resulted in a signed overflow. The result is written to *SValue1* unless the NR effect is specified.

SUMZ

Instruction: Sum a signed value with another whose sign is inverted depending on Z.

SUMZ *SValue1*, ⟨#⟩ *SValue2*

Result: Sum of signed *SValue1* and ±*SValue2* is stored in *SValue1*.

- *SValue1* (d-field) is the register containing the value to sum with either –*SValue2* or *SValue2*, and is the destination in which to write the result.
- *SValue2* (s-field) is a register or a 9-bit literal whose value is sign-affected by Z and summed into *SValue1*.

–INSTR– ZCRI –CON– –DEST– –SRC–	Z Result	C Result	Result	Clocks
100110 001i 1111 ddddddddd sssssssss	Result = 0	Signed Overflow	Written	4

Explanation

SUMZ (Sum with Z-affected sign) adds the signed value of *SValue1* to –*SValue2* (if Z = 1) or to *SValue2* (if Z = 0) and stores the result into the *SValue1* register.

If the WZ effect is specified, the Z flag is set (1) if *SValue1* ± *SValue2* equals zero. If the WC effect is specified, the C flag is set (1) if the summation resulted in a signed overflow. The result is written to *SValue1* unless the NR effect is specified.

TEST

Instruction: Bitwise AND two values to affect flags only.

TEST *Value1*, ⟨#⟩ *Value2*

Result: Optionally, zero-result and parity of result is written to the Z and C flags.

- *Value1* (d-field) is the register containing the value to bitwise AND with *Value2*.
- *Value2* (s-field) is a register or a 9-bit literal whose value is bitwise ANDed with *Value1*.

–INSTR– ZCRI –CON– –DEST– –SRC–	Z Result	C Result	Result	Clocks
011000 000i 1111 ddddddddd sssssssss	Result = 0	Parity of Result	Not Written	4

Explanation

TEST is similar to AND except it doesn't write a result to *Value1*; it performs a bitwise AND of the values in *Value1* and *Value2* and optionally stores the zero-result and parity of the result in the Z and C flags.

If the WZ effect is specified, the Z flag is set (1) if *Value1* AND *Value2* equals zero. If the WC effect is specified, the C flag is set (1) if the result contains an odd number of high (1) bits.

TJNZ

Instruction: Test value and jump to address if not zero.

TJNZ *Value*, ⟨#⟩ *Address*

- *Value* (d-field) is the register to test.
- *Address* (s-field) is the register or a 9-bit literal whose value is the address to jump to when *Value* contains a non-zero number.

–INSTR– ZCRI –CON– –DEST– –SRC–	Z Result	C Result	Result	Clocks
111010 000i 1111 ddddddddd sssssssss	Result = 0	0	Not Written	4 or 8

Explanation

TJNZ tests the *Value* register and jumps to *Address* if it contains a non-zero number.

When the WZ effect is specified, the Z flag is set (1) if the *Value* register contains zero.

TJNZ requires a different amount of clock cycles depending on whether or not it has to jump. If it must jump it takes 4 clock cycles, if no jump occurs it takes 8 clock cycles. Since loops utilizing TJNZ need to be fast, it is optimized in this way for speed.

TJZ

Instruction: Test value and jump to address if zero.

TJZ *Value*, ⟨#⟩ *Address*

- *Value* (d-field) is the register to test.
- *Address* (s-field) is the register or a 9-bit literal whose value is the address to jump to when *Value* contains zero.

–INSTR– ZCRI –CON– –DEST– –SRC–	Z Result	C Result	Result	Clocks
111011 000i 1111 ddddddddd sssssssss	Result = 0	0	Not Written	4 or 8

Explanation

TJZ tests the *Value* register and jumps to *Address* if it contains zero.

When the WZ effect is specified, the Z flag is set (1) if the *Value* register contains zero.

TJZ requires a different amount of clock cycles depending on whether or not it has to jump. If it must jump it takes 4 clock cycles, if no jump occurs it takes 8 clock cycles.

WAITCNT

Instruction: Pause a cog's execution temporarily.

WAITCNT *Target,* ⟨#⟩ *Delta*

Result: *Target + Delta* is stored in *Target.*

- *Target* (d-field) is the register with the target value to compare against the System Counter (CNT). When the System Counter has reached *Target's* value, *Delta* is added to *Target.*
- *Delta* (s-field) is the register or a 9-bit literal whose value is added to *Target's* value in preparation for the next WAITCNT instruction. This creates a synchronized delay window.

–INSTR– ZCRI –CON– –DEST– –SRC–	Z Result	C Result	Result	Clocks
111110 001i 1111 ddddddddd sssssssss	Result = 0	Unsigned Carry	Written	5+

Explanation

WAITCNT, "Wait for System Counter," is one of four wait instructions (WAITCNT, WAITPEQ, WAITPNE, and WAITVID) used to pause execution of a cog until a condition is met. The WAITCNT instruction pauses the cog until the global System Counter equals the value in the *Target* register, then it adds *Delta* to *Target* and execution continues at the next instruction. The WAITCNT instruction behaves similar to Spin's WAITCNT command for Synchronized Delays; see WAITCNT on page 322.

If the WZ effect is specified, the Z flag will be set (1) if the sum of *Target* and *Delta* is zero. If the WC effect is specified, the C flag will set (1) if the sum of *Target* and *Delta* resulted in a 32-bit carry (overflow). The result will be written to *Target* unless the NR effect is specified.

WAITPEQ

Instruction: Pause a cog's execution until I/O pin(s) match designated state(s).

WAITPEQ *State*, ⟨#⟩ *Mask*

- ***State*** (d-field) is the register with the target state(s) to compare against INx ANDed with *Mask*.
- ***Mask*** (s-field) is the register or a 9-bit literal whose value is bitwise ANDed with INx before the comparison with *State*.

–INSTR–	ZCRI	–CON–	–DEST–	–SRC–	Z Result	C Result	Result	Clocks
111100	000i	1111	ddddddddd	sssssssss	Result = 0	---	Not Written	5+

Explanation

WAITPEQ, "Wait for Pin(s) to Equal," is one of four wait instructions (WAITCNT, WAITPEQ, WAITPNE, and WAITVID) used to pause execution of a cog until a condition is met. The WAITPEQ instruction pauses the cog until the result of INx ANDed with *Mask* equals the value in the *State* register. INx is either INA or INB depending on the value of the C flag upon execution; INA if C = 0, INB if C = 1 (the P8X32A is an exception to this rule; it always tests INA).

The WAITPEQ instruction behaves similar to Spin's WAITPEQ command; see WAITPEQ on page 326.

If the WZ effect is specified, the Z flag will be set (1) if the result of INx ANDed with *Mask* is zero.

WAITPNE

Instruction: Pause a cog's execution until I/O pin(s) do not match designated state(s).

WAITPNE *State,* ⟨#⟩ *Mask*

- **State** (d-field) is the register with the target state(s) to compare against INx ANDed with *Mask*.
- **Mask** (s-field) is the register or a 9-bit literal whose value is bitwise ANDed with INx before the comparison with *State*.

–INSTR–	ZCRI	–CON–	–DEST–	–SRC–	Z Result	C Result	Result	Clocks
111101	000i	1111	dddddddd	sssssssss	Result = 0	---	Not Written	5+

Explanation

WAITPNE, "Wait for Pin(s) to Not Equal," is one of four wait instructions (WAITCNT, WAITPEQ, WAITPNE, and WAITVID) used to pause execution of a cog until a condition is met. The WAITPNE instruction pauses the cog until the result of INx ANDed with *Mask* does not match the value in the *State* register. INx is either INA or INB depending on the value of the C flag upon execution; INA if C = 0, INB if C = 1 (the P8X32A is an exception to this rule; it always tests INA). The WAITPNE instruction behaves similar to Spin's WAITPNE command; see WAITPNE on page 328.

If the WZ effect is specified, the Z flag will be set (1) if the result of INx ANDed with *Mask* is zero.

WAITVID

Instruction: Pause a cog's execution until its Video Generator is available to take pixel data.

WAITVID Colors, ⟨#⟩ Pixels

- **Colors** (d-field) is the register with four byte-sized color values, each describing the four possible colors of the pixel patterns in *Pixels*.
- **Pixels** (s-field) is the register or a 9-bit literal whose value is the next 16-pixel by 2-bit (or 32-pixel by 1-bit) pixel pattern to display.

–INSTR– ZCRI –CON– –DEST– –SRC–	Z Result	C Result	Result	Clocks
111111 000i 1111 ddddddddd sssssssss	Result = 0	---	Not Written	5+

Explanation

WAITVID, "Wait for Video Generator," is one of four wait instructions (WAITCNT, WAITPEQ, WAITPNE, and WAITVID) used to pause execution of a cog until a condition is met. The WAITVID instruction pauses the cog until its Video Generator hardware is ready for the next pixel data, then the Video Generator accepts that data (*Colors* and *Pixels*) and the cog continues execution with the next instruction. The WAITVID instruction behaves similar to Spin's WAITVID command; see WAITVID on page 329.

If the WZ effect is specified, the Z flag will be set (1) if the *Colors* and *Pixels* are equal.

Make sure the cog's Video Generator module is running before executing a WAITVID, otherwise the WAITVID instruction will wait forever.

WRBYTE

Instruction: Write a byte to main memory.

WRBYTE Value, ⟨#⟩ Address

- **Value** (d-field) is the register containing the 8-bit value to write to main memory.
- **Address** (s-field) is a register or a 9-bit literal whose value is the main memory address to write to.

–INSTR– ZCRI –CON– –DEST– –SRC–	Z Result	C Result	Result	Clocks
000000 000i 1111 dddddddd ssssssss	---	---	Not Written	7..22

Explanation

WRBYTE synchronizes to the Hub and writes the lowest byte in *Value* to main memory at *Address*.

WRBYTE is a Hub instruction. Hub instructions require 7 to 22 clock cycles to execute depending on the relation between the cog's hub access window and the instruction's moment of execution. See Hub on page 24 for more information.

WRLONG

Instruction: Write a long to main memory.

WRLONG *Value*, ⟨#⟩ *Address*

- *Value* (d-field) is the register containing the 32-bit value to write to main memory.
- *Address* (s-field) is a register or a 9-bit literal whose value is the main memory address to write to.

–INSTR– ZCRI –CON– –DEST– –SRC–	Z Result	C Result	Result	Clocks
000010 000i 1111 dddddddd ssssssss	---	---	Not Written	7..22

Explanation

WRLONG synchronizes to the Hub and writes the long in *Value* to main memory at *Address*.

WRLONG is a Hub instruction. Hub instructions require 7 to 22 clock cycles to execute depending on the relation between the cog's hub access window and the instruction's moment of execution. Hub on page 24 for more information.

WRWORD

Instruction: Write a word to main memory.

WRWORD *Value*, ⟨#⟩ *Address*

- *Value* (d-field) is the register containing the 16-bit value to write to main memory.
- *Address* (s-field) is a register or a 9-bit literal whose value is the main memory address to write to.

–INSTR– ZCRI –CON– –DEST– –SRC–	Z Result	C Result	Result	Clocks
000001 000i 1111 ddddddddd sssssssss	---	---	Not Written	7..22

Explanation

WRWORD synchronizes to the Hub and writes the lowest word in *Value* to main memory at *Address*.

WRWORD is a Hub instruction. Hub instructions require 7 to 22 clock cycles to execute depending on the relation between the cog's hub access window and the instruction's moment of execution. See Hub on page 24 for more information.

XOR

Instruction: Bitwise XOR two values.

XOR *Value1*, ⟨#⟩ *Value2*

Result: *Value1* XOR *Value2* is stored in *Value1*.

- **Value1** (d-field) is the register containing the value to bitwise XOR with *Value2* and is the destination in which to write the result.
- **Value2** (s-field) is a register or a 9-bit literal whose value is bitwise XORed with *Value1*.

–INSTR– ZCRI –CON– –DEST– –SRC–	Z Result	C Result	Result	Clocks
011011 001i 1111 ddddddddd sssssssss	Result = 0	Parity of Result	Written	4

Explanation

XOR (bitwise exclusive OR) performs a bitwise XOR of the value in *Value2* into that of *Value1*.

If the WZ effect is specified, the Z flag is set (1) if *Value1* XOR *Value2* equals zero. If the WC effect is specified, the C flag is set (1) if the result contains an odd number of high (1) bits. The result is written to *Value1* unless the NR effect is specified.

Appendix A: Reserved Word List

These words are always reserved, whether programming in Spin or Propeller Assembly.

Table A-0-1: Propeller Reserved Word List					
_CLKFREQ[s]	CONSTANT[s]	IF_NC_AND_NZ[a]	MIN[a]	PLL4X[s]	SUBSX[a]
_CLKMODE[s]	CTRA[d]	IF_NC_AND_Z[a]	MINS[a]	PLL8X[s]	SUBX[a]
_FREE[s]	CTRB[d]	IF_NC_OR_NZ[a]	MOV[a]	PLL16X[s]	SUMC[a]
_STACK[s]	DAT[s]	IF_NC_OR_Z[a]	MOVD[a]	POSX[d]	SUMNC[a]
_XINFREQ[s]	DIRA[d]	IF_NE[a]	MOVI[a]	PRI[s]	SUMNZ[a]
ABORT[s]	DIRB[d]	IF_NEVER[a]	MOVS[a]	PUB[s]	SUMZ[a]
ABS[a]	DJNZ[a]	IF_NZ[a]	MUL[a]	QUIT[s]	TEST[a]
ABSNEG[a]	ELSE[s]	IF_NZ_AND_C[a]	MULS[a]	RCFAST[s]	TJNZ[a]
ADD[a]	ELSEIF[s]	IF_NZ_AND_NC[a]	MUXC[a]	RCL[a]	TJZ[a]
ADDABS[a]	ELSEIFNOT[s]	IF_NZ_OR_C[a]	MUXNC[a]	RCR[a]	TO[s]
ADDS[a]	ENC[a]	IF_NZ_OR_NC[a]	MUXNZ[a]	RCSLOW[s]	TRUE[d]
ADDSX[a]	FALSE[d]	IF_Z[a]	MUXZ[a]	RDBYTE[a]	TRUNC[s]
ADDX[a]	FILE[s]	IF_Z_AND_C[a]	NEG[a]	RDLONG[a]	UNTIL[s]
AND[d]	FIT[a]	IF_Z_AND_NC[a]	NEGC[a]	RDWORD[a]	VAR[s]
ANDN[a]	FLOAT[s]	IF_Z_EQ_C[a]	NEGNC[a]	REBOOT[s]	VCFG[d]
BYTE[s]	FROM[s]	IF_Z_NE_C[a]	NEGNZ[a]	REPEAT[s]	VSCL[d]
BYTEFILL[s]	FRQA[d]	IF_Z_OR_C[a]	NEGX[d]	RES[a]	WAITCNT[d]
BYTEMOVE[s]	FRQB[d]	IF_Z_OR_NC[a]	NEGZ[a]	RESULT[s]	WAITPEQ[d]
CALL[a]	HUBOP[a]	INA[d]	NEXT[s]	RET[a]	WAITPNE[d]
CASE[s]	IF[s]	INB[d]	NOP[a]	RETURN[s]	WAITVID[d]
CHIPVER[s]	IFNOT[s]	JMP[a]	NOT[s]	REV[a]	WC[a]
CLKFREQ[s]	IF_A[a]	JMPRET[a]	NR[a]	ROL[a]	WHILE[s]
CLKMODE[s]	IF_AE[a]	LOCKCLR[d]	OBJ[s]	ROR[a]	WORD[s]
CLKSET[d]	IF_ALWAYS[a]	LOCKNEW[d]	ONES[a]	ROUND[s]	WORDFILL[s]
CMP[a]	IF_B[a]	LOCKRET[d]	OR[d]	SAR[a]	WORDMOVE[s]
CMPS[a]	IF_BE[a]	LOCKSET[d]	ORG[a]	SHL[a]	WR[a]
CMPSUB[a]	IF_C[a]	LONG[s]	OTHER[s]	SHR[a]	WRBYTE[a]
CMPSX[a]	IF_C_AND_NZ[a]	LONGFILL[s]	OUTA[d]	SPR[s]	WRLONG[a]
CMPX[a]	IF_C_AND_Z[a]	LONGMOVE[s]	OUTB[d]	STEP[s]	WRWORD[a]
CNT[d]	IF_C_EQ_Z[a]	LOOKDOWN[s]	PAR[d]	STRCOMP[s]	WZ[a]
COGID[d]	IF_C_NE_Z[a]	LOOKDOWNZ[s]	PHSA[d]	STRING[s]	XINPUT[s]
COGINIT[d]	IF_C_OR_NZ[a]	LOOKUP[s]	PHSB[d]	STRSIZE[s]	XOR[a]
COGNEW[s]	IF_C_OR_Z[a]	LOOKUPZ[s]	PI[d]	SUB[a]	XTAL1[s]
COGSTOP[d]	IF_E[a]	MAX[a]	PLL1X[s]	SUBABS[a]	XTAL2[s]
CON[s]	IF_NC[a]	MAXS[a]	PLL2X[s]	SUBS[a]	XTAL3[s]

a = Assembly element; s = Spin element; d = dual (available in both languages)

Appendix B: Accessing Math Function Tables

Log and Anti-Log Tables   ($C000-DFFF)

The log and anti-log tables are useful for converting values between their number form and exponent form.

When numbers are encoded into exponent form, simple math operations take on more complex effects. For example 'add' and 'subtract' become 'multiply' and 'divide,' 'shift-left' becomes 'square' and 'shift-right' becomes 'square-root,' and 'divide by 3' will produce 'cube root.' Once the exponent is converted back to a number, the result will be apparent. This process is imperfect, but quite fast.

For applications where many multiplies and divides must be performed in the absence of many additions and subtractions, exponential encoding can greatly speed things up. Exponential encoding is also useful for compressing numbers into fewer bits – sacrificing resolution at higher magnitude. In many applications, such as audio synthesis, the nature of signals is logarithmic in both frequency and magnitude. Processing such data in exponent form is quite natural and efficient, as it lends a 'linear' simplicity to what is actually logarithmic.

The code examples given below use each tables' samples verbatim. Higher resolution could be achieved by linearly interpolating between table samples, since the slope change is very slight from sample to sample. The cost, though, would be larger code and lower execution speed.

Log Table   ($C000-$CFFF)

The log table contains data used to convert unsigned numbers into base-2 exponents.

The log table is comprised of 2,048 unsigned words which make up the base-2 fractional exponents of numbers. To use this table, you must first determine the integer portion of the exponent of the number you are converting. This is simply the leading bit position. For $60000000 this would be 30 ($1E). This integer portion will always fit within 5 bits. Isolate these 5 bits into the result so that they occupy bit positions 20..16. In our case of $60000000, we would now have a partial result of $001E0000. Next, top-justify and isolate the first 11 bits below the leading bit into positions 11..1. This would be $0800 for our example. Add $C000 for the log table base and you now have the actual word address of the fractional exponent. By reading the word at $C800, we get the value $95C0. Adding this into the partial result yields $001E95C0 – that's $60000000 in exponent form. Note that bits 20..16 make up the integer portion of the exponent, while bits 15..0 make up the fractional portion, with bit 15 being the ½, bit 14 being the ¼, and so on, down to bit 0. The exponent can now be manipulated by adding, subtracting, and shifting. Always insure that your math operations will never drive the exponent below 0 or cause it to overflow bit 20. Otherwise, it may not convert back to a number correctly.

Here is a routine that will convert an unsigned number into its base-2 exponent using the log table:

```
' Convert number to exponent
'
' on entry: num holds 32-bit unsigned value
' on exit:  exp holds 21-bit exponent with 5 integer bits and 16 fractional bits
'
numexp          mov     exp,#0                  'clear exponent

                test    num,num4        wz      'get integer portion of exponent
                muxnz   exp,exp4                'while top-justifying number
       if_z     shl     num,#16
                test    num,num3        wz
                muxnz   exp,exp3
       if_z     shl     num,#8
                test    num,num2        wz
                muxnz   exp,exp2
       if_z     shl     num,#4
                test    num,num1        wz
                muxnz   exp,exp1
       if_z     shl     num,#2
                test    num,num0        wz
                muxnz   exp,exp0
       if_z     shl     num,#1

                shr     num,#30-11              'justify sub-leading bits as word
offset
                and     num,table_mask          'isolate table offset bits
                add     num,table_log           'add log table address
                rdword  num,num                 'read fractional portion of exponent
                or      exp,num                 'combine fractional & integer portions

numexp_ret      ret                             '91..106 clocks
                                                ' (variance due to HUB sync on RDWORD)

num4            long    $FFFF0000
num3            long    $FF000000
num2            long    $F0000000
```

Appendix B: Accessing Math Function Tables

```
num1          long     $C0000000
num0          long     $80000000
exp4          long     $00100000
exp3          long     $00080000
exp2          long     $00040000
exp1          long     $00020000
exp0          long     $00010000
table_mask    long     $0FFE              'table offset mask
table_log     long     $C000              'log table base

num           long     0                  'input
exp           long     0                  'output
```

Anti-Log Table   ($D000-$DFFF)

The anti-log table contains data used to convert base-2 exponents into unsigned numbers.

The anti-log table is comprised of 2,048 unsigned words which are each the lower 16-bits of a 17-bit mantissa (the 17th bit is implied and must be set separately). To use this table, shift the top 11 bits of the exponent fraction (bits 15..5) into bits 11..1 and isolate. Add $D000 for the anti-log table base. Read the word at that location into the result – this is the mantissa. Next, shift the mantissa left to bits 30..15 and set bit 31 – the missing 17th bit of the mantissa. The last step is to shift the result right by 31 minus the exponent integer in bits 20..16. The exponent is now converted to an unsigned number.

Here is a routine that will convert a base-2 exponent into an unsigned number using the anti-log table:

```
' Convert exponent to number
'
' on entry: exp holds 21-bit exponent with 5 integer bits and 16 fraction bits
' on exit:  num holds 32-bit unsigned value
'
expnum          mov      num,exp            'get exponent into number
                shr      num,#15-11         'justify exponent fraction as word
offset
                and      num,table_mask     'isolate table offset bits
                or       num,table_antilog  'add anti-log table address
                rdword   num,num            'read mantissa word into number
                shl      num,#15            'shift mantissa into bits 30..15
                or       num,num0           'set top bit (17th bit of mantissa)
                shr      exp,#20-4          'shift exponent integer into bits 4..0
                xor      exp,#$1F           'inverse bits to get shift count
                shr      num,exp            'shift number into final position
```

```
expnum_ret        ret                             '47..62 clocks
                                                  '(variance is due to HUB sync on
RDWORD)

num0              long     $80000000              '17th bit of the mantissa
table_mask        long     $0FFE                  'table offset mask
table_antilog     long     $C000                  'anti-log table base

exp               long     0                      'input
num               long     0                      'output
```

Sine Table   ($E000-$F001)

The sine table provides 2,049 unsigned 16-bit sine samples spanning from 0° to 90°, inclusively (0.0439° resolution).

A small amount of assembly code can mirror and flip the sine table samples to create a full-cycle sine/cosine lookup routine which has 13-bit angle resolution and 17-bit sample resolution:

```
' Get sine/cosine
'
'        quadrant:  1               2               3               4
'           angle:  $0000..$07FF    $0800..$0FFF    $1000..$17FF    $1800..$1FFF
'     table index:  $0000..$07FF    $0800..$0001    $0000..$07FF    $0800..$0001
'          mirror:  +offset         -offset         +offset         -offset
'            flip:  +sample         +sample         -sample         -sample
'
' on entry: sin[12..0] holds angle (0° to just under 360°)
' on exit:  sin holds signed value ranging from $0000FFFF ('1') to
' $FFFF0001 ('-1')
'
getcos            add      sin,sin_90             'for cosine, add 90°
getsin            test     sin,sin_90      wc     'get quadrant 2|4 into c
                  test     sin,sin_180     wz     'get quadrant 3|4 into nz
                  negc     sin,sin                'if quadrant 2|4, negate offset
                  or       sin,sin_table          'or in sin table address >> 1
                  shl      sin,#1                 'shift left to get final word address
                  rdword   sin,sin                'read word sample from $E000 to $F000
                  negnz    sin,sin                  'if quadrant 3|4, negate sample
getsin_ret
getcos_ret        ret                             '39..54 clocks
                                                  '(variance due to HUB sync on RDWORD)

sin_90            long     $0800
```

Appendix B: Accessing Math Function Tables

```
sin_180         long    $1000
sin_table       long    $E000 >> 1          'sine table base shifted right

sin             long    0
```

As with the log and anti-log tables, linear interpolation could be applied to the sine table to achieve higher resolution.

Index

Index

Index

Index

M

N

Index

Index

Index

Index